Dynamic Trading

Dynamic Concepts In Time, Price and Pattern Analysis With Practical Strategies for Traders and Investors

Robert C. Miner

Traders Press, Inc.®
PO Box 6206
Greenville, SC 29606

Serving Traders since 1975

This publication is designed to provide accurate and authoritative information in regards to the subject matter covered. It is sold with the understanding that the author and the publisher are not engaged in rendering legal, accounting or other professional service.

ISBN: 0-934380-83-X

Published by Traders Press, Inc.®
Teresa Darty Alligood
Editor and Graphic Designer

Printed in the United States of America

Second Printing 1999

Third Printing 2002

Traders Press, Inc.®
PO Box 6206
Greenville, SC 29606

Serving Traders since 1975

Publisher's Comments

Seldom have I encountered a more positive reaction to books than I have to this one. Most readers place it high on their list of the most valuable books they have ever come across in contributing to their education as traders. It deals with three primary subject areas about which much has been written: Gann, Fibonacci, and Elliott. However, much (but certainly not all) of the literature available heretofore on these topics has been of limited use because it was written in an unclear or non meaningful manner. Gann's own work, while it has fascinated traders for decades, is a prime example. This book addresses all three topics in a manner that will greatly benefit the trader interested in these subject areas.

One of the great pleasures gained from publishing books intended to help traders to increase their knowledge and ability as traders is the association with some of the brightest minds in trading. It is a great pleasure and a distinct honor to be associated with Robert Miner in publishing his masterpiece, "Dynamic Trading." I feel confident that it will help you in your quest for trading excellence.

Edward D. Dobson

Edward D. Dobson, President   March 8, 2002
Traders Press, Inc.®

Greenville, SC

Traders Press, Inc.®
PO Box 6206
Greenville, SC 29606

Serving Traders since 1975

Trademarks

The following are trademarks held by Robert C. Miner:

Dynamic Price Projections
Dynamic Time Projections
Projected Turning Point Period
Time Cycle Ratio
Trend Vibration
Time Rhythm Zone
Price Rhythm Zone
Gann Pull-Back

Previously Published Material

Some of the material found in this book is expanded from the trading tutorials that were originally published as a part of the *Dynamic Trader Analysis Report* newsletter written and published by the author. Some of the ideas were originally taught in the author's comprehensive *W. D. Gann Trading Techniques Home Study Course* first published in 1989 and no longer available.

Also Available From Dynamic Traders Group, Inc.

Dynamic Trader Weekly Report

A unique and comprehensive educational and technical analysis report delivered each Saturday with occasional mid-week updates.

Dynamic Trader Software and Trading Course

The only technical analysis software program sold to the public that includes a comprehensive trading course.

www.dynamictraders.com

Visit our web site every week for free current trade recommendations and trading tutorials. We provide a free comprehensive, ongoing trading education for all traders and investors interested in the Dynamic Trading approach.

More complete information regarding these products and services is found in the back of this book. Also, go to our Web site at

www.dynamictraders.com

or contact

Dynamic Traders Group, Inc.
6336 N. Oracle Rd. Suite 326-346
Tucson, Az. 85704
(V) 520-797-3668
(F) 520-797-2045
(E-mail) dt@dynamictraders.com
(Web Site) www.dynamictraders.com

Introduction To The Second Printing

With a minimal amount of promotion, *Dynamic Trading* has proven to be one of the fastest selling trading books of the decade which has required us to do a second printing much sooner than anticipated. I think *Dynamic Trading* has had such an enthusiastic and widespread response because of two reasons.

Firstly, *Dynamic Trading* is a comprehensive trading course. It not only teaches the reader a complete and unique approach to technical analysis, but the trading strategies and trade management necessary for successful trading as well. Most trading books are very limited in nature and only teach one or another aspect of the business of trading. It is extremely rare for a trading book to teach a complete approach as found in *Dynamic Trading*.

Secondly, *Dynamic Trading* teaches the reality of trading. Most trading books, courses and magazine articles are written by people who have never successfully traded. The misinformation in some of this material often far outweighs the useful information. *Dynamic Trading* teaches a logical and straight-forward approach that has stood the test of time and can be a stand-alone trading plan or integrated with an existing trading plan. We have received virtually hundreds of faxes, emails and letters from traders who have dramatically improved their trading results with the practical strategies taught in *Dynamic Trading*.

There is no change in the material that is taught in the second printing. A few additional examples have been included. The *Dynamic Trading* approach is applicable to all time frames from one-minute to monthly bar charts and in all types of markets including futures, stocks, indexes, mutual funds and options. Most of the examples are daily data of the futures markets which are the markets I primarily have been trading, analyzing and writing about since 1986. Many people who studied this material were concerned if the same techniques were applicable to short-term intraday data and stocks. The answer is absolutely yes!

I have included more examples with intraday data in the second printing and more stock examples. As you study this material, keep in mind that it doesn't make any difference what is the time frame or market with *Dynamic Trading*. They all act and react in the same manner. The technical analysis and trading strategies are the same regardless of time-frame or market.

Thank you to all the traders from absolute beginners to seasoned professional mutual fund managers who have sent us their enthusiastic feedback for what they have learned in *Dynamic Trading*.

Acknowledgments

Bertrand Russell said "in science the successors stand upon the shoulders of their predecessors." This is probably true in any field. It definitely is true in the field of technical analysis.

The "golden age" of technical analysis was surely the pre-computer age prior to the 1960's. Analysts and traders such as W. D. Gann, R. N. Elliott, Frank Tubbs, Samuel Benner, William Dunnigan, Richard Wyckoff, Prof. Alan Andrews and many others of their era are the shoulders I stand on. They were certainly a giant leap ahead in understanding market activity than the legions of computer junkies that have followed them. It seems the more prevalent personal computers and software have become, the more ways amateur and professional analysts have found to crunch the numbers into meaningless statistics and "indicators." The teachers of the previous era demanded the student to think and consider cause as well as effect.

Special recognition goes to the late Dr. Jerome Baumring who presented a series of seminars in the mid to late 1980's on market geometry and W. D. Gann. He definitely re-oriented my view of the market. Several of his former students have gone on to publish newsletters, give workshops and publish books. None have made a public recognition of his critical contribution. I recognized his contribution in the forward to my first published trading course in the late 1980's and do so again here. He influenced a recent generation of market geometers. Thanks to Baumring and others like him, people like me have shoulders to stand on.

Jerry Pegden spent thirteen years on Wall St. with Salomon Brothers, Inc. and Henry Kaufman and Co. Inc. before moving to Tucson in 1993 to work with me. His breadth of technical analysis expertise and respect for the practical application of knowledge has been a critical contribution to my work and the service we have provided our customers over the past few years. Jerry is responsible for bringing the Dynamic Trader Software program to fruition. His insights and keen sense of detail were a great influence in the book you are now holding.

Foreword

When Robert Miner asked me to review his manuscript for *Dynamic Trading*, I was excited to know that he had finally put his approach to technical analysis and trading strategies into a single, comprehensive source. I first met Bob in L.A. over a decade ago at a trading workshop about the geometric nature of the financial markets. I have followed his work on and off since then and come to appreciate not only his holistic and comprehensive approach to technical analysis, but his dogged pursuit of practical trading strategies.

I've made my living as a trader for over 30 years and have a library of trading books and courses that is rivaled by few, if any. I've always believed that if you get just one good idea from reading any book, it was worth your time and money. If this is the case, you won't be disappointed with *Dynamic Trading*. It is an outstanding bargain because you will not get just one or two good ideas but a comprehensive approach to market analysis and practical trading strategies.

Bob's pursuit of market knowledge started years ago with the vast amount of material from W. D. Gann. Over the years he became the foremost authority on Gann type analysis, and, better yet, how to put that knowledge into practical application. You learn to respect a man's research when you witness first hand what it entailed. "No stone was left unturned" is the appropriate cliché. His extensive personal library is inundated with books on geometry, physics, astronomy, mathematics, psychology, philosophy and many other related subjects besides those directly related to trading and investing. It is from this source material and Miner's extensive research and trading experience that *Dynamic Trading* is presented to its readers.

Dynamic Trading is a "show me how to do it" book that will be enjoyed, re-read and appreciated by both the expert and novice technician. The step-by-step presentation is as easy to follow as the logic it entails. Bob's approach to the market is complete. He does not focus on just one narrow aspect of technical analysis or trading strategies but provides a comprehensive approach to the technical position of a market and how to apply the appropriate trading strategies depending on the market position.

Dynamic Trading is divided into three broad sections. The first covers the three dimensions of market activity - time, price and pattern. Combining these three principles makes the technician's chart a powerful ally to determine risk and profit objectives. The second important area concerns trading strategies, in other words, how to put this comprehensive analysis into practice. Too many trading books just focus on the technical position of a market and fail to provide any real-world strategies of how to trade it. Miner makes clear what all professional traders know but is rarely emphasized in most trading books and workshops: trading decisions are based on probabilities and risk control, not on predictions of the future.

The third major section is how to put the analysis and trading strategies together in a comprehensive trading plan to be applied to every trading situation day-by-day. Miner doesn't just show a few isolated examples taken out of context to show-off his *Dynamic Trading* analysis techniques. Miner takes a prolonged period of market activity and clearly shows how to apply the *Dynamic Trading* analysis and trading strategies through all kinds of market conditions.

Miner has provided *Dynamic Trading* analysis and instruction for over ten years through his monthly and weekly advisory reports. In an industry where so many try to guard their so-called secrets or charge exorbitant fees for workshops and seminars, Miner has openly provided a valuable education to traders around the world. I'm glad he has finally put his work into writing into one comprehensive book.

This material will stand the test of time. *Dynamic Trading* is one of the great contributions to market literature. I may be accused of forecasting the future, but I think it will be regarded as a "must read" classic for all traders and investors in the years to come.

Larry Pesavento
Tucson, Az.

Dynamic Trading

By Robert C. Miner

Contents

Chapter 4 - Dynamic Price Analysis

Chapter 5 - Dynamic Time Analysis

Chapter 6 - Trade Strategies and Trade Management

Chapter 7 - Putting It All Together

Chapter 8 - The Real World of Dynamic Trading

Appendix - Dynamic Trading Guidelines

Glossary

Bibliography

—————— Chapter 1 ——————

Introduction To Dynamic Trading

Successful commodity trading is a business.
Roy W. Longstreet

In *Dynamic Trading*, you

- Learn what it takes to be a successful trader or investor.

- Learn how to understand the pattern position of the current trend of the market including the conditions necessary to signal when a market is reaching the completion of the trend using the *practical* application of Elliott Wave analysis.

- Learn how to project well *in advance* the price zones which have the greatest probability of support, resistance and trend change.

- Learn how to project well *in advance* the time periods with the greatest probability of trend change.

- Learn how to integrate the time and price projection techniques and pattern analysis into a practical trading plan.

- Learn how to distinguish the high probability trade set-ups that will provide you with the best opportunity for success.

Where We Are Going and What We Will Accomplish

Dynamic Trading will teach you how to confidently consider a market position and make a trading or investing decision. Every financial and commodity market is constantly in a process of dynamic change. When you have mastered the material in this book, you will not only be prepared for trend change before it happens, but will be prepared for the probable time and price extent of each trend and counter-trend swing.

One of the important objectives of Dynamic Trading is to project the extent of trends and the time and price of trend reversals *in advance*.

The chart below is an example of the power of dynamic market analysis. A bond top was projected to be made in the Nov. 20-Dec. 9, 1996 period, ideally Dec. 4-9. The top was projected to be in the price zone of 115.29-117.05. The top was made Dec. 3, 1996 at 116.28, precisely within the time and price zones projected for the termination of the rally.

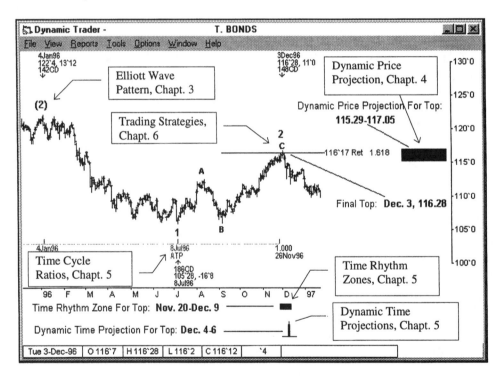

After-the-fact analysis? Absolutely not. The exact projections described above were made weeks *in advance* and published in the *Dynamic Trader Report* prepared by the author. By learning Dynamic Trading analysis and trading strategies, you will be prepared in advance for the extent of trends and counter-trends, the time and price with the greatest probability of trend reversal and low-risk trading strategies.

It's Time You Made A Change

Are you ready to make some changes? To do something different than the majority of traders and investors who are unsuccessful?

The majority of futures traders loose money. Some say the percentage is as high as 90%. The majority of stock and mutual fund investors under perform the stock indexes, year after year. How can this be when publications teaching trading, investing and technical analysis have flooded the market in recent years? How can this be when powerful technical analysis software is available for only a few hundred dollars? In the past twenty years, since the flood of technical analysis and investing books, newsletters, trading workshops and software have overwhelmed the market, the percentage of traders and investors who succeed has not gained at all! How can this be when the knowledge and tools seem to be so easily and cheaply available?

I believe it is because the vast majority of traders and investors have bought into the belief that the same overused and abused technical indicators actually provide an accurate assessment of market position. If the majority of traders and investors continue to loose or, at best, vastly under perform the market, it must be time for a change. It must be time to look at the market from a new perspective and put into practice new analysis methods and trading strategies.

My favorite definition of an insane person is *someone who continues to do the same thing but expects different results*. Are you insane? Are you approaching the market with the same popular analysis tools and trading techniques that have been used by the majority of traders and investors for more than the past twenty years? That same group of traders and investors who have consistently lost or under performed the market, year after year after year?

It's time to stop the insanity! *It's time to do something different.* Dynamic Trading provides both new techniques and new twists on some older techniques that are integrated into a comprehensive analysis and trading plan. If you want to be different than the 90% of unsuccessful traders and investors, you must do something different than what the 90% are doing.

I have taught these techniques to new and experienced traders in over a dozen countries for almost ten years. It is rare that someone involved in the business of market analysis and education has any trading experience. In order to demonstrate the value of these methods, in 1993 I entered and won first place in the Robbins Trading Company World Cup Championship of Futures Trading with a return of over 118% on account for the year. This annual trading contest is real-money, real-time. Not some silly hypothetical trading contest. In case you didn't know, less than 5% of trading and investing authors, newsletter writers and software developers have ever successfully traded or invested. All of their information is strictly from an academic or hypothetical viewpoint and is usually not applicable to practical analysis, trading or investing.

While I continue to trade futures and options and invest by mutual fund switching, my primary occupation is as a trading and investing analyst and advisor through my monthly and weekly *Dynamic Trader Analysis Reports*. These reports and their predecessors have provided a comprehensive analysis of the major financial and commodity markets since 1986. Each report is an education in itself with regular tutorials on dynamic technical analysis and trading strategies.

The monthly and weekly advisory reports have provided a ten year record of the value of the analysis, forecasts methods and trading strategies taught in this book. Throughout this period I have become especially known for my comprehensive and unique timing methods. A three year period of reports was examined and it was found that 89% of the trend changes made by the markets that were followed in the report were made within one trading day of my Projected Turning Point Periods. I'm sure you can see how valuable this kind of dynamic time analysis can be to you.

Of the hundreds of market analysts and newsletter publishers, the *1997 Supertraders Almanac* named me the 1996 "Market Guru of the Year", primarily for my technical analysis of market position and time and price projections for the stock indexes. The same analysis techniques that allowed me to so accurately determine the position of the stock market and time and price targets for the bull trend are taught in this book. The techniques are not difficult to understand or apply, but it will take work on your part.

This is the first comprehensive book I have offered to the public in ten years. In the past, a trader or investor had to either purchase my $900 home study course or attend a weekend workshop at a similar price to receive this information. Why have I put this information together in a book and made it available for less than $100? You're probably expecting me to humbly say it's for the benefit of the little guy or something like that. Not at all. I hope to reach a much wider audience of traders and investors who are ready to make a change. Some of you will want to continue your studies by subscribing to my monthly or weekly advisory service. Others may be interested in the unique software I have developed for traders and investors.

Whether you continue your study and application of Dynamic Trading beyond the material in this book or not, I promise you this: *You will get more than your money's worth from the material in this book alone.* You will learn new analysis and trading techniques that you can immediately put into practice as a complete approach by themselves or as a complement to an approach you already use. I have been in the business of advising and educating traders for over ten years. I have built a steady and loyal customer base over that time primarily from word of mouth. I have done that by offering a quality product and service in everything I do in an industry that is known for a decided lack of quality and integrity. If for any reason you feel the material in this book is not worth the price you paid, send it back within sixty days and I will be glad to refund your purchase price. I'll bet you've never had a money back guarantee made to you in the introduction to a book.

The other reason I have made this material available in a low cost book format is that over the past few years, many of the techniques I have been teaching for many years are being taught by others and incorporated into software programs without any reference to the source. They are often being taught at extraordinary high cost like several thousand dollars for weekend workshops or telephone conference tutorials. Unfortunately, many of the techniques are often taught incorrectly. Probably because the teacher did not develop the methods and had no actual experience putting them into practice.

In late 1993, I gave a lecture at the Trader's World technical analysis conference in Chicago and described the relationship of market timing and atomic energy structure. I explained this analogy and the practical application to time analysis and trading strategies. By the way, it is not as weird or esoteric as it may sound! Within about thirty days, a technical analysis software developer who was at the conference had not only included some of the timing techniques I taught at the conference into his software, but even called it something like Energy Pivots, exactly as I described them at the conference. I didn't even get a copy of the software as thanks for designing the routines!

While imitation is the highest form of flattery, I decided then to discontinue my public appearances at conferences and my educational contributions to technical analysis magazines until I had produced a book for the general trading and investing public that set forth my methods. It is almost four years later and here it is!

I have long since accepted that what ever you place before the public whether through articles, books or workshops becomes public domain and no one who appropriates the material is required to reference the source of their instruction except in the case of copyrighted or trademarked material. At least now I know this material will be properly presented in its entirety at a fair price.

I know the value of this material as do hundreds of traders from around the world who have studied it and put it into practice. What ever your level of trading or investing experience, you will find great value in this material. I have taught this material to brand new traders and investors who hardly knew the difference between long and short as well as experienced fund managers who are responsible for millions of dollars of customer funds. Many of them have made these techniques their sole approach to analysis and trading. Others have integrated one aspect or another into their trading approach and trading plans.

Whatever your current level of experience or expertise, it is now your turn to make a change and learn to be a *Dynamic Trader.*

Chapter 2

Getting Started With Dynamic Trading

Use all of the tools, all of the time.
W. D. Gann

The Three Dimensions of Market Activity

Every aspect of the market must be taken into consideration for consistently successful trading and investing decisions. There are two criteria that should be met for any technical analysis methodology to be included as part of the decision making aspect of a trader's trading plan:

1. The analysis technique must be simple and easy to understand both in regards to theory and application.

2. The analysis technique must provide the critical information well *in advance* that is needed to make a trading decision. In other words, we are primarily concerned with *leading indicators* of market activity, not lagging indicators. There are a thousand indicators that will tell us what the market has done. We want to know with a *high degree of reliability* what the market should do in the immediate future.

   The three important dimensions of market activity - time, price and pattern - meet the two criteria described above. Most trading plans only include one, or at the most, two of these important market factors. A comprehensive trading plan that is concerned with having the greatest probability for success will include information from all three dimensions before a trading decision is made.

Time

We must have a time projection methodology that allows us to project with a high degree of consistency the future periods of time that have the greatest probability of trend change. Typical time-cycle analysis provides for wide "windows" of time of as much as several weeks for a potential trend change. This is of little use to the trader or investor. When using daily data, dynamic time projections focus in on periods of just a few days which have a very high probability of trend change. When using intraday data, the focus may be on just a few hours. These relatively narrow time ranges provide the trader or investor with a highly useful piece of information from where to make a decision. Dynamic time projection techniques also project the high probability minimum and maximum time targets for any trend or counter-trend.

Price

We must have a price projection methodology that allows us to project with a high degree of consistency price levels that have the greatest probability of support and resistance. Our price projection methodology must not only project temporary support and resistance zones, but must allow us to project zones that have the greatest probability of terminating the trend. Dynamic price projections provide a very narrow price *zone* where important trend changes usually unfold. A dynamic price projection technique also projects the high probability minimum and maximum price targets for any trend or counter-trend.

Pattern

Our pattern recognition analysis must consistently represent the position of the market in relation to trend, counter-trend, trend termination and trend confirmation. In the chapter on pattern, we will see how to simplify Elliott wave analysis so we can quickly recognize the position of the market related to Elliott wave guidelines. There are certain rules and guidelines associated with Elliott wave analysis that usually reveal the position of the market relative to trend or counter-trend. When that position is not clear, we may choose to ignore that particular market and only consider trading those markets where the pattern clearly reveals the position.

Holistic Technical Analysis

Without a comprehensive analysis procedure, an important decision-making element may be missing. It is critical to view the market from all perspectives. *Each dimension of market activity must be viewed in the context of the other dimensions.* Failure to be aware of all dimensions of market activity may result in a trading decision arrived at by an isolated view of the market that ignores an important market factor. Another dimension of market activity may contradict the isolated view. The market must be viewed from the whole of its activity.

Buy The Bottom, Sell The Top

An important part of dynamic trading analysis is to be prepared in advance and recognize important trend changes as they occur. The lowest risk and lowest capital exposure trade and investment set-ups are often at the significant trend change pivots. I know, I know. Most of the trading and investing books teach never to try to buy the low or sell the high. What nonsense. Those books were written by academics and other non-traders who know little about technical analysis except for lagging indicators which only provide information well after the trend is established. They teach this bit of nonsense because most analysts do not have an analytical method that projects in advance when and where market reversals will take place. Buy the bottom and sell the top is an important factor of a trading plan. This book will give you the tools to do just that quite often.

The Coincidence of Time, Price and Pattern

When time, price and pattern coincide, change is inevitable. When each of the three market dimensions project a high probability of trend change, the change is at least very highly probable, if not inevitable. The coincidence of time, price and pattern projections provide low risk/low capital exposure trade set-ups. If the trend change is confirmed, the trader and investor will have the confidence of knowing the direction of the main trend and the direction that market positions should be taken.

The Objective of Technical Analysis

The purpose of technical analysis is not to be able to accurately identify every market position, all of the time. While this may be the daydream of some analysts and most amateur traders, it is an impossibility. Every method of technical analysis has limitations and at times will provide contradictory information. Unless the analyst, trader or investor is willing to accept that some times his or her analysis will not provide a confident opinion of the market position,
he or she is doomed to failure.

> *The objective of technical analysis is to identify those market conditions and the specific trading strategies that have a high probability of success.*

There are three positions a trader may take at any one time: long, short or out of the market. The out-of-the-market position is taken when the technical analysis does not recognize that the market is in a high probability profit position. Jim Rodgers has said that he "waits until the money is just sitting there on the floor waiting to be picked up" before he considers entering a position. In other words, Rodgers waits until his analysis recognizes the conditions that have a very high probability of success. If you want to be successful, so will you.

Traders who demand action usually have no technical analysis approach or trading plan and are doomed to the same fate as all other junkies - busted. Over the years, I have often had prospective customers call to inquire about my newsletter advisory services, trading workshops or software program. If one of their first questions is something like "how many trades a month does this approach signal", I know they have never had success and never will until they change their objectives. These trading junkies are more concerned with activity than profitability. The only objective of a trader or investor should be net profitability, not the amount of activity.

Once you recognize that the purpose of technical analysis is to identify high probability trade set-ups, patience and discipline should follow.

Analyst, Investor or Trader

Both investors and traders must be good technical analysts to be successful. The technical analysis methods provide the information to make a trading or investing decision. But many analysts are not necessarily good investors or traders. For the purposes of this book, analyst includes everyone interested in the technical analysis of the markets including both trader and investor. The same methods apply to all time frames whether a 15 minute chart or a monthly chart.

What Markets Do These Techniques Apply?

The *Dynamic Trading* techniques apply to all actively traded markets including all of the major futures, stocks, mutual funds and indexes. These techniques have been used by short-term futures traders who consider a three hour trade a long-term position to mutual fund switchers who make only two or three switches each year.

System Trading

The myth that a so-called mechanical trading or investing "system" may be purchased that will provide great profits over time is a sad reminder that a significant portion of the population has more money than brains or at least some money and few brains. What is a "mechanical trading system?" It is a specific and objective set of rules that signal when to buy and sell. The rules may be programmed into software or simply written down. The basis of all these systems is that the user does not have to know anything about the market or trading and investing and will profit by simply following the rules or system signals.

As long as there has been trading and investing, there have been trading and investing systems sold to the public for anywhere from a few hundred dollars to many thousands. I don't believe there has ever been a system sold to the public that the purchaser has profited from over a period of more than one or two years which always seem to be followed by consistent losses that wipe out any accumulated profit in a short amount of time. The majority of "systems" sold are nothing but scams. Some probably have value in the hands of the developer who knows the market conditions under which the system was developed and would recognize when the conditions have changed and the system is no longer applicable.

Not long ago, I challenged all of the readers of the Club 3000 newsletter to provide any evidence of ever having had a single, profitable year from taking every signal of a system that they had purchased. The Club 3000 newsletter was originally begun to provide comments and reviews by system purchasers. I am sure just about every system purchaser and developer in the trading and investing universe subscribes to this newsletter. Not a single system purchaser or developer was able to provide any evidence of a profitable year trading a purchased system! Surprised? I'm not.

Why does the trading system illusion continue? I believe there are two reasons. The first is that many of us want to believe that there really is an easy way. Many of us want to believe that there is a formula that can be purchased and will guarantee success. Whole industries are built on this illusion. Stay up late at night and channel surf and you will see how alive and well is this illusion. *Success can't be purchased*. It must be earned. Trading and investing is the same as any other business. You must gain a certain amount of knowledge and make decisions. Judgment will always be required for success.

The second reason for the perpetuation of the successful system illusion is the recent plethora of system testing software. Most of the popular and inexpensive technical analysis software programs make it relatively easy to test the profitability of a set of trading rules. The left-brain junkies have a field day with the system testing software. Most of these users do not understand that a set of rules may be developed to show a profit on any set of data! Even data randomly generated. But wait until you apply those rules to a new set of data generated under different market conditions. Software promoters feed on the system illusion by heavily promoting the system testing routines in their software. Trading magazines continually have articles on system development written by academics or professional writers with no actual trading experience.

Still interested in system trading? *Futures* magazine tracks the results of most of the public futures trading funds. Public trading funds are all system traders. For practical purposes, they have unlimited financial, computer and brain power resources to develop trading systems. In 1995, the S&P was up 35% for the year. In 1995, the average gain of the 205 funds tracked by Futures magazine was just 12.11%. About one quarter of the funds were down for the year. Only nineteen or less than one out of ten funds beat the S&P for the year. Futures magazine does not report on multi-year returns for these funds, but I will give very high odds that none of them has ever beaten the S&P in each of three years in a row.

Most of these public trading funds have more than ten million dollars under management. Some a lot more. All together they represent several billions of trading dollars. And this is just a drop in the bucket compared with the private trading funds. How much do you think it would be worth to any one of these funds to purchase a system that is profitable? Can you count that high? Given this information, do you really think that you can buy a profitable trading system for a few hundred dollars? For a few thousand dollars?

Hopefully you are now well grounded in reality. Success cannot be purchased. It's that simple.

How This Book Is Laid Out

It is important to progress through the book in the order the material is presented. Each chapter builds upon the previous material.

Doesn't it aggravate you when you are reading in a book the descriptive commentary about a chart illustration and the chart is not on the same page as the commentary? You have to keep flipping back and forth to view the illustration and the commentary together? That won't happen in *Dynamic Trading*. Care has been taken so that the descriptive chart commentary is on the same page as the chart illustration. This often results in a good bit of blank space left at the bottom of a page. This "wasted" space aggravates traditional publishers to no end but is necessary for the best learning experience. The purpose of this book is to teach you these techniques as well as possible, not to conform to the ideal layout standards of traditional book publishers.

It's Time To Get Started

We will begin the *Dynamic Trading* journey with an understanding of "What A Trader Must Know To Be Successful."

What A Trader Must Know To Be Successful

Below are a few definitions with the help of Webster's you must know with my brief comments.

Forecast: *To predict a future condition, occurrence or event.* No one at any time knows what the future outcome of any event will be. All forecasts of future events can only be an educated guess. The outcome of any condition can only be a *probability*, never a certainty.

Probable: *Having more evidence for than against, but not proven conclusively.* All trading and investing activity deals in probabilities, *never* certainties. The objective of all market analysis and trading plans is to put the probabilities of success on our side. This includes eliminating those activities with a low probability of success and only engaging in those activities with a high probability of success.

Speculate: *To engage in a risky business transaction in the hope of making a large profit.* All activities whose outcome is in the future are speculative activities. The degree of risk is relative. The only reason to accept greater risk is with the intention that the potential, future gains will be far greater than relatively less risky activities.

Chance: *The unpredictable element of an occurrence. A possibility or probability.* Every possible occurrence of a future event has a degree of unpredictability which is why no method of attempting to predict the future is without risk.

Risk: *To expose to the chance of loss.* The probability of an event occurring. If the success of any activity is contingent on a future event occurring, that activity is always risky. The objective of the trader and investor is to reduce the inevitable chance of loss by only engaging in those activities (trades or investments) that reflect the greatest probability of success relative to all of the choices available.

Capital Exposure: *The minimum dollar risk to see if your guess of the future is correct or not.* You've got to pay to play. In trading or investing terms, capital exposure is the protective stop-loss amount. What does it cost to find out if you made a profitable decision or not?

Consistency: *Steadfast adherence to the same principles, course, etc.* A trader or investor must adhere to his or her trading plan consistently. Without the quality of consistency of action, success is unobtainable.

Plan: *A scheme or method of acting, proceeding, etc., developed in advance.* "If you fail to plan, plan to fail." Any endeavor which does not include a defined plan will not succeed. No one, particular plan will ensure success. No one plan will include rules or guidelines that will respond successfully to every possible, contingent future activity. But, every plan must at least provide the guidelines of how to proceed in all circumstances.

Trade: *Relatively short-term speculation.*

Invest: *Relatively long-term speculation.*

Bozo: *Someone who does not take the above definitions seriously.* A Bozo may or may not have red hair and bad taste in clothes. There are no Bozos who are successful traders or investors.

Knowing the above definitions and their meaning to us as traders and investors is *critical* to the success in the business of trading and investing. Their critical nature requires more comment and elaboration. The following discussion describes elements necessary for successful trading and investing that are far more essential to success than any trading techniques. On the next page is the real "Holy Grail" of trading and investing.

Speculation … is the self-adjustment of society to the probable.

Oliver Wendell Holmes

Probability Is A Key Concept Successful Trader and Investors Understand

If there is a key word associated with trading and investing, it must be *probability*. All consistently successful investors and traders know that every trading and investing decision only has a probability of success, never a certainty. *Losses are inevitable* and are just as much a part of a successful trading plan as profits. If a trader has a successful trading plan, he or she should have no more emotional response to a loss than to a win. Each will be inevitable. While it may be difficult to maintain a completely non-emotional relationship to trading and investing, an understanding that trading is a business of probabilities will go a long way towards developing a stable attitude toward the business.

All successful traders have a defined, written *trading plan*. The trading plan can take many forms. At the very least, it will provide the minimum guidelines that must be satisfied before a trade will be considered. It may be as complex as a long set of very restrictive rules that must be satisfied before a trade is considered. Each has its strengths and weaknesses. Neither method, whether guidelines or rules will ensure success, but the lack of either will ensure failure. There will be much more on developing a trading plan latter in the book.

A trader who does not *consistently* abide by his or her trading plan is doomed to failure. Why have a plan and not follow it? Each guideline and rule must be included with reason and purpose. All successful traders and investors consistently follow their trading plan and know that if they violate their trading plan it will *always* be costly in the long run.

The above discussion is as important and maybe more so than learning any method of technical analysis or trading strategies. Even a trading plan that included analytical procedures and trading strategies that were 100% accurate, in other words, would indeed predict the exact outcome of the current position of the market 100% of the time, would not result in profits if the trader or investor implementing the plan did not know and act in accordance with the qualities discussed above.

Dynamic Ratios and Counts

The foundational principle of dynamic time and price analysis of the financial markets is the proportional relationship of all market swings to each other. W. D. Gann was certainly the first to demonstrate and teach this fact as early as his first published material in the early 1900s. Up until Robert Pretcher revived and popularized the work of R. N. Elliott, most ratio analysis was limited to static divisions for price retracement. By static, I mean the even divisions such as thirds and fourths. Pretcher's revival of Elliott's work also made the trading public aware of the so-called Fibonacci ratios based on 1.618 which are much more relevant than static ratios to market activity.

In a series of private seminars taught in the early to late eighties based on the work of W. D. Gann and even more obscure market analysts from the first half of the century, Dr. Jerald Baumring taught about many of the other dynamic ratios based on dynamic geometry processes that are also found in the financial markets. Many of these ratios are based on square roots and geometric diagonals. While these other number and ratio series can be an important addition to the tools of the analyst, they are more applicable to advanced study.

I have only included the Fibonacci ratios and counts plus just a few others with this work because they are by far the most prevalent in time and price studies. More importantly, they are all that are necessary to make consistently accurate analysis and projections. Once these methods become second-nature, the student may want to expand his or her knowledge of market geometry and ratio through more advanced study.

Fibonacci Ratios and Counts

As far as we know, R. N. Elliott was the first to apply what have become known as the Fibonacci ratios and number counts to the financial markets. It is a dis-service to the ancient philosophers, particularly Pythagoras, to call them Fibonacci ratios. The proper name for the root ratio, 1.618, is the Golden Mean or Divine Proportion. This proportion was part of the fundamental teaching of the great Greek philosopher, Pythagoras, many centuries before the Italian Fibonacci came on the scene.

Many books on technical analysis, particularly those on Elliott Wave analysis, have described how the Fib ratios and counts are derived and found thoughout the natural world and have been used in all of the greatest art and architecture thoughout history. I'm not even going to touch on the subject here because the background is not directly relevant to practical application. All that we need to know are which ratios and counts are important and how to apply them to technical analysis. So, I will just list the ratios and counts that are relevant to our work. If the student wishes to delve deeper into the greater significance and history of these ratios and numbers, the bibliography provides plenty of sources.

Fib Ratios	Fib Number Series
.236	3
.382	5
.50*	8
.618	13
.786*	21
1.00*	34
1.272*	55
1.618	89
2.000*	144
2.618	233
4.236	377
The series continues by multiplying the previous ratio by 1.618.	The series continues by adding the two most recent numbers to come up with the next number.

Ratios with an asterisk (*) are not directly a part of the Fib ratio series but are related and important for time and price technical analysis work.

Two ratios included above that you may not be familiar with are:
0.786 = square root of .618
1.272 = square root of 1.618

The Dynamic Time and Price Analysis chapters will describe the special situations where each of these ratios apply.

Waves or Swings of Similar Degree

At important market turning points, prior waves of similar degree will relate in time and price proportion at the turning point. Similar degree waves are those waves that are to some extent similar in time and price within the context of the trend. For instance, intermediate term waves are generally 30-90 days in time and 5%-10% change in price for most markets. If you were to look at a weekly chart, intermediate degree waves would be the obvious swings in the market.

Daily charts reveal the lesser degree or minor degree waves that unfold within the intermediate degree waves. In other words, the intermediate degree waves are sub-divided into the minor degree waves. The time, price and pattern projections of the lesser degree waves should coincide with and confirm those of the larger degree.

Many of the examples throughout the book will demonstrate how the smaller degree wave projections will fine tune the time, price and pattern analysis of the larger degree projections. This aspect of the analysis should be very familiar to Elliott Wave traders who look at ever smaller degrees of wave counts to understand the position of the market.

The terms wave and swing will be used interchangeably throughout this book.

T-Bond: 10% or Greater Swings

The chart below is a daily close-only chart from the July 1984 low with a 10%+ swing file overlaid. In other words, each swing made a price change of at least 10% before it was included. As you can see, the 10% or greater swings represented major trends and counter-trends in this period.

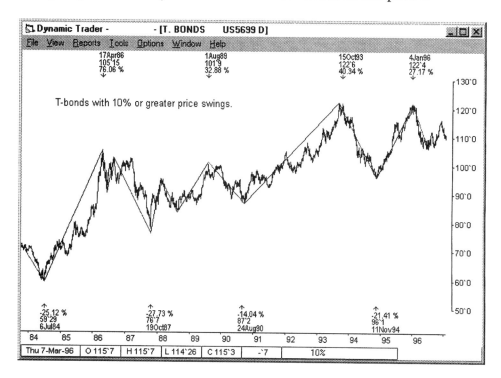

The major degree swings in any particular market may not necessarily be represented by 10% or greater price swings. A greater or lesser percentage change may be more suitable for other markets. The above chart and the one on the following page are included to illustrate how dynamic traders view different degrees of change in each market.

The following page shows a 5% or greater swing chart for the same period.

T-Bonds: 5% or Greater Swings

The chart below is for the same period as the chart on the previous page. This chart includes the 10% or greater swings shown on the previous chart as well as the lesser degree 5% or greater swings. The daily bars are not shown to avoid overcrowding the chart.

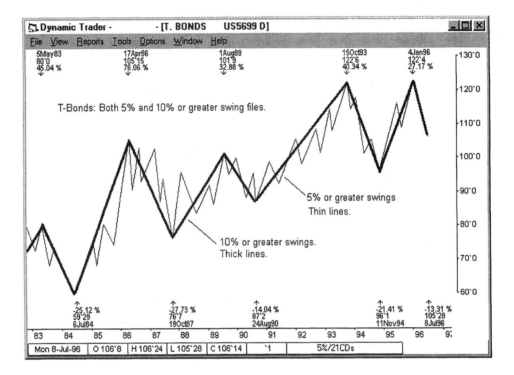

Dynamic Trading analysis often references the position of one degree of market activity within the context of the larger and smaller degrees.

Chapter 3

Pattern and Practical Elliott Wave Analysis

Practically all developments which result from our social-economic processes follow a law that causes them to repeat themselves in similar and constantly recurring series of waves or impulses of definite number and pattern.

R. N. Elliott

In the *Pattern and Practical Elliott Wave Analysis* chapter you

- Learn practical pattern and Elliott Wave analysis in order to identify specific set-ups that have a high probability outcome as well as the specific market activity that will invalidate the anticipated outcome.

- Learn the relationship between pattern and trend position.

- Learn how to use pattern to validate or invalidate the working assumption of the position of the market.

- Learn how to use pattern to help determine the maximum stop-loss level.

- Learn which patterns are the most consistently reliable across a wide range of markets to identify the position of the market.

- Learn the strengths and weaknesses of Elliott wave analysis.

- Learn practical strategies to implement Elliott wave analysis into the trading plan.

This Chapter Teaches *Practical* Elliott Wave Analysis

Two of the important benefits of practical Elliott Wave analysis is to be able to quickly determine if the market position is trend or counter-trend and the pattern position that signals the termination of each of these trend positions.

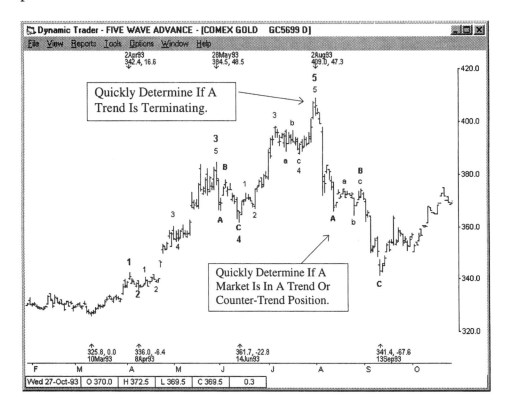

Gold terminated a strong, bull rally Aug. 2, 1993. Elliott wave analysis signaled days *in advance* that the bull move was nearing completion. Is this an after-the-fact example? Absolutely not. The author's *Dynamic Trader Analysis Report* identified gold's position well in advance. This chapter will teach **you** how to quickly identify the position of any market most of the time by practical Elliott wave analysis. I say "most of the time" because you will also learn when the Elliott wave pattern position is not providing adequate information for a trading decision.

How valuable is it to you to be able to identify if the current position of a market is a trend or counter-trend? This is critical information that will help determine what trading strategies to implement.

Dynamic Traders Make Their Own Decisions

Do you remember the sharp decline made by the S&P in July 1996? Do you remember how many well publicized market "gurus" and analysts claimed this was just the beginning of the "long over-due" bear market? Practical Elliott wave analysts understood the July decline was the completion of a correction (probably wave-four) which should be immediately followed by the continuation of the bull trend to new highs.

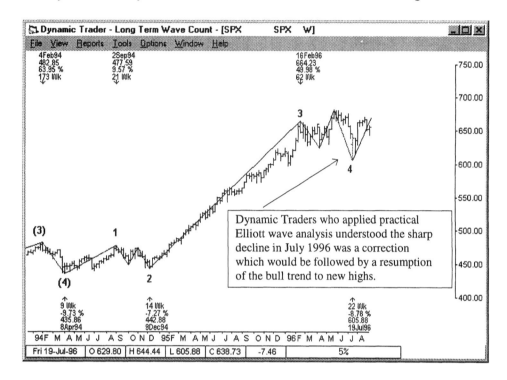

Dynamic Traders who applied practical Elliott wave analysis understood the sharp decline in July 1996 was a correction which would be followed by a resumption of the bull trend to new highs.

How did it turn out? Up to the time this section of the book was prepared, the S&P has advanced over 30% from the July 1996 low leaving many of the gurus and overpaid analysts with egg on their faces and big drawdowns in their customer's accounts. Do you see how an understanding of the trend and counter-trend position of a market will provide you with the perspective to make high probability trade and investment decisions?

Dynamic Traders were prepared for the continuation of the bull trend in July 1996. By mastering the simple rules and guidelines of practical Elliott wave analysis and trading strategies, you will understand the position of a market and not have to rely on the often grossly inaccurate analysis of the media gurus.

It is necessary to first gain a background of pattern analysis of market position. Much of the high probability time and price analysis will be contingent on an understanding of the pattern position of the market.

Your first time though this pattern chapter, it may seem more complicated than it really is. Don't skip this chapter, but also, don't get hung up on memorizing every detail. By the time you are through with this chapter, you will have a firm grasp of the practical principles of Elliott wave analysis. The subsequent chapters on *Dynamic Price and Time Analysis* and *Putting It All Together* will reinforce what you have learned in this chapter.

The summary of Elliott's wave principle in this chapter does not attempt to explain the rationale of Elliott's theory or how it is a reflection of social or mass psychology. That explanation is available in other publications about Elliott Wave.

Most traders are already familiar with the basics of Elliott wave analysis. Even if you are, do not skip this section. It is important to understand the perspective, terminology and notation used in the book so there will not be confusion later on.

There is no practical trading value in knowing all of the complex corrective variations. The purpose of this training is not to become academic experts of market analysis but recognize and apply analysis and trading strategies that have practical value for making trading decisions. We'll let the academics and non-trading analysts argue over the proper interpretation of market structure, while we will concentrate on what helps us to make trading and investing profits.

The focus of our use of wave analysis will be the same as it is with any other analysis method. What practical information is the market providing us that helps put the probabilities in our favor for successful trades and investments? The chart pattern provides us with an important piece of information regarding a market, which is: *What is the most likely current position of the market relative to the trend, and what market activity will confirm or invalidate the assumed position?*

If we know the most likely current position of a market relative to the trend, we know what the most likely future position will be. Note that I have said, *most likely*. Always keep in mind that we are dealing with probabilities. We can never know with certainty what is the current position and what will be the future position. The objective of pattern analysis, just as with time and price analysis, is to put the probabilities on our side.

R. N. Elliott has provided traders and investors with the most objective methodology of determining the position of a market by what has become known as the Elliott Wave Principle. This pattern chapter will only consider Elliott's Wave Principle as it is the most objective description of the position of a market related to pattern. However, contrary to the opinion of some Elliott wave proponents, Elliott's Wave Principle will not always provide a confident description of the market position. However, the Elliott Wave Principle will almost always provide a description of the market position that will tell us with confidence if the market is in a *trend* or *counter-trend* and the degree of the trend or counter-trend. This information alone is invaluable to the trader or investor.

First we will look at a summary of the Elliott wave principle, then we will look at it's strengths and weakness followed by how we can put it to practical trading application.

Essentially, Elliott's Wave Principle is a catalogue of defined chart patterns. When recognized by the analyst, these patterns should not only indicate what the current position of the market is relative to trend or counter-trend, but imply what the most probable direction of the market should be if the analyst has correctly identified the current pattern. In other words, each pattern has implications regarding the position of the market and the most likely outcome of the current position.

Elliott Wave Basics

The basis of Elliott's Wave Principle is that most trends unfold in *five waves* in the direction of the trend and *three waves* in the direction counter to the main trend. It's that simple. Markets usually unfold in three's and five's. Five wave patterns are *impulsive* structures. Three wave patterns are *corrective* structures.

There are certain rules and guidelines that help to identify the wave structure. If the activity of all markets could be easily identified at all times with one of Elliott's wave patterns, trading would be a simple exercise of entering and exiting a market at the completion of the pattern that would signal a trend reversal. Needless to say, it does not work out this easily for two obvious and important reasons:

1. *Markets only exhibit a useful Elliott wave pattern about 50% of the time.* Traders or investors who try to apply an Elliott wave count to each market at all times and under all conditions are usually forcing a wave count just for the sake of exhibiting a wave count. When this is the case, the Elliott wave pattern information is not only useless, but misleading and can prove very costly. Market analysts who limit their entire technical approach to Elliott wave analysis are notorious for doing this. They try to prove something that does not exist. Practical traders and investors recognize when Elliott wave analysis is applicable to a market condition and when it is not.

2. *At times, particularly with complex, corrective patterns, there is simply little clue as to the position of the market within the context*

of the pattern of the larger degree trend. All indications may be that a market is in a correction, but once the market gets beyond a simple ABC correction there usually is not a confident, specific pattern interpretation. When this is the case, the analyst should not try to force a complex count just for the sake of trying to identify something that is not reliably identifiable.

Don't Become A Trading Junkie

If a market is not providing the information necessary to make a confident decision that provides an acceptable level of capital exposure, *that market must simply be ignored for the time being.* There will be opportunities within the context of the trading plan at another time or in another market.

If we are able to identify a confident Elliott wave count of the market position, that particular count will also provide us with the market activity that will invalidate the wave count. This is extremely critical. In effect, we are talking about a *pattern stop-loss.* There will be more about this as we look at each individual pattern.

Now, let's begin our study of Elliott's wave patterns by studying the general characteristics of impulse and corrective waves, the rules and guidelines associated with Elliott's Wave Principle and how the most reliable wave patterns provide us with specific price targets for the confirmation and termination of trend.

Wave Labeling and Notation Conventions Used In This Book

Each wave may be sub-divided into another wave pattern of lesser degree. Each wave is also a part of a larger degree wave. Generally, we will only be looking at three degrees of trend: minor, intermediate and major. While R. N. Elliott described many degrees of waves from the super-cycle wave that lasted decades to sub-minuette waves that may only last minutes, these extreme waves are of little practical value to traders. It frequently takes a lot of imagination and a three martini lunch to come up with wave counts on very long-term charts or very short-term intraday charts. If you can clearly identify two or three degrees of wave structure, you will have the critical information needed to make a trading decision.

The charts on the following page show how waves may be labeled by three degrees: major, intermediate and minor. The intermediate degree waves are sub-divisions of the major degree waves while the minor degree waves are sub-divisions of the intermediate degree waves.

Three Degrees of Wave Sub-Divisions

Major Degree Waves

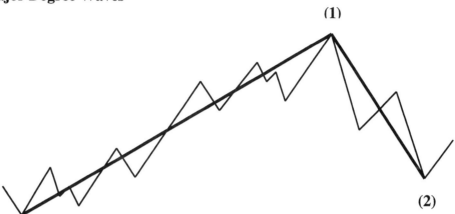

Intermediate Degree Waves

Sub-divisions of major degree waves.

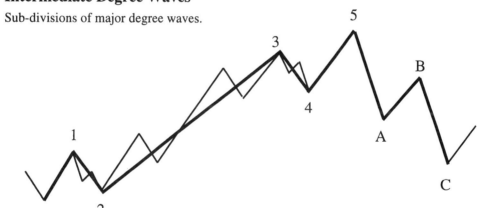

Minor Degree Waves

Sub-divisions of intermediate degree waves.

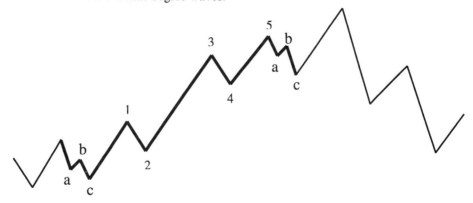

Three Degrees Of Wave

The swing chart below shows three degrees of waves labeled. Only the last wave of the series shows all the notations for all degrees.

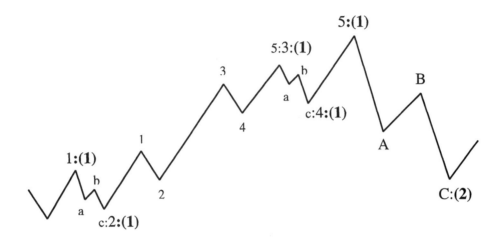

The entire sequence shown above is a wave one and two of major degree (waves (**1**) and (**2**)). A smaller degree sequence will always complete at the end of a larger degree wave. When notating more than one wave together, begin with the smallest wave and work up to the largest. For example, <u>5:3:(1)</u> is the end of minor degree wave 5 of intermediate degree wave 3 of major degree wave (**1**).

Major degree waves usually last from several months to several years and are obvious on a monthly or weekly chart. Intermediate degree waves usually last from several weeks to several months and are obvious on a longer term daily or weekly chart. Minor waves usually last from a few days to a few weeks and are revealed on a daily chart. There is no defined time period for each of these degrees of waves. A grain market may have a major degree bull and bear market every three to five years because of panic weather cycles while a financial market's major cycle may last much longer as the recent major-degree, stock bull-market which has lasted well over a decade demonstrates.

My terminology and labeling conventions may be a bit different from Elliott's and what other Elliott wave analysts use today. Don't be hung up on labels and terms. Leave that for the academics to argue over. My objective is to keep things simple so we will be able to easily note what is the wave structure of the market. The most important factor to keep in mind is that you should be concerned with one degree of wave larger and one degree of wave smaller than the degree you intend to trade.

Ideally, the market structure will clearly reveal three degrees. This is not always the case. *Do not try to force an Elliott Wave count on a market when none clearly exists*! Academics and advisors do this all of the time and usually end up tripping over their multitude of "alternate" counts. It is just as important to recognize and admit to what is not clearly revealed as to recognize what is obvious. True knowledge is recognizing how little it is you know. The wise person does not worry about their ignorance.

The wave structure illustrations on the following pages are idealized swing charts. The first objective is to become thoroughly familiar with the rules and guidelines for wave structure before applying them to actual price charts. This is best taught with the idealized swing charts. Latter examples will use actual price charts.

Some of the illustrations in the time and price chapters will assume you have a working knowledge of wave structure and the label notations used in this chapter. Don't skip the rest of this chapter even if you are already familiar with Elliott Wave analysis.

A Summary Of The Elliott Wave Principle
Impulse Waves - General Description

1. Impulse waves unfold in a pattern of five waves. A five wave pattern is always a part of a larger degree trend.

2. Waves 1, 3 and 5 within a five wave pattern are themselves impulse waves of lesser degree and should each sub-divided into a five wave pattern.

3. Once a five wave pattern completes, the entire sequence should be corrected by a pattern of either three waves (ABC) or one of a series of three and five waves known as "complex corrections."

4. Corrective waves within a five wave sequence are waves two and four.

5. One of the impulsive waves will usually extend or be noticeably longer in price than the other two impulse waves. In the financial markets, the extended wave is usually wave three. In the commodity markets, the extended wave is often wave five.

6. The two non-extended waves are frequently close to equality of price range.

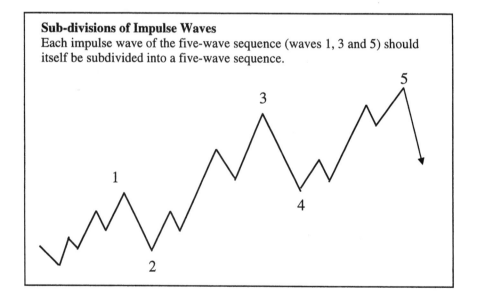

Sub-divisions of Impulse Waves
Each impulse wave of the five-wave sequence (waves 1, 3 and 5) should itself be subdivided into a five-wave sequence.

Elliott Wave "Rules" For An Impulse Sequence

There are just three rules that are considered inviolate according to today's traditional, Elliott wave analysts. However, Elliott never listed these as inviolate rules. When describing these situations in his earlier works, Elliott used the terms "should" and "rarely", not "never". In order to avoid the criticism that Elliott's pattern analysis was not completely objective, I suspect these rules were developed as inviolate long after Elliott had completed his own life-cycle fifth wave.

I will describe these rules here, as they are a good guide to keep the analyst objective as to the position of the market relative to Elliott Wave analysis. Later in this section, I will illustrate how markets apparently have not read Elliott's works and seem to ignore the rules with some regularity.

Elliott Wave "Rules"

1. Wave 2 cannot retrace past the beginning of wave 1.

2. Wave 3 cannot be the shortest of the three impulse waves (1, 3 and 5) in the five wave sequence.

3. Wave 4 cannot overlap or trade into the territory of wave 1.

If any of these rules are violated, the wave structure as labeled is incorrect and must be re-evaluated.

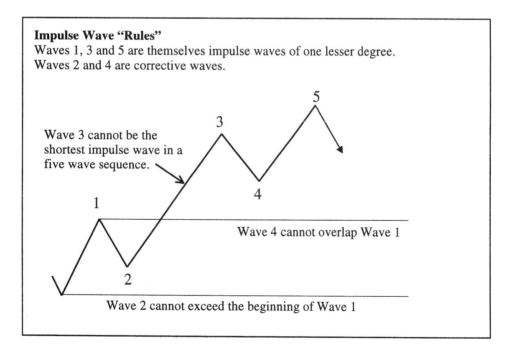

Impulse Wave "Rules"
Waves 1, 3 and 5 are themselves impulse waves of one lesser degree.
Waves 2 and 4 are corrective waves.

Wave 3 cannot be the shortest impulse wave in a five wave sequence.

Wave 4 cannot overlap Wave 1

Wave 2 cannot exceed the beginning of Wave 1

The Rules and Guidelines Illustrated

The following illustrations assume that the pivot marked **0** is a change of trend from where a five-wave, impulse sequence should begin. As a market unfolds, it will either validate that assumption or provide us with potential alternate counts if that assumption is invalidated.

Wave Two cannot exceed the beginning of Wave One.

If the market exceeds the beginning of wave one, the count must be reconsidered. Below, the initial five wave advance from **0** cannot be a wave one of larger degree because the market has declined below the beginning of wave one. Possibly, the five wave advance is a wave A of an irregular ABC correction. Waves A and C are often five wave structures as we will see when we discuss corrective waves. Or, **0** is not the completion of a five wave sequence as we originally suspected.

If a market trades below what was assumed to be the beginning of wave one, we *must* change our opinion of the position of the market and can no longer assume a new five-wave trend sequence had begun. Depending on the preceding wave structure, that opinion may now be very bearish.

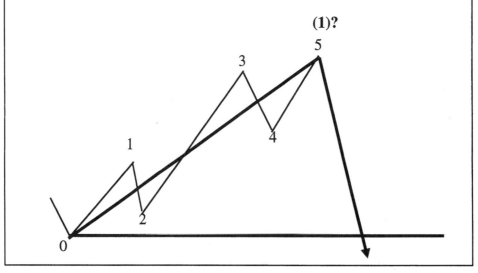

Wave 2 cannot exceed the beginning of Wave 1.
This five-wave sequence cannot be a wave (1) of larger degree as it has declined below the beginning of wave-1. It may be an A wave or even the termination of a complex correction.

Wave Three cannot be the shortest of the three impulse waves 1, 3 or 5.

If what we have considered to be a wave three is less than the length of wave one and wave five then exceeds the length of wave three, the five wave impulse count is invalidated. Wave three cannot be the shortest of waves 1, 3 or 5. If this occurs, more than likely the proper count would indicate that wave three is to be extended and the original label of waves 3-5 are the sub-waves of a wave three of larger degree as shown below.

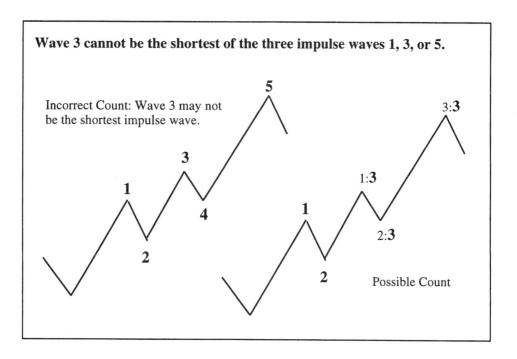

Wave 3 cannot be the shortest of the three impulse waves 1, 3, or 5.

Incorrect Count: Wave 3 may not be the shortest impulse wave.

Possible Count

Wave Four cannot trade within the price range of Wave One.

If we have labeled a 1-2-3 count and subsequently the market declines from the end of wave 3 into the price range of wave 1, the count must be reconsidered. Either the original wave three and four are waves one and two of wave three of larger degree or the market is in a corrective phase and waves 1-3 are really ABC of a corrective pattern.

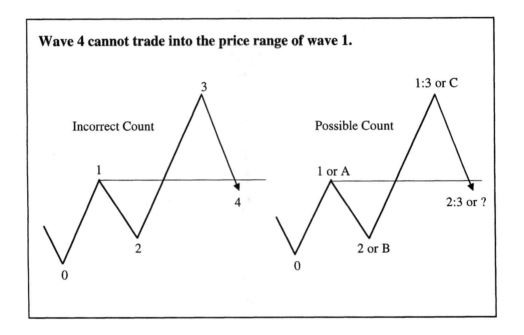

The smaller degree patterns confirm the position of the larger degree.

As a market unfolds, it will continually confirm or invalidate the suspected count. The assumption below is that the market has made a five wave advance which is wave one of larger degree. From the wave one high, the market declines in a five wave structure. The five wave decline should not be a completed correction as corrections are usually three wave structures. The five wave decline could be a wave A of an ABC correction or the high labeled wave one may have actually completed a larger degree correction and the decline is a continuation of the main bear trend.

The position of the market preceding what is illustrated below will help to determine the alternate pattern positions. For now, all we want to be able to do is recognize the immediate position of the market.

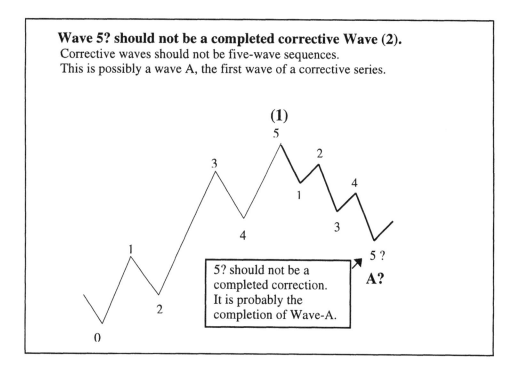

Wave 5? should not be a completed corrective Wave (2).
Corrective waves should not be five-wave sequences.
This is possibly a wave A, the first wave of a corrective series.

5? should not be a completed correction. It is probably the completion of Wave-A.

Trading is applying the knowledge of the greater probabilities of market position derived from the analytical procedures. In the above case, there is one important piece of information: more than likely, what was labeled as Wave (2) is **not** a Wave (2). *Knowing what a market probably is **not** can be as valuable as knowing what it probably is.*

Fifth-Wave-Failures

The expectation for impulsive waves is that each of the internal impulsive waves of a five wave sequence (waves 1, 3 and 5) will exceed the extreme of the prior impulsive wave. In other words, in a bull trend the wave three high will be higher than the wave one high and the wave five high will be higher than the wave three high. Occasionally, this will not occur in the fifth wave, and the fifth wave will terminate short of the extreme of the third wave. This is called a *fifth-wave-failure*.

The fifth wave is an impulse wave and should be sub-divided into five waves of lesser degree. Rather than try to guess if a fifth-wave-failure will unfold, it is better to monitor the internal structure and price objective of the fifth wave itself to determine if it is probable to fail.

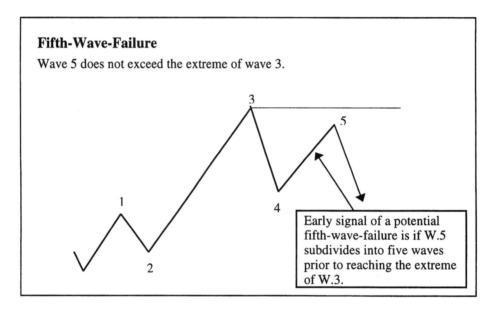

Fifth-Wave-Failure
Wave 5 does not exceed the extreme of wave 3.

Early signal of a potential fifth-wave-failure is if W.5 subdivides into five waves prior to reaching the extreme of W.3.

An early warning that a fifth-wave-failure may unfold is the nature of the wave four. An unusually deep wave four which retraces more than 50% of the price range of waves 1-3 or approaches the extreme of wave one will often result in a fifth-wave-failure.

Important trading implication of a fifth-wave-failure

A fifth-wave-failure has very bearish implications regarding the subsequent correction. The correction will probably be relatively deeper than is typically anticipated following a completed wave five.

Fifth-Wave-Diagonal-Triangles

A fifth-wave-diagonal-triangle is an exception to the rules. The importance of recognizing a fifth-wave-diagonal-triangle is the trading implication following the completion of the triangle.

A diagonal triangle may occur as the fifth wave of a five wave sequence. The impulsive waves 1, 3 and 5 of the larger degree wave five may divide into "threes" instead of "fives" which of course can cause confusion regarding the count and position of the market if this should occur.

Wave 4:5 may trade into the range of W.1:5. This is the only exception to the non-overlap rule of waves four and one accepted by traditional Elliott wave analysts.

Fifth-wave-diagonal-triangles are infrequent and <u>usually only occur at market peaks, not market bottoms</u>.

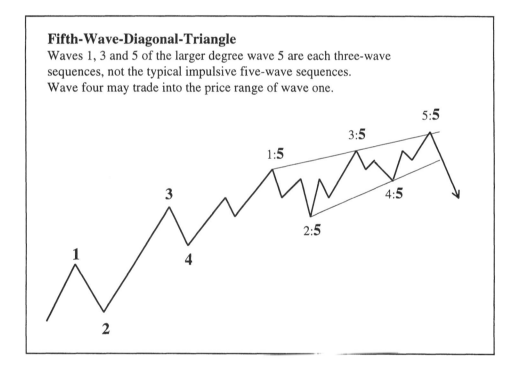

Fifth-Wave-Diagonal-Triangle
Waves 1, 3 and 5 of the larger degree wave 5 are each three-wave
sequences, not the typical impulsive five-wave sequences.
Wave four may trade into the price range of wave one.

Since fifth-wave-diagonal-triangles violate the Elliott wave "rules" for an impulsive wave structure, they will usually not be evident until they are either near completion or after they have completed and the counter-trend is underway.

An extended complex correction often has about the same form and structure as a fifth-wave-diagonal-triangle. While you may consider the possibility that a market is in a fifth-wave-diagonal-triangle, *always* view the position of the market as if it is in a complex correction and will eventually resume the trend *until proven otherwise*. It can be very hazardous to your trading and investing profits to try to identify a fifth-wave-diagonal in advance, as many Elliott wave stock market analysts and traders who had been calling the top of the U.S. stock market throughout the 1993-1994 period found out.

Important trading implication of a fifth-wave-diagonal-triangle

If fifth-wave-diagonal-triangles are so difficult to identify as they are forming and are usually only evident after they have completed, why is it important to be aware of this market structure? *The ramifications of a fifth wave diagonal triangle is that the market should have an unusually strong correction following the completion of the diagonal fifth wave.*

If a market signals that the structure is probably not a complex correction but a completed diagonal fifth wave, the trader or investor will be prepared for a deep and prolonged correction against the prior trend. A sure sign that the market structure has completed a fifth-wave-diagonal is if the market exceeds what could be labeled as the wave two of five extreme. At this point, the trader should have no more illusions that the market is in a prolonged complex-correction but should recognize that a larger degree impulse trend has completed.

Implications Of The Rules and Guidelines
For A Five Wave Impulse Sequence

It must be kept in mind that the most important objective of Elliott-wave, pattern analysis is to understand the position of the market relative to the trend.

1. If we believe that the last swing high or low began an impulsive, five-wave trend sequence, the market cannot trade below (above) what we believe is the beginning of wave one. If this should occur, the wave count is incorrect, as a wave two may not exceed the beginning of wave one.

    Trading Implication
    A protective stop loss should never be placed more than one tick beyond what we consider the beginning of wave one.

2. If we believe that a market is in the initial stages of a five wave sequence and has completed waves one and two and has begun wave three, *we can anticipate that wave three will be longer in price range than wave one*. Of the three impulse waves in a five wave sequence (waves 1, 3 and 5), wave three is most often the "extended" wave. This is particularly true of the stock and financial markets. In commodity markets, wave five is as likely to be extended due to panic, weather condition blow-offs. Wave one is rarely the extended wave.

    The fact that wave three is usually the extended wave allows us to make a minimum price objective for a wave three within a five wave sequence. Wave three will usually be greater in price than wave one. A 100% Alternate Price Projection (APP) will be the minimum expectation of wave three. Once a market exceeds the 100% APP, we have a strong indication that a five wave sequence is underway. This is also called a trend confirmation.

    Trading Implication
    We should not be too quick to bring a protective stop loss close to the market prior to price reaching what we consider the minimum projection which is where wave three would equal wave one. The protective stop loss should be adjusted closer to the market once the price range of the suspected wave three exceeds the price range of wave one.

3. If we believe that a market has completed wave three of a five wave sequence, yet wave three is less in price than wave one, wave five must be less in price range than wave three which is the shorter wave

of waves one and three. *Wave three cannot be the shortest of the three impulse waves in a five wave sequence.* In this situation, we have a definite *maximum* price objective for wave five which is 100% of the price range of wave three, the shortest impulse wave to date.

We may consider wave three is complete even if its price range is less than the price range of wave one, if wave three has completed a five wave advance. This is the only situation where we can consider wave five has a maximum price objective.

Trading Implication
The protective stop loss of wave five should be moved very close to the market if the price approaches the maximum objective for this wave structure.

4. If we believe that a wave three has completed and the wave four is underway and the market trades into the price range of wave one, *the market has invalidated our count of the waves three and four as a wave four may not trade into the price range of wave one.* The wave count must be re-considered.

Trading Implication
The *maximum* protective stop loss on a trend trade is the wave one extreme. However, in most cases the stop loss would be closer to the market. In the case of a bull market, the maximum protective stop loss is one tick below the wave one high once the wave three high is identified and the wave four decline is underway.

5. The smaller degree pattern will confirm the position of the larger degree. Waves 1, 3 and 5 should each be constructed of five wave patterns of lesser degree. If the market violates any of the rules of impulse pattern within the lesser degree, it indicates that the larger degree is not a five-wave impulse sequence as anticipated. Smaller degree patterns are not always evident on a daily chart.

Trading Implication
If the smaller degree patterns are evident, they are used to advantage by enabling the trader or investor to enter positions with closer initial protective stop losses, adjusting protective stop losses closer to the market and providing narrower time and price targets for trend confirmation and trend termination.

Wave Comparison Notation

Throughout the time and price sections of the book, you will learn how to project the time and price ranges of prior waves forward in order to determine at what price and time a market should reverse trend. When comparing one wave to another, a simple notation system is used to quickly recognize what is being compared. Below are some examples.

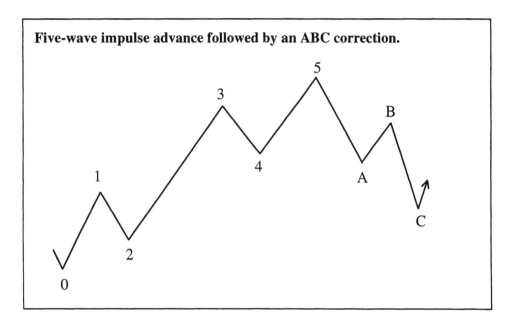

Five-wave impulse advance followed by an ABC correction.

The illustration above shows a five wave advance followed by an ABC correction. It has not been sub-divided into minor degree waves. Earlier in this chapter, the wave-labeling and notation conventions used to identify waves was described. This section will describe the notations used to compare waves when making time and price projections.

Wave Ranges

Price ranges are measured by the vertical axis. Time ranges are measured by the horizontal axis.

A wave is indicated by a W.

W.1 above is the distance from 0 to 1.

W.1-3 (waves 1 through 3) is the distance from the beginning of wave 1 (labeled 0) to the end of wave 3 (labeled 3). W.1-3 does not mean the distance from point 1 to 3, but the net range traveled of waves 1 though 3.

W.3-5 (waves 3 through 5) is the distance from point 2 to point 5 or the distance covered from the beginning of wave 3 (end of wave 2) through the end of wave 5.

Wave 5 is often related to both wave 1 and waves 1-3 by either equality or one of the Fibonacci ratios. If we have identified the end of wave 4 (beginning of wave 5), we can project potential time and price targets for wave 5.

Examples Of Price Wave Comparison Notation

642.00: W.5 = 61.8% W.1. At 642.00, the price range of wave 5 equals 61.8% of the price range of wave 1.

643.20: W.5 = 100% W.1. At 643.20, the price range of wave 5 equals 100% of the price range of wave 1.

644.10: W.5 = 61.8% W.1-3. At 644.10, the price range of wave 5 equals 61.8% of the price range of waves 1 through 3.

622.10: W.2 = 50% Ret. W.1. At 622.10, wave 2 is a 50% retracement of the price range of wave 1.

633.50: W.3 = 100% Exp. W. 1. At 633.50, the extreme of wave 3 is at a 100% expansion of the price range of wave 1.

Price retracements, alternate projections and expansions are described in detail in the *Dynamic Price Analysis* chapter. These same wave comparison notations are used for time projections and are described in the *Dynamic Time Analysis* chapter.

Each wave and its sub-divisions tend to have definite characteristics that help to identify the wave and it's position within the larger trend. The following sections describe the main characteristics and price relationships of each wave type, impulsive and corrective, and their sub-waves. The price chapter will provide the detail of how to make the price projections. For now, we just want to be aware of the wave characteristics that are reasonably consistent.

Impulsive Waves 1, 3 and 5
Their Main Characteristics and Price Ratio Projections

As a market progresses, completing more and more waves, there are additional waves to make comparisons with and projections from. The earliest stages of a trend provide the least information to make price projections. The later stages provide the most information. The ultimate objective of making price projections for a five wave sequence is to project the end of wave five which is the end of the entire sequence which should then be followed by a correction greater in time and price than the prior corrective waves two or four within the sequence.

The following discussion of wave characteristics and price objectives of the various impulse waves within a five wave sequence assumes that we have identified a change in trend that we believe is the beginning of a five wave sequence. As a market progresses, how the market acts, reacts, meets or exceeds the various projections will help to confirm or invalidate if an impulse sequence is actually underway.

The price projections described on the following pages are the *internal* relationships of the waves within the five wave sequence. We must always keep in mind that any wave sequence is a part of a larger degree sequence. The internal price projections of the larger degree waves will be the *external* price projections of the smaller degree waves. This will become more clear with examples.

The price projections described on the following pages are the typical projections found the most often for each wave described. The most reliable price zones to anticipate support or resistance are those that are a cluster of several projections as described in the *Dynamic Price Analysis* chapter. These price projections will frequently provide us with very reliable minimum and maximum expectations for the price objective of the current wave structure.

Another very important factor is that the most reliable price projections will be made from more than one degree. For instance, when the internal, *minor* waves of a fifth intermediate degree wave project the same price zone as the *intermediate* degree waves preceding the fifth wave, we have a very reliable price objective. *The highest probability price projections include projections from one larger and one smaller degree .* The smaller degree waves confirm the projections of the next larger degree waves.

Impulse Wave One

A. Wave one should sub-divide into a five wave sequence.

B. Wave one is usually greater in price and time than the recent <u>corrective</u> swings of similar degree.

Wave one is the initial swing against the prior trend. Wave one is rarely the longest impulse wave of the five wave sequence. Wave one will frequently be similar in price and time to the prior corrective wave or waves, as the conviction of the majority of traders has not changed. They continue to believe the prior trend is still in force and that the wave one is another correction within the established trend. The most important indication that a wave one may be forming is if the prior trend appears to have completed a larger degree corrective structure and the *suspected wave one sub-divides in a five wave sequence of lesser degree.* Corrective waves are usually three-wave structures such as an ABC, so if the current wave is a five wave sequence it should not be a corrective wave but a new impulse wave.

The chart on the following page shows that the rally from <u>0</u> appears to have unfolded in a five wave structure which signals it may be a wave one of larger degree.

An *overbalance* of price and/or time is an initial signal that a market has made a reversal of greater degree than prior counter-trends. An overbalance of price and time is when a market makes a counter-trend swing that is greater in price and time *range* than prior counter-trend swings. If a market makes a five-wave sequence that overbalances in price and time prior corrections, it is a strong indication that the trend change is larger in degree than prior counter-trends and the market may be in the initial stages of a new impulsive sequence.

Because wave one is the initial swing in a new impulsive sequence, there are few swings to compare to in order to make price projections. Ideally, the lesser degree five wave sequence within the larger degree wave one will be evident, which will allow price projections from these minor swings.

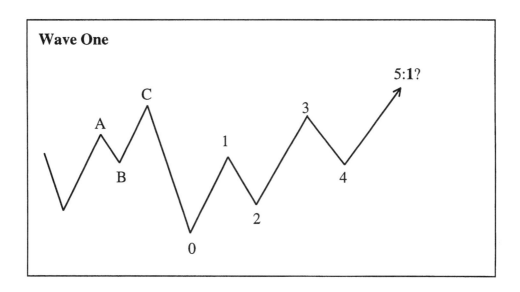

Wave One

Wave One Summary

A. Wave one should sub-divide into five waves of lesser degree.

B. Wave one is usually greater in time and price than prior corrective waves of similar degree. The prior corrective wave above is the ABC sequence. The waves 1-5 sequence is greater in price and time than the ABC sequence and is therefore probably the sub-divisions of a wave one.

Impulse Wave Three

A. Wave three is never the shortest of the three impulse waves (1, 3 or 5).

B. Wave three is usually the extended impulse wave (greater in price range than either waves one or five).

Wave 3 verses Wave 1.

Since wave one is rarely the longest of the three impulse waves (1,3,5) and wave three is usually the extended impulse wave, we can anticipate that the *minimum* price objective for wave three will be 100% of the price range of wave one (W.3 = 100% W.1).

If the suspected wave three has exceeded the 100% price range of wave one, a signal has been made that the current wave is probably wave three of a five wave sequence. If this is the case, the next minimum price objective will be where W.3 = 162% W.1. The majority of the time, wave three will be between 162% and 262% of wave one. In fact, wave three will often terminate on or very near these projections: W.3 = 162% W.1 or W.3 = 262% W.1.

Wave 3 verses Wave 2.

Wave three is frequently related to wave two by 162%, 200% or 262% (W.3 = 162% W.2, etc.). These are external price retracements and will be described in detail in the price chapter.

Wave 3 verses the expansion of Wave 1.

The price terminus of wave three is frequently related to the expansion of the price range of wave one. Wave one is also called the "initial impulse." The most important ratios for this projection are: 100%, 162%, 200% and 262% of the range of wave one added to the end of wave one. Price expansions are described in detail in the price chapter.

Wave three is usually the longest and strongest wave.

Wave three usually travels at a greater rate of change than waves one or five. In other words, the slope of wave three is usually more steep than wave one. The rate of change of wave three usually increases once the extreme of wave one is exceeded. This is the point where the larger numbers of traders or investors become convinced that the trend has actually changed and begin to enter a bull market *en mass* or exit a bear market in a panic liquidation. This is usually also the third of the third wave and usually has the widest range days and often gap moves.

Because wave three of three is frequently a powerful move, traders ideally want to be positioned before wave three is underway. Because all of the Dynamic Trading analysis techniques of time and price are leading indicators that are calculated in advance, this is not just a pipe dream but will frequently be a reality.

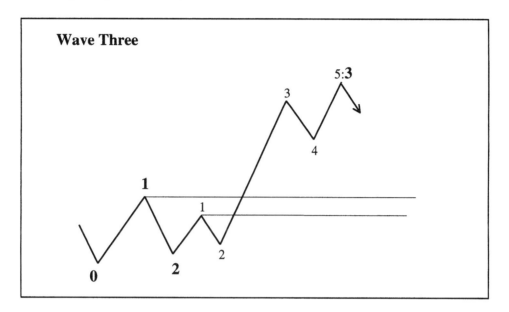

Wave Three Summary

A. Wave three should sub-divide into a five wave sequence of lesser degree

B. Wave three should travel at a greater rate-of-change than either impulse waves one or five.

C. The rate-of-change of wave three will often increase when wave one is exceeded.

D. Wave three of three is often a very powerful move with wide-range and gap days.

E. The price range of wave three will usually be 162% or greater of the price range of wave one.

Key Trading Strategies For Wave Three

If waves one and two of wave three are identified, a low risk/high profit potential trade is to buy on the breakout from the extreme of wave one of three. This is also a strategy often used to add positions if a position was taken on the wave two correction. If the sub-divisions of wave three are not clearly identified, enter on the breakout of the wave one extreme. Ideally, the initial trades will be entered on the wave two correction as described in the correction section.

Impulse Wave Five

Wave 5 verses Wave 1.

The two non-extended impulse waves of a five wave sequence are usually near equality in price range. If wave three is 162% or greater than wave one, go under the assumption that wave three is the extended wave.

   If we assume that wave three is extended, wave five will frequently be near equality of price range to wave one (W.5 = 100% W.1). If wave five does not complete at or near the 100% projection of the wave one price range, it will probably complete near either the 62% or 162% projection of wave one.

   If neither waves one or three are extended, wave five will have a greater probability of being the extended wave and 162% or more of either waves one or three.

Wave 5 verses Wave 3.

The relationship of wave five to wave three is not as consistent as it is to either wave one or waves one-three. If wave three appears to be extended (greater than 162% of wave one), wave five will usually be near 38%, 50% or 62% of wave three. If wave five extends (greater than the range of waves one or three), it will tend to be near 100% or 162% of waves one-three.

Wave 5 verses Waves 1-3.

If wave three is extended, wave five will frequently be either 62% or 38% of the price range of waves one-three.

Wave 5 verses Wave 4.

Wave five is frequently 127%, 162%, 200% or 262% of the price range of wave four. W.5 = 162% W.4 is the most frequent.

Waves 3-5 verses Wave 2.

The net range of waves three through five is usually related to wave two by a 162%, 262% or 424% retracement of wave two. The end of wave five rarely exceeds a 424% retracement of wave two.

Wave 5 verses the expansion of Wave 1.

The price termination target of wave five is frequently targeted by an expansion of wave one. The most important ratios of wave one expansion related to the end of wave five are 162%, 200%, 262%, 300% and 424%.

Wave 5 Rate-of-Change.

Wave five usually has a lesser rate of change than wave three even if new highs are being made. In other words, the slope of wave five is usually less than the slope of wave three.

The psychology of the public, trading and investing advisors and the media is usually at an extreme in the fifth wave. In a bull market, the trend must end when there is no more money to invest in the market. The volume in wave five is frequently less than the volume in wave three, even if wave five is making a new price extreme. There are no buyers of consequence left to bid up prices. Just when the market position looks the most bullish to the majority, the market peaks. This does not imply that a market will peak as soon as the bullish psychology is overwhelming, only that *a market peak will not occur without the bullish psychology being overwhelming.*

Wave 5 should sub-divide into five waves of lesser degree.

A wave five should not end until it has subdivided into five waves of lesser degree. The key to the most accurate price projections to anticipate trend change is when the waves of one lesser degree project price targets that are at or near the same price targets as the larger degree projections. When the price target for wave 5 of 5 coincides with the price target of wave 5, the odds are high that the coincidental price target will complete wave 5.

Key Trading Strategies For Wave Five

Enter against the trend direction at or near the completion of wave five.

One of the lowest risk/highest profit potential trades that pattern analysis can alert us to is identifying the end of wave five. Wave five completes a trend structure and should be followed by a move against the five wave trend direction that should be greater in price and time than any counter-trend swing since the beginning of the five wave structure.

If it appears that wave five is nearing completion, stops on current positions should be brought close to the market with the expectation that the trend is near completion. Traders should also look to enter positions against the five wave trend direction on reversal signals. Ideally, the wave five sub-divisions will be evident and the time, price and pattern projection zone for the end of wave five of five will provide a narrow price objective for trend reversal.

Corrective Waves

While there is basically just one pattern for impulse waves, a five wave structure, Elliott described eight different potential patterns with variations for corrective waves. Identification and labeling of corrective waves is what has not only brought so much confusion to Elliott wave analysis, but has driven so many people to deny its practical application. In the spirit and necessity of keeping market analysis simple, I am not going to include descriptions of the many "complex" corrections.

Essentially, corrective waves are three wave patterns or various combinations of three wave patterns. The simplest three wave, corrective pattern is called an ABC correction. Even within this simple pattern there are four variations: zigzag, flat, irregular and running. I am only going to describe in detail the ABC corrective patterns and ignore all of the various complex, corrective patterns for two important reasons:

1. Once a market has demonstrated that the corrective pattern will not be an ABC correction, it is almost impossible to predict what form the correction will take. All labeling of the correction beyond a simple ABC pattern is little more than guess work. The form of the complex correction usually only becomes evident after the correction has completed.

2. There is no practical trading value in knowing all of the complex corrective variations. The purpose of this training is not to become academic experts of market analysis but recognize and apply analysis and trading strategies that have practical value for making trading decisions. We'll let the academics and non-trading analysts argue over the proper interpretation of market structure while we'll concentrate on what helps us to make trading and investing profits.

Corrective Waves

General Characteristics

1. Corrective waves within a five wave structure are waves two and four.

2. Corrective patterns unfold following the completion of a five-wave, impulse structure.

3. Corrective patterns unfold in at least a three wave, ABC structure.

4. Three wave, ABC corrections may take the form of 5-3-5 or 3-3-5. That is, the A wave may be three or five waves, the B wave should always be three waves and the C wave should always be five waves.

5. Three wave, ABC corrections may take several shapes including a zigzag, irregular, flat or running.

6. Corrective waves may unfold in an almost unlimited progression of threes and fives called "complex" corrections which can include a series of ABCs separated by so-called "X" waves. An X wave may also be labeled a DK wave (**D**on't **K**now). X waves are frequently used by Elliott wave analysts to make a count fit as a corrective series when there really is no logical pattern other than the knowledge that the market is not undergoing a five wave, impulse sequence.

7. Corrections tend to terminate near the range of the fourth wave of one lesser degree.

8. Once a correction terminates, a new five wave sequence should follow.

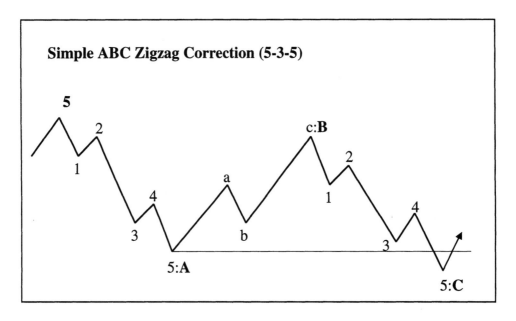

Simple ABC Zigzag Correction

A. The correction begins following the completion of a five wave impulse pattern.

B. Wave A may be five or three waves. If wave A is five waves, the ABC correction is called a 5-3-5. If wave A is three waves, the ABC correction is called a 3-3-5.

C. Wave B is a correction of the larger degree correction. Wave B should be a three wave structure.

D. Wave C exceeds the extreme of wave A.

E. Wave C should be sub-divided into five waves.

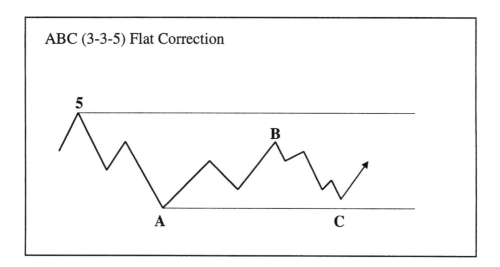

ABC (3-3-5) Flat Correction

ABC Flat Correction

A. The correction begins following the completion of a five wave impulse pattern.

B. Wave A may be a three or a five.

C. Wave B tests the extreme of wave five. Wave B is a three wave.

D. Wave C tests the extreme of wave A. Wave C is a five wave.

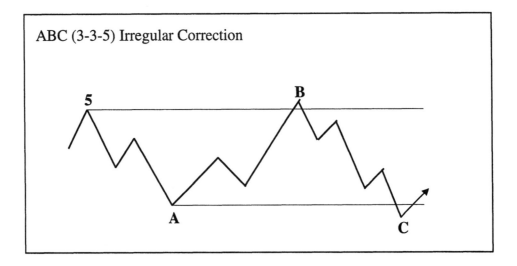

ABC (3-3-5) Irregular Correction

ABC Irregular Correction

A. The correction begins following the completion of a five wave impulse pattern.

B. Wave A may be a three or five wave.

C. Wave B exceeds the extreme of wave five. Wave B is a three wave.

D. Wave C exceeds the extreme of wave A. Wave C is a five wave.

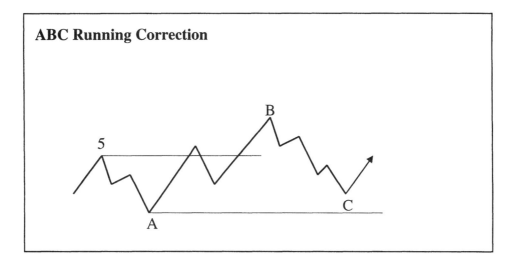

ABC Running Correction

An ABC "running correction" appears to be the continuation of the trend rather than a correction to a five wave sequence. For practical purposes, it is considered a correction because it is the interim pattern between the completion of a five wave sequence and the beginning of the next five wave sequence. A running correction implies a strong continuation of the trend following the end of the correction. Running corrections are made infrequently.

A. A running correction begins following the completion of a five wave impulse pattern.

B. Wave A may be a three or a five wave and is relatively shallow.

C. Wave B exceeds the extreme of wave 5.

D. Wave C retraces wave B and does not exceed the extreme of wave A.

Correction or Impulse?

An ABC (5-3-5) zigzag corrective pattern will have the same structure as Waves 1-3 of a five wave impulse pattern. If the position of the market at the beginning of the structure is not clearly evident, only the pattern of the market as it unfolds will reveal whether a correction or impulse pattern is underway.

The wave pattern shown below could be the initial stages of a five wave impulse sequence or an ABC corrective sequence. Which pattern is more likely to be the case will depend a great deal on the wave structure going into the beginning of this pattern.

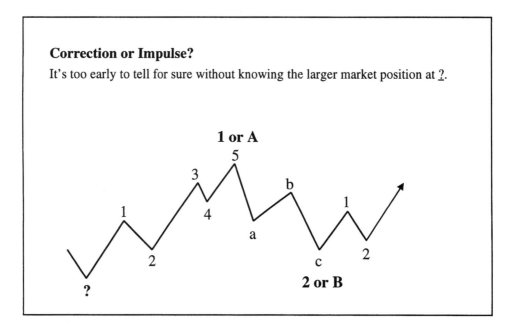

Correction or Impulse?

It's too early to tell for sure without knowing the larger market position at ?.

The one thing we know regarding the above illustration within the context of Elliott wave rules is that a five wave sequence should develop from the low that is labeled **2 or B**. That five wave sequence may be a wave three or a wave C. The position of the market at **?** will help determine whether the current activity is a correction or impulse. Even if the position of **?** is not clear, *a five wave sequence should unfold from 2 or B*.

If the five wave sequence from **2 or B** extends beyond a 100% Alternate Price Projection (W.C >100% W.A), more than likely it is the beginning of a five wave sequence. If the five wave sequence from **2 or B** completes at less than a 100% Alternate Price Projection (W.C < 100% W.A), more than likely the pattern starting at **?** is an ABC correction and not waves one-three of a five wave sequence.

If a five wave sequence completes following <u>2 or B</u> and the market then declines below the top of **1 or A**, it cannot be waves one-three, as a wave four cannot trade into the price range of wave one.

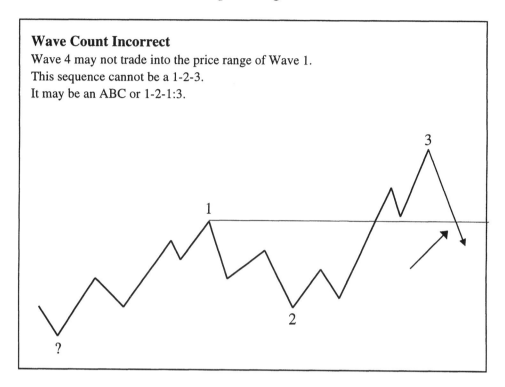

Wave Count Incorrect
Wave 4 may not trade into the price range of Wave 1.
This sequence cannot be a 1-2-3.
It may be an ABC or 1-2-1:3.

The wave count shown above assumes the market made a wave three high. Price then declined below the top of wave one. Why is the wave count incorrect? Wave four may not trade into the price range of wave one. Rather than a 1-2-3 sequence as labeled above, the sequence must be reconsidered as either an ABC or 1-2-1:3.

As a market unfolds, it will continually provide conditions that confirm or invalidate the assumed wave count position.

Corrective Patterns

Waves 2 and 4, General Guidelines

Five wave impulse structures are usually more symmetrical in form and predictable in price objectives than corrective patterns. The analyst must keep clearly in mind that one of the most important purposes of Elliott wave, pattern analysis is to determine *if the market is in a trend or counter-trend position and what is the relative degree of that trend or counter-trend.*

1. Once we believe a five wave sequence has completed, we can antici-pate that *at least* an ABC correction will follow. In most cases, the C wave will test or exceed the extreme of the A wave.

2. The correction *to* a five wave sequence will usually be greater in price range and time range than the corrections *within* the preceding five wave sequence.

3. An A wave can be either a five or three wave sequence. If an initial three wave sequence unfolds, the question arises whether that three wave sequence is the completed ABC correction or just the completion of the A wave of a larger degree ABC. If the initial ABC sequence is less in price or time range than both of the waves 2 and 4 of lesser degree, it is most likely a three-wave, wave A of the correction.

4. Once the market makes a five wave sequence *against the trend direc-tion of the correction*, we have a strong indication that the correction has terminated. B Waves (correction of the correction) should be a three wave structures.

5. *Principle of Alternation*: If wave two is an ABC correction, wave four will probably be a complex correction (any sequence that is not either a five-wave impulse or ABC). If wave two is a complex correction, wave four will probably be an ABC correction. Wave two is usually an ABC correction.

A five wave sequence is always part of the larger degree trend.
A three wave sequence is always part of a counter-trend.

A correction always follows a five wave sequence. The correction will be a *three* wave, ABC pattern at a *minimum*. Completed corrections are usually not a five wave sequence. A five wave sequence may be only one wave of the larger degree corrective trend.

In the illustration below, once we recognize that the market has declined in an initial five wave sequence, we know that the correction should not be over. We know there will probably be a three part B-wave advance, *followed by another decline to test or exceed the A-wave low.*

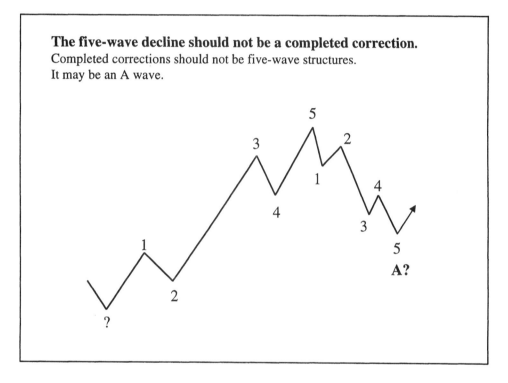

The five-wave decline should not be a completed correction.
Completed corrections should not be five-wave structures.
It may be an A wave.

A five wave sequence should not be a completed correction. The five wave decline shown above is probably wave A of a 5-3-5 (ABC) correction.

Trading Implication

The A wave is only the initial section of the decline. Following the correction to wave A which will be labeled as wave B, the market should make another decline to test or exceed the wave A low.

A correction will usually be greater in price and time than the prior corrections of lesser degree.

A five wave sequence is followed by a correction to the entire sequence. The correction to the entire sequence should exceed in price and time the corrective waves two and four within the five wave sequence.

If it appears an ABC correction has developed but it is less in price and time than the waves two and four of the five wave sequence, more than likely it is not a complete ABC correction, but probably waves 1-2-3 of wave A or a completed three-wave, wave-A. *Whichever the case may be, the most important information is that it is probably not the completion to the correction to the previous five wave sequence.*

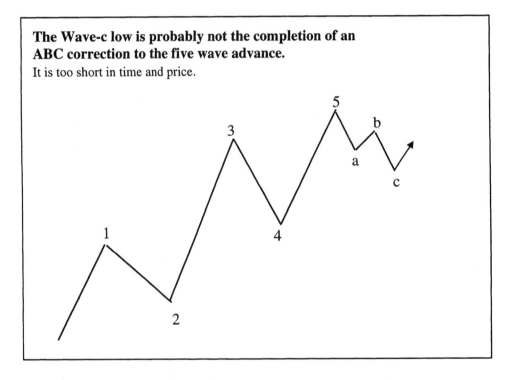

The Wave-c low is probably not the completion of an ABC correction to the five wave advance.
It is too short in time and price.

The ABC correction shown above is probably not the completion of the correction to the five wave advance. If what appears to be an ABC correction is less than the price and time of waves two or four, it is probably not the completion of a correction.

Trading Implication

Don't consider entering against a three wave correction unless it has overbalanced in price and time the prior waves two and four.

Five wave sequences are always in the direction of the larger degree trend.

If a five wave sequence unfolds against the direction of the counter-trend, it is an initial indication that the counter-trend has terminated.

In the chart below, the minor five wave advance from c signals the correction should be complete and the larger degree bull trend should continue. If the rally from c was an ongoing part of a complex correction, it should only be a three-wave structure.

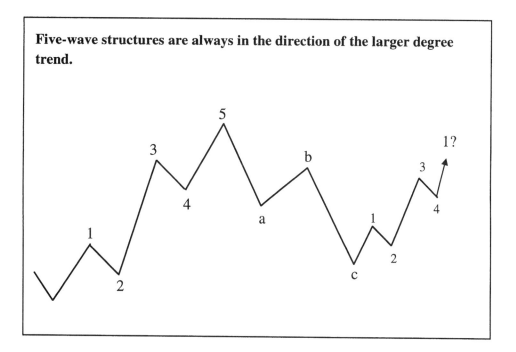

Five-wave structures are always in the direction of the larger degree trend.

Trading Implication

The five wave sequence from c suggests that the ABC correction should be complete and a new impulse sequence of larger degree is probably beginning. This market should continue higher without exceeding the Wave-c low. Prepare to enter on the correction to the initial, minor five wave sequence from c.

Principle of Alternation

Wave four usually alternates corrective patterns with wave two. If wave two is an ABC correction, wave four will probably be a complex correction. If wave two is a complex correction, wave four will probably be an ABC correction. Wave two is usually an ABC correction.

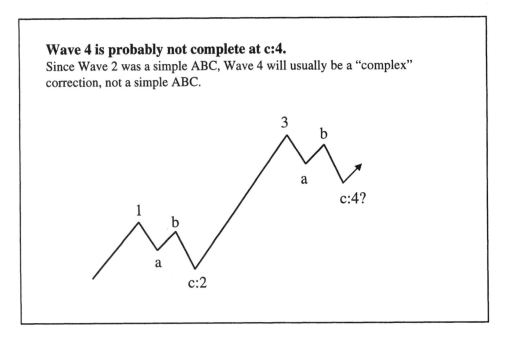

Wave 4 is probably not complete at c:4.
Since Wave 2 was a simple ABC, Wave 4 will usually be a "complex" correction, not a simple ABC.

In the chart above, wave two was an ABC correction. Wave four will probably not be an ABC correction but some form of complex correction. It is unlikely the abc decline from the wave three high has completed a wave four correction.

Trading Implication

You usually do not want to enter at the end of wave C of wave four if wave two was an ABC correction unless time and price factors strongly suggest wave four is complete. The odds are high that wave C of four is not the end of the correction.

Corrective Waves 2 and 4

Main Characteristics and Price Ratio Projections

In projecting price targets for a correction, we must go under the assumption that the market has completed a five wave impulse pattern of one degree or another. Corrections are always against the trend of the previous five wave structure.

We always go under the assumption that the correction will be a *minimum* of an ABC. An ABC correction will not necessarily be a simple, ABC zigzag, but may be an ABC irregular or flat. The B wave *might* exceed the beginning of the A wave (end of wave five) and the C wave *might not* exceed the end of the A wave.

Usually, a completed corrective structure that is less than a 38.2% retracement of the prior five wave sequence indicates a strong market that should result in a strong impulse wave once the correction is complete. Replace weak for strong for a bear market.

Corrective Wave Two

Wave two is the first correction within a new five-wave pattern. Wave two has the same characteristics of a B wave. Both wave-two and wave-B corrections should be followed by a five wave structure in the direction of the previous trend which will be either a wave-C or wave-three.

1. Wave twos tend to be "simple" ABC corrections, usually 5-3-5 zigzags where the C wave exceeds the extreme of the wave A.

2. Wave two cannot exceed the beginning of wave one.

3. Wave two will usually retrace over 50% of wave one. Therefore, we would rarely look for a completed wave two pattern or to enter a market until the suspected wave two has retraced at least 50% of the suspected wave one.

4. Wave two usually does not exceed a 78.6% retracement of wave one.

5. If wave two retraces less than 50% of wave one, wave three will usually be the extended, impulse wave of the five wave pattern. This is even more likely to be the case if wave two is a flat or irregular pattern.

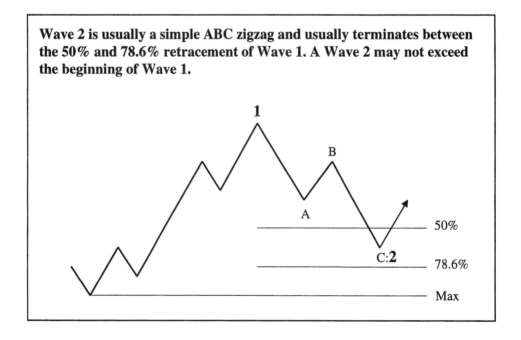

Wave 2 is usually a simple ABC zigzag and usually terminates between the 50% and 78.6% retracement of Wave 1. A Wave 2 may not exceed the beginning of Wave 1.

Key Trading Strategies For Wave Two

The ideal objective is to enter at or near the completion of wave two to be positioned in the early stages of wave three which should be the strongest and longest impulse wave.

Since a Wave-2 usually; retraces at least 50% of Wave-1, don't consider entering prior to the suspected Wave-2 reaching the 50% retracement. Since a Wave-2 usually does not exceed a 78.6% retracement, don't considering entering if the market has exceeded a 78.6% retracement. If the market has either failed to reach a 50% retracement or has exceeded the 78.6% retracement (but not the beginning of Wave-1), wait to enter the market after the break-away from the Wave-1 extreme.

If waves A and B are identified, all efforts should be made to identify the completion of wave C. Ideally, the sub-waves of C will be able to be identified to project the end of wave five of C. Entering at or near the completion of wave two places the trader in the position to take advantage of the next trend-wave whether it turns out to be a wave-three or a wave-C.

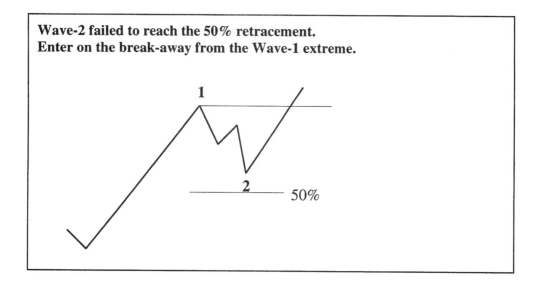

**Wave-2 failed to reach the 50% retracement.
Enter on the break-away from the Wave-1 extreme.**

Corrective Wave Four

Wave four is often called the "profit taking" correction. During wave four, many of the traders and investors who have been long through all or most of the waves one through three will take profits. Wave four is often a prolonged correction, usually longer in time than the wave two.

1. Wave four should not trade into the price range of wave one. If a suspected wave four trades into the price range of wave one, the labeling is probably incorrect and the position of the market must be reconsidered.

2. Principle of Alternation: If wave two was a simple correction (ABC) then wave four will usually be a complex correction. *This is a tendency, not a rule.* Wave four is frequently a relatively flat, "complex" correction.

3. If the wave four correction is one of the many "complex", flat corrections (otherwise known as consolidation or trading range), it usually does not retrace more than 38.2% of waves 1-3.

4. Wave four usually retraces at least 23.6% of wave three but usually does not retrace more than 50% of wave three. This provides us with typical minimum and maximum targets for wave four.

5. The wave four retracement of wave three will almost always be a smaller *percentage* than the wave two retracement of wave one.

6. Wave four is often near equality in price to wave two (W.4 = 100% W.2). If not, wave four will usually be at or near 62% or 162% of wave two.

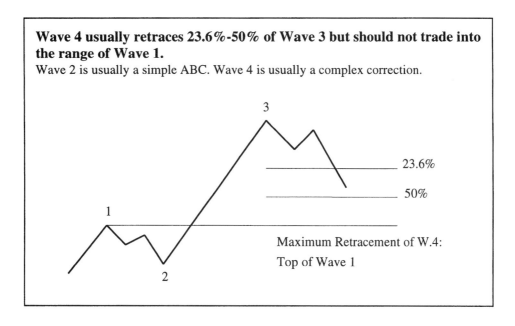

Wave 4 usually retraces 23.6%-50% of Wave 3 but should not trade into the range of Wave 1.

Wave 2 is usually a simple ABC. Wave 4 is usually a complex correction.

23.6%

50%

Maximum Retracement of W.4:
Top of Wave 1

If the suspected wave four trades into the range of wave one, the wave count must be reconsidered. Keep in mind that the wave count represents the position of the market and the most likely trend direction. If the wave count must be reconsidered, the position of the market is in question. If the wave four has traded into the price range of wave one, what may have been considered a new bull trend and the beginning of a five wave advance may now be considered a correction to be followed by a continuation of a bear trend.

This is one of the many ways that Elliott wave pattern analysis provides a "pattern" stop loss to the market position.

If wave two was an ABC correction, the odds are that wave four will be a complex correction. Knowing this, traders and investors should not be too quick to want to enter long positions on a suspected wave four.

Key Trading Strategy For Wave Four

Enter at or near the completion of wave four to position for the wave five trend sequence.

Because wave four is frequently a complex correction which is very difficult to project in advance the ultimate outcome, the wave four pattern is often of little use to identify the end of wave four. Identifying the end of wave four is more reliant on time and price projections if wave four is a complex correction.

Waves A, B and C

Wave A

1. Wave A is usually a five wave structure, but may be a three wave structure. Wave A is an impulsive wave as it is in the direction of the larger degree trend. In this case, the larger degree trend is the corrective trend direction.

2. Wave A is similar to wave one. Wave A and wave one are the initial waves of a sequence, price projections are pretty much limited to retracements of the prior impulse swing and projections of the minor internal waves of lesser degree within the A Wave.

Wave B

1. B waves are counter-trend waves to the larger degree trend which is also a counter-trend. In other words, a B wave is a correction to the correction. B waves are frequently three wave, ABCs, but may be any of the numerous "complex" corrections.

2. *Wave B verses Wave A*: B waves usually terminate in the 50% - 78.6% retracement zone of the A wave. However, a B wave will retrace over 100% of the A wave in an *irregular ABC* correction.

Wave C

C waves should *always* be five wave structures. C waves may or may not exceed the end of wave A. If wave B has not exceeded the *beginning* of wave A, wave C will normally test or exceed the wave A extreme.

1. *Wave C verses Wave A.* The price range of Wave C will usually be either 62%, 100% or 162% of the wave A price range. If the correction is a simple ABC, zigzag, wave C is usually 100% of wave A.

2. *Wave C verses Wave B:* The price range of Wave C will frequently be 162%, 200% or 262% of the wave B price range.

3. *Wave C should be a five wave structure:* Use the price projection targets described for five wave impulse patterns to project the termination of the fifth wave within the C wave.

Beyond ABC Corrections

If a market continues beyond an ABC correction, the counter-trend is no longer as predictable in pattern. It is at this point that the Dynamic Time and Price projections become important, as the time of the termination of the correction will usually be within one of the Dynamic Time Projections and at one of the Dynamic Price Projections.

Five Wave Corrections

Wait a minute! We've just spent a considerable amount of time and space describing corrections as three wave structures and impulse trends as five wave structures. What's this about five wave corrections?

A market may unfold in any possible pattern. The impulse and ABC corrective patterns that have just been described are the most frequent trend and counter-trend patterns that are usually identifiable in the initial stages of the sequence. More importantly, the termination of the entire sequence is very predictable once the sequence is identified within the parameters of the rules and guidelines. Recall that these patterns will be easily identifiable only about 50% of the time. Other times, trends and counter-trends may unfold in any of a multitude of patterns.

Any five wave sequence that does not follow the rules and guidelines of an impulse sequence is probably a correction or part of a correction with the exception of a fifth-wave-diagonal. One example of a corrective, five-wave sequence is an ABCDE correction which usually looks like a contracting triangle correction. There are others.

Once the corrective wave structure has demonstrated it is going to extend beyond one of the ABC structures, do not take any labeling scheme too seriously. Always keep in mind that your objective is to extract the information from the market that will lead to high probability trading and investing decisions. Never feel you must always be able to label a market "correctly."

I have purposely not provided any illustrations of the many so-called Elliott-wave, complex-corrections. By illustrating them, it would imply that they are legitimate, predictable patterns that provide reliable analytical information to the analyst. They do not. There is no lack of other Elliott wave source material that will describe the myriad examples of complex corrections in an attempt to convince the analyst that all markets may be labeled with an Elliott wave pattern, all of the time. It is time to dispel this mis-leading and expensive myth and only concern ourselves with high probability, relevant information that helps to formulate reliable trading and investing decisions.

Parallel Channels

Parallel channels were suggested by Elliott to help identify where wave four and five would complete. They have proven over the course of years and many markets to be very valuable. Consider them as important confirmations to the time, price and pattern position.

Projecting Wave 4

Draw a trendline from the top of W.1 to the top of W.3.

Draw a parallel trendline from W.2.

W.4 will often terminate at or very near the parallel channel line from W.2.

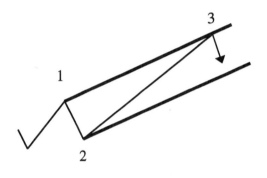

Projecting Wave 5

Draw a trend line from the bottom of W.2 to the bottom of W.4.

Draw a parallel channel line from the top of W.3.

W.5 will often terminate at or very near the parallel channel line drawn from W.3.

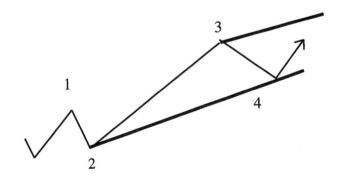

And Now For Another Opinion

While Elliott wave analysis is relatively objective with specific rules and guidelines, pattern analysis does require the thought, knowledge and judgment of the trader. Much more so than time and price analysis. Any analyst who has studied wave patterns on charts for a length of time knows that it ain't over till it's over. I don't care how ideal the pattern looks. Wave five can extend just when you thought it was all over. That ideal ABC correction can all of a sudden go haywire and twist and turn for days, weeks, even months.

When we begin to expect a market to continually unfold in an ideal Elliott wave pattern is when we have lost track of the practical value of Elliott wave analysis. The purpose of Elliott wave analysis is not to identify and label every twist and turn in any particular market, all of the time.

Elliott Wave Analysis Objective
The objective of Elliott wave analysis for traders and investors is to identify specific set-ups based on pattern that have a high probability outcome and a specific market activity that will invalidate the anticipated outcome!

If you demand more of Elliott wave analysis than this, take out your checkbook and keep it out. You will have a very costly experience!

This chapter has described the market patterns that are the most consistently reliable in identifying the position of the market and the most probable outcome from the current position. I have also described what are the most consistently reliable price relations between the various waves that allow us to project the price zones with the greatest probability of support and resistance and pattern termination.

IIow often will we be able to place the position of the market within the context of Elliott wave patterns as has been described here? About 50% of the time!

The major failure of analysts who primarily rely on Elliott wave to make trading recommendations or forecasts is their attempt to put all market activity, in all markets, all of the time within the context of Elliott's wave patterns. When this is attempted, the wave counts frequently become an outrageous exercise in hallucinogenic imagination with X waves all over the place, waves related to each other that are no way in any symmetrical relationship within the pattern and, generally, forced wave counts that don't relate to the concepts of Elliott's Wave Principle by any stretch of the imagination. Successful traders are rarely guilty of these imaginary, forced counts, as they do not lead to profitable trading decisions. They only feed the ego of the analyst. Traders and investors must deal with the reality of market activity, not dreams and illusions.

The trader who wishes to incorporate Elliott wave pattern analysis into his or her trading plan must recognize and admit to him or herself when the market pattern does not fit into one of the relatively simple impulse or corrective patterns. When this is the case and the time and price analysis does not provide sufficient information to make a trading decision, that market must be ignored as a tradable market until the position does become clear!

Don't Become An Elliott Wave Obsessive

Recall that at the beginning of this chapter, I stated that one of the most important objectives of Elliott Wave analysis is to distinguish if the market was in a trend or counter-trend position. I also stated above that a clearly identifiable Elliott Wave pattern is usually only evident about 50% of the time in most markets. When a market is not unfolding in one of the specific impulse or counter-trend patterns described in this chapter, the rules, guidelines and general characteristics of impulse and counter-trend patterns will often strongly suggest whether the market is in an impulse or counter-trend position. That is a valuable piece of information itself.

Do not become obsessive with having to make a specific wave count if one is not obvious. The road to trading and investing ruin is littered with Elliott-Wave-Obsessives who would leave no chart unlabeled. The harder you have to work to apply a wave count the less likely it is to be a valid count and the more likely you will believe it to be a true when in fact it is only an illusion of your label-obsessive mind.

In recent years, software programs have been developed with extensive and complex algorithms (mathematical rules) that supposedly provide Elliott wave labels automatically on any data chart. If a software program provides an Elliott wave count on each and every data file, the program (and its programmer) assumes there is a valid and practical Elliott wave count on every data series, at any time. The program is *forced* to provide a wave count, even when none logically exists. A forced wave count is not only misleading, but will prove very costly to the trader who foolishly takes action on this irrelevant information.

Beware of forced wave counts, whether they are made by you, an Elliott wave analyst or a software program.

And Now For the Real Elliott Wave Story

The beauty and significance of R. N. Elliott's work is that he recognized that markets are composed of groups of people that respond as crowd behavior in the same way that other social groups respond to a cycle of events. There is a *process* that evolves in almost every cycle of crowd behavior that runs its course. This *process* results in a fairly predictable pattern of behavior of cycles of optimism and pessimism. This process and pattern of behavior is represented on price charts of financial markets, as the price charts are simply reflections of the state of the psychology of the group participating in the market.

Throughout the course of R. N. Elliott's work developing his Wave Principle, it is obvious he continually looked to refine and expand upon the guidelines of his wave principle as applied to the markets. In Elliott's earlier work, there were no X waves, there were no "rules" and there was no mention of Fibonacci numbers or ratios!

Elliott developed his theory over less than a ten year period from the late 1920's to the latter half of the 1930's. It was in 1938 that Elliott's first monograph, *The Wave Principle*, was published by Charles Collins and the following year that Elliott was commissioned to write a series of articles on the principle for *Financial World* magazine.

It is these early works of Elliott that I find the most valuable. Here is found the spirit of the fundamental truths of what Elliott discovered about pattern and process in the cyclic development of the financial markets, unencumbered with the need to explain every little twist and turn on the financial charts. There were no X waves, no complex corrections, *just fives and threes*. Occasionally, a fourth wave traded into the territory of wave one. Occasionally, a third wave was the shortest impulse wave. *The form was more important than any rules.* The process would not be denied.

From 1938 - 1946 Elliott published his educational and forecast letters (*R. N. Elliott's Market Letters*, edited by Robert R. Prechter, Jr.). In these letters it became evident that Elliott felt he must show his theory to be right under all conditions, at all times. In these letters we find that he made his theory fit whatever market activity unfolded. There are some pretty wild counts in these letters. Here we are introduced to the dreaded X wave (actually a # wave) which mysteriously shows up whenever a market correction does not comply with a three (ABC) or five (ABCDE). No correction will be denied its count!

It is also during this time that Elliott begins to expound on the Fibonacci number series. Elliott's knowledge of Fibonacci number and ratio is elementary at best. While he demonstrated some of the Fib counts and ratios relating to some market activity of time and price, this aspect of market activity was obviously not well thought out or researched by Elliott. After what can only be considered a brief study of number, ratio and geometry, Elliott was amazed and thrilled that he had discovered the "secrets of the universe" and the great "laws of nature", all conveniently available on the shelves of his local bookstore, courtesy of Jay Hambridge, Samuel Coleman, Manly P. Hall and others. (A little irreverence is due all great men in order to maintain perspective and avoid idolatry.)

What is the point of this brief history of R. N. Elliott? The practical application of Elliott's Wave Principle to trading and investing decisions has its strengths and weaknesses. Elliott did not describe a "law of the markets" with inviolate rules. With a limited history of data and within a fairly short period of time, Elliott recognized an important process that developed in the cycles of market activity. He recognized that the form of this process was fairly regular, which allowed for a certain degree of predictability of future behavior. He recognized that markets have a fairly, consistent symmetry of ratio based on the Golden Mean (1.618). He suspected (rightfully so) that this was the same process and same proportions that are evident in almost all natural growth processes outside crowd behavior.

When Elliott died in 1948, the understanding and application of his principle of form and ratio in the financial markets was really only in its infancy. Since the time of his death, far more has been written about Elliott and his Wave Principle than Elliott wrote himself. Market analysts over the years have had the opportunity to study thousands of charts of many more markets than did Elliott. The great value of his principle has been demonstrated time and again, as well as the frequent weaknesses.

Knowledge is never static. There is never the final word on anything. Today, we find that Einstein's Theory of Relativity may not be the inviolate law it has been accepted to be for most of the century. How can we say that Elliott's Wave Principle may also not be as complete and inviolate as some would like us to think?

In light of the above discussion, here are a few comments and suggestions that will help the analyst, trader and investor to apply Elliott's Wave Principle in a practical manner.

Elliott Wave "Rules"

There are none according to Elliott in *The Wave Principle* monograph. The three "inviolate" rules of labeling wave patterns were developed after his death in order to make his principle and its application more acceptable to the left brain junkies who believe life unfolds with predictable, mathematical precision.

Why then have I described and illustrated these rules throughout this chapter? They are usually not violated in real-time market activity. They provide an objective guide to understand market position and to make objective decisions. Implement the rules in your wave counts.

Occasionally, you will be betrayed by the truth of the market which does not always follow the rules, but more times than not the "rules" will keep your view of the market in proper perspective.

Experience will provide the knowledge and intuition when to break the rules. But don't be too quick to do so.

If you are going to violate the three so-called "inviolate rules" of Elliott wave analysis, *be consistent regarding those violations.* For instance, let's take the rule that a wave four of a five wave impulse sequence may not trade into the price range of wave one. I only consider that rule violated if the suspected wave four closes within the closing extreme of wave one, not trades into the intraday range. I know of other traders who have thoroughly studied markets and only consider a trade greater than 10% into the wave one range of many markets as a violation of the wave four-wave one overlap rule.

So-called Elliott wave purists, or, as I call them, traditional Elliott wave analysts, would say that expanding the parameters of this rule in either of the above ways is not trading R. N. Elliott's Wave Principle. I'll let you decide what you want to call it. The Elliott wave purists are mostly academic advisors who do not apply the principle successfully to their own trading or investing and have generally been creamed in the stock market in the last few years calling the top of the market more frequently than the full moon cycle.

Elliott provided a firm and original foundation for pattern analysis in the markets. Don't hesitate to expand on Elliott's work when your market research proves it necessary and profitable.

Trend or Counter Trend?

The most important piece of knowledge a trader can have is a confident idea of trend direction. Elliott's work is very helpful in this regard, as Elliott wave patterns each relate to trend or counter-trend. Trends unfold in five waves. Counter-trends usually unfold in three waves or a series of three waves.

Market Position

Elliott wave patterns will frequently provide a clear indication of the position of the market within the trend or counter-trend and what activity should follow to complete the trend or counter-trend pattern. Having a confident idea of trend direction, the position of the market within the trend and the likely activity that should unfold prior to the termination of the current trend signals to the trader which side of the market to trade, short or long. There can be no more valuable information.

Alternate Counts

A very important factor of Elliott wave analysis is that it usually provides for an obvious "alternate count" if the market invalidates the "preferred count" or the first assumption of the position of the market. If a market does not unfold as anticipated because it violates one of the rules or guidelines associated with its current position, the trader may then have a firm conviction of what the new position of the market is which will allow him or her to take an alternate trading or investing action.

Do not abuse alternate counts. When a market does not unfold as anticipated by the Elliott wave analysis and there is no reliable alternate count that fits within a reliable wave structure, the trader must then admit that the position of the market is not clear and avoid forcing a count just for the sake of having a count. There will be many times when a market should be avoided because the pattern of the market does not fit within a reliable structure.

Cash Stock Indexes versus Other Markets

Almost all of Elliott's research and analysis was done on the cash stock indexes, primarily the DJIA. The Wave Principle is a reflection of mass or social psychology. It is best reflected by a large group of people from a wide variety of backgrounds with a single interest. Of all the financial or futures markets, this is best reflected in the stock market, and it is in the stock market indexes that we find the Wave Principle most applicable on a consistent basis over the greatest variety of time periods.

Long Term versus Short Term

Fortunately for traders, the Wave Principle and its catalogue of patterns are most consistently evident in short to intermediate term degrees, a few days to a few months. This is particularly true of commodity markets. If you have ever seen an attempted wave count of a 20-30 year or longer monthly chart of soybeans for instance, you have probably seen a great lesson in futility and imagination!

Yet, the individual bull and bear trends that typically last one to three years in agricultural markets usually unfold in the basic fives and threes, trend and counter-trend even in the panic, weather markets. The intermediate term trends often unfold in text book Elliott wave pattern and price projections! Just don't try to explain how the five-wave, two year bull trend fits into the fifty year cycle from an Elliott wave perspective. It doesn't.

Cash versus Futures

Ideally, all wave counts should be done on cash prices to avoid the distortions that are inevitable in continuous futures prices. Today's price of a futures contract includes adjustments due to carrying charges, interest charges, etc. No future's contract price represents today's idea of value except on expiration day. Cash charts are much less likely to violate the "rules" than futures charts.

Other than individual stock and stock index analysis, most wave counts are done on futures contract data including long term, continuous data because this data is much more available from data services than long term cash data. Ideally, the analyst will double check his or her work on cash data to see if the form and pattern are the same as the continuous futures data.

Closing Price versus Daily Price Range

While most of our work is done using the time and price of swing extremes of the daily range of data, daily closing prices should be carefully considered for wave counts. This will become evident when the rules come into play. If there is no other evidence related to pattern to contradict a five wave impulse count other than Wave-4 trade during the day into the range of Wave-1, check closing prices and only consider the count to be invalidated if Wave-4 makes a daily close within the closing range of Wave-1.

Objective versus Subjective

Because Elliott's Wave Principle and its application is not 100% objective like time and price projections, it has been derided by many as useless and little more than guess-work. This is particularly the tack taken by system junkies and system promoters who live under the illusion that market activity and a successful business of trading or investing may be reduced to a mathematical algorithm that will provide them with keys to profits with no strain on the brain.

Elliott's Wave Principle and its catalogue of patterns and guidelines provide an objective method to recognize the position of a market most of the time; be prepared for the most probable outcome of the current market position on a consistent basis, and; provide for the specific market activity that will invalidate the current opinion. The Wave Principle requires study, thought, knowledge and, yes, even occasionally, judgment. Every successful business requires this. If you are under the illusion that you can succeed in the business of trading or investing without knowledge and the occasional application of judgment based on that knowledge, you probably don't remember the 60's! And, probably don't care and should get a job and a haircut.

When the market is not unfolding in a clearly recognizable pattern within the context of the Elliott Wave Principle, do not force a wave count just for the sake of having a wave count. Trading and investing will only be successful when you recognize that action is only taken when the market is in a position that places the probabilities clearly on your side. There is no place for guesswork or ambiguity. Only your own, personal patience and discipline will provide for success.

Elliott Wave Chart Examples

The following pages show numerous Elliott wave examples from many markets. Most are examples that were shown and described in my *Dynamic Trader Analysis Report* newsletter.

The purpose here is to get you to recognize patterns that provide a high probability opinion of the position of the market and the market events that will validate or invalidate the opinion of the market position.

None of these charts show the price relationships described in the text. Price projections will be illustrated in the *Dynamic Price Analysis* chapter. For now, I just want you to get used to viewing the market from a pattern perspective. Many of the charts shown here will also be used to illustrate time and price projections in the next two chapters so you will begin to see the value of the holistic approach to market analysis.

Set-ups that worked and those that didn't work are shown. By becoming very aware of the pattern position of each market, traders and investors soon learn to make a quick and accurate determination if a market is in a trend or counter-trend and the market pattern that will signal the end of the trend or counter-trend.

If a trader did nothing but learn to recognize the completion of a five-wave-impulse sequence, think what a profitable benefit that would be! What are the ramifications? When a five-wave-impulse sequence is completed, a counter-trend larger in time and price than any since the beginning of the five-wave sequence should unfold.

If a trader knows that most counter-trends are at least a simple ABC and only a minor five wave counter-trend has unfolded, the trader knows that the odds are very high that that minor five-wave counter-trend is probably only wave A and the entire correction will not be complete until waves B and C complete. How profitable do you think this simple piece of information will be?

Focus on the basics. Learn to recognize the obvious and be wary of the less than obvious. Always consider what is the specific market activity that will validate or invalidate the pattern position. What is the market activity that should follow the validation or invalidation signal?

Remember that the objective of Dynamic Technical Analysis is to identify low-risk/low-capital exposure trading opportunities, not to form an opinion of the position of every market, all of the time.

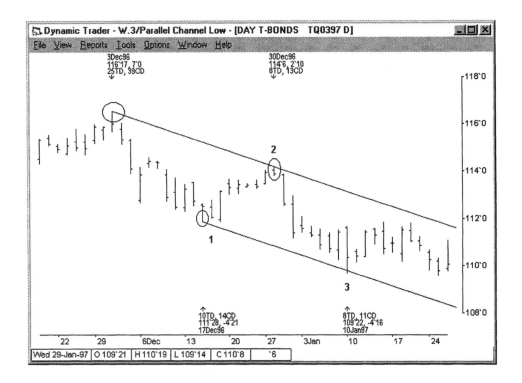

Parallel Channels Often Project The End Of Wave 3 and 5

The parallel channel was constructed by drawing a trendline from the Dec. 3 high (beginning of the bear trend) to the wave 2 high. A parallel line was drawn from the wave 1 low. The wave 3 low was made on the parallel support line.

Parallel channel targets for waves 3 or 5 should only be considered a confirmative target within the context of the time, price and pattern analysis. If the time, price and pattern factors are signaling a low at the same area as the channel line, the probabilities increase for the trend change.

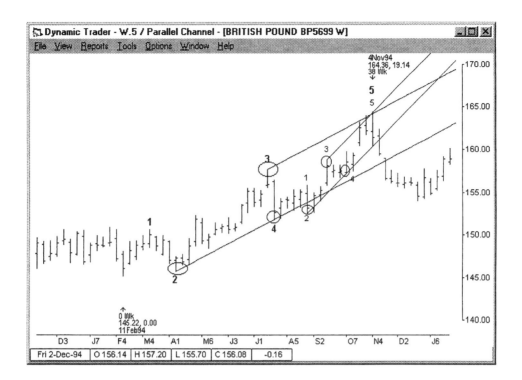

Parallel Channels Of Two Degrees Project The Wave 5 High

The parallel channel is constructed by drawing a trendline from the waves 2 and 4 lows and a parallel line from the wave 3 high. In the chart above, parallel channels were constructed for wave 5 and wave 5:5.

The wave 5 and 5:5 top was made at the coincidence of both degrees of parallel channel resistance.

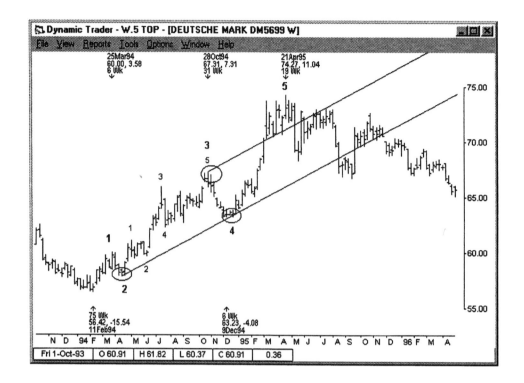

It Doesn't Always Work But Still Provides Valuable Information

A parallel channel of waves 2-4 from wave 3 was constructed to project a wave 5 high. The Deutsche mark shot right through the resistance channel line but soon made the final, wave 5 high.

A market will usually not make an extended trend beyond a wave 4 or 5 channel projection. Exceeding the waves 2-4 trendline usually signals the completion of the prior trend.

Consider waves 4 and 5 projection channels as alert signals. They often provide the targets where waves 4 or 5 terminate. They are usually not exceeded for long. Traders and investors should be very alert to the time, price and pattern position of a market if the channel target is exceeded, as the market is probably "overextended" and nearing the completion of the whole trend sequence.

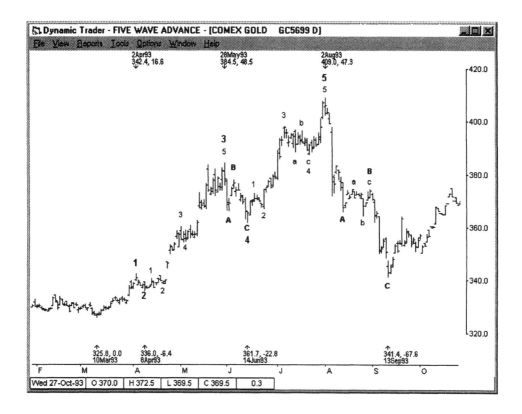

Ideal Five-Wave Advance and ABC Correction

The rally and correction in gold from the March 1993 low through the Sept. 1993 low is a textbook illustration of a five wave impulse and ABC correction. If would be nice if gold and other markets conformed so nicely all of the time. They don't, but what is important is to recognize the set-ups when they do.

Note how impulsive waves three and five sub-divided almost perfectly into five waves themselves.

What should we anticipate after the conclusion of a five wave advance followed by an ABC correction? Another five wave advance that should exceed the Aug. 5, wave 5 high. The next page shows what happened.

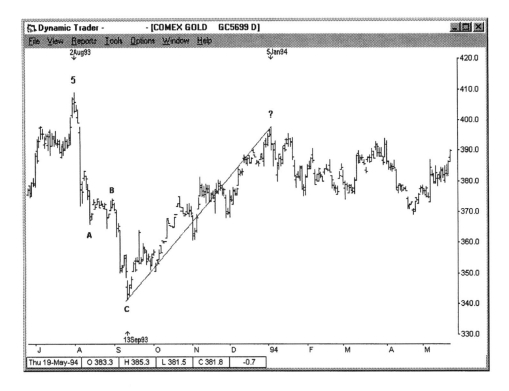

Advance Follows ABC Correction As Anticipated

The gold market had not read R. N. Elliott's work. Gold did advance from the ABC, Sept. 13 low as anticipated but not in an impulsive, five wave advance. The advance was a choppy, labored affair. While it made higher highs and higher lows, the very definition of a bull trend, the pattern appeared more corrective than impulsive with overlapping waves, difficult to identify sub-waves, etc.

While we could label this advance in any of a number of ways, for practical purposes the pattern does not conform to a practical wave pattern that provides decision making information to the trader. Do not force a count when none exits!

The failure of an impulsive five wave advance to develop from the Sept. 1993 low as anticipated, signaled the larger degree trend was probably not as bullish as anticipated. This turned out to be the case as gold did not exceed the Aug. 1993 high for over two years. Never-the-less, there were still many good trading opportunities during this period from a shorter term perspective.

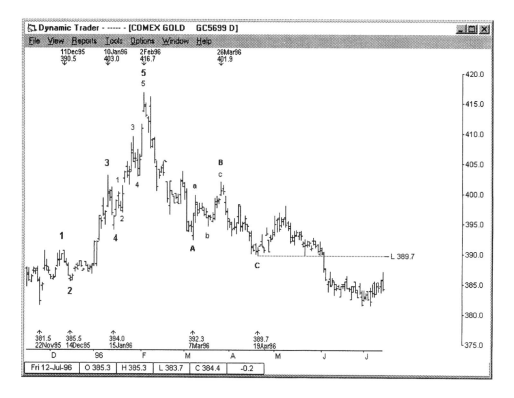

Elliott Wave Pattern Analysis Provides The Market Action That Invalidates An Anticipated Outlook

Gold made another textbook, five wave advance from the Nov. 22, 1995 low to the Feb. 2, 1996 high. Wave five sub-divided perfectly into five waves. What should we anticipate following a textbook, five wave advance? Unless it is a wave C, another five wave advance should follow a correction.

Gold declined sharply into a low on March 7 that appeared to be a wave A low. The wave B rally was an ABC correction. Once the low of April 19, labeled C, was exceeded, it became obvious the gold market was not going to comply with the anticipated Elliott wave outlook.

Once a market is not conforming with a pattern that falls within the rules and guidelines, do not force an Elliott wave count just for the sake of having a count.

From a trading strategy perspective, traders should be aware that a failed signal is often a signal for a sharp move in the opposite direction. Once the April 19, potential wave C low was exceeded, gold had demonstrated its weakness and bear trend. Go with the market signals, not personal expectation. Trade the market, not the forecast.

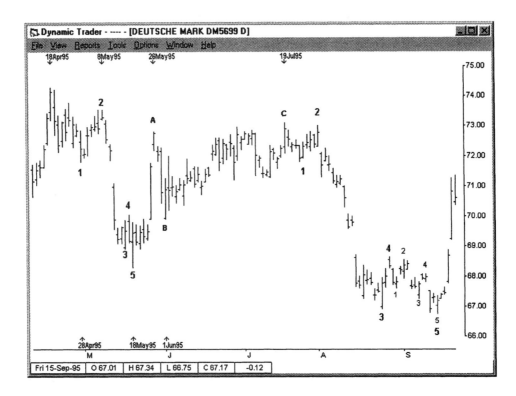

Wave Three Is Usually The Longest and Strongest Wave

From the April 18, 1995 high, the mark made an almost ideal five wave decline. Note the force of wave three with the wide range and gap days down. While the earlier data is not shown, the April 18 high was made following a prolonged bull market trend.

The five wave decline from the April high should be considered either a wave A in a major ABC correction or wave one of a new bear trend. In either case, another five wave decline would be anticipated following a correction up from the May 18 low.

The rally from the May 18 low was not an ideal ABC correction. Many Elliott wave analysts would probably put in a few X waves to make a pattern fit the market activity into the July high. No pattern count would provide a predictive indication that July 19 would be the final corrective high. It is at this point that other analysis techniques such as the Dynamic Time and Price projections are important.

From a practical trading perspective, the key pattern analysis factors prior to the July high were: 1. The five wave decline from the April 18-May 18 signaled the major trend should be bearish. 2. The mark should complete a corrective high below the April 18 high followed by at least one more decline to a new low.

From the July 19 high, the mark again declined in an almost ideal five wave impulse pattern. Again, wave three includes the widest range and gap days. Wave five is a fifth-wave-diagonal. Remember that diagonal-fifth-waves are usually followed by sharp corrections. That is an understatement in this case. The mark exploded upward following the completion of wave five of five.

Five Wave Sequences Are Usually Part of a Larger Degree Trend

From the Aug. 2, 1995 low, cotton made an ideal five wave advance into the Sept. 1 high. A decline followed, making a low near the wave four low. Corrections to five wave impulses typically terminate at or near the prior wave four extreme.

How does the five wave advance into the Sept. 1 high fit into the larger picture? It could be either a wave one of larger degree or wave A. From a trading perspective, it doesn't make any difference. In each case, another rally to new highs following the correction is anticipated, and that is exactly what unfolded.

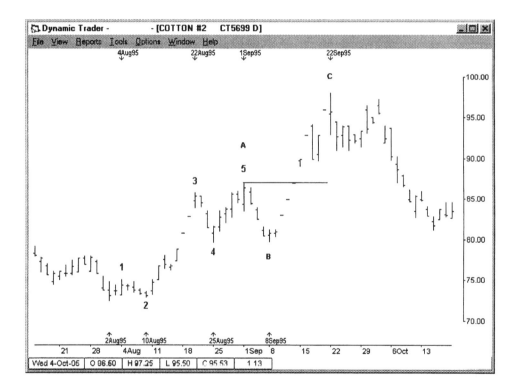

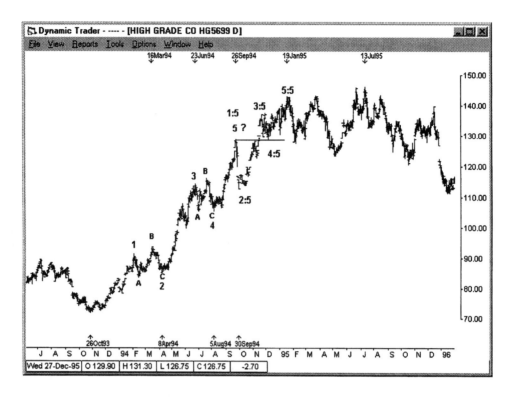

You Must Be Quick To Reassess The Pattern Position If A Market Invalidates The "Preferred Count"

Copper was in a very strong bull trend from the Oct. 26, 1993 low. Wave two was an ABC, running correction which was very bullish. Wave four was an irregular ABC.

It appeared that Sept. 26, 1994 (labeled 5?) completed a wave five high in a text book blow-off. A very sharp and short decline unfolded from the Sept. 26 high followed by a continued rally to new highs.

With the continued rally to new highs, the five wave advance into the Sept. 26 high is invalid and a new count must be considered. The most logical alternate count is an extended wave five beginning from the Aug. 5, wave 4 low. Why is this the most logical alternate count? Waves one through four (Oct. 1993 through Aug. 1994) are a perfect fit and do not lend themselves to an alternate count. We should assume that they are correct.

Copper advanced in five waves from the Aug. 5 low to make the final top Jan. 19.

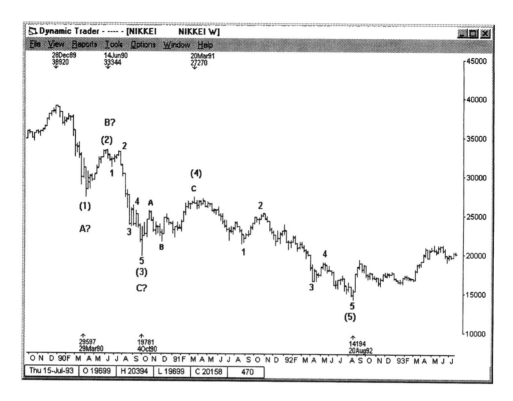

The Lesser Degree Pattern Position of a Market Will Often Signal The Larger Degree Trend Position

In Dec. 1989, the Nikkei made a major bull market top. At least an ABC correction would be expected from the Dec. '89 high. The Nikkei made a three section decline from the Dec. high into the Oct. 1990 low. Was Oct. 1990 an ABC correction or wave one through three of a five wave, impulse decline? What would be the signal for each?

If Oct. 1990 completed an ABC corrective low, a five wave advance should be made from the Oct. low. The Nikkei made a three wave advance (ABC) followed by a continued decline to new lows. This signaled that March 20, 1991 should be a wave four high and a wave five to new lows should be made. The Nikkei then declined in another text book, five wave pattern to make the wave 5 of (5) low in Aug. 1992.

What was the first signal following the Oct. 1990 low that alerted traders and investors that the rally was probably a wave four and not the beginning of a new bullish impulse sequence? The signal is obvious from the chart above. The detail is shown on the next page.

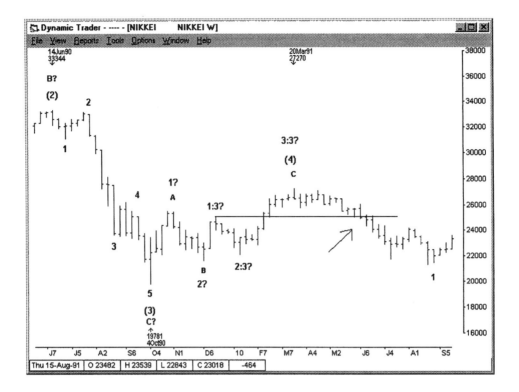

Elliott Wave "Rules" and Guidelines Will Often Signal Very Quickly Whether A Market is in a Trend or Counter-Trend

The chart above is a close-up of the chart on the previous page of the market activity following the Oct. 4, 1990 low in the Nikkei. The alternate wave counts are shown with a question mark. The initial weeks of the rally looked like it could be waves one and two followed by waves one, two and three of the larger degree wave three. What was the first signal this potentially very bullish wave count was incorrect?

Wave four should not trade into the price range of wave two. The Nikkei declined from the March 1991 high which is alternately labeled as wave 3:3 into the price range of wave 1:3. This voided the bullish wave count and signaled that the March 1990 high was probably not wave 3:3 but wave C of a completed ABC, wave four. This had major implications. Another five wave decline (wave five of larger degree) should then unfold to new lows! This is exactly what unfolded. See the chart on the previous page.

By being aware of the pattern position of a market and the ramifications of when a pattern is voided, the trader and investor is prepared for the early signals of the direction of the larger degree trend. Every market does not always provide such a ideal wave count and alternate count set-up. But when they do, traders and investors are provided with a powerful piece of information.

How would you like to have known in June 1991 that the Nikkei should probably continue to decline to new lows in the months ahead?

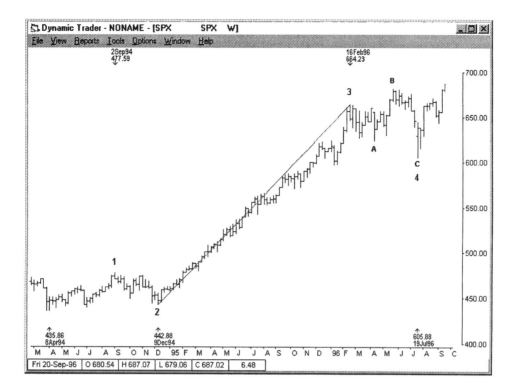

What wave count?

The S&P began a relentless bull trend from the Dec. 1994 low. Up to the Feb. 1996 high, there were no waves to count! If you followed any of the traditional Elliott wave analysis services, you may recall any number of wave counts that continually projected a wave five top. Prior to Feb. 1996, where could you possibly count waves four and five? Only in the illusions of your mind. Certainly not on the chart.

Why did many of the services see a five wave advance as complete prior to Feb. 1996? They made the wave count fit their forecast. If you are strongly predisposed for a particular market forecast, you will find the evidence, however flimsy, to support that outlook.

Don't trade your prophesy of the future. Trade the market. Don't see what isn't obviously not there, or it will be very detrimental to your wallet.

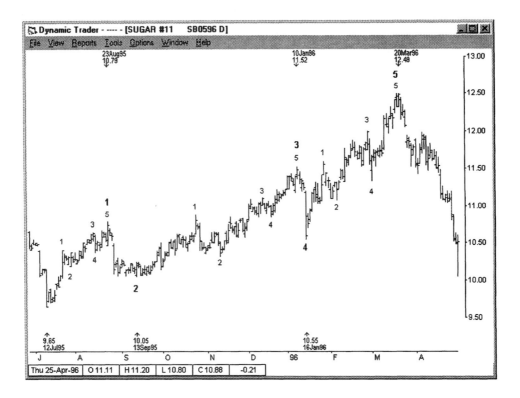

Markets Do Not Always Play By The Rules

Sugar made a five wave advance into the March 1996 high that broke most of the rules. Markets just have no respect. Each larger degree impulse wave (1, 3 and 5) sub-divided into five waves. But, in every case, the wave fours traded into the range of the wave ones for a day or two and then immediately continued the bull trend.

Traditional Elliott wave analysts would feel forced to re-label the waves to some sort of complex and indecipherable correction. Real-world traders will look to identify the completion of a five wave sequence in order to step out of the trade and possibly reverse the trading direction. If a market is closely fitting the structure of a wave sequence, at least consider it valid even if it very briefly breaks the "rules."

The Dynamic Time and Price projections which will be learned in the next two chapters will be critical to validating the probability of the wave count.

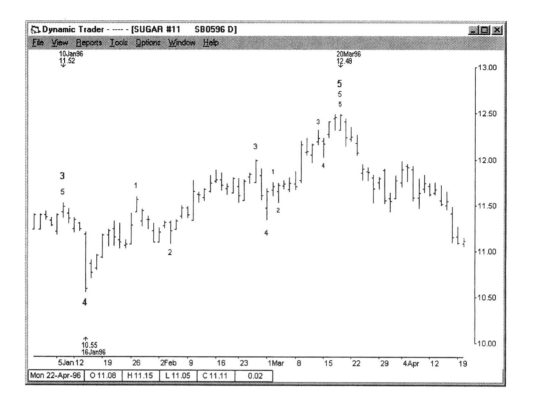

Do Not Ignore The Ramification of the Completion Of Multiple Degrees of 5th Waves

This is a close-up from the previous page of the larger degree wave five that began from the Jan. 16, 1996 low. This is a beautiful example of minor degree sub-divisions signaling the trend reversal of larger degree. Sugar made a final top at wave five of five of five.

Look again at the chart on the previous page and note the extent of the decline from the March 1996 high. Do you care if this five wave sequence precisely meets all of the Elliott wave "rules" or would you rather be prepared to recognize completion of the final, minor wave five of a long term sequence?

Don't Force a Wave Count Where No Logical Count Exits

What is your idea of a wave count for this three year bull trend in bonds? This was an unmistakable bull trend, yet there is no logical Elliott wave impulse count that was evident as the market was unfolding or is evident after-the-fact.

However, almost all of the intermediate degree trends marked off on the chart made very clean five wave advances and three wave declines. The chart above are weekly bars. Check your daily charts for the intermediate degree patterns to see how tradable bond swings are.

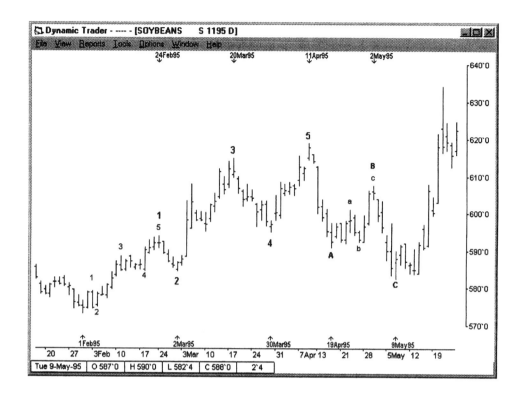

When Handed A Gift, Take It

It doesn't get much better than this. Beans made an almost ideal five wave advance from the Feb. 1, 1995 low into the April 11, 1995 high followed by an ABC correction into the May 9, 1995 low.

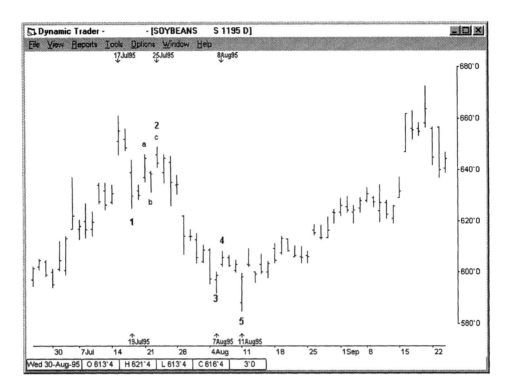

Markets Do Sometimes Correct In A Five-Wave Sequence

Corrections are supposed to be three waves or a series of three waves, right? Somebody forgot to tell the bean traders. Beans made an ideal, five wave impulse decline which completed a correction. The bean market hadn't read the Elliott wave textbooks.

Traders may still have taken advantage of the five wave decline from the short side and know to bring stops close to the market as beans entered the fifth wave down.

Take advantage of what ever information the market is providing. Profits will be maximized and losses minimized.

Do not try to re-label this decline to fit the "rules" of corrections. This is a five wave, impulse sequence, period. Now and them, a correction will be a perfect five wave sequence. Academic Elliott wave hardheads will always re-label a market to make it fit their perceptions of how they think it is supposed to be rather than move on to the present condition and the next money-making set-up.

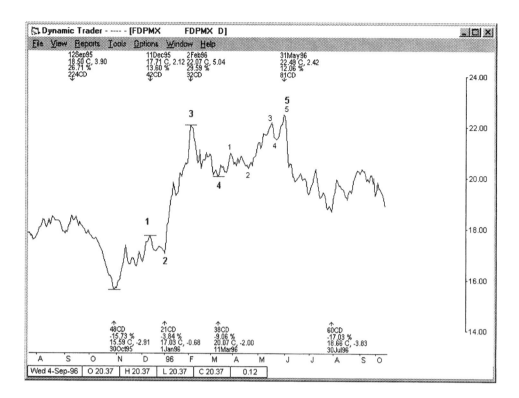

Elliott Wave Analysis Applies To All Actively Traded Markets

This is a chart of the close-only data of Fidelity's Select Precious Metals mutual fund. Elliott wave pattern analysis applies to all actively traded markets including futures, stocks, stock indexes and mutual funds.

The PM fund made a five wave advance where wave five subdivided into five waves in text book fashion.

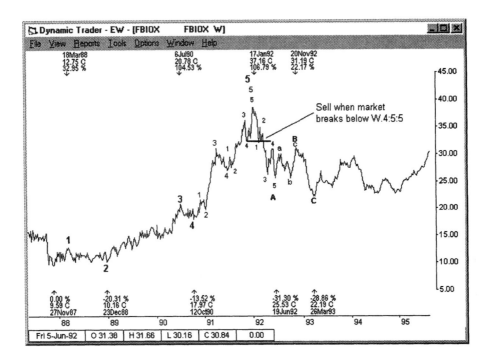

Form More Important Than Rules

The chart above is weekly close-only data of Fidelity's Select Bio-Tech fund. The bull trend from the Nov. 1987 low to the Jan. 1992 high had three distinct rally sections, waves 1,3 and 5. Waves 1 and 3 definitely didn't conform to Elliott wave impulse pattern rules or guideline, but still were distinct rally trends. Wave 5 (Oct. 1990 - Jan. 1992) was a text book Elliott impulse pattern, right down to the five-wave subdivision of wave 5. The ABC correction (Jan. 1992-March 1993) was also a text book pattern. The initial five wave decline into the June 1992 low is the A wave. The B wave was an abc (correction to the correction). Note the initial, minor five wave pattern up following the C wave low.

How is this analysis put to practical used?

1. As the mutual fund rallied to new highs in Jan., it appeared that it was in a minor wave-five that should also complete the intermediate and major wave fives.
2. Let the mutual fund signal if a top has been made. Exit long positions if the mutual fund declines below Wave 4:5:5 (see the chart above).
3. The mutual fund made a five wave decline into the June 1992 low. Corrections usually do not complete with five waves. The June low should be an A wave which should eventually be followed by another swing down to lower price (C wave). This is exactly what occurred.

Elliott wave analysis of this mutual fund prepared investors for a major top and provided the discipline to wait until the correction had run its course. While the entire form of the impulse series did not follow all of the Elliott wave "rules", the pattern was an unmistakable five wave trend.

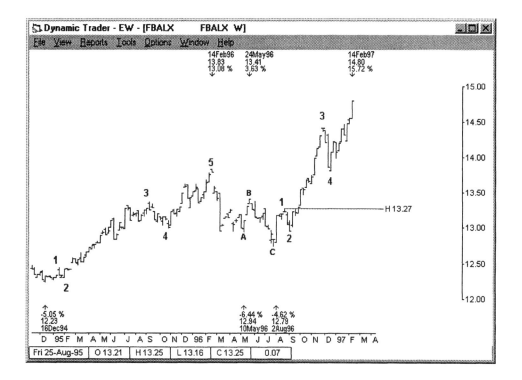

Five's and Three's

Trends usually terminate in five wave patterns. Counter-trends usually terminate in three wave patterns or a series of three wave patterns (complex-corrections).

Following a five wave advance, Fidelity's Balanced Fund made an ABC correction. It appears another five wave advance is nearing completion as of the time the examples for this chapter are completed.

Note how the advance accelerated when the wave one high was exceeded. It appears waves 1-4 are complete and the current advance is in wave five. If this is the case, when wave five is completed, a decline greater in time and price than any since the Aug. 2 low should unfold.

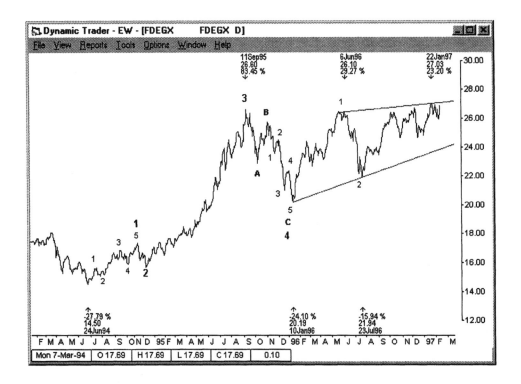

Diagonal-Fifth-Waves In Mutual Funds

Elliott wave patterns are alive and well in Fidelity's Emerging Growth fund. Wave 1 clearly sub-divided into five waves. Wave 3 was almost a parabolic advance, typical of wave 3s which are usually the longest and strongest of the three impulse waves.

The wave four correction was an ABC. Note how wave C clearly subdivided into five waves, typical of C waves.

What has unfolded since the Jan. 10, 1996 wave-four low? It appears to be a fifth-wave-diagonal. Waves 1 & 2 of 5 appear complete. What is usually the outcome of the completion of a fifth-wave-diagonal triangle? A stronger than typical counter-trend. A strong bear trend should unfold following the completion of the fifth-wave-triangle.

Only marginal new highs would be expected from this point on in this mutual fund. Investors in this fund should be anticipating a major top and have relatively close stops. A decline below the support line should signal a top is complete.

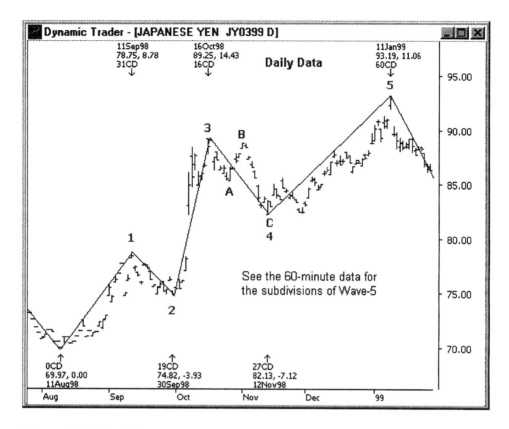

Waves Within Waves

The ideal trade set-up is made when at least one smaller degree wave pattern signals the completion of the larger degree.

In early Jan. 1999, the yen appeared to be in the later stages of an impulse five-wave series that began at the Aug. 11 low. The subdivisions of Wave-5 helped to pinpoint the completion of the larger degree pattern shown on the daily chart.

See the 60-minute chart on the following page.

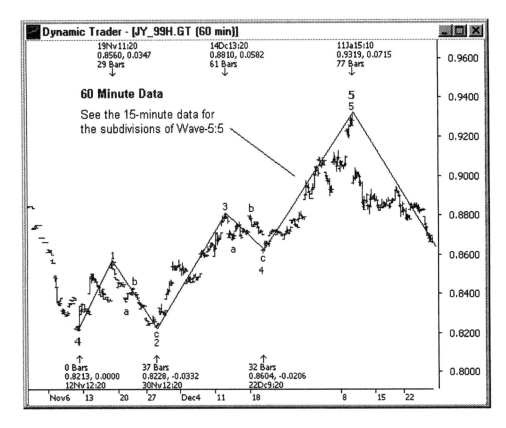

60-Minute Date: Subdivisions of Wave-5

A Wave-5 should subdivide into a five-wave structure of lesser degree.Wave-5 began from the Nov. 12 low (see the daily chart on the preceding page) and clearly unfolded in a five-wave structure. Both Wave-5 and Wave-5:5 were "extended" or greater in price than a typical Wave-5. The price chapter will teach you how to project the price targets for the termination of a five-wave impulse trend.

We can go to an even shorter-term time frame and see if Wave-5:5 also subdivided into a five-wave structure.

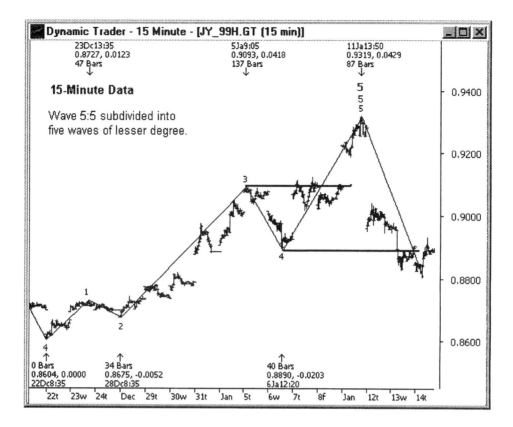

15-Minute Data: Subdivisions of Wave 5:5

While a wave pattern may not be an ideal structure meeting all of the rules and guidelines, the basic form is usually clearly evident.

The 15-minute data shows that Wave-5:5 from the Dec. 22 low into the Jan. 11 high clearly unfolded in a five-wave structure. There are immense trading ramifications to the trader who is alert to the wave structure of any trend or counter-trend.

Once the yen has advanced above the Wave-3:5:5 high, we know that we should be in the last minor swing up (Wave-5:5:5) before the completion of the entire bull trend that began almost five months ago in mid-Aug. How would you like to be alert to the probability that a major trend is only days away from completion? If you were long, you would be very careful to protect the unrealized profits and alert to trading strategies to enter a short position.

A trade below the Wave-4:5:5 low signals the completion of the entire bull trend since Aug.! Wave-5:5:5 is complete! The yen should then make a decline greater in time and price than any decline since the Aug. low. How did it turn out?

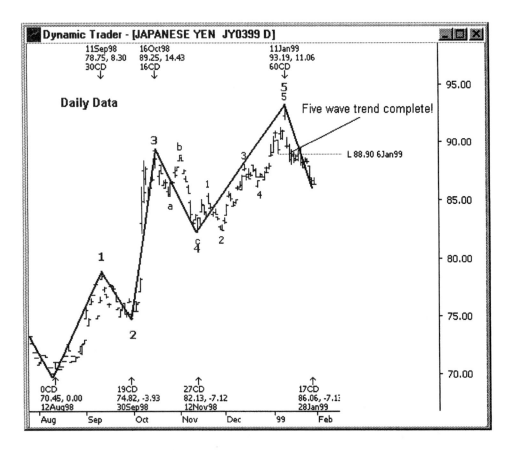

Pattern Analysis Identifies The Completion of the Five-Wave Trend

Just two days following the Jan. 11 high the yen declined below the Wave 4:5:5 low signaling the completion of the five-wave bull trend from the Aug. low. This signal came right at a time when many yen traders were very bullish. *Dynamic Traders* knew that the bull trend should be complete, at least temporarily as the yen makes a decline greater in time and price than any decline since the Aug. low.

Even in the very volatile and often choppy currency markets, pattern analysis will often clearly identify the position of a market and the trend objectives. Short-term trades may be made off of the signals and objectives provided by the intraday data. Intraday data is also used to identify the trend position and completion of larger degree trends.

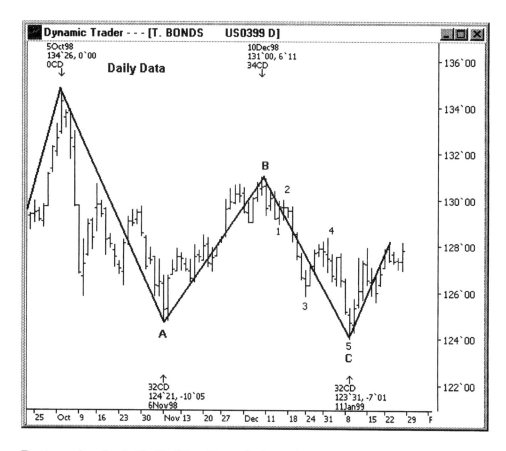

Pattern Analysis Nails The Completion of a Major Low

Bonds made a significant low on Jan. 11. . Since this example is being
included just a few weeks after the low, we don't know yet if this will be a
long term low or not. The pattern position indicates it is the completion of
a major ABC correction. Regardless of whether it turns out to be a long-
term low or not, the pattern analysis provided the signal for a great set-up
for a long position.

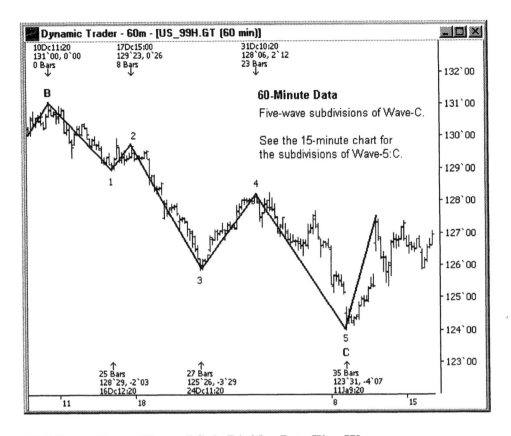

60-Minute Data: Wave-C Sub-Divides Into Five Waves

A Wave-C should subdivide into five-waves which is exactly what happened. The 60-minute chart clearly shows the five-wave subdivisions of Wave-C.

The 15-minute chart on the following page shows the subdivisions of Wave-5:5:C.

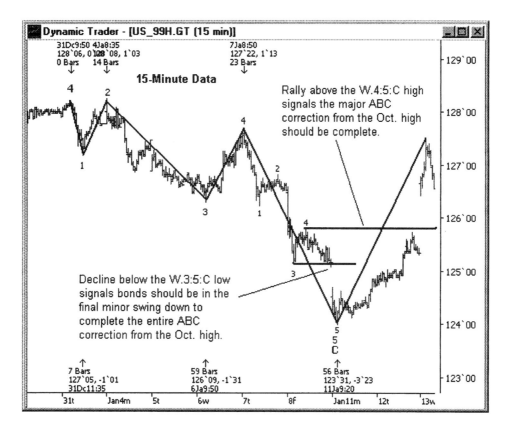

15-Minute Data: Wave-5:5:C Completes A Major Low

Wave-5:5 subdivided into a perfect five-waves itself. Once bonds had declined below the Wave-3 low, traders know that the completion of the whole Wave-C was near completion. The rally above the Wave-4 high signaled Wave-C should be complete.

The Trading Strategies and Putting It All Together Chapters will teach you much more how we use the pattern position to help make specific trading decisions.

Wave Structure Checklists

On the following two pages are two checklists to help you monitor the wave structure of a market as it is unfolding. In effect, they are a concise summary of the rules and guidelines of typical three and five wave structures. There is an Impulse and Correction checklist

As a market unfolds, it is continually providing information as to its nature, impulsive or corrective, in accordance with the wave guidelines for each wave structure. While these checklist tables do not provide for every potential wave structure, they will help you keep on track with how the typical wave structure unfolds. If a wave structure violates a guideline for how it should unfold, you must consider that it is not unfolding as you originally anticipated. You must then re-evaluate the position of the market according to the next best alternative wave structure.

Because a corrective wave structure can take any number of complex structures, only the simple corrective zigzag (ABC) or triangle (ABCDE) are noted in the Correction Checklist. One a market demonstrates it is going to unfold in a complex correction, there is little predictability left in the wave structure. The trader must then focus on the time and price position for signals that the correction may be terminating.

These two tables do not consider the time or price position of the market. They only consider the pattern position out of context of the other market factors. Never make a trading or investing decision based on pattern position alone. This has been the downfall of many Elliott wave analysts.

Also keep in mind that all markets have not agreed to unfold according to R. N. Elliott's rules and guidelines. Markets have a mind of their own and will often unfold in a completely non-predictable and non-symmetrical pattern that provides little valuable information to the analyst.

These checklists will go a long way in helping to identify whether a market is in an impulsive or corrective position. Even more importantly, they will help to identify when a market is unfolding in a predictable Elliott wave pattern and the signals necessary to confirm or invalidate the assumed pattern.

Always keep in mind the purpose of technical analysis for traders and investors: *To identify high probability trade and investing set-ups.* Not to know the position of every market at all times.

It will not be long before you will be familiar with Elliott wave structures and will not have to refer to the tables. Until then, these tables will be a quick and easy reference to the probable position of any market at any time.

IMPULSE WAVE CHECKLIST (Bull Market Example)

C or E	Wave 1	Wave 2	Wave 3	Wave 4	Wave 5
	5 Sub-Waves	Corrective Wave: Refer To Corrective Table	5 Sub-Waves	Corrective Wave: Refer To Corrective Table	Usually 5 Sub-Waves Unless Diagonal Triangle.
End of Correction Assumed	**5 Waves Up** OK.	**3 Waves Down** Completed Zigzag OR Wave A of 2?	**5 Waves Up** OK. W3 Must Be 5 Waves.	**3 Waves Down** Complete Zigzag or Wave A. If Wave A, Probably The Start of a Complex, Sideways Correction.	**3 Waves Up** Possibly Start Diagonal 5th Wave But More Likely Incomplete Wave 5.
Monitor Each Wave As It Unfolds To Confirm Or Invalidate Wave Count.	**3 Waves Up** Correction Is Probably Not Over. Prepare For The Resumption of The Previous Trend. REFER BACK TO CORRECTION TABLE.	**5 Waves Down** Wave A of Zigzag OR Resumption of Prior Trend?	**3 Waves Up** Something Wrong With Count. Review Wave Count. Wave 3 Must Be 5 Waves. REFER BACK TO CORRECTION TABLE.	**5 Waves Down** Probably Wave A of Zigzag Correction.	**5 Waves Up** OK.
		When W2 Complete, **Draw Parallel Channel** (0 - W2 From W1) For Potential W3 Objective.	Price Range of W3 Is Usually Greater Than W1. If Less, Beware That It May Be A Wave C.	**Check Alternation Guideline** For Potential Structure of W4.	If W3 Was Extended (>162% of W1) Then W5 Will Probably Be Similar Price Range To W1.
		W2 Should Not Exceed The Beginning of W1. If It Does, The Prior Trend Should Continue. REFER BACK TO CORRECTION TABLE.	If W3 Is Shorter Than 162% Of W1, W5 Will Often Be The Extended Wave.	When W4 Complete, **Draw Parallel Channel** (W2-W4 From W3) For Potential W5 Objectives.	If W3 Less Than 162% of W1, Anticipate Potential W5 Extension.
			When W3 Complete, **Draw Parallel Channel** (W1-W3 From W2) For Potential W4 Objectives.	W4 Cannot Enter The Price Zone of Wave 1. If It Does, Consider That A W3 Extension Is Underway And This Is W2:3. If Not, The 5 Wave, Impulse Count Is Probably Wrong.	If W3 Shorter Than W1, W5 Should Be Shorter Than W3.
					If W4 Retracement To W3 Greater Than 50%, Anticipate Potential W5 Failure.

CORRECTION CHECKLIST (Bull Market Example)

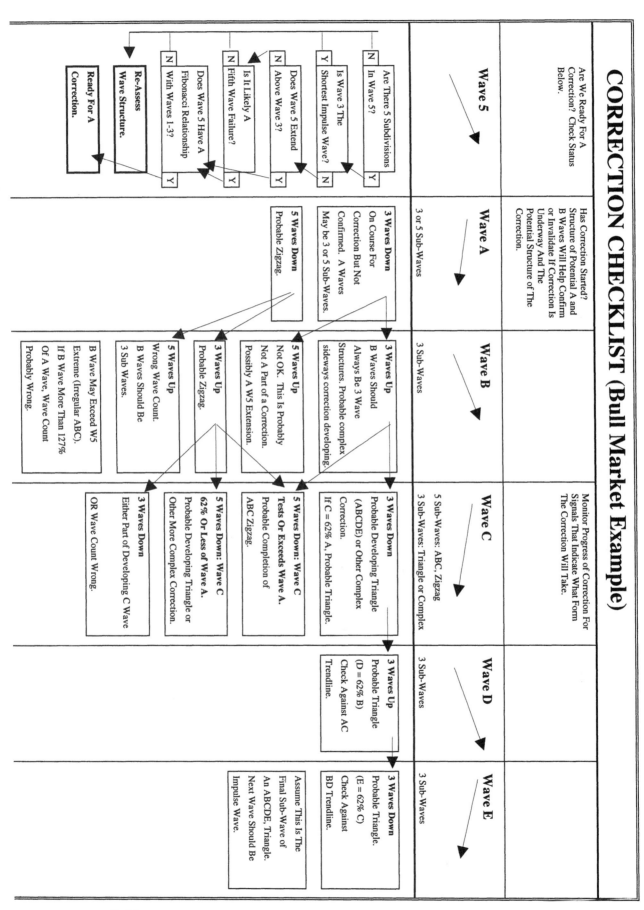

Are We Ready For A Correction? Check Status Below.

Wave 5

Flowchart:
- Are There 5 Subdivisions — Y / N
- N → In Wave 5?
- Is Wave 3 The Shortest Impulse Wave? — Y / N
- Does Wave 5 Extend Above Wave 3? — N / Y
- Fifth Wave Failure? — N / Y
- Is It Likely A
- Does Wave 5 Have A Fibonacci Relationship With Waves 1-3? — N / Y
- Re-Assess Wave Structure.
- Ready For A Correction.

Has Correction Started? Structure of Potential A and B Waves Will Help Confirm or Invalidate If Correction Is Underway And The Potential Structure of The Correction.

Wave A — 3 or 5 Sub-Waves
- **3 Waves Down** On Course For Correction But Not Confirmed. A Waves May be 3 or 5 Sub-Waves.
- **5 Waves Down** Probable Zigzag.

Wave B — 3 Sub-Waves
- **3 Waves Up** B Waves Should Always Be 3 Wave Structures. Probable complex sideways correction developing.
- **5 Waves Up** Not OK. This Is Probably Not A Part of a Correction. Possibly A W5 Extension.
- **3 Waves Up** Probable Zigzag.
- **5 Waves Up** Wrong Wave Count. B Waves Should Be 3 Sub Waves.
- B Wave May Exceed W5 Extreme (Irregular ABC). If B Wave More Than 127% Of A Wave, Wave Count Probably Wrong.

Monitor Progress of Correction For Signals That Indicate What Form The Correction Will Take.

Wave C — 3 Sub-Waves / 5 Sub-Waves: ABC, Zigzag / 3 Sub-Waves: Triangle or Complex
- **3 Waves Down** Probable Developing Triangle (ABCDE) or Other Complex Correction. If C = 62% A, Probable Triangle.
- **5 Waves Down: Wave C** Tests Or Exceeds Wave A. Probable Completion of ABC Zigzag.
- **5 Waves Down: Wave C** 62% Or Less of Wave A. Probable Developing Triangle or Other More Complex Correction.
- **3 Waves Down** Either Part of Developing C Wave OR Wave Count Wrong.

Wave D — 3 Sub-Waves
- **3 Waves Up** Probable Triangle. (D = 62% B) Check Against AC Trendline.

Wave E — 3 Sub-Waves
- **3 Waves Down** Probable Triangle. (E = 62% C) Check Against BD Trendline.
- Assume This Is The Final Sub-Wave of An ABCDE, Triangle. Next Wave Should Be Impulse Wave.

Chapter 4

Dynamic Price Analysis

Every market makes a top or bottom on some exact
mathematical point in proportion to some previous move.

W. D. Gann

In the *Dynamic Price Analysis* chapter you

• Learn how to project well *in advance* the price
zones which have the greatest probability of support,
resistance and trend change, allowing the trader plenty
of time to prepare for trading action.

• Learn the three most important price projection
techniques: price retracements, alternate price
projections and price expansions.

• Learn which ratios to use with each price projection
technique.

• Learn how the price projections cluster to form
support, resistance and trend reversal price zones.

• Learn how to integrate price projections of waves
of more than one degree.

• Learn how to integrate dynamic price analysis with the
pattern analysis learned in the prior chapter.

Be Prepared In Advance For The Price Targets Of Trend Reversals

This chapter will teach you to quickly and easily project the price targets with the greatest probability for support, resistance and trend reversal. It is not complicated or time-consuming to prepare *in advance* the Dynamic Price Projections.

The example above is not an isolated example of a price projection for the termination of a trend. Dynamic Price projections will often allow you to determine well *in advance* the price target to complete trends of all degrees.

Pinpoint The Exact Price Levels For Corrective Highs and Lows

The previous chapter taught you how to identify if a market is in a trend or counter-trend phase. The Dynamic Price Analysis chapter will teach you to project the price levels with the greatest probability of completing a trend or counter-trend.

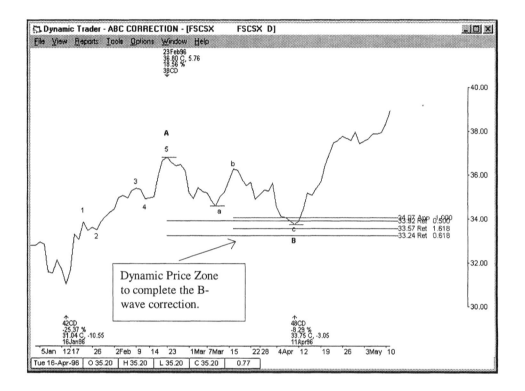

How valuable to your trading would it be if you could project *in advance* the specific price zone a correction to the main trend should reach? Dynamic Price Analysis allows you to do just that. You will often project almost to the tick the price of corrective highs and lows.

Be Prepared In Advance For The High Probability Support and Resistance Zones

Waves or swings of similar degree will relate to each other in price relative to important ratios. The market analyst, investor and trader must consider price ratio relationships of more than one degree. The smaller degree price projections should confirm the larger degree price projections.

No *single* price methodology can be consistently relied upon to indicate with confidence, in advance, where support or resistance is likely to be found. The most important potential support or resistance zones will be found where price projections from more than one of the three primary price projection methods and from more than one degree of swing cluster within a relatively narrow price zone.

Traders must be prepared *in advance* for the price zones from where trend change has the greatest probability of occurring. If traders are prepared in advance for the price zones of change, they may then concentrate their efforts on technical signals that trigger trade entry and confirm trend change.

It is true, as Mr. Gann said, that "every market makes its top and bottom at some exact mathematical point in proportion to some previous move." The question is, which proportion of which previous move? Mr. Gann failed to answer that question, probably because there is no single, right answer. If you have studied any of W. D. Gann's original work, you know that he was a bit of a master of the overstatement. There is not one particular prior swing or one particular proportion (ratio) that will project the price of all future tops or bottoms. The concept of proportioning past moves (swings) and projecting forward is the key concept to projecting the price levels that have the greatest *potential* for trend change.

I underlined potential above for three important reasons:

1. The price support and resistance projections do not project that price *will* reach the projected levels. The price support and resistance projections are simply mathematical projections of relationships of past swings. They are price zones that should offer support or resistance *if reached*. The importance or degree of support or resistance will be indicated by the time and pattern position of the market as the price zones are reached.

2. There are usually two or three projected price zones from any one swing point. While we will see later on how to determine in advance which projection is likely to be the most important, it will only be the market itself that will validate one or another of the projections by the time and

pattern position as the market approaches the price zone. If a projected price zone is exceeded, the odds favor a continuation of the trend to the next price zone. In other words, exceeding one projected price zone is usually a trend-continuation signal.

3. Occasionally, a market will make a top or bottom at a price that either is not within a price cluster which is a support or resistance zone or not even at one of the more common price projections. While I can almost always find the obscure price relationship at tops and bottoms that were made outside of a projected price cluster, this after-the-fact analysis is only of academic interest. Traders must accept the fact that a top or bottom will occasionally be made away from the typical price projections that are calculated in advance. This is one of the important reasons why we always consider all dimensions of market activity and do not rely solely on price analysis.

Gann's quote at the beginning of the chapter may be better worded as: *"Every market makes the majority of its tops or bottoms at or very near a cluster of price projections from several previous swings. These price projections may be determined well in advance and, usually, the significance of each projection relative to the trend will be known in advance."*

In this chapter, we will also discuss methods that will provide a strong indication of the minimum and maximum price projections to anticipate in any trend or counter-trend swing. We will also discuss the ramifications of understanding the trend position when price exceeds certain levels. As you will see, there is much more to price analysis than simply computing retracements.

The most important narrow price zones for potential support or resistance will occur when various price methods and relationships all point to the same area as support or resistance. Never rely on one price methodology or one ratio. If a price zone is important, it will be indicated by several relationships and result in a relatively narrow cluster of targets at or near the same price level.

Primary Price Projection Techniques

There are three key price relationships that will quickly and easily provide the price projections. They are:

1. Retracements (Ret)

2. Alternate Price Projections (APP)

3. Price Expansions (Exp)

Each price technique is considered from the degree of trend that is to be traded and, ideally, one larger and one smaller degree. The following pages include examples of how each price projection is calculated and how multiple projections will cluster within relatively narrow price zones.

A very important factor to keep in mind as we review the following examples is: *All of the price projections are calculated IN ADVANCE.* As soon as a new swing is confirmed, new projections are made. We do not know in advance which price zone will be the ultimate target of the market, but we do know in advance which price zones have the greatest potential for trend change if price should reach one of those zones. The time and pattern position of the market will usually clearly reveal which price zone has the greater probability of making a trend reversal.

As a market advances its trend and makes new swing pivots, new projections are made from each new pivot. You will soon learn how the new pivots will confirm or invalidate prior price projections.

Retracements

Most traders are familiar with price retracements. Retracements are the percentage of the prior swing that a market moves counter to the range of the prior swing. As a market advances, there will usually be more than one prior swing extreme from where to measure retracements. In other words, we will have more than one degree of retracement projections.

There are both *internal* and *external* retracements.

The following pages first illustrate retracements on idealized swing charts in order to clearly understand the concept. These are followed by numerous actual market examples.

Internal Price Retracements

Internal retracements are less than 100%.
The four most important internal retracement ratios are:
38.2%, 50%, 61.8% and **78.6%**.

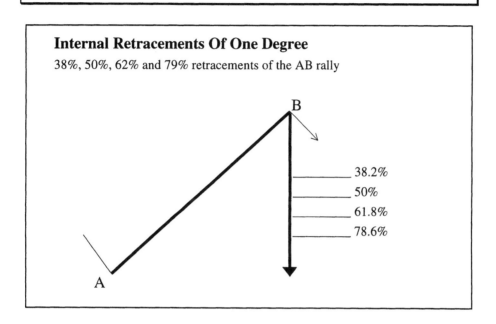

Internal Retracements Of One Degree
38%, 50%, 62% and 79% retracements of the AB rally

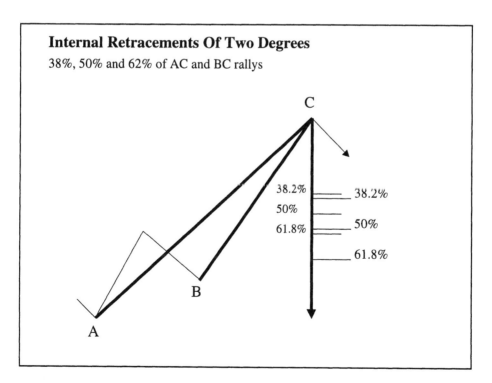

Internal Retracements Of Two Degrees
38%, 50% and 62% of AC and BC rallys

Internal Retracements

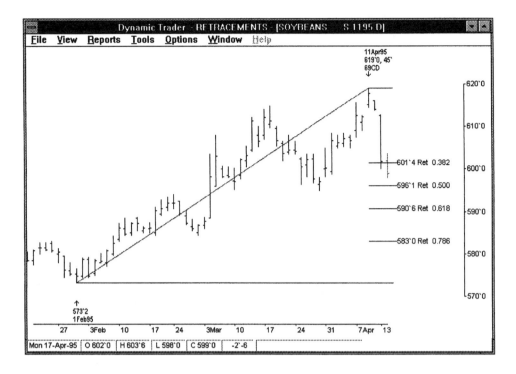

Retracements measure the percentage of the range of the prior swing that the market reacts against or retraces. *Internal retracements* are always less than 100%. A market that retraces less than 100% of the prior swing is always a counter-trend swing or a correction to the prior swing. The most important internal retracement percentages are 38.2%, 50%, 61.8% and 78.6%.

The position of the market relative to the pattern will indicate which of these ratios is particularly important at any given time. The sections on Trading Guidelines, Elliott Wave Guidelines and Putting It All Together describe in more detail the importance of each ratio at different market positions.

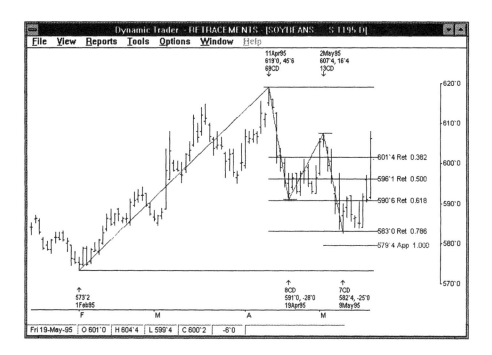

On April 19, beans made a low one tick above the 61.8% retracement. Beans eventually continued to decline in an ABC correction with a final low at the 78.6% retracement. APP is an Alternate Price Projection and will be described later in this chapter.

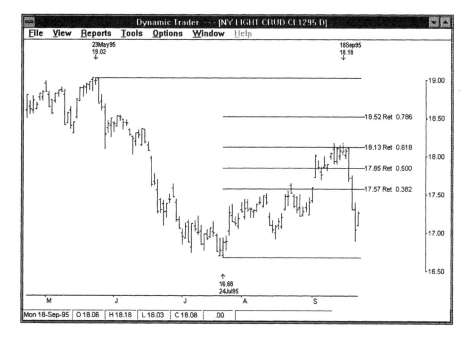

Retracement resistance in crude oil at the 38.2% and 61.8% retracements.

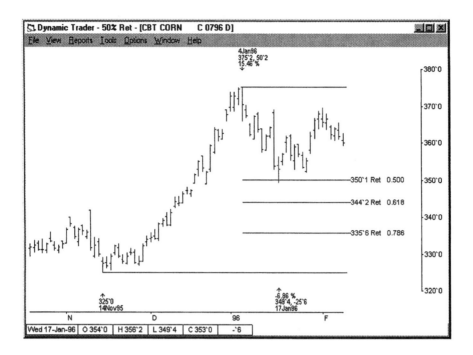

Corn made a counter-trend low at the 50% retracement. There will almost always be at least a minor reaction against the 50% retracement in all markets.

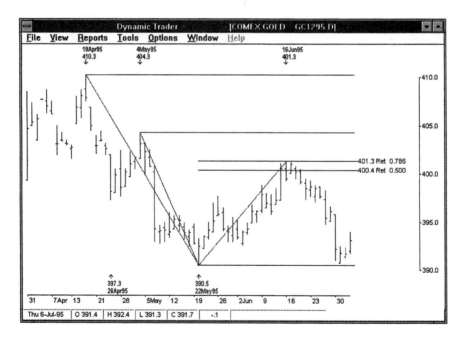

Retracements of two degrees: Gold made a top June 16, 1995 at the coincidence of a 50% retracement from the April 19 high and a 78.6% retracement from the May 4 high. The nearer price projections are to each other, the more likely they are to result in support or resistance if the market reaches the price zone.

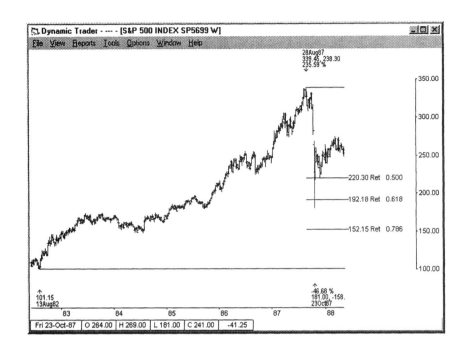

The Oct. 1987 Panic: In Oct. 1987, the S&P crashed down to make a low just below the 61.8% retracement of the Aug. 1982-Aug. 1987 bull market (top chart). Note that the secondary lows were made right on the 50% retracement. The chart below shows the retracement levels from the July 1984 low. The Oct. bottom was made just a few points below the 78.6% retracement and the initial reaction low right at the 61.8% retracement level. The retracements from two degrees provided two retracement support zones which held the market: 192.18-189.32 and 221.41-220.30.

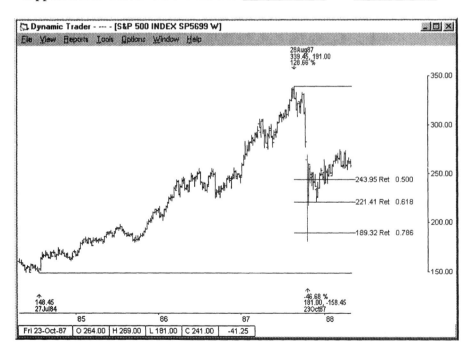

Retracement Levels Signal Strength and Weakness: The June 1 low was made just a few ticks below the 61.8% support retracement. In June and July, the mark tested the 78.6% resistance retracement three times but failed to exceed this important retracement level.

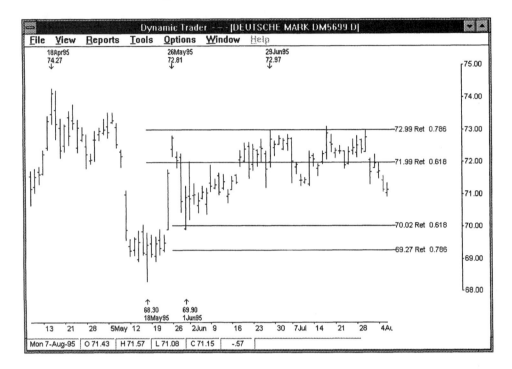

How a market reacts against retracement percentages will often indicate the position of the market. Currencies have a very high reliability of finding support and resistance at Fib retracements. This is probably because the currency traders of the world are very Elliott wave oriented. The mark came down very hard from the May 26 high and then bounced very hard off of the 61.8% retracement. The wide range reversal day on June 1 at the 61.8% retracement provided at least an initial signal that the correction down may be over.

Most traders have been erroneously taught by Elliott wave academics that the 61.8% retracement is the critical zone to signal if a swing is a counter-trend or new trend direction. In other words, counter-trends or corrections are not supposed to exceed a 61.8% retracement. If the 61.8% retracement is exceeded, it is supposed to be a signal that the market is in a new trend direction, not a counter-trend.

While the 61.8% retracement is an important potential support or resistance price zone, it should not be considered as a trend signal as described above. The 78.6% retracement is a far more important retracement projection that is usually not exceeded if the prior trend is to continue. Wave 2s often terminate at the 78.6% retracement.

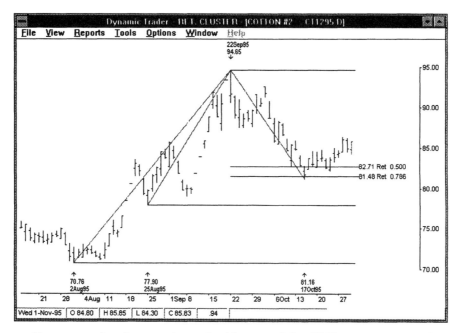

Cotton made a low at the coincidence of the 50% retracement of the larger degree and 78.6% retracement of the smaller degree.

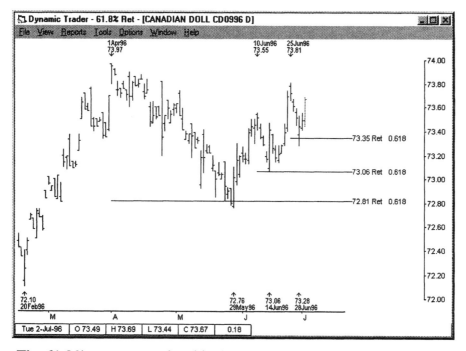

The 61.8% retracement level is the support at each counter-trend low. Note that the June 14 low was made at the 61.8% retracement to the tick! Do not fail to be alert to the market position at the 61.8% retracement level in all markets.

External Price Retracements

Many traders have a difficult time accepting that a retracement can be over 100%. A retracement can be any amount. A few ratios over 100% are very important in projecting support and resistance.

> **External Retracements** are greater than 100%.
> The most important external retracements are:
> **127%, 162%, 200%, 262%,** and **424%.**

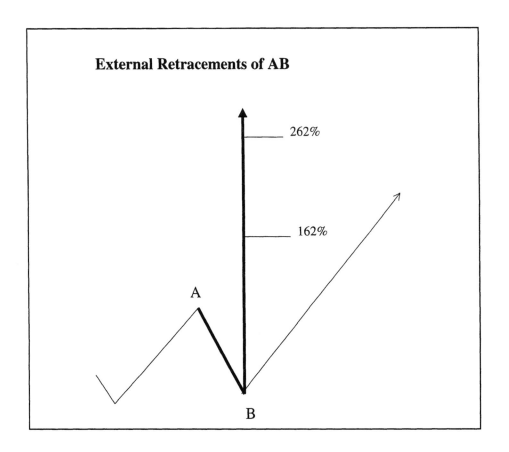

External Retracements of AB

262%

162%

A

B

External Retracements

The Aug. 22 low in the British pound was made just a few ticks above the 162% external retracement of the 6/28L- 8/1H

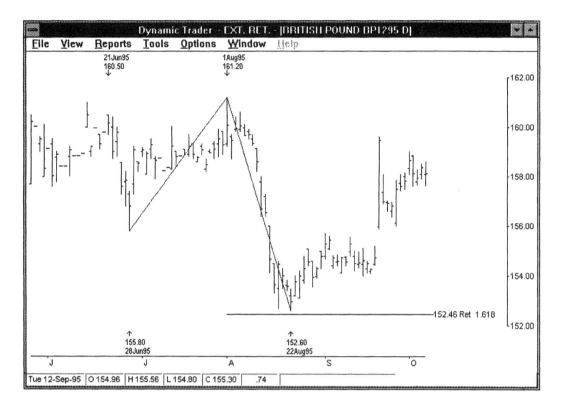

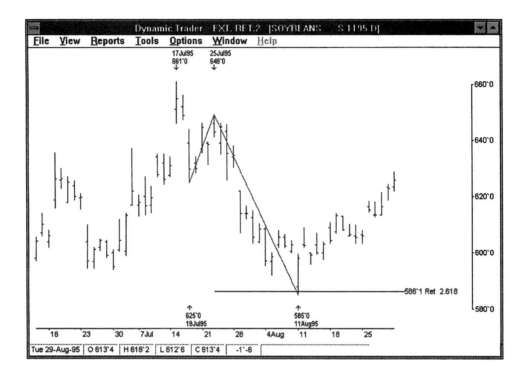

The soybean decline terminated at the 262% retracement of the initial counter-trend swing. Five wave structures frequently terminate at 162%, 262% or 424% external retracements of wave two. Wave two is also called the initial counter-trend swing.

External retracements are little used by most traders but are a very valuable price projection method.

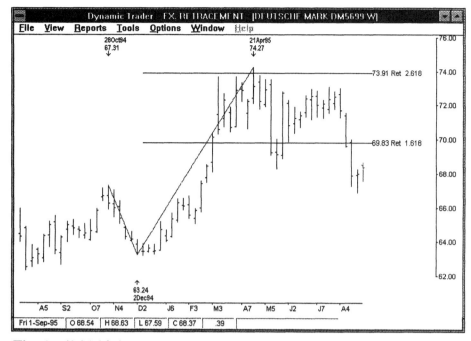

The April 21 high was made at the 262% retracement of the prior counter-trend.

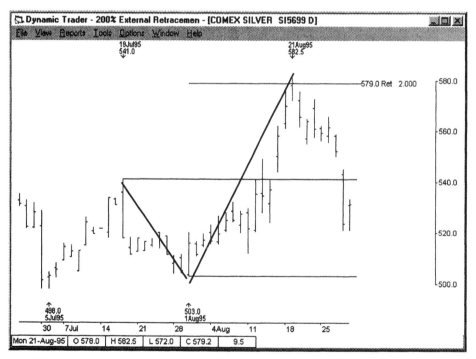

A 200% retracement is also known as a "measured move."

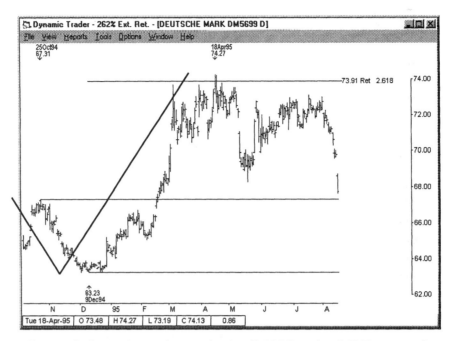

The mark formed a major top in April 1995 at the 262% external retracement of the last major counter-trend prior to the top.

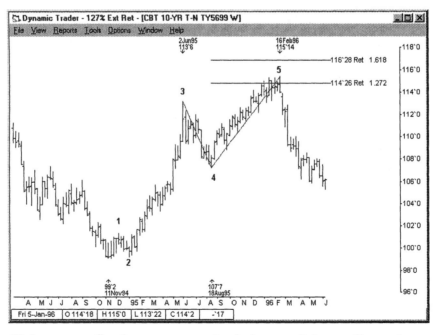

Unless wave five becomes an extended wave, it is usually made within the range of the 127% and 162% external retracement of wave four. The final wave five top is often made right on one of these two retracements.

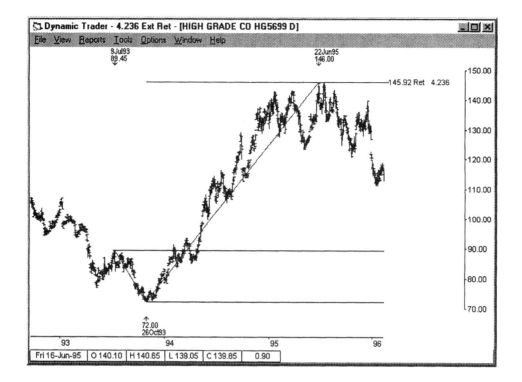

The final top of a major bull market in copper was made just a few ticks above the 4.236 external retracement of the final decline prior to the beginning of the bull market. *External retracements of the final swing prior to the beginning of a trend as shown above or external retracements of the first swing following the beginning of a trend (wave 2 or B in Elliott wave terms) will usually project the termination of the entire trend sequence.*

A trend rarely exceeds the 4.236 external retracements of these two swings. This is important to consider. If a trend is nearing the 4.236 external retracement, the odds are very high that the trend is near completion.

Alternate Price Projections (APP)

Alternate price projections project the proportions of a past swing that moved in the same direction as the current market is moving. APP projections compare trend swings with trend swings and counter-trend swings with counter-trend swings. Alternate price projections are labeled according to which previous alternate swing is being projected. The most recent alternate swing projection is labeled APP.1. The second most recent is labeled APP.2 and so on.

Alternate price projections compare trend swings to trend swings and counter-trend swings to counter-trend swings. The most important ratios to use for APPs are: **62%, 100%, 162%, 200%, 262%** and **424%.**

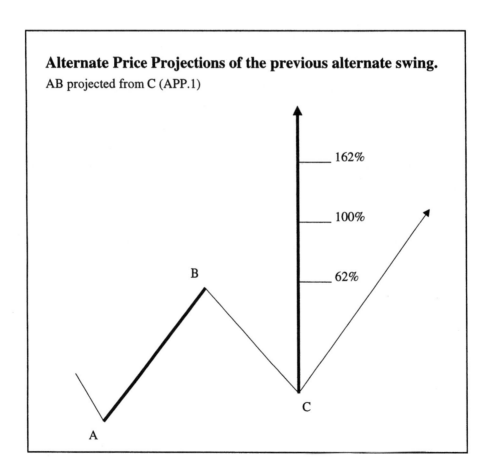

Alternate Price Projections of the previous alternate swing.
AB projected from C (APP.1)

Alternate Price Projections

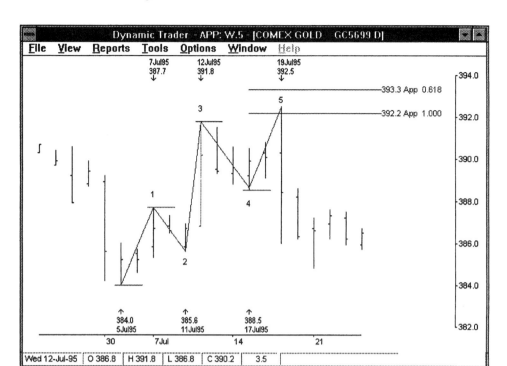

The July 19, 1995, wave 5 top was made at the coincidence where wave 5 equaled 100% of wave 1 and wave 5 equaled 61.8% of waves 1-3 (7/5L-7/12H). These are the two most frequent price targets for a wave 5 as described in the pattern chapter.

Alternate price projections are very important and reliable targets for the termination of Elliott five-wave impulse patterns and ABC corrections. Which ratios and swing comparisons are the most important for each target is described at the end of this chapter.

The Jan. 5, 1994 high and beginning of a prolonged trading range in gold was made slightly above the coincidence of the 61.8% alternate price projection and 78.6% retracement.

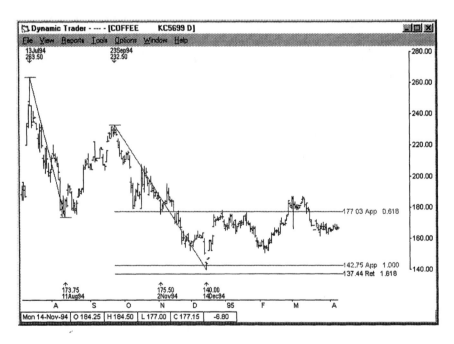

Coffee made a major low in Dec. 1994 that lasted for several months at the coincidence of the 100% alternate price projection and 162% retracement of the 8/11L-9/23H.

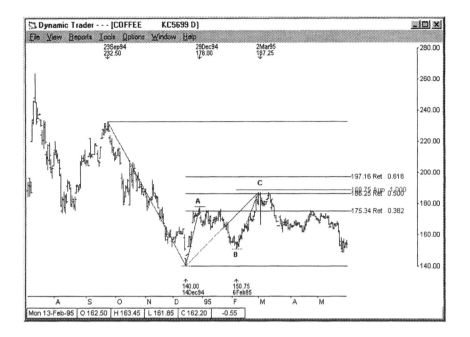

The March 2, 1995 high (W.C) was made at the coincidence of a 50% retracement and 100% APP where the price range of Wave C equaled the price range of Wave A. The Dec. 29, Wave A high was made at the 38.2% retracement. The chart below shows other price projections at the March 2 high.

The March 2 high was made at the 38.2% retracement of the larger degree decline (7/13H-12/14L) and the 127% retracement of Wave B. The Wave C high was 187.25. Four price projections fell within the 184.75-188.75 zone. It is inevitable that a market will react against such a strong cluster of price projections.

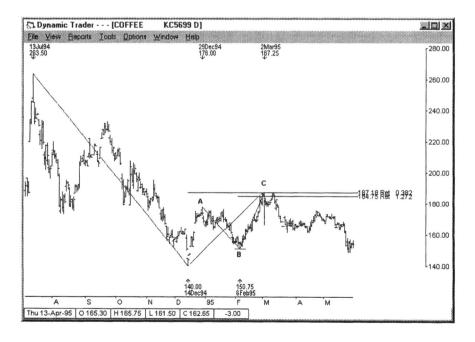

The Jan. 4, 1996 bond high was made at the 61.8% APP where Wave C equaled 61.8% of Wave A. The chart below shows the smaller degree Alternate Price Projections at the Jan. 4 high. Every minor rally was related to each other by 100% or 61.8% right up to the final top. The larger degree 61.8% APP shown above fell right within the 121.09-121.30 minor degree zone shown below. *When several APPs of two or more degrees coincide, change is inevitable.*

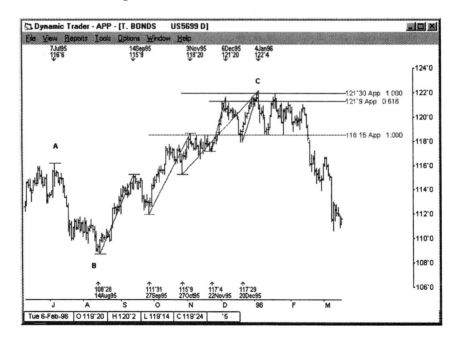

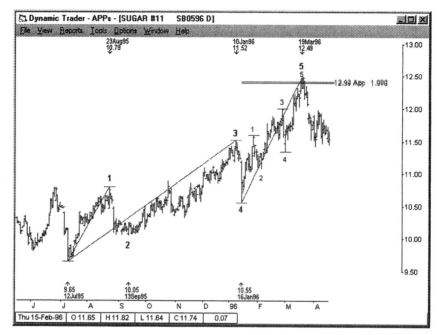

The March 19, 1996 high in the sugar market is an outstanding example of the coincidence of APPs of <u>three</u> different degrees. The chart above shows the top was made at the price zone where Wave 5 equaled 162% of Wave 1 and Wave 5 equaled 100% of Waves 1-3. The chart below shows the price zone at the top where Wave 5 of 5 equals 100% of Wave 1 of 5 and 62% of Waves 1-3. Wave 5 of 5 of 5 equals 100% of Wave 1 of 5 of 5. The solid horizontal bar at the <u>12.20-12.50</u> price zone represents the zone of the coincidence of Alternate Price Projections from all three degrees.

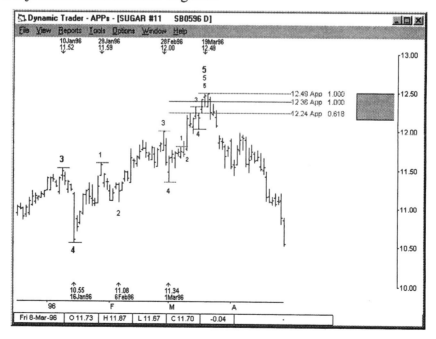

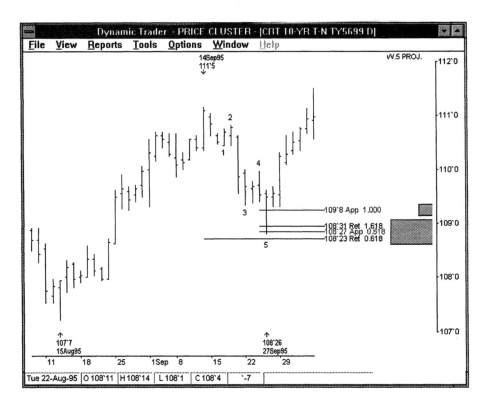

The 10-year notes made an important low at a cluster of three important price projections.

108.31-108.23

108.31 (Ret): W.5 = 1.618 W.4 (external retracement)
108.27 (APP): W.5 = .618 W.1-3
108.23 (Ret): .618 retracement (8/15L-9/14H)

The **Price Histogram Detail** below shows the details of the price projections in the zone of the wide bar which is shaded gray shown in the chart above.

	Projection	Ratio	Type	Project	from	H.I	1st	price	H.I	2nd	price	H.I
1	10831	1.618	RET	26-Sep-95	109.31	H	22-Sep-95	109.11	L	26-Sep-95	109.31	H
2	10827	.618	APP	26-Sep-95	109.31	H	14-Sep-95	111.5	H	22-Sep-95	109.11	L
3	10823	.618	RET	14-Sep-95	111.5	H	15-Aug-95	107.7	L	14-Sep-95	111.5	H

Price Clusters

There were three potential resistance zones projected from the June 14, wave 4 low. Two of these zones were confirmed by projections of the next smaller degree by projections from the wave 4:5 low made in July. The pattern and time position of the market as it approaches each price zone will help to qualify which zone is most has the greatest probability of trend reversal.

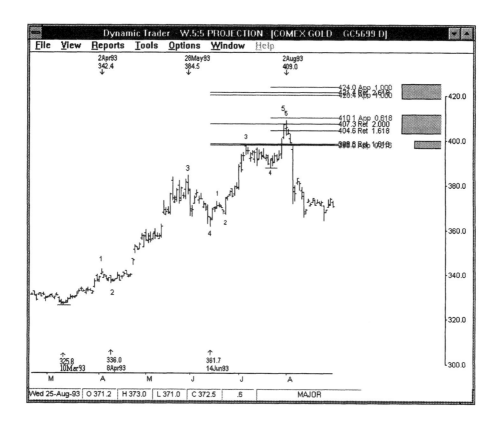

Gold made the wave 3 of 5 top at the first projection of <u>397.9-398.6</u>.

The final wave 5 of 5 high at 409.0 was made precisely within the next price cluster of <u>404.6-410.1</u>. This was the ideal price zone for a wave 5:5 high for this wave structure. It was unlikely that the final top would have reached the higher zone near 424.0.

The *Putting It All Together* chapter of the book instructs how to update the price projections as a market unfolds and how to discern which of the projected price zones are most likely to terminate the trend.

The **Price Histogram Detail** below describes all of the individual price projections included on the chart on the previous page. Notice how the price projections are in three relatively tight groups as represented by the horizontal price target bars on the chart on the previous page.

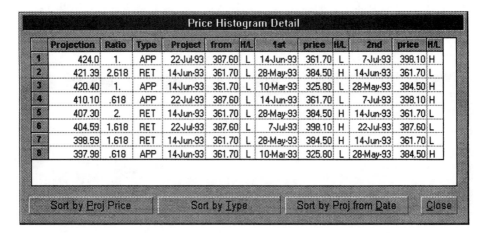

	Projection	Ratio	Type	Project	from	H/L	1st	price	H/L	2nd	price	H/L
1	424.0	1.	APP	22-Jul-93	387.60	L	14-Jun-93	361.70	L	7-Jul-93	398.10	H
2	421.39	2.618	RET	14-Jun-93	361.70	L	28-May-93	384.50	H	14-Jun-93	361.70	L
3	420.40	1.	APP	14-Jun-93	361.70	L	10-Mar-93	325.80	L	28-May-93	384.50	H
4	410.10	.618	APP	22-Jul-93	387.60	L	14-Jun-93	361.70	L	7-Jul-93	398.10	H
5	407.30	2.	RET	14-Jun-93	361.70	L	28-May-93	384.50	H	14-Jun-93	361.70	L
6	404.59	1.618	RET	22-Jul-93	387.60	L	7-Jul-93	398.10	H	22-Jul-93	387.60	L
7	398.59	1.618	RET	14-Jun-93	361.70	L	28-May-93	384.50	H	14-Jun-93	361.70	L
8	397.98	.618	APP	14-Jun-93	361.70	L	10-Mar-93	325.80	L	28-May-93	384.50	H

Sort by Proj Price	Sort by Type	Sort by Proj from Date	Close

For years all of my price projections were done with a calculator and a form to keep track of the price targets. While it was slow and a bit cumbersome, the proper information was always at hand. Then I designed my own spreadsheets to do the price projections and the output looked similar to the table above. This was much faster, more accurate and allowed me to follow many more markets. It was only after designing my own technical analysis software that the projections are now done almost automatically with the output shown right on the chart.

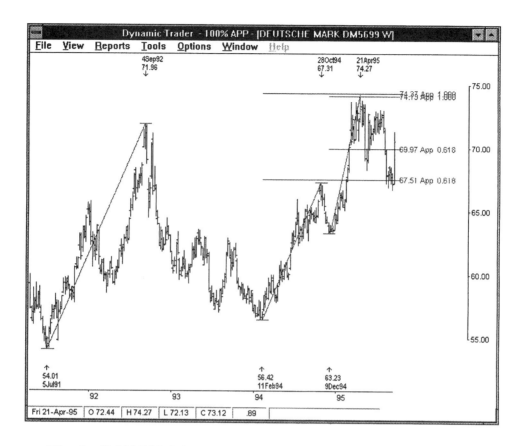

The April 1995 high in the mark was made at the coincidence of two 100% alternate price projections, each of different degree. The 100% APPs were the July 5, 1991 low - Sept. 4, 1992 high projected from the Feb. 11, 1994 low and the Feb. 11, 1994 low - Oct. 28, 1994 high projected from the Dec. 9, 1994 low.

Note that the Oct. 28 high was made just a few ticks below the 61.8% APP of the July 5, 1991 low - Sept. 4, 1992 high projected from the Feb. 11, 1994 low.

Almost every trend of any degree terminates at or very near an alternate price projection of at least one of the prior two alternate swings. *When APPs coincide with internal and/or external retracements within a relatively narrow price zone, a change of trend is very probable.*

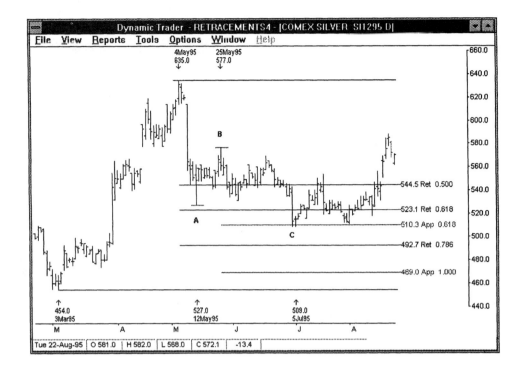

Every market does not make a corrective high or low at one of the retracement objectives every time. If they did, trading would be easy. However, most counter-trend highs or lows will be made at or very near one of the important internal retracement percentages. If another price projection falls near a retracement percentage, a price zone results where there is a high probability of support or resistance.

Silver fell sharply from the May 4, 1995 high and found initial support at the 50% retracement. There is at least a minor reaction against the 50% retracement in almost every counter-trend move simply because so many traders are aware of this retracement objective. Silver continued lower in late June and closed below the 61.8% retracement. The final low was made at the 61.8% Alternate Price Projection just below the 61.8% retracement. The Ret. and APP formed a support zone at 523.1-510.3.

Price Expansions (Exp)

Price Expansions literally expand the price range of a price swing by chosen ratio amounts. The most frequent use of price expansions are expansions of the initial impulse wave off of a major trend change.

> **Price Expansions** expand the price range of a swing.
> The most important ratios to use for Price Expansion are:
> **62%, 100%, 162%, 200%, 262%, 424%.**

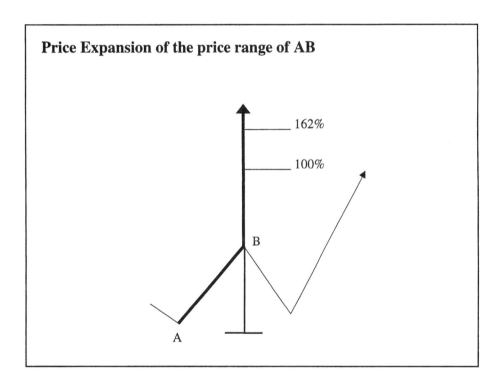

Price Expansion of the price range of AB

Price Expansions

Of the three methods of price projections, retracements and alternate price projections are the most consistently reliable. I consider price expansions as a confirming factor to the other two. In other words, I would not consider a price expansion target of any consequence if it did not coincide with a retracement and/or alternate projection.

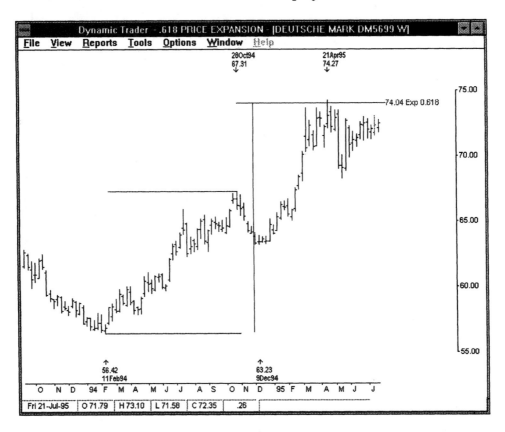

The April 21, 1995 high was made at the .618 price expansion of the Feb. 11, 1994 low - Oct. 28, 1994 high.

Price expansions are a confirming price projection method. Tops and bottoms are made right on a price expansion less often than on a retracement and alternate price projection. Price expansion projections are confirming factors to the price retracements and alternate price projections.

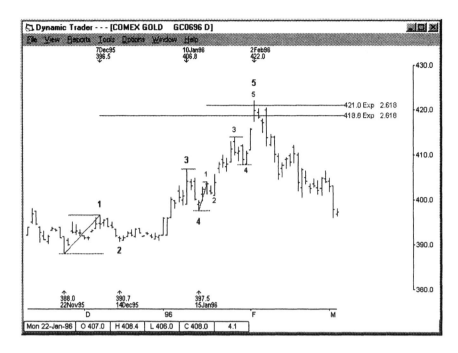

The Feb. 2, 1996 gold high was made at the coincidence of the 2.618 price expansions of Wave 1 and Wave 1 of 5.

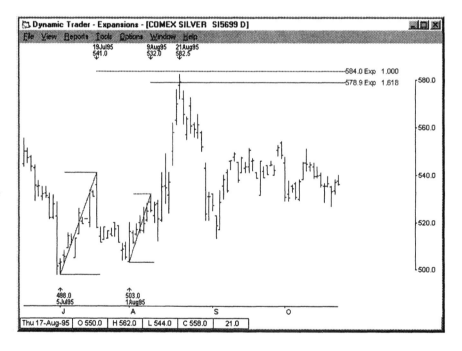

The Aug. 21, 1995 silver top was also made at the coincidence of price expansions of two degrees. The 100% expansion of the 7/5L-7/19H price range and the 162% expansion of the 8/1L-8/9H price range each fell near the Aug. 21 high.

Nikkei Weekly

The Aug. 1992 low in the Nikkei Stock Index is a great example of the coincidence of price projections in a very narrow range. The projections are grouped so tight, that they overlap in the chart below.

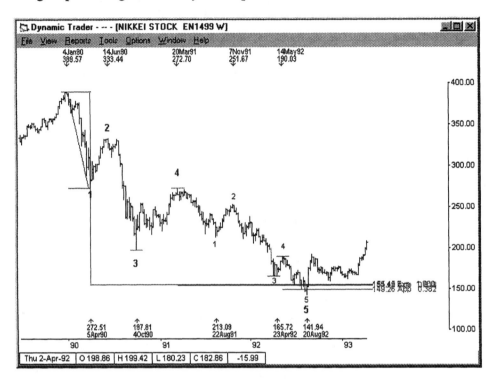

The Aug. low was made in the price zone where:

Exp: W.5 = 100% Exp W.1
App: W.5 = 62% W.1-3
Ret: W.5 = 162% W.4
Exp: W.5:5 = 100% Exp W.1:5
App: W.5:5 = 38.2% W.1-3:5
Ret: W.3-5:5 = 262% W.2:5
Ret: W.5:5 = 162% W.4:5

    The Aug. 1992 low was made at the coincidence of at least seven price projections including expansions, external retracements and alternate price projections of two degrees! Is it any wonder that a major low was made at such a strong coincidence of support?

S&P Weekly

The Sept. 1995 high in the S&P was made at the 2.618 expansion of the initial bull swing from the April 1994 low to the Sept. 1994 high. While the reaction against the 2.618 expansion was relatively mild in price and time, it was the greatest reaction since the Dec. 1994 low and lasted about six weeks. The S&P soon continued to rally and made the next top at the 4.236 expansion of the initial thrust (wave 1).

Again, the greatest reaction in time and price to the bull trend since the Dec. low was made at the 4.236 expansion. This top lasted about twelve weeks. *Trends rarely exceed a 4.236 expansion of the initial thrust.* The continued bull trend to new highs for the S&P was another demonstration of the unprecedented strength of this historic bull market.

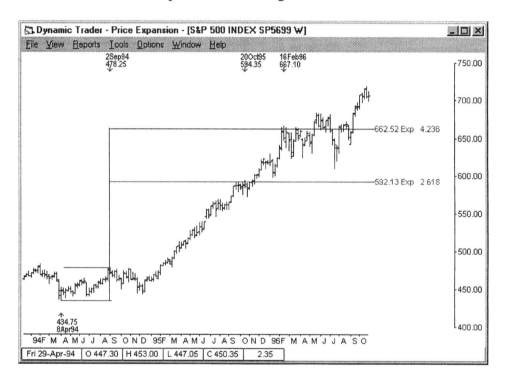

What would be the next expansion ratio to consider? <u>6.854</u> (4.236 x 1.618). A 6.854 expansion falls at 776.40. It seems outrageous that the S&P will reach that high of a level without having made a major correction, but it seemed outlandish to many people in early 1995 that the S&P would reach 662.00 with only minor corrections, but it did! The 776.40 projection is not a forecast that the S&P will reach that level, but a price to anticipate a reaction if the level is reached.

A comprehensive price analysis of any market will include price expansion projections.

Price Projections By High/Low Extremes, Closing Extremes and Percentage Change

Most traders are familiar with calculating price retracements and projections using the high or low of the pivot bar. All of the price examples in this chapter up to this point used the extreme range from pivot to pivot. High-Low or Low-High price projections may also be calculated using closing data only. Closing data may more accurately represent the form, pattern and position of the market as it eliminates the very short-term, intraday, volatile swings. However, it is usually not reasonable to expect to trade
on analysis of just closing data as the daily swings may be large and require entry, stop placement and exit at a more prudent position than waiting for the close.

Price percentage change more accurately represents the range of price change than the actual amount of price traveled. A price advance of $100 from $200 to $300 is a 50% increase in price while a price advance of $100 from $500 to $600 is only a 20% increase in price. Each price change was the same amount yet a dramatically different percentage change. The percentage change in price more accurately represents what we may consider the force of movement or the degree of psychological shift required of traders to move price.

Traders should consider supplementing their price analysis by making all price projections by closing data and by price percentage change as well as by the more traditional price range. This is particularly worth-while for major degree swings. The extra work involved will often provide critical information that will not be revealed by high/low extreme price analysis.

Price Projections By Percentage Change

Gold, Weekly: The chart above is gold weekly data bars. Dates shown are week-ending, Friday dates. Price projections calculated by percentage change are labeled with a % and the price projection method (Ret, APP or Exp). The pivot markers show the date, price and percentage change from the prior pivot.

The Jan. 1994 high was made just above the 78.6% retracement (Ret) of the Aug. to Sept. decline. Note that the high was made *dead on* the 100% *percentage change retracement* (Ret%). Gold declined 16.53% from the Aug. 6, $409.0 high to the Sept. 17, $341.4 low. Gold then rallied 16.52% up from the Sept. 17 low to the Jan. 7 high. A 16.52% rally from the lower number is a lesser amount of price than a 16.53% decline from the higher number. This is why the 100% retracement in *percentage change* does not make a 100% retracement in price amount.

The trading range lows in 1994-1995 were made at the coincidence of the 50% range retracement and 38.2% percentage change retracement. The Sept. 1993 low was made at the coincidence of the 78.6% range retracement and 61.8% percentage change retracement.

As you can see, including percentage change price projections can be a very valuable addition to the price analysis techniques.

Close-Only Data and Price Projections

This is a daily, close-only chart for gold. The <u>C</u> next to the date/price markers denote the prices shown are closing prices. The <u>C</u> next to the

price projection level also denotes the price projection is closing prices. The 38.2% and 50% high/low extreme range retracements and 50% and 61.8% percentage change retracements are shown. Gold shot right through the first pair of retracements, the 50% percentage change and 38.2% retracements and stopped dead on the 61.8% retracement.

Subsequently, the Feb. 1990 top was just a few ticks above the 61.8% percentage change retracement. Traders should be aware of the percentage change retracement targets on intermediate to major degree swings.

The chart on the next page shows a close-up of the Feb. top.

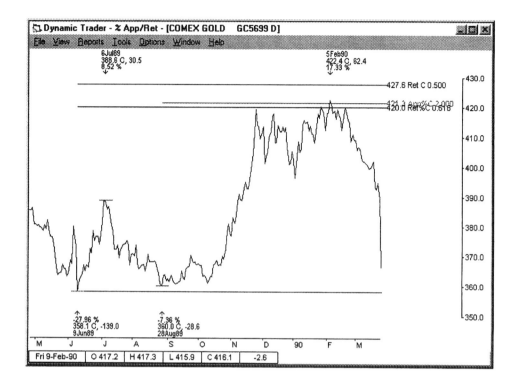

This is a close-up of the same daily close-only chart on the previous page. The 200% Alternate Price Projection of percentage change (APP%C) coincided with the 61.8% percentage change retracement at the Feb. high.

Traders who only calculate high/low retracements and projections did not have any targets near where the high was made in Feb. Traders who included percentage change retracements and projections were aware of a narrow price zone that was the coincidence of two percentage change projections that was several dollars away from the traditional projections.

It is always worth the extra effort to make price projections from close-only data and percentage change when analyzing major swings.

Close-Only Data and Percentage Change Projections

Unfortunately, every market does not make every extreme high and low reversal on a price projection or cluster of price projections. The gold rally from the Jan. 15, 1993 closing low made temporary highs almost to the tick at the 78.6% and 100% percentage change retracements on the close-only chart as shown above. The final top exceeded normal retracement targets by only a few points. Most corrections will not exceed either a 78.6% range retracement or 100% percentage change retracement.

The chart on the following page is the same as the one above except with range retracements instead of percentage change retracements.

The previous chart showed that the two minor tops prior to the final top on July 30 were made at the 78.6% and 100% percentage change retracements. The 61.8% and 78.6% range retracements fell within one tick of each of the percentage change levels. Now that is a coincidence of range and percentage change retracements to make note of!

While neither of these two important retracement coincidences were the final top, they projected levels that traders would want to be particularly alert to for potential trend termination. Both levels may have been strong profit taking zones depending on the time perspective of the trading plan.

Be very prepared for market pivots at price zones where both range and percentage change retracements coincide.

Price Projections of Three Degrees

The following three charts illustrate the value of examining a market from all price perspectives and ever smaller degrees of change.

Weekly bonds found support at the coincidence of the 50% range retracement and 38.2% percentage change retracement in early 1994. The next support was made at the 61.8% range retracement. The ultimate low was made in Nov. 1994, just below the 50% percentage change retracement and above the 78.6% range retracement.

Are the price projection methods invalidated if a major trend change does not fall right on an important retracement level? As described earlier in the chapter, price analysis should consider waves or swings of more than one degree to confirm or invalidate the larger degree projections. As a market approaches a major price projection, the next smaller degree price analysis may provide a focus to a specific price zone near the larger degree price zone where trend change is probable. See the daily bond chart on the next page.

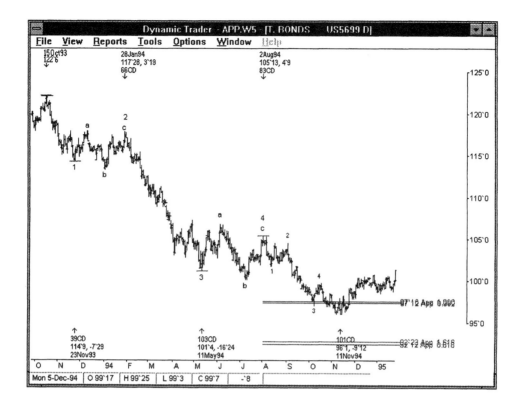

Alternate price projections of swings beginning with the Oct. 1993 high pointed to two narrow price zones with a high probability of completing the decline: <u>97.16-97.12</u> or <u>92.23-92.12</u>. The first zone coincided with the 50% percentage change retracement at 97.12 (see chart on previous page) while the second zone did not coincide with either percentage change or range retracements shown on the previous chart.

97.16: W.5 = 100% W.1
97.12: W.5 = 38.2% W.1-3
97.12: 50% percentage change retracement 9/28/90L - 10/15/93H

Once the Aug. 2, wave 4 high was confirmed by bonds trading below the <u>b</u> low, the price zone of <u>97.16-97.12</u> would be calculated in advance as having a high probability of making the wave 5 low. The next job is to go to the smaller degree swings made beginning with the Aug. 2 high to further fine tune the price projections from the larger degree swings.

The chart on the next page focuses in on the next smaller degree swings.

Smaller Degree Projections Confirm The Larger Degree

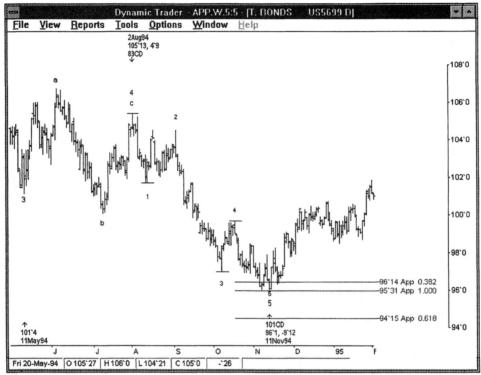

Alternate price projections of swings beginning with the Aug. 2, 1994 high projected 96.14-95.31 as the ideal target for a wave 5 low. This narrow price zone fell just below the larger degree target shown on the prior page of 97.16-97.12.

96.14: W.5 = 38.2% W.1-3
95.31: W.5 = 100% W.1

The most reliable price projection targets will be calculated from swings of at least two degrees and from different projection techniques, retracements, alternate projections and expansions of ranges and percentage change.

Intraday Examples

Up to now, only daily bar charts have been used to illustrate the *Dynamic Trading* analysis. All *Dynamic Trading* techniques apply to all time periods including intraday data. The same dynamic growth process, patterns, ratios and proportions that we have seen on the daily charts are found on all time periods.

The following pages include a number of intraday charts with comments. There are only a few examples because nothing is done differently than if it were daily data. Since we used a number of examples of the position of bonds in the second half of 1995, let's first look at the intraday data for this time period.

Bonds: 5-Minute Bars From The July 11, 1994 Low

A minor wave-four low was made on July 18 on the 8:35 AM (EST) bar. The projection for a wave-five high is **102.81-103.02** (price in decimals, not 32nds). This price zone includes the typical wave-five price projections where W.5 = 100% W.1, 38.2% W.1-3 and 162% W.4.

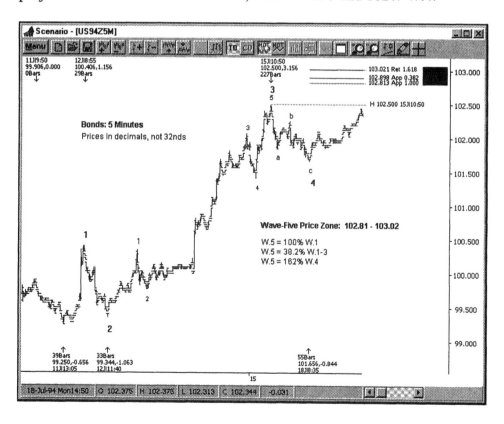

The chart on the next page shows how it turned out.

Bonds: 30 Minute Bars From The July 11, 1994 Low

Bonds made the wave-five high at **102.94** on July 20 on the 8:50 AM bar. This was a direct hit of the **102.81-103.02** projected price zone show on the 5-minute chart on the previous page. The 30-minute bar chart below also begins from the July 11 low and shows the continued rally into the July 20 high.

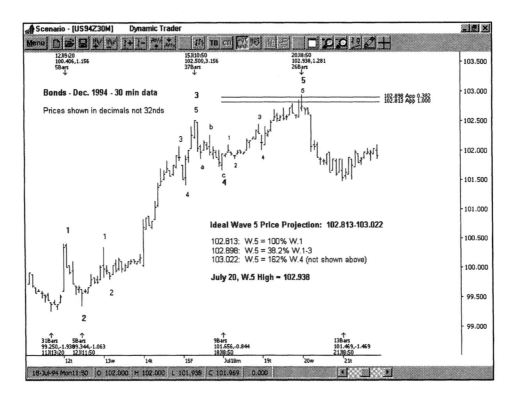

Let's continue to follow the bond activity after the July 20 high.

Bonds: 30-Minute Bars From The July 20 High

From the July 20, W.5 high a minor five wave decline was made into the 38.2% retracement on the morning of July 21 to complete W.A. An ABC-W.B rally followed then bonds continued to decline to a new low. From the W.B high on July 25, bonds made a text book, minor five-wave decline into the W.C low on July 28.

There were four price projections in a relatively tight group where the W.C low was made.

101.231: W.C = 127% W.B
101.188: W.5:C = 100% W.1:C
101.094: 50% Ret.
101.070: W.5:C = 61.8% W.1-3:C

The W.C low was 101.125, precisely within this price zone.

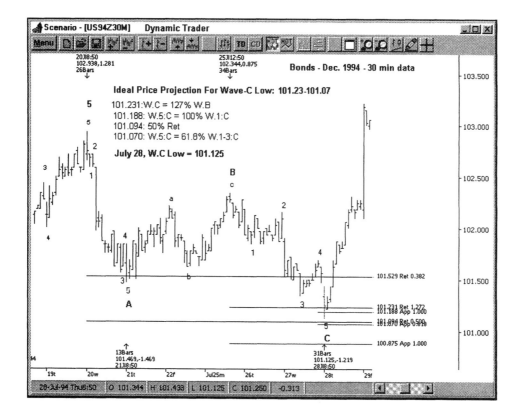

Bonds: 30-Minute Bars From The July 11, 1994 Low Through the Aug. 2, 1994 High

The July 28 Wave-C low was the completion of a larger degree Wave-B which is labeled (B) on the chart below. Bonds made another five wave advance to complete Wave-(C). The ideal price projection for Wave-5:(C) fell in the **104.499-104.813** price zone which included all of the typical price projections to complete a W.5 and W.(C).

104.499: W.5:(C) = 162% W.4:(C)
104.572: W.5:(C) = 38.2% W.1-3:(C)
104.625: W.5:(C) = 100% W.1:(C)
104.813: W. (C) = 100% W.(A)

The Aug. 2, W.5:(C) high was complete at **104.625**, precisely within the price zone projected for the top. Aug. 2 completed an ABC correction which we found in the previous daily data analysis earlier in the chapter was the completion of a Wave-4 correction.

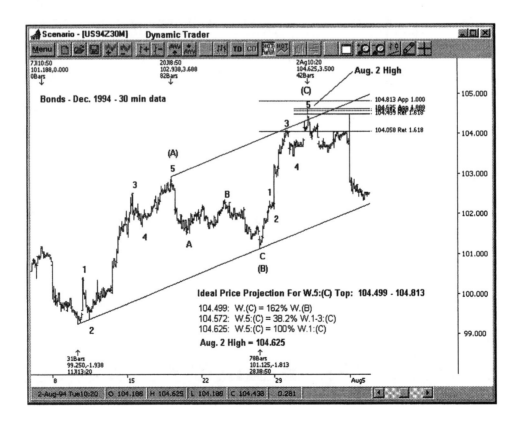

Bonds: Daily Data From July 11, 1994 Low To The Aug. 2, 1994 High

The chart below shows the daily data for the same period illustrated by the previous intraday charts. The minor sub-divisions shown on the intraday charts clearly helped to discern the pattern of the swings shown on the daily chart. More importantly, the intraday swings fine-tuned the price projections of the larger degree waves and provided much more narrow range price targets.

Every intraday chart will not provide symmetrical, minor price patterns that are of practical value to help project the termination of the larger degree swings shown on the daily charts. But, many will. For traders who do not collect real-time data, several data vendors provide tick data at the end of the day for a very modest cost. Readers may want to consider collecting the tick data in order to take advantage of the information provided by the intraday charts.

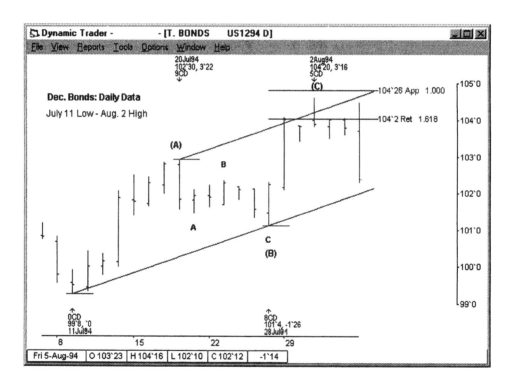

S&P: 60-Minute Data From The July 16, 1996 Low

The S&P appeared to make a Wave-4 low on the 10:30 bar on Sept. 3. The low was made at the price cluster that included the 50% retracements from the July 16 and July 24 lows as well as the 100% alternate price projection (W.4 = 100% W.2).

What is labeled as the Wave-4 low briefly traded into the price range of the Wave-1 which violated the Wave-4 guideline. While the eventual outcome may show that Sept. 3 was not a Wave-4 low, what is important is that the simple dynamic price projections of retracements and alternate price projections provided a high probability, minor support zone in a bull trending market.

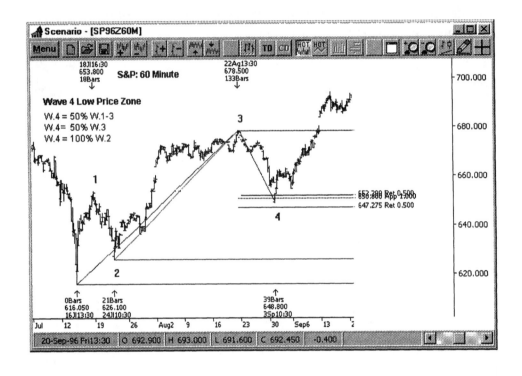

S&P: 60-Minute Data

The ideal target for a Wave-5 high projected from the Sept. 2, Wave-4 low fell in the **686.90-696.50** price zone. On Sept. 16, the S&P reached this price zone which coincided with the parallel channel resistance line. As you can see from the hourly chart below, the S&P remained in the price zone for a week before continuing the advance. While the wave count shown on the chart may be questionable, the projected resistance level was right-on target.

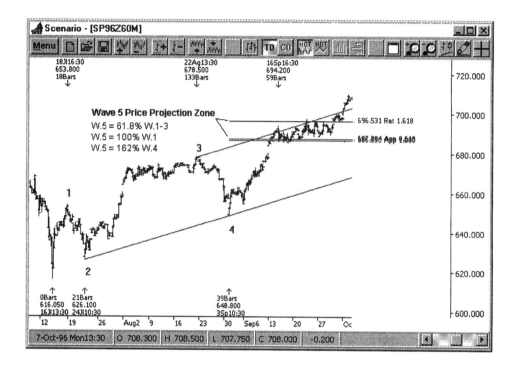

Gold: 60-Minute Data

One of the best uses of intraday data is to fine tune price projections. In April 1996, the major trend in gold was down. Gold began a minor rally on April 19. The May 8 high was made dead-on the narrow range price projection that included the 50% and 61.8% retracements of the prior two minor swing highs and the 127% external retracement where W.C = 127% W.B.

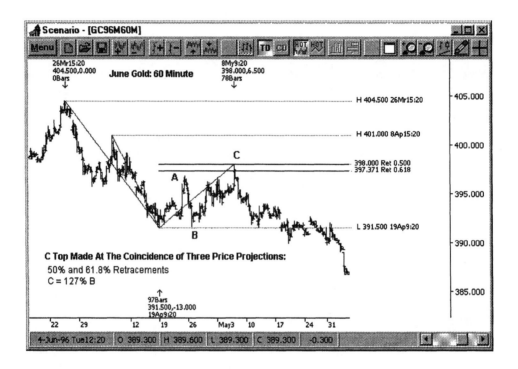

Silver: 30-Minute Data

Silver made a triple bottom just a few ticks below the narrow range retracement zone of the 50% and 61.8% retracements of the prior two minor lows. The triple top at 497 is at the 61.8% retracement (not shown) of the corrective decline from the Jan. 27 high to the triple bottom. Breakouts from triple tops or bottoms are usually dramatic.

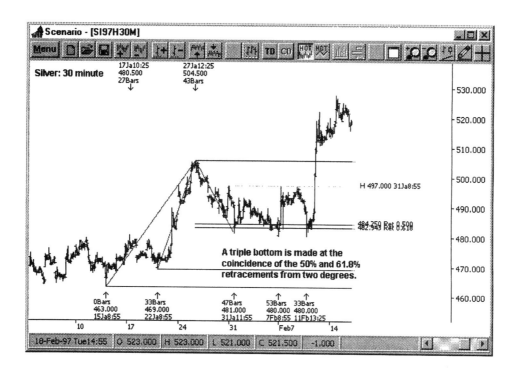

DM: 30-Minute Data

The DM made a low on the morning of May 28 followed by one of the most significant rallies in several weeks. The 30-minute data shows an almost ideal ABC correction was made between the May 31 high and June 11 low. The Wave-C low was made at the 61.8% retracement of the May 28-May 31 rally which coincided where Wave-C equaled 100% Wave-A and 162% Wave-B.

Note how this 30-minute data clearly shows the minor five wave structure of Wave-C.

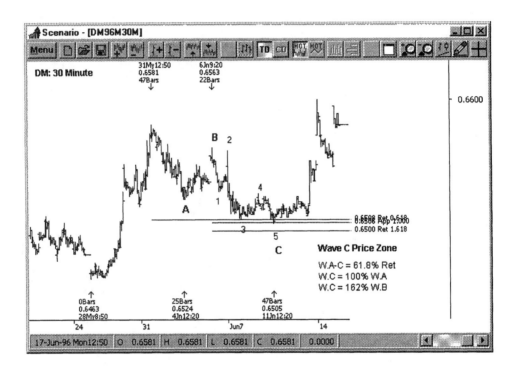

Intraday Data

I have only provided a few examples of intraday analysis as the procedures and techniques are exactly the same as with the daily data examples.

Intraday data will often provide an invaluable advantage to the trader, particularly for confirming the price projections of the larger degree swings shown on the daily charts. The same caution must be made with intraday data as with daily data. Don't read more into the data than what is there. Don't force a wave count when no practical wave count exists. Even if a practical wave count is not being made, the intraday data can be invaluable to project the minor projected support and resistance zones that help the trader lessen the capital exposure on entry strategies and protective stop loss placement. Intraday data is also invaluable for short term traders.

Dynamic Price Projections For Mutual Funds

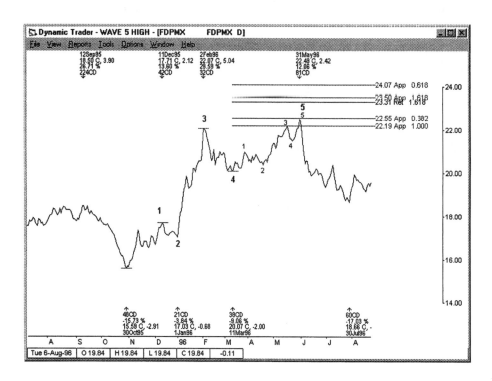

All types of dynamic analysis applies to all active futures, stock, mutual funds and cash data. The chart above is Fidelity's Select Precious Metals Mutual Fund. There were two price projections for a wave 5 top.

21.95-22.55	**23.26-23.50**
21.95: 200% W.1 Expansion	**23.26**: 262% W.1 Expansion
22.19: W.5 = 100% W.1	**23.31**: W.5 = 162% W.4
22.55: W.5 = 38.2% W.1-3	**23.50**: W.5 = 162% W.1
	24.07: W.5 = 61.8% W.1-3

These two zones are calculated *in advance* as soon as the wave 4 low is suspected to be complete. Which of the two zones should have had the greater probability of making a wave 5 top? Each includes typical wave 5 projections. Ideally, the smaller degree swings within wave 5 will provide the ideal target. The chart on the next page provides the smaller degree projections.

Small Degree Projections Confirm The Larger Degree Projections

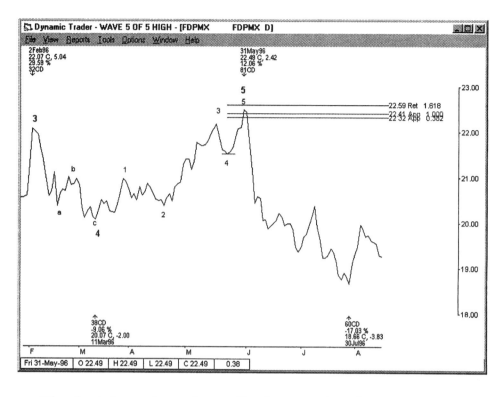

The chart above shows the smaller degree swings from the March 11, wave 4 low for Fidelity Select Precious Metals fund. The ideal target for the wave 5 of 5 high would be <u>22.32-22.59</u>.

22.32: W.5 = 38.2% W.1-3
22.41: W.5 = 100% W.1
22.59: W.5 = 162% W.4

This price zone overlapped with the larger degree <u>21.95-22.55</u> projection shown on the previous page. The final wave 5:5 top was made May 31 at <u>22.49</u> precisely within the overlap zone for the ideal wave 5 of 5 high. Fidelity's Precious Metals mutual fund declined at least 17% from the wave 5:5 top in May 1996.

Dynamic price analysis applies to all actively traded markets. Every market will not make a top dead on a dynamic price projection. But when two degrees of price projections overlap, there is a very high probability for trend change within the overlapped price zone.

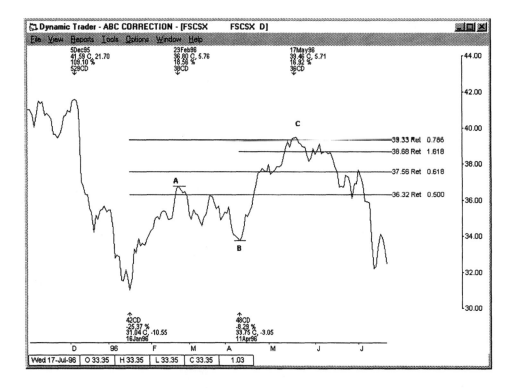

The chart above is Fidelity's Select Software and Computer Services mutual fund. From the Jan. 16, 1996 low, the price rallied to the Feb. 23 high just above the 50% retracement. Price then declined into the April 11 low and rallied again above the Feb. (wave A) high. Once the Feb. high was exceeded, price projections for a wave C high may be made. The ideal target for a C wave high was 38.68-39.51.

38.68: W.C = 162% W.B
39.33: 78.6% retracement of the Dec. 5, 1995 high to Jan. 16, 1996 low.
39.51: W.C = 100% W.A (not shown on chart).

Most corrections do not exceed the 78.6% retracement if the prior trend is to remain in force. This simple ABC zigzag correction terminated where wave C equaled wave A, the typical target for wave C.

The following page shows a close up of the B wave price target.

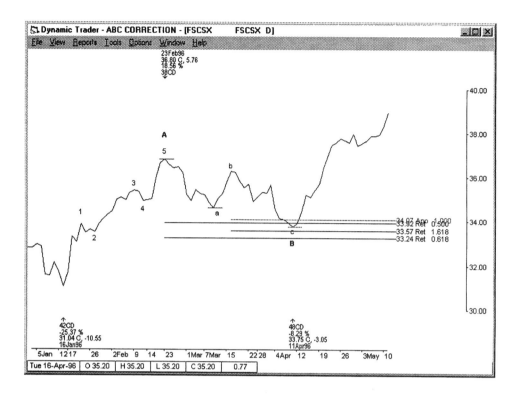

The chart on the previous page showed the price targets for an ABC correction. B waves are considered corrections to the larger degree trend which is also a correction. In other words, a B wave is a correction to the correction. B waves are often ABCs themselves.

The chart above zooms in on the B wave of the ABC correction shown on the previous page. Once the minor A wave low was exceeded, the price target for the minor C wave of the larger degree B wave could be calculated. The ideal price zone for the B wave of the ABC correction to terminate was the 34.07-33.24 price zone.

34.07: W.c:B = 100% W.a:B

33.92: 50% Retracement (1/16L-2/23H)

33.57: W.c:B = 162% W.b:B (162% rctracement)

33.24: 61.8% Retracement (1/16L-2/23H)

The April 11, Wave c:B low of 33.75 was made precisely within the ideal target zone of 34.07-33.24 which included all of the typical price projections for an ABC correction.

Individual Stock Examples

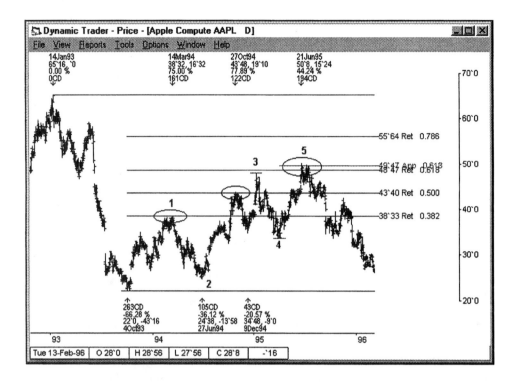

All Dynamic Trading analysis techniques and trading strategies work well on individual stocks which are actively traded on the major exchanges.

Apple computer stock made each significant high on a Dynamic Price Projection during the 1993-1994 rally. The Wave-5 top was made at the coincidence of the 61.8% retracement and where W.5 = 61.8% W.1-3.

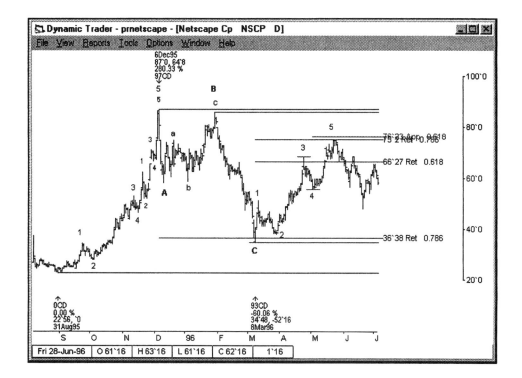

Netscape stock had a wild ride during its first couple of years. It dramatically demonstrates the significance of the 78.8% retracement. The ABC corrective low in March 1996 was made just a few ticks below the 78.6% retracement. The five-wave high was made in the price zone where W.5 = 61.8% W.1-3 and the 78.6% retracement.

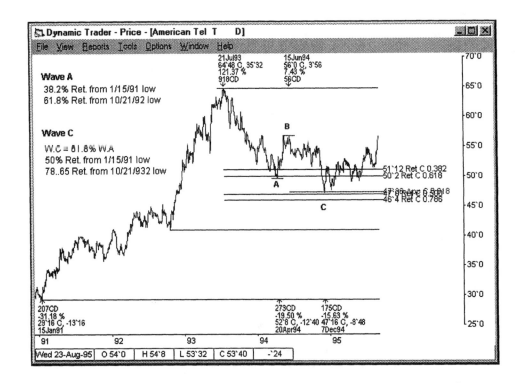

AT&T is a widely traded stock. The Waves A and C lows were both made at the coincidence of retracements.

The Wave-C low was made at the price zone where W.C = 61.8% W.A and the 50% and 78.6% retracements of two degrees.

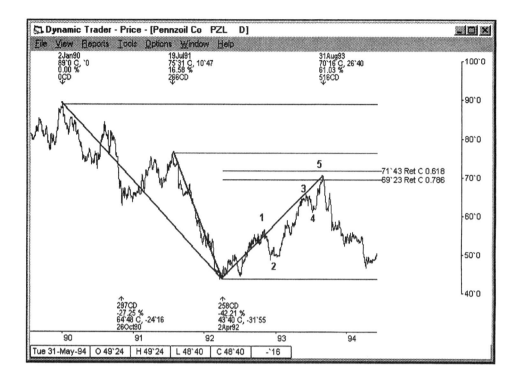

Pennzoil's Aug. 1993 high was made at the coincidence of the 61.8% and 78.6% retracements of two degrees. The chart on the next page shows four additional lesser degree price projections at the Aug. high.

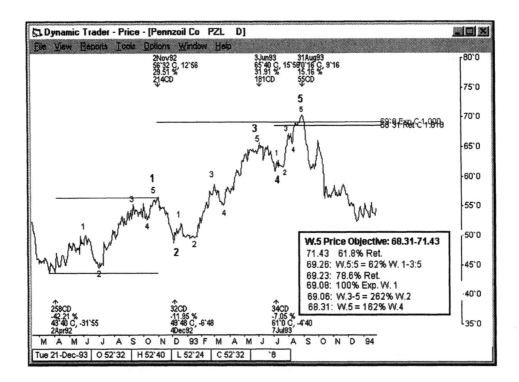

The box in the chart shows the six price projections that fell near the Aug. 1993 high. The chart on the previous page showed the two major retracement targets. The chart above shows the 100% Expansion of W.1 and where W.5 = 162% W.4.

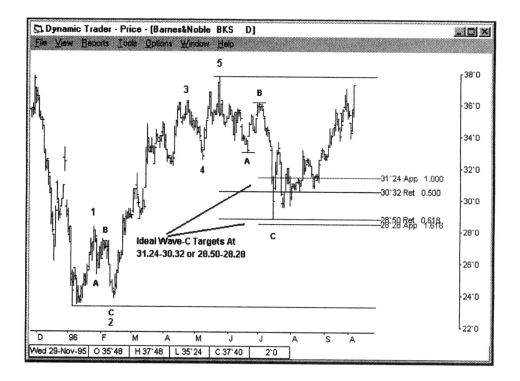

Maybe if I show a great example from a big book seller, they will help to sell this book.

There were two ideal price targets for a Wave-C low for Barnes and Noble in mid-1996. The first target was where the 50% retracement fell near the 100% Alternate Price Projection (W.C=100% W.A) and the second where the 61.8% retracement fell near the 162% Alternate Price Projection (W.C=162% W.A).

The ABC correction terminated at the second target.

Price Overbalance

A *price overbalance* is when the price range or percentage change of a correction exceeds the price range or percentage change of the prior corrections. A price overbalance is an alert that a larger degree trend change may be underway.

A price overbalance is not a definitive indication that a larger degree change-in-trend is underway. But, it is an alert signal that there is more buying or selling pressure against the trend than has previously occurred. If a counter-trend swing exceeds in price range or percentage change the price range or percentage change of all previous counter-trend swings since the larger degree trend began, it is a signal to be alert to the price and pattern position of the market for clues to the trend position.

Price overbalance is a lagging indicator. It is only signaled after the fact. While it is not a trade signal, it is an important reference point to alert the trader to the position of the market.

Overbalance Of Price Range

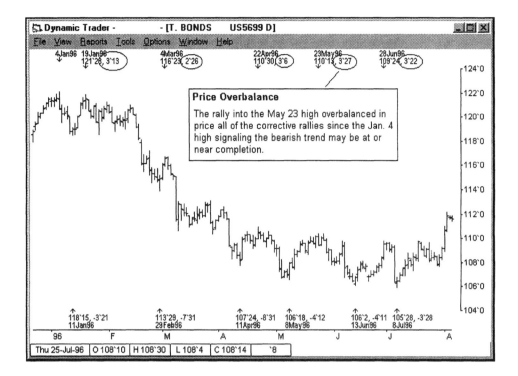

From the Jan. 1996 highs, bonds declined making minor corrective rallies of approximately three points. The May rally advanced 3-27/32, a greater rally in price than any since the Jan. high. This was a price overbalance and signaled more buying power was coming into the market than at any time since the Jan. high. The price overbalance was an alert to traders that the bearish trend may be coming to an end.

While bonds made a slight new low in June and July, the price overbalance signaled the trend was at or near the end.

Overbalance Of Price Percentage Change

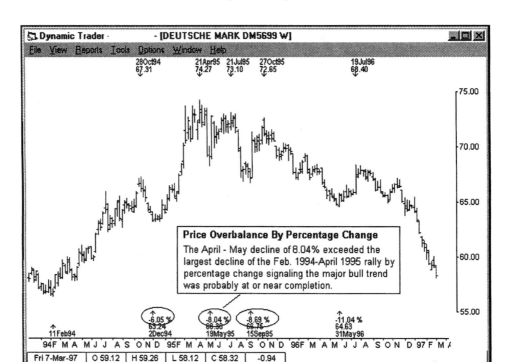

> **Price Overbalance By Percentage Change**
> The April - May decline of 8.04% exceeded the largest decline of the Feb. 1994-April 1995 rally by percentage change signaling the major bull trend was probably at or near completion.

All price analysis of long term trends should be done by percentage change as well as price range. The largest percentage decline during the Feb. 1994 to April 1995 rally was 6.05%. The mark declined 8.04% from the April high to the May low. This was an overbalance of price by percentage change and signaled the bull trend was probably at or near completion.

The mark rallied to a high in July and declined 8.69%, another price overbalance. The bull trend was complete and a major bear trend was just in the initial stages.

Price overbalance is a lagging indicator, but often valuable as a signal of an impending or just completed larger degree trend change. While specific, trading decisions are not made by an overbalance in price signal, traders are alerted to the larger degree position of a market by a price overbalance.

Overbalance Of Price Percentage Change

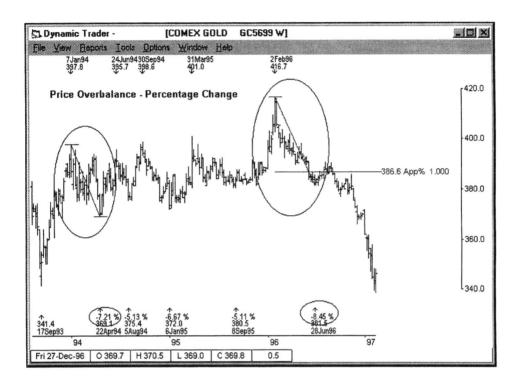

Gold had been in a prolonged and wide trading range in 1994-1996. The largest percentage decline was 7.21% from the Jan. 1994 high to April 1994 low. If a percentage decline greater than 7.21% was made, the odds favored a bear trend and breakout of the trading range to the downside.

A 7.21% decline from the Feb. 1996 high fell at 386.6. In June 1996, gold declined below 386.6 signaling a bear trend and the probability that the decline would continue.

The price overbalance shown above at 386.6 is a 100% Alternate Price Projection (APP) by percentage change of the Jan. 1994 high to the April 1994 low projected from the Feb. 1996 high.

Dynamic Price Projections™

These Dynamic Price Projection targets are a simple, yet very powerful method of projecting the price zones that have the highest probability of support or resistance and trend termination. There are four important factors to keep in mind with price projections:

1. *These price projections are not forecasting that a market will reach any one projected price zone.* They are simply important symmetrical, mathematical relationships of past price swings. Support and resistance and most trend changes occur at clusters of these projections in all markets. Therefore, we want to be prepared in advance for those price zones that are a cluster of projections. The pattern chapter described the typical price targets for each wave sequence.

2. *All analysis and trading concerns probability, not certainty.* We want the probabilities on our side. If support and resistance and *most* trend changes occur at these price clusters, we have a very important edge for our trading strategies. We have a definite piece of information to act upon.

3. *If a market trends beyond a projected support or resistance zone, more than likely it will continue to trend at least into the next projected support or resistance zone.* Trend changes are almost always made at a coincidence of projected price targets. It follows that if one is exceeded, the market will probably continue to the next.

4. *Take a holistic approach. Price projections must not be taken out of the context of the other two dimensions of market activity: time and pattern analysis.* Price is just one of the three important analysis factors. As a market approaches the projected price zone, the other two factors will qualify how important that price projection is likely to be. Traders must be careful not to focus on just one dimension of market activity. The value of the type of market analysis and trading strategies taught in this book is that we look at the whole of the market activity.

Review Of The Ratios That Are

The Most Important For Price Projections

Retracements
Internal: 38.2% **50% 61.8% 78.6%**
External: **127% 162%** 200% **262%** 424%

Alternate Price Projections:
61.8% 100% 162% 200% **262%** 424%

Price Expansions:
61.8% **100% 162%** 200% **262%** 424%

Be Prepared In Advance

All price projections are calculated *in advance*. As soon as a new swing is made, the price projections are updated. It is a simple matter to keep the price projections updated. If you will do this, you will always be prepared with a very high degree of confidence for those price zones that have the highest probability of support, resistance and trend change.

The next page shows a summary of the most important wave comparisons and price ratios to project the target for each wave.

A Summary Of The Most Important Price Projection Ratios By Wave

The ratios in **bold** occur the most frequently for the particular wave noted.
As a market advances making new swings, more comparisons are
possible. High probability support and resistance zones are found at price
zones
where several projections fall at or near the same price level.

End of Wave 2 Price Projections

W.2 = (38.2% **50% 61.8%** 78.6%) W.1 (Ret)

End of Wave 3 Price Projections

W.3 = (100% **162% 262%**) W.1 (APP)
W.3 = (**162% 262%**) W.2 (Ret)

End of Wave 4 Price Projections

W.4 = (**100%** 162%) W.2 (APP)
W.4 = (**38.2% 50%** 61.8%) W.3 (Ret)
W.4 = (23.6% **38.2% 50%** 61.8%) W.1-3 (Ret)

End of Wave 5 Price Projections

W.5 = (**100%** 162%) W.1 (APP)
W.5 = (**38.2% 61.8%** 100%) W.1-3 (APP)
W.5 = (**127% 162%** W.4 (Ret)
W.3-5 = (**262% 424%**) W.2 (Ret)

End of Wave B Price Projections (ABC zigzag)

W.B = (38.2% **50% 61.8%** 78.6%) W.A (Ret)

End of Wave B Price Projections (ABC irregular)

W.B = (**127%** 162%) W.A (Ret)

End of Wave C Price Projections

W.C = (61.8% **100%** 162%) W.A (APP)
W.C = (**162%** 262%) W.B (Ret)
W.C = (38.2% **50% 61.8%** 78.6%) W.1-5 (Ret.)

Chapter 5

Dynamic Time Analysis

"The future is a repetition of the past and each market movement is working out time in relation (proportion) *to some previous time cycle."*

W. D. Gann

In the *Dynamic Time Analysis* chapter you

- Learn how to project well *in advance* the time periods with the greatest probability of trend change.

- Learn the difference between dynamic and static time cycles.

- Learn the most important time projection technique, Time Cycle Ratio projections.

- Learn which ratios and swing comparisons are the most important for time projections.

- Learn which time counts are the most important and how to integrate them with the Time Cycle Ratio projections.

- Learn how the time projections cluster to provide narrow bands of time that project future trend reversals.

Project The Time Of Trend Changes *In Advance*

Does your technical analysis methods include a time analysis methodology that will project the high-probability time of trend change, often to the exact day? Dynamic Time Analysis does just that.

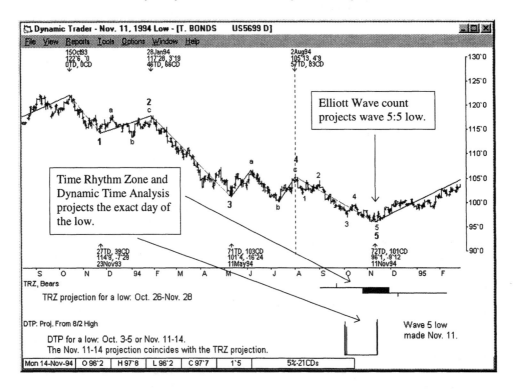

The previous chapters taught you how to analyze the pattern position of the market by the Elliott Wave Principle to understand if a market was in a trend or counter-trend position and when to identify the termination of a trend. In the Dynamic Price Analysis chapter you learned how to project well in advance the specific price zones for support and resistance and trend termination.

This Dynamic Time Analysis chapter will teach you to project the minimum and maximum time targets for a trend or counter-trend and the specific, high-probability dates to anticipate trend termination.

Time, Price and Pattern Coincide To Signal Major Trend Change

A comprehensive analysis of the whole market position signals to the trader the lowest-risk and highest profit potential trade set-ups. When time, price and pattern projections coincide, change is just about inevitable.

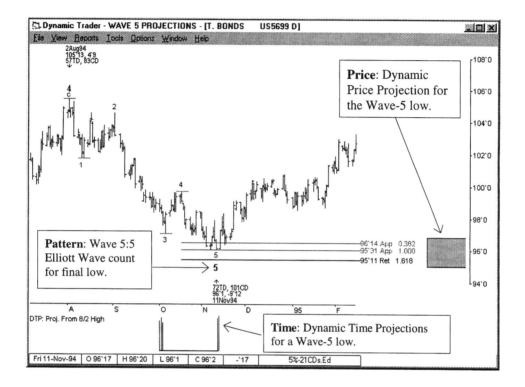

Is the example above unique? Of course not! Every market provides frequent low-risk and high profit potential trade set-ups. When you have mastered the Dynamic Time Analysis techniques taught in this chapter, you will often be prepared days, even weeks, in advance for the dates when trend changes will unfold.

When you integrate dynamic price and pattern analysis with dynamic time analysis, you will have a comprehensive view of the market position and the information you need to make high probability trading decisions.

Market Timing Based On Reality

Before describing the specific techniques of change-in-trend, time projection, I will briefly discuss the background of time analysis.

Traditional cycle analysis is based on the concept that time cycles of human activity are linear and of fixed periodicity. This concept is derived from two concepts that attempt to relate the cycles of the financial and commodity markets to linear, fixed-periodicity cycles.

Calendar Cycles

We record periods of time by days, weeks, months, years, etc. in accordance with the relationship of the earth, moon and sun. These calendar periods are precisely defined and predictive of fixed-periodicity and serve us well for record keeping purposes and accurately reflect the seasonal and agricultural growth cycles. They seem to imply that events progress in regular fixed periods.

Physical Cycles

Fixed length cycles are found in many other relationships in the physics of nature, such as sound and light frequencies. While these cycles may appear to be irregular, they are composites of many individual, fixed length cycles. These cycles are a reaction to a physical phenomena, not a result of an internal growth process.

These calendar and physical cycles are easy to understand and observe. They appeal to the analytical type with a highly developed left brain who wants everything to easily work out in mathematical precision and prediction. It is a mistake to believe that the cycles of human nature also unfold in periods of fixed periodicity. All freely traded markets are driven by mass psychology - periods of optimism and pessimism of the groups of participants. The social cycles of mass psychology are not of the same nature as the physical and calendar cycles. Mass psychological cycles unfold in a dynamic process of growth by cycles that are not of fixed length periodi-city but are continually expanding and contracting in relationship to prior cycles.

Cycles of fixed length periodicity are called *static cycles* as they imply that the same cycle or condition will endlessly repeat over time. Static cycles imply change, but not growth. Static cycles imply that a previous condition will continuously repeat at predictable fixed periods. Static cycles are represented geometrically by a circle.

Dynamic cycles represent growth, evolution and expansion. They represent a repetition of the process, and the process will be connected to the past but not duplicate the past. As we shall see, dynamic cycles imply that conditions will repeat in relation to prior cycles by dynamic, growth proportions, not static, fixed repetition. Dynamic cycles are represented geometrically by a spiral. A spiral is a circle that is evolving and expanding.

The Theory Behind Static Cycles

So-called component cycles (individual, fixed-length cycles) are combined into a composite cycle (the summation of the underlying component cycles) in an attempt to mirror the past time activity and project the time activity of the future. If time cycles of human activity, including financial market activity, were a composition or summation of component cycles of fixed-length periodicity, a composite cycle that would mirror the past and accurately project time of change into the future would be possible *if all component cycles and their proper phasing were known.*

After decades of sophisticated research from this perspective, including massive computer power and millions of research dollars, consistently, reliable future projections of time activity have not been achieved by summing alleged, fixed-length component cycles into a composite cycle! How is this possible? Why hasn't this problem or challenge been solved? Is it the failure to identify all underlying, component cycles and their proper phasing? I don't think so.

The problem has not been solved because the solution is attempted from a belief in a concept that does not exist in the reality of time and growth process of human psychology. Time is not linear, but multidimensional and non-linear. Time does not unfold in linear cycles of fixed-length periodicity. Time unfolds in evolving, growth cycles of dynamic proportion.

All methods of time analysis of the price activity of the financial and commodity markets that assume that cycles of fixed-periodicity are the underlying cause of market cycles have consistently failed with one exception. The history of "cycle" analysis of the financial and commodity markets is a history of perpetuating the myth that fixed-length cycles exist and provide predictability for investors and traders. Study the history of cycle analysis including the analysis and predictions of past decades and you will find a history of no more than coincidental success.

The exception to this condemnation of fixed-length cycles is that markets often exhibit a *temporary* rhythm of *relatively* fixed-length, *short-term* cycles. They are temporary in that they usually are evident for only a few days or weeks. They are relatively fixed-length because the cycle length (low-low) will vary by 10% or so. The cycles are short-term because they usually are only a few days to a few weeks in length. Any one market exhibits these short-term rhythms less than one-third of the time.

The Theory Behind Dynamic Cycles

The Universe does not sponsor stasis or regression. Everything in the universe is constantly evolving, expanding, growing. Time cycles of mass psychology, including those related to the financial markets, are related to evolving, dynamic ratios of growth, not static, fixed period divisions.

If market activity is to be understood, that understanding must be based on an accurate concept and theory based on reality, as well as specific analytical techniques that allow one to project the future historical effects with consistent reliability.

Ratio and proportion are important concepts from antiquity. *Markets evolve in proportion to past time cycles by dynamic growth ratios.*

Price movements in the financial markets reflect the optimism and pessimism of the participants. In other words, price movements are a result of the mass psychology of the traders and investors participating in the market. Psychological unfoldment is always a dynamic process, one of growth and evolution. Therefore, market cycles must be related in a dynamic manner.

The current position of a market is related to its past condition, as no effect is without a cause. The current position of a market is related to its past position by dynamic, growth cycles, not by static, fixed cycles. Current cycles are in dynamic proportion or ratio to prior cycles. The most important series of dynamic ratios, known as the Fibonacci ratios, are those related to the Divine Proportion, 1.618.

Waves of similar degree will relate in dynamic proportions in time just as they do in price. This does not just mean that one cycle is only related to one past cycle, but that any one cycle should be related by most, if not all, prior cycles of waves of similar degree. As a market unfolds, it will weave a dynamic web of time and price proportion just as any one of the three dimensional, regular polyhedra (Platonic solids) weave a dynamic proportion of space between edges, sides and vertices.

Ideally, we would know the cause of cyclic activity in human affairs which should then allow us to project those cycles of change with precision. I don't know what is the cause. I'm in good company, because neither does any one else that I'm aware of! While the study of such fields as chaos, non-linear dynamic, geometric growth patterns and other related subjects provide greater understanding and insight into the unique nature of time and growth processes, they have not yet provided a specific answer
as to what is the cause.

From the standpoint of trading, cause is not particularly relevant. We are concerned with the other side of the equation, *effects*. We measure the effects of market activity (historical data) to see if there are consistent relationships that allow for some degree of predictability of the future. We develop a model of how things work which provides a basis for understanding how the process unfolds and a guide for the application of certain projection techniques.

I have discovered from the study of past historical data that attempting to relate market cycles to composite cycles which are a summation of fixed-length, component cycles simply does not work to a reliable degree. This suggests that the model of relating financial cycles to composite, physical cycles is not correct.

I have found that the majority of trend changes occur when several past cycles are related at or near a single point in time by the same dynamic cycles (ratios) that are found in other natural growth processes. The best model for this is the geometric growth processes that are found in crystal structures which grow in the same geometric relationships found in the regular polyhedra.

While a model of a process does not necessarily reveal the cause, it helps us to gain a better understanding of what is going on as well as keep us on track in further study and research.

I would strongly encourage all traders to pursue the study of geometric solids and growth as well as chaos, non-linearity and multi-dimensional time. You will gain a greater understanding of how markets unfold and may even discover the cause. But, be very careful! Such a study can become an obsession, and you can easily lose sight of the goal which is *Trading Profits*. We can discover all we need to know for trading from a study of effects (historical data) and save the intellectual pursuits for our free time.

Projecting The Time Of Trend Change

For most traders, time is the most difficult dimension of market activity to anticipate. Yet, time is a critical factor in our market analysis. If we are able to enter and exit a trade at the right time, we are able to take all the gain or profit that is available from any market movement regardless of the extent of the price move. That is the best that can be done.

W. D. Gann recognized the importance of time cycles or the time factor as he called it for trading analysis. As with price, he recognized that a market unfolds in proportion to prior cycles, just as a crystalline structure unfolds in well defined, predictable structure and proportion. Unfortunately, Mr. Gann once again did not describe which proportion (ratio) or which previous time cycle a current market is "working out in relation to."

Price and time are the effects of the same cause. Time = Price or as W. D. Gann said: "When time and price square, change is inevitable."

A well accepted and implemented method of **price** projection in market analysis is to use the Fibonacci, *dynamic*, growth ratios of .382, .618, 1.618, etc. Yet, the same analysts will use *static*, fixed length and equal division ratios for time analysis. This reflects a lack of under-standing of the equality of time and price and that time and price are the effects of the same past causes.

> *If time and price are the effects of the same cause, the same techniques used for price analysis should be applicable to time analysis.*

There are two methods of dynamic time analysis: Time Cycle Ratios and Time Rhythm Zones. Each complements the other. Time Rhythm Zones projects a broad period with a very high probability of trend change. Time Cycle Ratio projections are very narrow time zones of just a few days from where most trend changes take place. When the Time Cycle Ratio period coincides with the Time Rhythm Zone period, the odds increase for trend change.

Each of the two methods are dynamic in that they adjust for recent market activity. Each method is a leading indicator in that the time projections are made well *in advance* in the same manner as the price projections.

Time Cycle Ratios™

Prior time cycles are proportioned and extended forward in time in the same manner as price cycles are proportioned for retracement, alternate cycle and extension. The general term I use for this method of time analysis is Time Cycle Ratios™ (TCR).

The time of change will occur at a "cluster" of important ratio relationships of past cycles all falling within a narrow time zone, usually of 2-5 days, with intermediate term swings and often as little as 2-5 hours with short-term swings. I call these projected time clusters a Projected Turning Point Period™ (PTPP). Projected Turning Point Periods should be viewed as periods of change when energy enters or exits the system (market). If the market is in balance (consolidation, trading range), price will frequently begin a break-out of the trading range at a Projected Turning Point Period (energy entering a balanced system). If a market is trending into a PTPP, a trend reversal is likely.

Projected Turning Point Periods should be considered in the same manner as projected price zones. Each represents a high probability zone of support or resistance. PTPPs are time support or resistance zones.

Time Cycle Ratio™ Projections

Time projections are done in exactly the same manner as price projections. A prior time cycle is proportioned and projected forward from the end of the cycle or from an alternate cycle pivot just as we do with price. It is important that traders learn the terminology and labels for the time projections in order to be able to quickly recognized what is being described on the charts and time projection reports.

The time between any pair of pivots can be measured, proportioned and projections made. However, there are a few swing relationships in time that are the most important for projecting future dates with a high probability of trend change. First, I will describe the individual TCR methods. We will then see how they are combined to project future time zones called Projected Turning Point Periods™ that have a high probability of trend change.

Time Retracements (TR)

A Time Retracement is the same as a price retracement. It is the amount of time that a market moves counter to the prior trend. As a market advances or declines, there will be more than one prior swing extreme from where to measure time retracements. In other words, we will have two or more degrees of retracement to consider.

Time Retracement ratios are similar to those used for Price Retracements: Note that 78.6%, a ratio that is very important for price retracements, is usually not important for time retracement.

38.2%, **50%, 61.8%, 100%, 162%,** 200%, 262%.

Time Retracements are projected in the same manner as price retracements. The time range of A to B is measured, proportioned and projected forward from B to calculate time retracements. As long as price is declining away from the swing high at B, the time retracements are potential periods for a low.

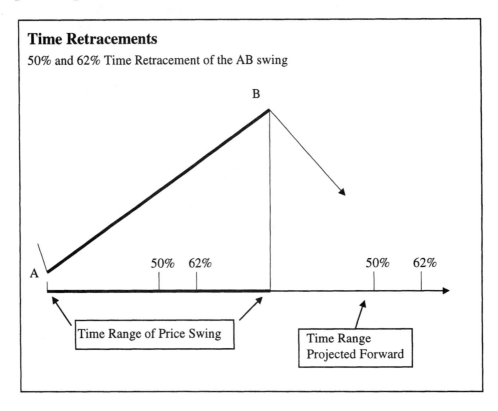

Time Retracements

50% and 62% Time Retracement of the AB swing

Time Retracements

Most markets make corrective highs or lows at or very near time retracements in the same manner as the highs and lows are made at or very near price retracements. The March 2, 1994 low in gold was made just one day prior to the 50% retracement in time of the rally from the Sept. 13, 1993 low to Jan. 5, 1994 high. The April 22 low was made one week prior to the 100% time retracement.

The chart below appears to have many days with no bars. It is a *calendar day* chart which includes spaces for all non-trading.

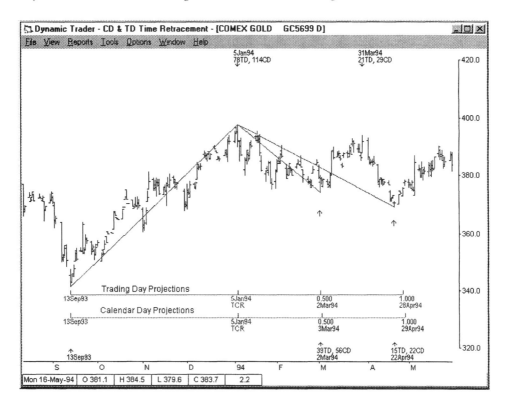

How The TCRs Are Labeled On The Chart

TCR (Time Cycle Ratio) projections involve two or three pivots. The time period between two pivots is proportioned and the projections are made from the second point. The TCR label is always placed at the second date from where the projections are made. In the illustration above, the time period from the Sept. 13 low to the Jan. 5 high is multiplied by 50% and 100% and the product is counted forward from the second date, Jan. 5. You can see the TCR label below the Jan. 5 date which indicates the projection was made from Jan. 5.

Alternate Time Cycle Ratio projections involve three pivots. They will be described and illustrated later in the chapter.

Calendar Days Verses Trading Days

There will be little difference to the projected dates whether calendar or trading days are used. Keep in mind that we are *proportioning* a period of time and projecting forward the proportion of time. We are not making static counts.

The gold chart on the previous page shows the 50% and 100% Time Cycle Ratios by trading and calendar day counts. The TD and CD time retracements are only one day different in each case.

9/13/93-1/5/94	50%	Projected Date
78 TD	39 TD	March 2
114 CD	57 CD	March 3

The 50% time retracement is only one day different whether counting forward 39 trading days or 57 calendar days from Jan. 5, 1994. The ratio of trading days to calendar days of any time period will be about 70% or 5/7. Trading day and calendar day projected dates will only be different by 1-3 days depending on the length of the period projected forward and how many non-trading days there are in the elapsed period to the projected date. TCRs should be done by *calendar days* for the most accurate results.

Time Retracements

The Aug. 2, 1993 high in gold was made dead on the 61.8% time retracement of the July 20 high to March 10 low. A minor high was made at the 50% time retracement. Every high or low in every market will not be made right on a time retracement date. But, like price retracements, most significant trend changes will be made at or very near a time retracement.

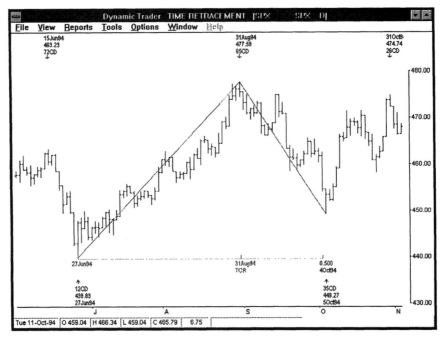

The Oct. 5 low was made just one day after the 50% time retracement.

The Nov. 22 low was made dead on the 61.8% time retracement of the Oct. 9 low to Jan. 31 high (DJIA close-only data). Note that Nov. 22 was a higher low than the one made in April. This is an example of a trading range terminating at a TCR projection.

Time Retracements

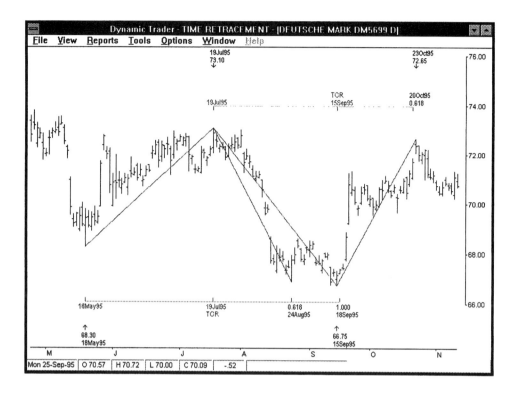

The decline from the July 19 high stopped at the 61.8% time retracement and completed one trading day prior to the 100% time retracement.

The rally that followed made a top on Oct. 23, one trading day after the 61.8% time retracement.

Time Retracements

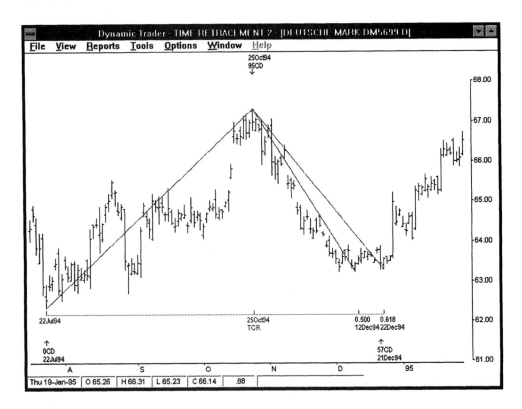

The decline from the Oct. 25 high stopped one trading day prior to the 50% time retracement. The slightly higher low was made at the 61.8% time retracement which was followed by a sharp advance.

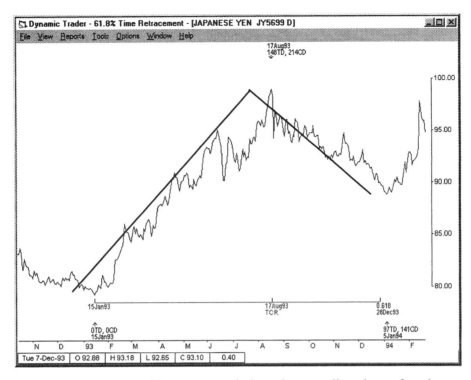

The counter trend low was made just three trading days after the 61.8% time retracement.

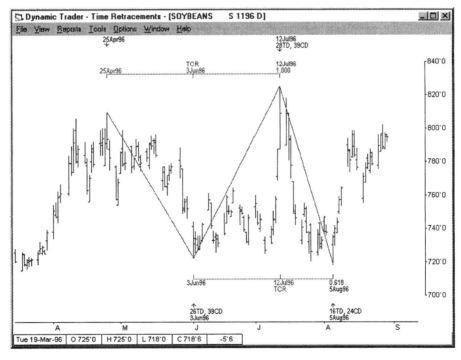

The July 12 high was made at the 100% Time Retracement and the Aug. 5 low at the 61.8% Time Retracement.

Alternate Time Projection (ATP)

Alternate Time Projections are calculated in the same manner as Alternate Price Projections. In the case of ATPs, the time range of trend swings are compared with prior trend swings and the time range of counter-trend swings are compared with prior counter-trend swings.

Alternate Time Projections

The most important ratios to use for ATP projections are:

38.2%, 50%, **61.8%**, **100%**, **162%**, 200%, **262%**, 424%.

The time range of the prior alternate cycle is measured, proportioned and projected forward from the beginning of the new swing. The time range from pivot number one to two is measured, proportioned and projected from pivot #0.

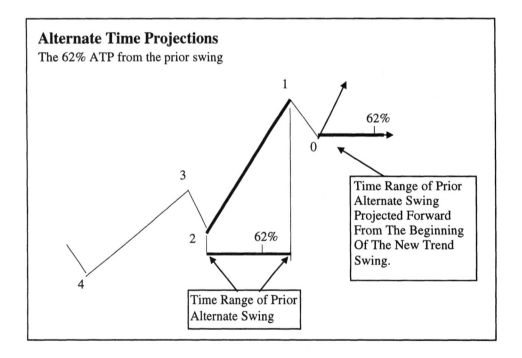

Alternate Time Projections
The 62% ATP from the prior swing

1

62%

0

Time Range of Prior Alternate Swing Projected Forward From The Beginning Of The New Trend Swing.

3

2   62%

4

Time Range of Prior Alternate Swing

Alternate Time Projections may be made from other prior swings in the same direction as the current swing. In the illustration below, the time of the second alternate swing from pivot #3 to #4 is measured, proportioned and projected from the current pivot #0.

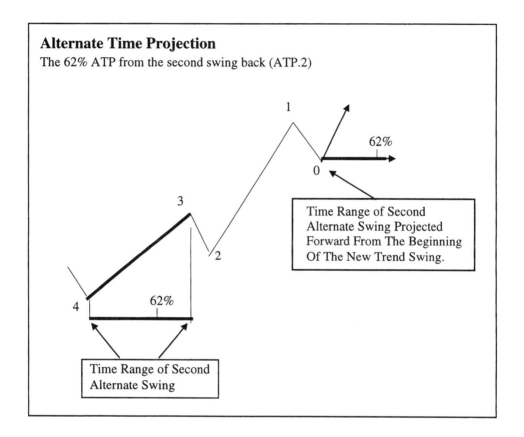

Alternate Time Projection
The 62% ATP from the second swing back (ATP.2)

Time Range of Second Alternate Swing Projected Forward From The Beginning Of The New Trend Swing.

Time Range of Second Alternate Swing

The chart examples on the following pages will illustrate many variations of the Alternate Time Projections. The important factor to keep in mind is that time projections are made in the same manner as the price projections.

Alternate Time Projections

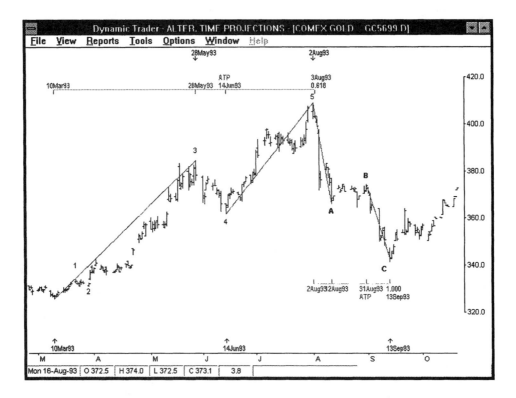

Alternate Time Projections always involve three pivots. In the illustration above, the rally from the March 10 low to the May 28 high is proportioned and projected from the next low of June 14. In these chart examples, the ATP label (Alternate Time Projection) is always shown at the pivot from where the projections are made. The Aug. 2 high was made just one day prior to the 61.8% ATP. The Sept. 13 low was made dead on the 100% ATP where the time range of wave C equaled the time range of wave A.

It should be clear from this chart how the Alternate Time Projection method is the same as the Alternate Price Projection. The number and letter labeling above are Elliott Wave counts. A typical relationship of a wave 5 price range is 61.8% of the price range of waves 1 through 3. In the case above, the wave 5 time range was 61.8% of the time range of waves 1 through 3. A typical price relationship of an ABC correction is for the time range of the C-wave to be equal to 100% of the time range of the A-wave. This was also true of time for the Sept. 13 low in gold shown above.

Alternate Time Projections

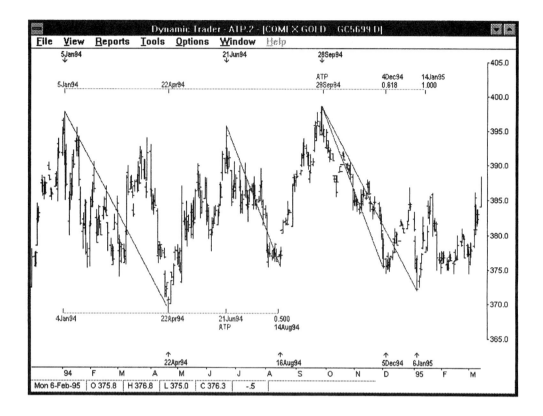

The three bear-trend, gold swings shown in the chart above are each related to each other by dynamic ratios. Aug. 14, 1994 was the 50% ATP of the prior bear swing of Jan. 5 to April 22. Aug. 14 fell on the weekend. The next trading day, Aug. 16, the final low was made that preceded the sharp advance.

The Dec. 5 low was made one day after the 61.8% ATP. Every high and low will not be made dead-on an alternate time projection, but most will fall at or within a few time periods of one of the major ATP ratios. Alternate time projections are always viewed within the context of other time factors. As we will see in later examples, the more time projections that fall within a period, the greater the probability a trend change will be made.

Alternate Time Projections

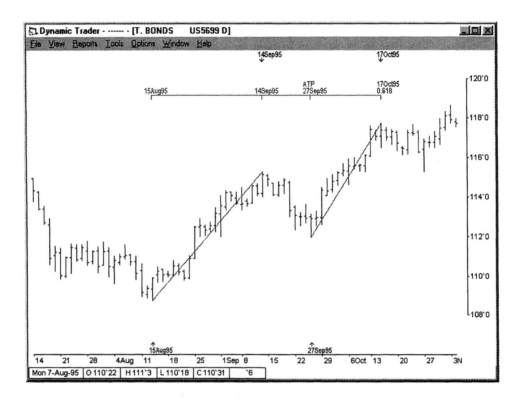

The Oct. 17 high was made right on the 61.8% ATP. Bonds have continued higher. The next significant top will probably be made at or near an ATP.

Alternate Time Projections

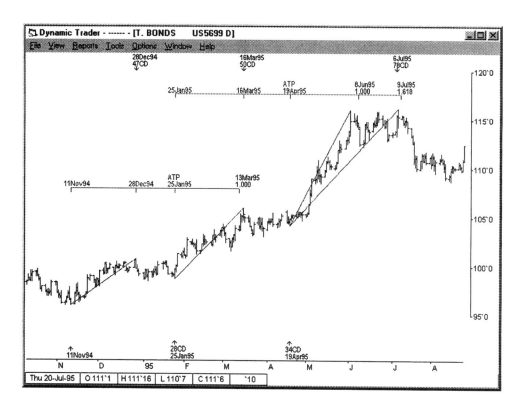

The March 16 high was made one trading day after the 100% ATP. The June/July tops were made within a couple days of the 100% and 162% ATPs.

Alternate Time Projections

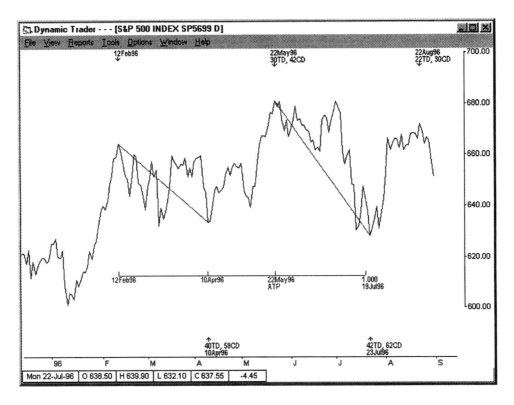

The S&P made a low just two trading days after the 100% Alternate Time Projection. Trading range or consolidation periods often make highs and lows at or very near 100% ATPs.

The chart above is a close-only chart. If a market becomes very volatile with wide range days near trend changes, all analysis should be considered from close-only data as well as daily range data.

Note that a low was made in early March that was slightly below the April 10 low. While March made a slightly lower-low than April, the April 10 low completed the corrective period. It was from April 10 that the new bull trend began the rally to a new high.

Alternate Time Projections

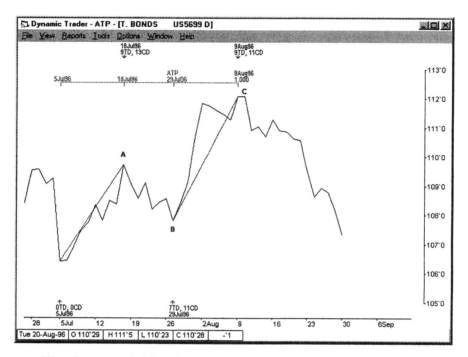

The C wave of this ABC rally was exactly equal to the number of trading days of the A wave.

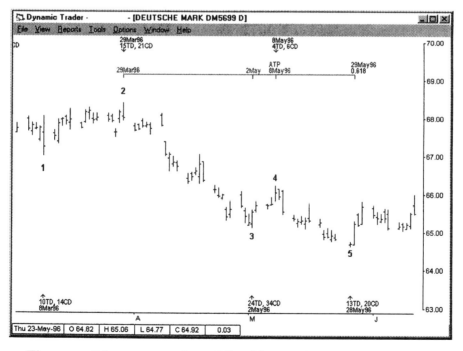

The wave 5 low was made on May 28, one day prior to the 61.8% Alternate Time Projection of wave 3.

Other Time Cycle Ratios

Time Retracements and Alternate Time Projections are the two most consistently reliable Time Cycle Ratio projections. A TCR may be made from any two pivots and an alternate TCR from any three pivots. The following pages illustrate many other Time Cycle Ratios that are not Time Retracements or Alternate Time Projections.

Time Cycle Ratio Projections: High-to-High Cycle

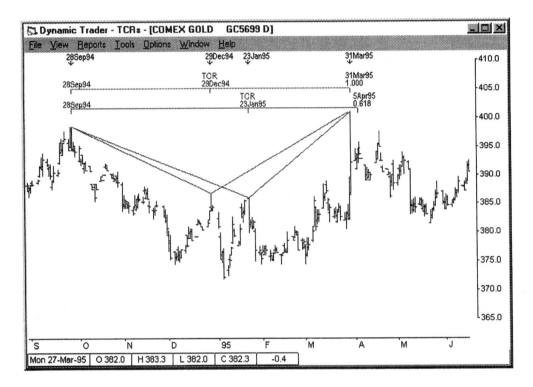

The March 31 high was made at the coincidence of the 100% high-high Time Cycle Ratio projection of the Sept. 28 high to Dec. 29 high and three trading days before the 61.8% high-high Time Cycle Ratio projection of the Sept. 28 high to Jan. 23 high.

Time Cycle Ratio Projections: Low-to-Low

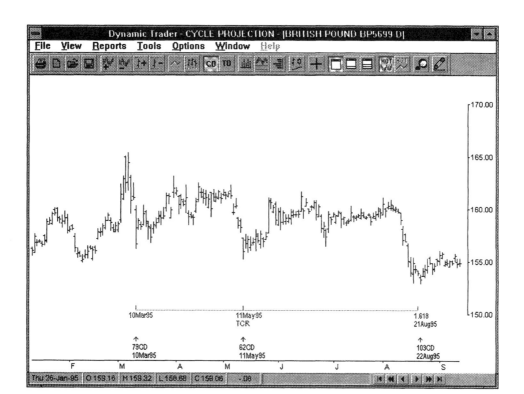

The Aug. 22 low was made just one day following the 162% TCR projection of the March 10 to May 11 lows.

High-to-high and low-to-low projections are commonly considered cycle projections. Contrary to popular opinion of traditional cycle analysts, high-to-high and low-to-low cycles are usually not repetitive, fixed periods.

Time Cycle Ratio Projections: Low-to-Low

The Oct. 17 low was made within one day of the 61.8% cycle projection of the prior two lows.

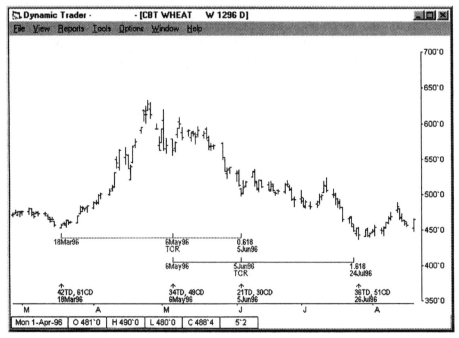

The June 5 and July 26 lows were each made at TCRs of the prior two lows.

Time Cycle Ratio Projections: Low-to-Low

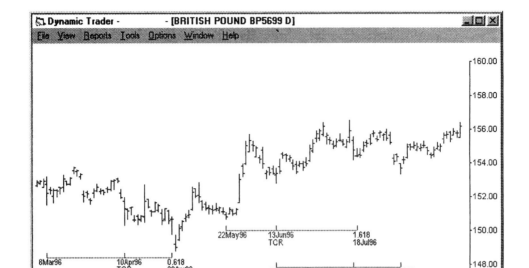

Each of the minor lows during this period for the British Pound were made at TCRs of the prior two lows. Traditional "cycle" analysts continue to perpetuate the myth that low-to-low "cycles" are repetitive and fixed period. We can see the low-to-low cycles are more frequently dynamic proportions of past cycles, not static, fixed length cycles.

Time Cycle Ratio Projections: High-to-High

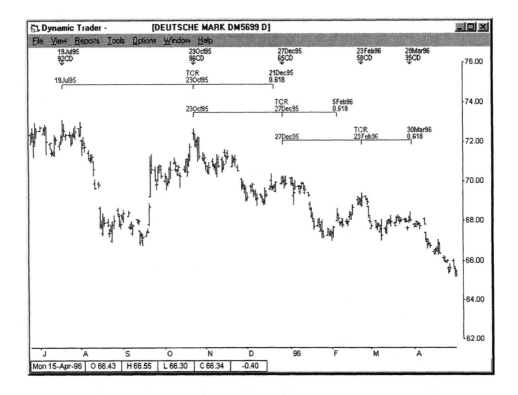

As the mark declined, highs were made within a few trading days the 61.8% TCR of the prior two highs. The early Feb. high only lasted about a week. The Dec. 27 and March 29 highs were followed by intermediate declines to new lows.

Time Cycle Ratio Projections: Low-to-Low

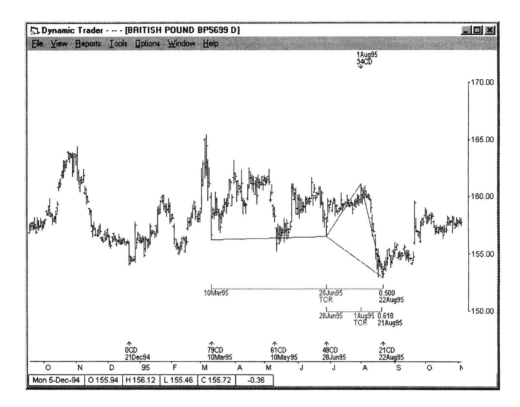

The Aug. 22 low was made at the 50% TCR of the prior Dual Cycle or double low-to-low period. This low was also at the 61.8% Time Retracement.

Time Cycle Ratio Projections

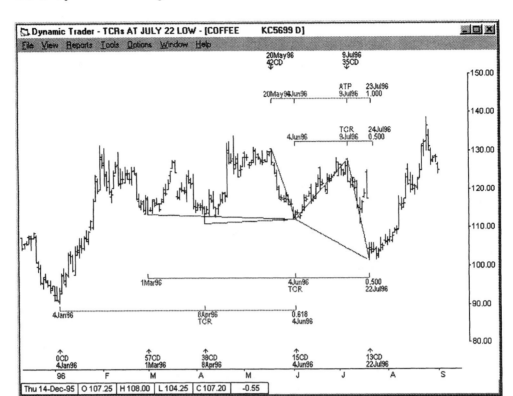

The June 4 low was made at the 61.8% TCR of the prior Dual Cycle (1/4L-3/1L-4/8L).

The chart above shows three of the TCRs that coincided at the June 22 low. The 100% Alternate Time Projections (5/20H-6/4L projected from the 7/9H), the 50% Dual Cycle Projection (3/1L-6/4L) and the 50% Time Retracement (6/4L-7/9H).

Most significant highs and lows are made at the coincidence of several TCRs.

Time Cycle Ratio Projections

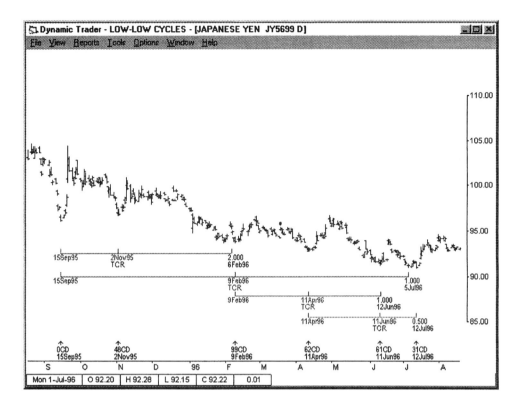

All of the lows during this unusually prolonged trading range period for the Japanese Yen were related by proportions of one and its even divisions and multiples. The Feb. 9, 1996 low was made at the 200% TCR of the prior Cycle (L-L). The July 5 low was made at the 100% TCR of the Dual Cycle. A Dual Cycle is three consecutive lows or two consecutive low-to-low cycles. In this case, the Dual Cycle was from the Sept. 15, 1995 low to the Nov. 2, 1995 low to the Feb. 9, 1996 low (L-L-L).

The June 12 low was made at the 100% TCR of the prior Cycle (L-L). The next low on July 12 was made on the 50% TCR of the prior Cycle (L-L). The April 11 low was made at the 61.8% TCR of the prior Cycle. This projection is not illustrated in the chart above, but you can see that 62CDs is 61.8% of 99CDs.

All of the distinct pivot lows during the period shown above are linked to prior cycles and dual cycles.

Alternate Time Projection Variation

This TCR has taken the period from a low-to-low and projected from the intervening high. This is another form of the Alternate Time Projection where a period between two pivots is projected from a third pivot.

The low-to-low period from April 11 to May 8 is 27 calendar days. That period is projected from the intervening high on April 26. The 100% Alternate Time Projection falls on May 23, the exact day of the next high.

Remember that the date with the ATP label is the date the projection is made from. In the chart above, the ATP label is just above the April 26 date. The initial time period measured is from April 11, 1996 to May 8, 1996. This period is projected from April 26. May 23 is the 100% ATP projected from April 26.

Alternate Time Projection Variation

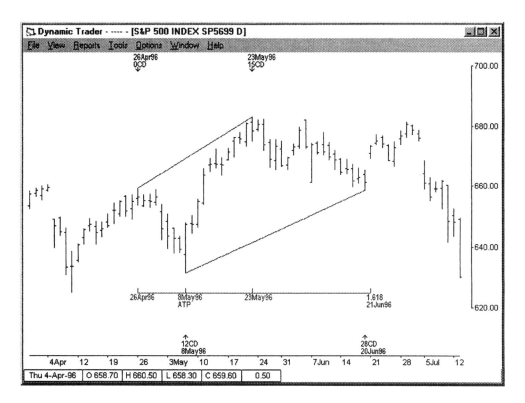

The 162% TCR of the April 26 high to May 23 high is projected from the intervening low of May 8 for a projected date of June 21. The next low fell just one day earlier on June 20.

Time Cycle Ratios In The Stock Market

Like all factors of Dynamic Trading, Dynamic Time Analysis works in all actively traded markets.

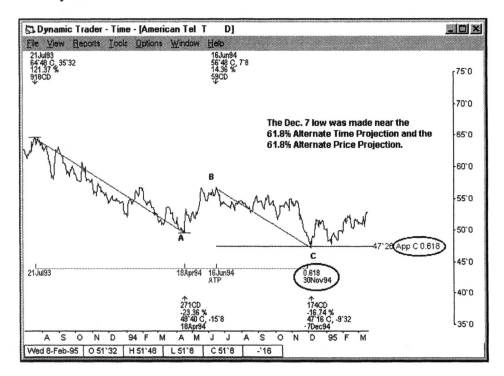

The Dec. 7, 1994 low in AT&T was made where the time range of Wave-C was 61.8% of the time range of Wave-A. The Dec. 7 low at the 61.8% ATP coincided with the 61.8% Alternate Price Projection.

There is a *very high probability* of trend change in any market when the same ratios of price and time factors coincide like they did at the Dec. 7 low for AT&T. While this set-up is not frequent, it is a very high probability trend reversal set-up.

Barnes and Noble Makes Important Low at the Coincidence of Time, Price and Pattern

I'm still hoping for a big push by Barnes and Noble for my book so let's take a look at another example of their stock.

This chart is a perfect example of the integration of time, price and pattern analysis. The July 16, 1996 low was made at the coincidence of a 38.2% time retracement and 61.8% price retracement. Note how the Jan. 5, 1996 to May 23, 1996 rally was an ideal five-wave sequence and the May-July decline was a perfect ABC correction into time and price support.

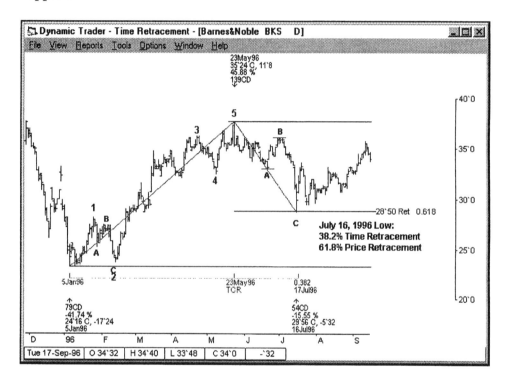

Is every important high and low made at the ideal coincidence of projected time, price and pattern? Of course not. But many are. The trader's job is to keep alert and be prepared and identify the best opportunities as they are unfolding.

Trading is not about forecasting the future. Trading is not about having an opinion of the position of every market all of the time. Trading is about recognizing and taking action on high-probability/low-capital-exposure opportunities. If you approach trading from any other perspective, it will only become a very costly hobby, not a profitable business.

Trend Vibration™

The Trend Vibration (TV) method of time projection uses the concept of Time Cycle Ratio projections but in a unique manner. Trend Vibration time projections assume that the initial thrust and counter-trend of a market trend often provides the time range that projects subsequent highs and lows within the ensuing trend.

Initial thrust and counter-trend is another way of saying cycle. Cycle is another way of saying vibration. In Elliott wave terms, waves one through two is the initial vibration of a five-wave, impulse-trend. More importantly, the final pivot of the trend should be made on a proportion of the initial "vibration."

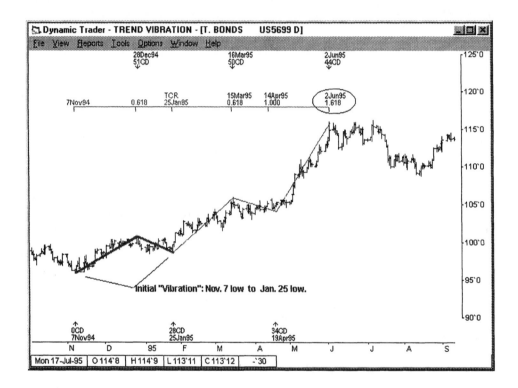

The initial "vibration" of the bond trend that began in early Nov. of 1994 lasted from the Nov. 7 low to the Jan. 25 low. Note that the Dec. 28 high was made at the .618 division of the initial low-to-low cycle or vibration.

The subsequent TCRs of the initial low-to-low cycle are shown in the chart above. The March 16 high was made one day following the .618 TCR, the April 19 low three trading days after the 100% TCR and the June 2 top precisely at the 1.618 TCR of the initial vibration. The general rhythm of the trend was related to the initial vibration. More importantly, the trend terminated right on a TCR of the initial vibration.

Trend Vibration

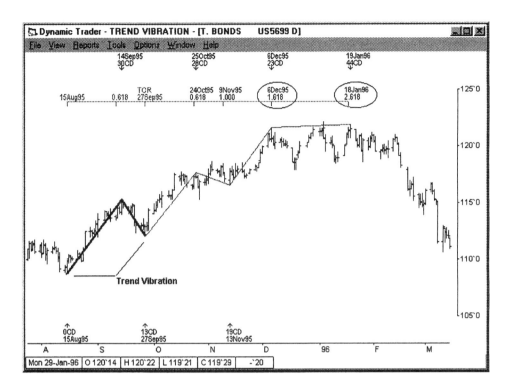

The initial vibration from the Aug. 15 low projected both the first and final top of the rally that completed on Jan. 19. The Dec. 6 top was made precisely on the 162% TCR of the initial vibration and the final top of Jan. 19 was made just one day after the 262% TCR.

The initial high of Sept. 14 was made near the .618 division of the initial vibration. *If the initial high is made near the 50% or 62% division of the initial vibration, there is a greater chance that the trend will progress in dynamic proportion to the initial vibration and the trend will terminate on a dynamic proportion.*

Trend Vibration

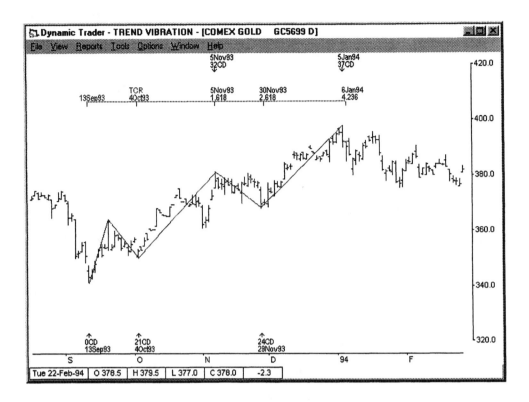

The initial vibration set up the rhythm of the trend into the Jan. 5 high. A high was made at the 162% TCR of the initial vibration and the low of Nov. 29 was made one day prior to the 262% TCR. The final top on Jan. 5 was made one day prior to the 424% TCR of the initial vibration.

Trend Vibration

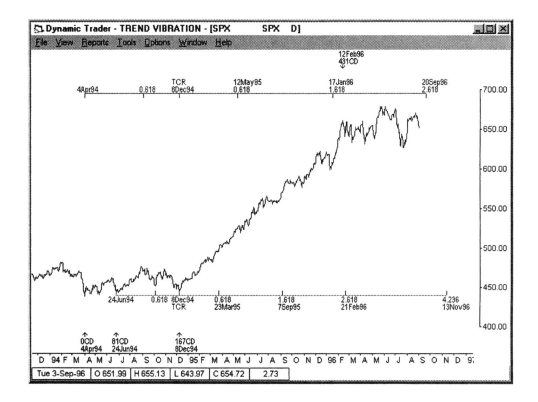

Wouldn't it be nice if every trend vibrated to the initial rhythm and completed dead-on a dynamic TCR of the initial vibration? If this were the case, we wouldn't need any other analysis techniques or trading strategies. Unfortunately, it's not that simple. Fortunately, the market will let us know in advance if a trend is "vibrating" and if it should make the final top at a projected TCR of the initial vibration.

I've shown a dynamic Trend Vibration for the SPX using two different initial vibrations. The Trend Vibrations are projected forward from both the April 4, 1994 to Dec. 8, 1994 low-to-low vibration and the June 24, 1994 to Dec. 8, 1994 low-to-low vibration. None of the minor highs and lows during the consistent bull trend were made at the TCRs from either of these two potential initial vibrations.

Since the S&P bull trend does not appear to be consistently vibrating to the initial vibration, we cannot have a high degree of confidence that the final top of the bull trend begun in April 1994 will be made on a TCR of the initial vibration.

Trend Vibration

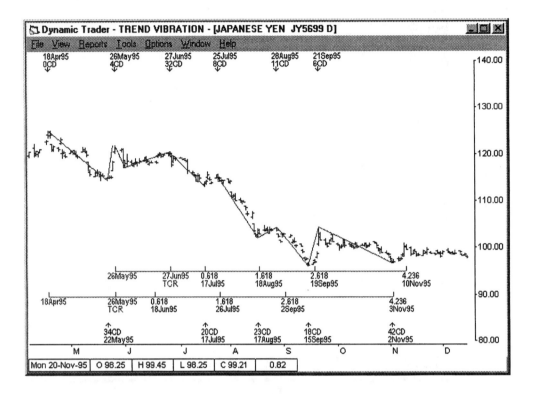

All of the minor highs and lows of the bear trend in the yen were made within one or two trading days of a Trend Vibration of either the initial vibration (April 18 high to May 26 high) or the subsequent vibration (May 26 high to June 27 high) just prior to the beginning of the consistent bear trend.

The Sept. 15 low was made just two trading days prior to the 262% TCR of the second high-to-high while the double bottom of Nov. 2 was made just one day prior to the 424% TCR of the initial vibration.

Trend Vibration

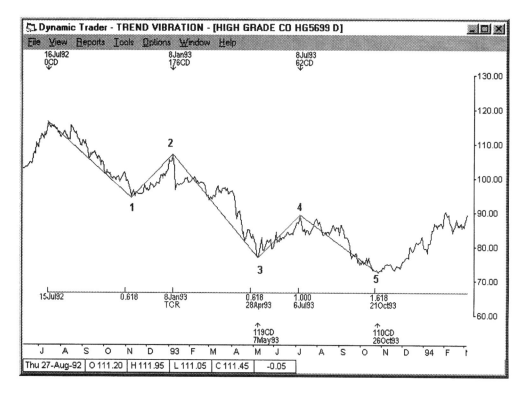

The final wave 5 low was made just three trading days after the 162% Trend Vibration. While wave 3 and 4 did not hit dead on the other TCRs, the rhythm was definitely evident as copper declined.

A timing decision should never be made solely on the basis of a TV projection. Trend Vibration projections must be considered within the context of the other timing factors. However, considerable weight should be given to TV projections for time projections of the termination of a trend if the market has been trending in rhythm to the initial vibration.

Note that the Wave-1 low was made near the .618 division of the initial high-to-high vibration. This signaled early on that the trend would have a high probability of vibrating to the initial vibration.

Time Counts

Time counts are calendar day or trading day counts from prior swing pivots. The counts that most traders are familiar with are the Fibonacci number series (3, 5, 8, 13, 21, 34, 89, 144, etc.) and some of Gann's time counts such as the squares of 90, 144, 360, etc.

What do we mean by the "square" of a number? A square of a number is simply the series of divisions and multiples of that number. For instance, the series of numbers of the "Square of 144" include 36, 72, 108, 144, 180, etc. Each of these numbers are multiples of 36 which is ¼ of 144.

Some markets make trend changes at a particular series of numbers more frequently than others. For instance, gold often makes trends changes at calendar day counts of the Fibonacci number series. Currencies often make trend changes on calendar day counts from the "squares of 90 and 144" or at divisions and multiples of 90 and 144 such as 30, 60, 72, 90, 144. It is a simple matter to research past trend change dates for any market and discover if particular calendar day or trading day counts are frequently repeated. If they are, those time counts should be considered for that particular market.

Anniversary Dates

Markets often make a trend change at or very near the date of prior trend changes. Sometimes it is uncanny. Anyone who will look at a long history of any market will find how often trend changes unfold exactly on or within one or two days of trend changes in past years.

By keeping the swing file for each market up-to-date, traders will have a complete record of the anniversary dates of past years. Sort the dates by month and date to put the file in the proper order for an anniversary date file.

> *While many trend changes fall at or within a day or two of these time counts and anniversary dates, Time Cycle Ratio projections are far more important. Time counts and anniversary dates should only be used as confirming factors for Projected Turning Point Periods.*

The following page includes a table with the most useful time counts and anniversary date periods.

Fib	Sq. 90	Sq. 144	Anniversary Dates
5	**30**	36	**365**
8	**60**	**72**	**730**
13	**90**	108	**1096**
21	120	**144**	1461
34	150	180	1826
55	**180**	216	2191
89	210	252	2557
144	240	**288**	2922
233	270	324	3287
377	300	360	3652
610	330	396	4018
987	**360**	**432**	4383

Time Counts and Anniversary Dates Table
These counts could be carried out indefinitely, but the longer term counts are less effective than those relative to intermediate degree trends. The counts in bold tend to be the most important for that series. The anniversary dates are through year twelve.

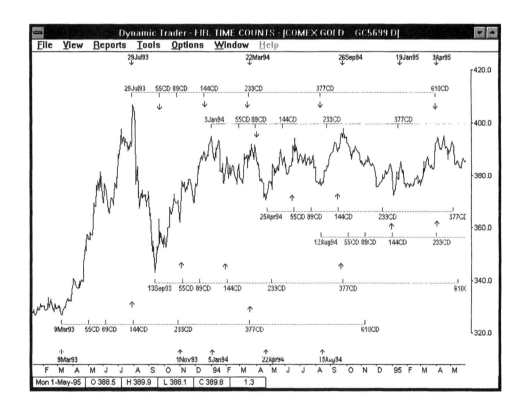

Almost every intermediate high and low shown above was made at or very near one or more Fib calendar day counts from a prior high or low. Time counts are supplementary time factors to the TCR projections.

Time Counts

The following two daily charts of the Deutsche Mark show how almost every pivot high and low was made within two calendar days of either a Fib or Square-of-90 count. Currency traders who do not remain aware of the dates of these counts are missing out on the value of a very reliable time projection technique.

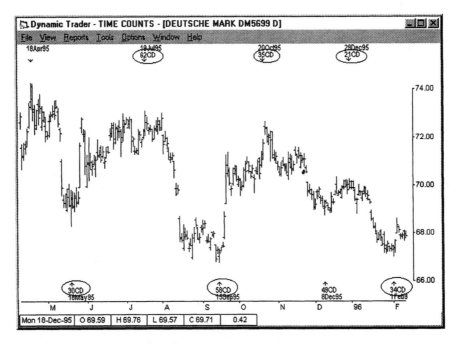

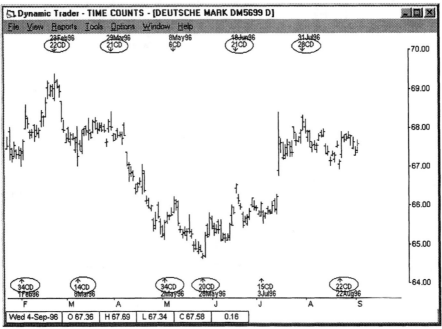

Time Counts

Bonds usually make at least an intermediate degree trend change within 1-3 calendar and trading days of a Fib count. The two charts below show several intermediate and major trend changes that fell on or near the 55, 144 and 233 counts. Bond traders should always have the Fib CD and TD projections up to date.

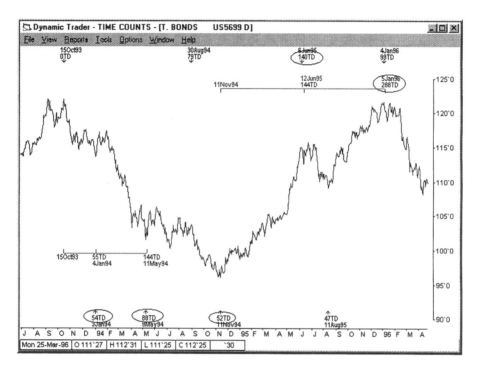

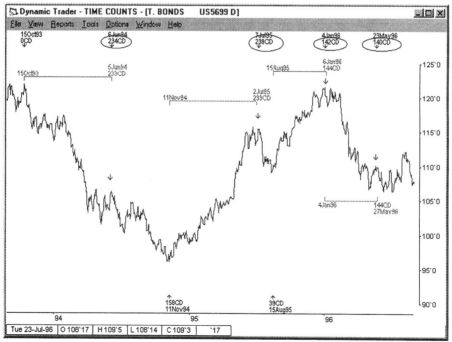

Time Counts

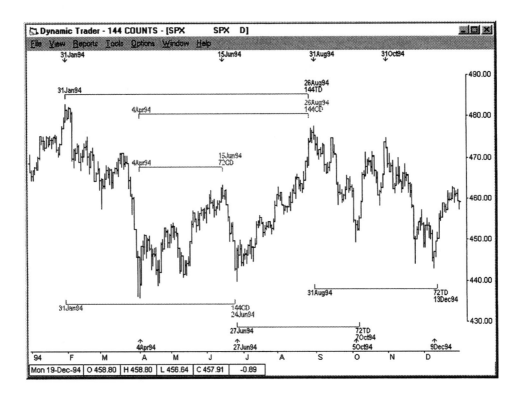

Each of the significant highs and lows during this consolidation period for the S&P were made on or within a couple days of a 72 or 144 calendar or trading day count. This is not coincidence. The S&P is not a random market. Every trend change in the S&P will not be made on a 144 or Fib time count but many, if not most, will be. If you are a stock market investor or trader do you think it is worth your while to keep these counts up-to-date?

Trading decisions should not be made by time counts alone. Time counts are considered in relation to the Time Cycle Ratio projections. W. D. Gann has taught us to "use all of the tools, all of the time." By keeping all time analysis factors up-to-date, the periods with a high coincidence of several time factors will stand out.

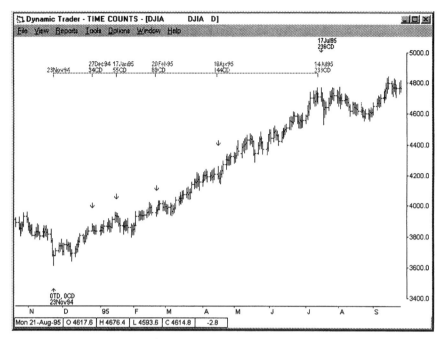

The DJIA began a consistent, record breaking bull trend from the Nov. 1994 low. Minor reactions were made at the 55 and 89 calendar day counts from the low. The trend made a top followed by the largest thru Sept. 1995 just one trading day following the 233 calendar day count from the low.

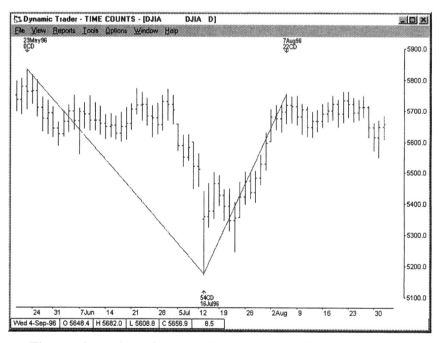

The stock market often completes sharp declines on or near a 55 calendar day count. Do you know the date of the most famous 55-CD, panic decline?

Time Counts

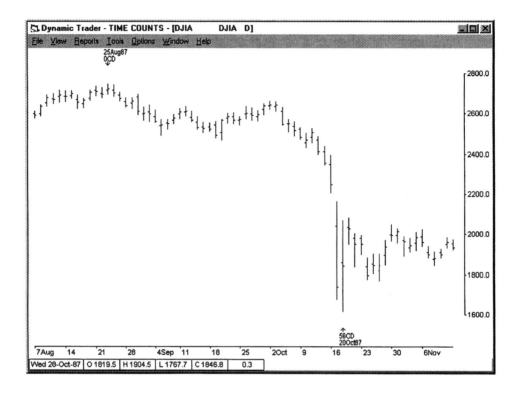

Who can forget the Aug. 25, 1987 to Oct. 20, 1987 panic decline? The Oct. 20 low was made 56 calendar days from the Aug. 25 top. The closing low on Oct. 19 was 55 calendar days from the closing high of Aug. 25. Note how the second leg of the decline was the panic leg. Take another look at the May - July 1996 decline on the previous page for the similarity.

Individual markets and securities will often have their own peculiar timing factors that will only be revealed to the dedicated analyst that takes the time to become thoroughly familiar with each market he or she intends to trade or invest. Let the system junkies continue their illusive and fruitless quest for the holy grail of system trading. It's up to you to learn the business of speculation if you desire to be successful. Part of that learning curve is to become thoroughly familiar with the details of market history. Take the time to gain the knowledge, and your efforts will be rewarded.

Anniversary Dates

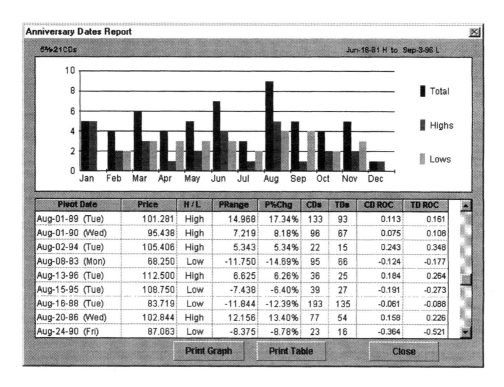

Anniversary Dates Report

5¾21CDs   Jun-16-81 H to Sep-3-96 L

Pivot Date	Price	H / L	PRange	P%Chg	CDs	TDs	CD ROC	TD ROC
Aug-01-89 (Tue)	101.281	High	14.969	17.34%	133	93	0.113	0.161
Aug-01-90 (Wed)	95.438	High	7.219	8.18%	96	67	0.075	0.108
Aug-02-94 (Tue)	105.406	High	5.343	5.34%	22	15	0.243	0.348
Aug-08-83 (Mon)	68.250	Low	-11.750	-14.69%	95	66	-0.124	-0.177
Aug-13-96 (Tue)	112.500	High	6.625	6.26%	36	25	0.184	0.264
Aug-15-95 (Tue)	108.750	Low	-7.438	-6.40%	39	27	-0.191	-0.273
Aug-16-88 (Tue)	83.719	Low	-11.844	-12.39%	193	135	-0.061	-0.088
Aug-20-86 (Wed)	102.844	High	12.156	13.40%	77	54	0.158	0.226
Aug-24-90 (Fri)	87.063	Low	-8.375	-8.78%	23	16	-0.364	-0.521

Print Graph   Print Table   Close

At the beginning of every month, the anniversary date file should be reviewed for potential dates of trend change during the month. The above swing file includes all pivot reversals that were followed by a minimum of
a 5% price reversal that lasted at least 21 days.

The graph above the table totals the swing pivots for the 15 year period from June 1981 through Sept. 1996. Note that Aug. is by far the most frequent month for bond trend change. In the 15 year period, only one trend reversal of 5% or more in price has been made in Dec. The odds favor a continuation of a bond trend through Dec. each year with only minor (less than 5%) price reversals. During this 15 year period, all trend changes made in Jan. have been highs. If bonds are declining into Jan., the odds strongly favor a continuation of the decline without a 5% or greater price reversal.

Simple statistical record keeping such as anniversary dates will provide a wealth of information and is critical timing information to complement the Time Cycle Ratios and Time Counts.

Short-Term, Fixed-Length Time Cycles

Having spent a good amount of time at the beginning of this time analysis chapter warning against the use of traditional fixed-length cycle analysis, I will now describe the limited conditions when fixed-length cycles are evident in market activity and how they may be used to understand the position of the market and contribute to the trading decision.

Occasionally, a market will fall into a rhythm of relatively short-term, fixed-length cycles. We will not know in advance if a relatively consistent rhythm will be established. The rhythm will only be evident after it has made several complete cycles or repetitions. If a rhythm is established, how do we use it to aid in our trading decision?

The time targets for trend changes will complement the dynamic time factors. If a trend change target of an established short-term rhythm coincides with a Projected Turning Point Period of dynamic time projections, the probabilities increase for trend change.

When the rhythm is broken, it is a signal that the market condition is changing. If the rhythm was established in a trading range, the market is probably breaking away from the trading range and in the initial stages of a trend when the rhythm is broken. If the rhythm was established in a trending market, the trend is probably at or near completion when the rhythm is broken.

Markets do not often establish relatively short-term rhythms of fixed-length periodicity, but, when they do, they provide an additional signal of when to prepare for minor highs and lows as well as a signal of trend change.

Short-Term Fixed-Length Cycles

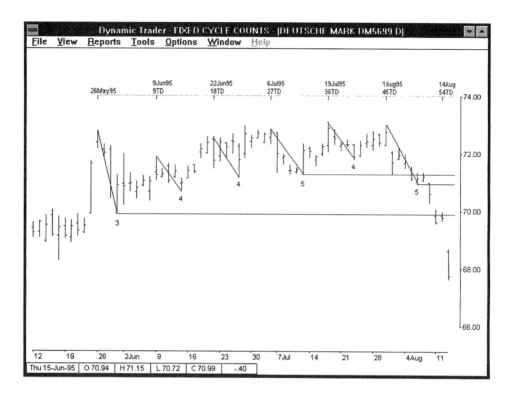

The Deutsche mark fell into a very regular pattern of making highs each 9 trading days and lows 3-5 trading days after the highs. When a regular short-term rhythm is exceeded, it is a signal that a new trend is developing.

If the mark rallied beyond a nine trading day count from high-to-high, the market is signaling that a new bull trend breakout of the trading range is probably developing. If the mark declined beyond five trading days, the market is signaling a bear trend breakout is probably developing. In the situation above, the mark made a new low seven trading days after the Aug. 1 high signaling a breakout into a bear trend should be unfolding. That is exactly what took place.

All of the timing factors we have discussed so far are *leading indicators* that project potential trend change in advance. The break-away from an established short-term cycle rhythm is a *lagging indicator* in that it is only after the established rhythm is violated that the signal is made. However, it is still a valuable piece of information. The new trend swing should be of the same degree or greater as the trend swing just prior to the established rhythm.

Traders may also use an established time rhythm to help provide parameters for trade entry and stop placement.

Short-Term Fixed-Length Cycles

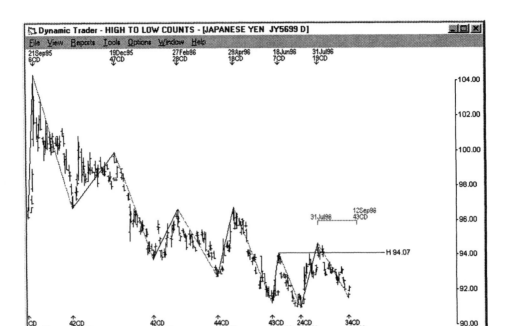

From Sept. 1995 through early Sept. 1996, the Japanese Yen had been in one of the longest non-trending periods in the history of yen futures trading. This period also developed a very regular time rhythm. The minor bear swings were made every 42-44 calendar days from the prior high with only one exception. The July 12 low was made just 24 CDs from the prior high which is the first signal the yen may be making a bottom.

A 43 CD count from the most recent high that was made July 31 falls on Sept. 12. The period of Sept. 10-14 (Sept. 12 +/- 2 CDs) is a time target for a low if the rhythm continues. If the yen makes a low prior to Sept. 10 and subsequently exceeds the July 31 high, it is a strong signal the bear trend is complete. If the yen makes new lows from the July 31 high after Sept. 14, it is a strong signal that the major bear trend will continue and probably accelerate the decline.

Established short-term cycle rhythms not only provide a target for when a trend change is likely, but, more importantly, provide the timing conditions that will help signal a new trend direction.

Time Overbalance

A *time overbalance* is the same as a price overbalance except a time range is used instead of a price range. A time overbalance is when the time of a correction exceeds the time of the prior corrections. A time overbalance is an alert that the larger degree trend change may be underway. Time overbalance is similar to the short-term cycle rhythm just discussed in that it compares the time of prior similar cycles or swings to the current swing.

As with price overbalance, a time overbalance is not a definitive indication that the larger degree change in trend is underway. But, it is an alert signal that there is more buying or selling pressure against the trend than has previously occurred. If a counter-trend swing exceeds the time of all previous counter-trend swings since the larger degree trend began, it is a signal to be alert to the price and pattern position of the market for clues to the trend position.

Time overbalance is a lagging indicator. It is only signaled after the fact. While it is not a trade signal, it is an important reference point to alert the trader to the position of the market.

Time Overbalance

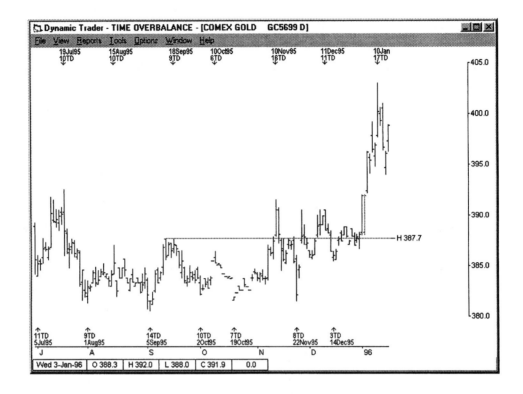

Gold began a basing or accumulation period in early Aug. that ran through Oct. The minor rallies lasted 6-10 trading days. A rally that exceeded 10 trading days would be a signal that the larger degree trend should be turning bullish. From the Oct. 19 low, gold made a 16 trading day rally that exceeded the prior minor highs. The new price high and time overbalance signaled an important low may have been made and gold may in the initial stages of a bull trend which is exactly what happened.

When a time overbalance signal is considered in relationship to the position of the market, it may be a critical factor to signal a new trend is in the early stages.

Time Overbalance

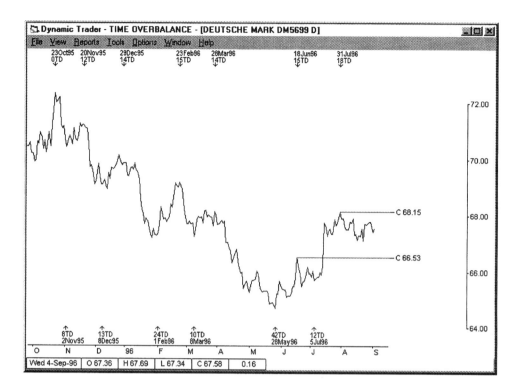

The mark made 12-15 trading day reactions against the bear trend. From the May 28 low, the mark has rallied greater than 15 trading days signaling a larger degree low may be in place. However, the rally from the May low is composed of two minor rallies of 15 and 18 TDs and not a consistent new trend. This is not a strong signal as the recent minor rallies would fit in nicely with an ABC correction of larger degree.

Keep in mind that a time overbalance signal must be considered within the context of the position of the market.

Time Overbalance

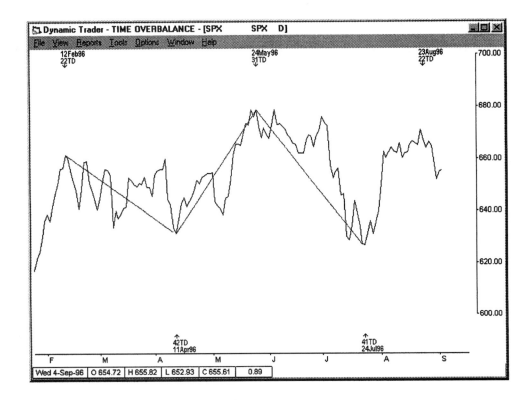

Has the S&P made a major top in May 1996? A decline greater than 42 trading days will be a strong time overbalance signal that a major change in trend has been made. A bullish trend signal will be made if the S&P rallies to new highs without having made a decline greater than 42 trading day.

The Dynamic Trader Software program that is used to make the illustrative charts for this book includes several routines that automate the time projection analysis process. One of the routines, the Dynamic Time Projection Report, makes all of the most important TCR projections including the Time Retracements and Alternate Time Projections as well as the Calendar Day and Trading Day counts. Those dates with the greatest cluster of time projections are shown as a histogram in the indicator window below the bar chart.

Below are the Dynamic Time Projections from the Aug. 15, 1995 low in T-bonds. One of two Projected Turning Point Periods (PTPP) had a cluster of Dynamic Time Projections and the greatest probability of making a top. These two PTPPs were <u>Dec. 1-3</u> or <u>Jan. 2-6</u>. Some of the time projections are shown on the chart below.

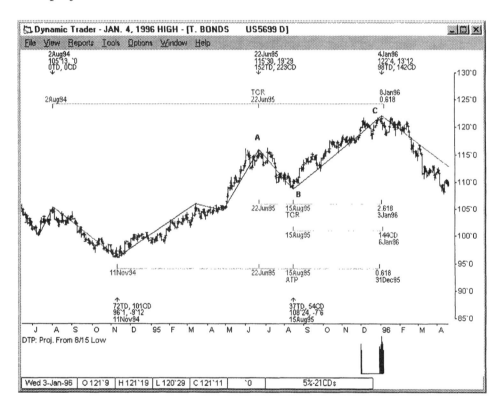

The final top was made Jan. 4, 1996, right in the <u>Jan. 2-6</u> projection for a high. The Dynamic Trader Software allows the user to customize the Dynamic Time Projection routine to include any chosen ratio and swing comparison in order to provide maximum flexibility of time analysis.

While a properly programmed software program should make any routine quicker, easier and more accurate, keep in mind I originally did all of these time projections with a calculator and then graduated to a spreadsheet for several years. While it required more time and thought calculating the time projections that way than completing them with a specially designed software program, the output was just as useful. There is no excuse not to have the necessary decision making information at hand.

Dynamic Time Projections™

As you can now see, these Dynamic Time Projection targets are projected in the same manner as the price projection targets. Instead of price ranges, we are proportioning and projecting time ranges. Instead of looking for those narrow price zones that include several price projections, we are looking for those narrow time zones that include several time projections.

I have been doing these time projections, which I call Projected Turning Point Periods, since I first began publishing a newsletter advisory service in 1986. Needless to say, the methodology has been refined and the accuracy of the projections has gotten better and better over the years. I once took a three year period of published projections and found that 89% of the intermediate term trend changes in the markets I followed in the advisory service came within *one trading day* of a Projected Turning Point Period. The Projected Turning Point Periods were generally 1-3 trading days each.

Do not have doubts as to the effectiveness of these time projections. Projecting periods of change by this Dynamic Time Projection methodology out-performs any other time or cycle analysis method, period! I'll be glad to retract that statement if proven wrong, but I've followed every published financial cycle analysis publication for the past ten years and none has come close to the accuracy and practical application of Dynamic Time Projections. If you keep your time analysis up-to-date, you too will have a great edge over the rest of the trading and investing pack!

There are four important factors to keep in mind when projecting Dynamic Time Targets:

1. *These Dynamic Time Projections are not forecasting that a market will make a trend change at one particular time projection period.* These future periods are simply periods where several past cycles will be in proportion in the future. These are periods that have a high probability of trend change if a market trends into the period and if the other dimensions of market activity, price and pattern indicate change at the same time. The Projected Turning Point Periods should be considered in the same manner as price support and resistance zone, except they are time support and resistance.

   The next section in this chapter will describe a simple time analysis method called *Time Rhythm Zones* that will project the probable minimum and maximum periods of trend and counter-trend swings.

2. *If a market trends beyond a Projected Turning Point Period, more than likely it will continue to trend at least into the next PTPP.* This follows the assumption which has been proven out by historical studies of past market activity that trend changes will almost always be made within a PTPP.

3. *Time projections must not be taken out of the context of the other two dimensions of market activity, price and pattern analysis.* Time is just one of the three important analysis factors. As a market approaches a time period, the other two factors will qualify each time projection as to how important that time projection is likely to be. Traders must be careful not to focus on just one dimension of market activity. The value of the type of market analysis and trading strategies taught in this book is that we look at the whole of the market activity.

4. *All analysis and trading concerns probability, not certainty.* We want the probabilities on our side. If *most* trend changes occur on or very near the Projected Turning Point Periods, traders and investors who keep this information up-to-date have a significant edge. The PTPPs provide a definite piece of information from where to make a decision.

A Summary Of The Most Important Time Ratios and Time Counts By Method

Time Retracements (TR)

38% **50% 62% 100% 162%** 200% 262%

Alternate Time Projections (ATP)

38% 50% **62% 100% 162%** 200% **262%** 424%

Trend Vibration (TV)

62% **100% 162%** 200% **262%** 424%

Time Counts (TC)

Fib: 21, 34, **55, 89, 144**, 233
Also see Time Count section for a table of the complete Fib. list plus Squares of 90 and 144 and anniversary dates.

Short-Term Fixed Length Time Cycles

Market defined.

Time Overbalance

100% Alternate Time Projection of prior counter-trend swings of similar degree.

More Dynamic Time, Price and Pattern Examples

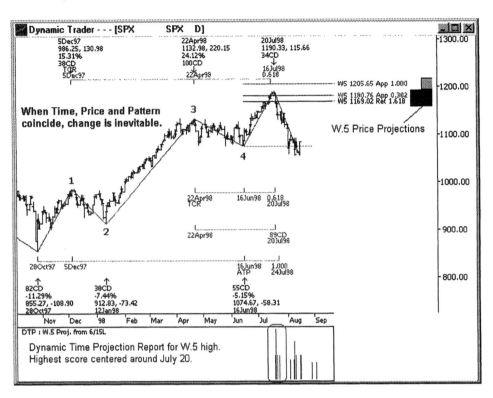

Dynamic Time Projections Target July 20 High Weeks In Advance

The chart below shows some of the time projections for a high that fell near July 20, 1998. How valuable is this timing approach?

This is not an after-the-fact example. Shortly after the June 16 low, I placed the time and price targets for a Wave-5 top on our web site. The time target for the top was the relatively broad zone of July 16-24. The final top was made July 20 and was followed by the largest decline in over ten years!

The Dynamic Trader Weekly Report used the very short-term swings from the intraday data to project the top would be complete by mid-day on July 20. The extreme high was made just before noon on July 20!

The bar-histogram below the chart is the relative scores of the Dynamic Time Projection report in the Dynamic Trader program. These time projections are made from the June 16 low. The highest score is made on July 20 which was the exact date of the high.

Time Retracements

As the S&P declined from the July 20 high, the minor corrective highs were made on the time and price retracements.

The first correction was complete on the 38.2% time retracement and the second was complete one day before the 50% time retracement.

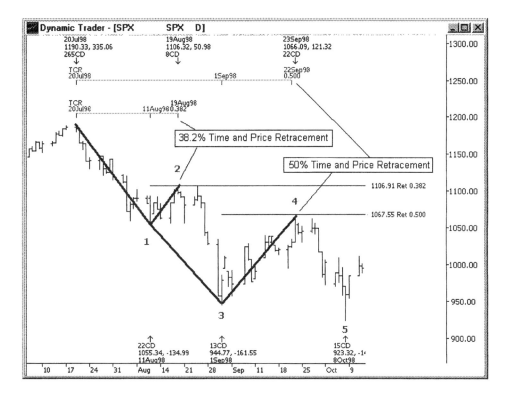

"When time and price coincide, change is inevitable!" A very low-risk, high profit potential trade opportunity is when a market makes a time and price retracement or projection of the same ratio. Both of the corrections shown above were made at the same time and price retracement ratios.

Silver Top At Time and Price

Silver made the July 24, 1998 high at projected time and price zones.

July 24 High at 585.5

<u>July 22-23</u>: 100% Time Retracement and 100% High-to-High Projection
<u>573-583</u>: 100% Alternate Price Projection and 50% Retracement

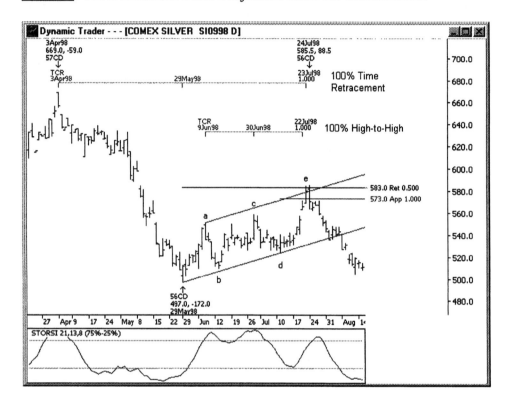

Time and Price Projections Are Always Made In Advance

Every high and low is not made on a exact, direct hit of projected time and price. However, the vast majority of highs and lows of every degree are made at or very near time and price projections that are made well in advance. The following pages show you many more examples of the time, price and pattern position at some important highs and lows for several markets.

The next chapters in the book will show how we integrate the time, price and pattern projections into a low-risk trading plan.

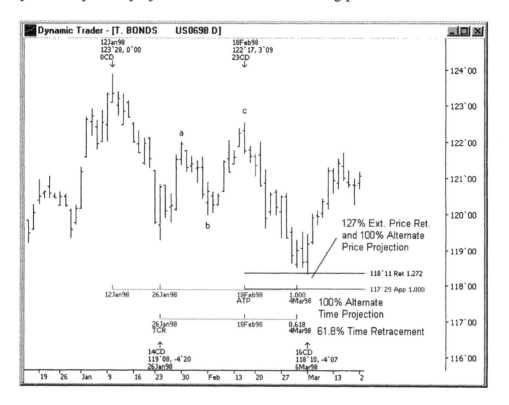

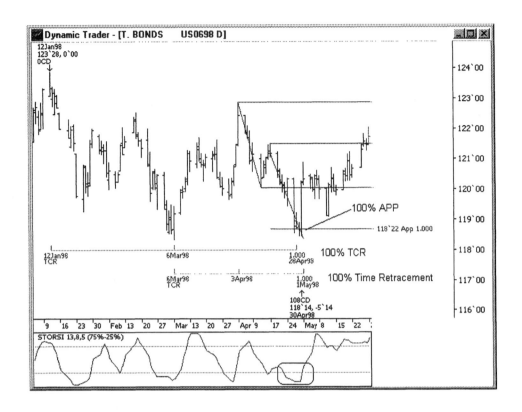

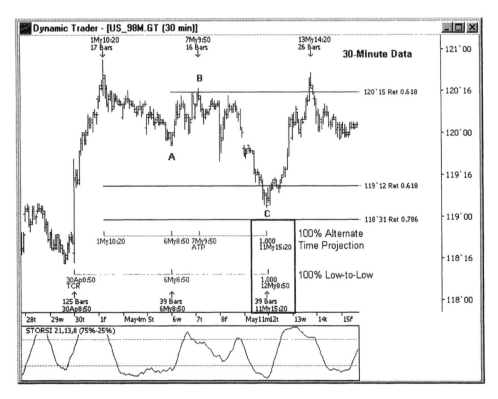

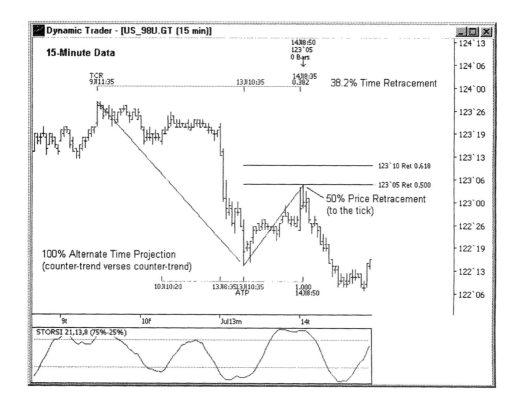

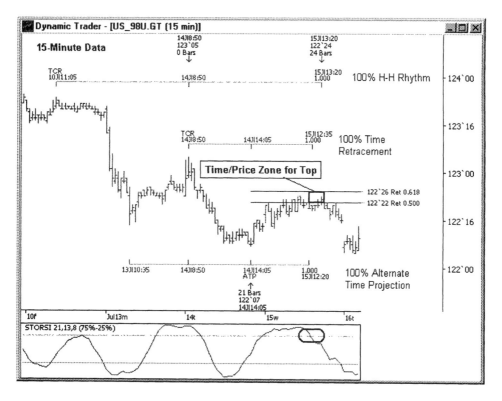

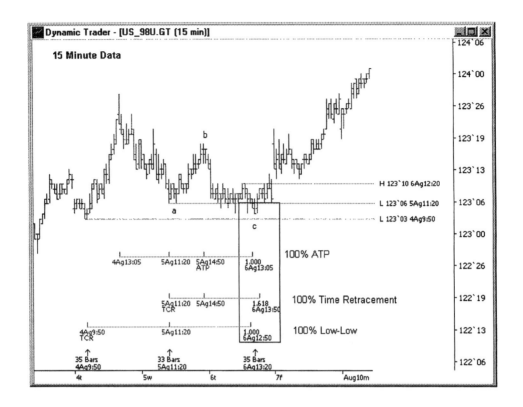

Dynamic Trader - [US_98U.GT (15 min)]

15 Minute Data

H 123`10 6Ag12:20
L 123`06 5Ag11:20
L 123`03 4Ag9:50

4Ag13:05	5Ag11:20	5Ag14:50 ATP	1.000 6Ag13:05

100% ATP

5Ag11:20 TCR	5Ag14:50	1.618 6Ag13:50

100% Time Retracement

4Ag9:50 TCR	5Ag11:20	1.000 6Ag12:50

100% Low-Low

35 Bars 4Ag9:50   33 Bars 5Ag11:20   35 Bars 6Ag13:20

4t   5w   6t   7f   Aug10m

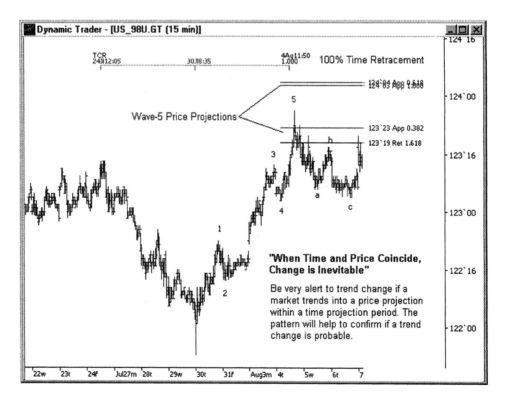

Dynamic Trader - [US_98U.GT (15 min)]

TCR 24Jl12:05   30Jl8:35   4Ag11:50 1.000   100% Time Retracement

124`04 App 1.618

Wave-5 Price Projections

123`23 App 0.382
123`19 Ret 1.618

5
3
4
1
2
a
b
c

"When Time and Price Coincide, Change is Inevitable"

Be very alert to trend change if a market trends into a price projection within a time projection period. The pattern will help to confirm if a trend change is probable.

22w 23t 24f Jul27m 28t 29w 30t 31f Aug3m 4t 5w 6t 7

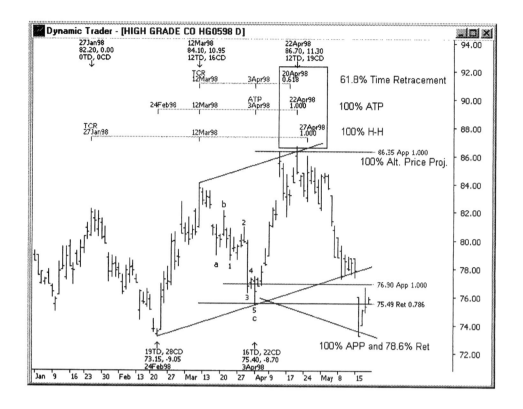

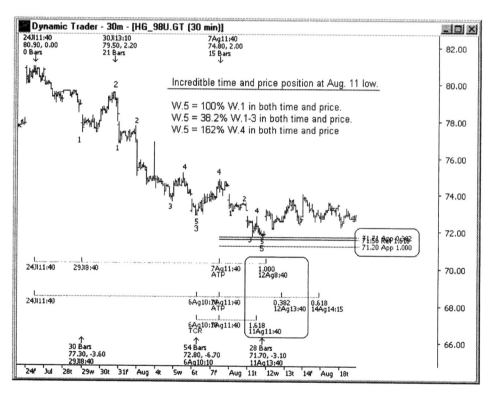

Time Rhythm Zones™

Earlier in this Dynamic Time Analysis chapter, it was described that there are no cycles of fixed-length periodicity in market activity and how the idea that market activity can be represented by a summation cycle is little more than a myth not backed up by actual market activity. However, market structure often displays a "time rhythm." What do I mean by a "time rhythm" and how is it different than what is commonly considered a "cycle?"

A time rhythm represents a fairly regular ebb and flow of price activity. For instance, a market may tend to make a low on a fairly regular basis within a relatively broad time period. That certainly sounds like a hedged statement if there ever was one. An example might be that gold usually makes an intermediate term low 16-22 weeks from the prior intermediate term low. The variables in this statement are what do we mean by "usually" and "intermediate."

"Usually" should be a high percentage of occurrences such as 80%. "Intermediate" must be defined by a minimum percentage change of price for the new trend such as a 10% price change. A more accurate statement might be: "Eighty percent of the time since 1975, gold has made a low in the broad period of 16-22 weeks from the prior 10%-low followed by a rally of 10% or more in price. A "10%-low" is a low that is preceded and followed by a minimum 10% change in price against the preceding trend.

This information is not hedged but specific and objective. It provides us with a significant, statistical edge of the high probability time to antici-pate and prepare for a trend change low that should be followed by a rally of at least a ten percent price advance. A seven week (16-22 weeks) time period is too broad to make a specific trading decision, but provides a framework from where to focus in on the more specific and/or short-term time factors.

Whenever we apply historic, statistical output to present conditions, we are operating under the assumption that the same conditions of the past are relevant today. A market will only continue to make a low in the 16-22 week period if the same forces that have acted upon the market during the past continue to do so in the future. We never know if this will be the case, but must assume it will be so unless there is some indication to the contrary.

Some traders and analysts would call this statistical information a 19 week gold *cycle* because 19 weeks may be the average length of time of the low-to-low period. An average may be very misleading. Unfortunately, an average does not provide any information on how tightly grouped are the events. If the events are tightly grouped around the average, it is a valuable figure. If they are widely dispersed from the average, the average is not only useless, but very misleading.

To call an average period of time a cycle is not only a misnomer but misleading to the trader. Calling a general tendency for a market to make a low within a broad period of time a cycle misleads the trader into believing the so-called cycle period is more precise and more reliable than it is.

Low-to-Low Time Rhythm Example

Bonds began a bear market Oct. 15, 1993. On Aug. 2, 1994, bonds made a counter-trend top followed by a continued decline to new lows. What would be the time range with the greatest probability of making the next low? We must first decide what degree of trend change we are concerned with. Swings of 5% or greater generally represent intermediate degree trend change for bonds. The 5% swing file also has a minimum time filter of 21 calendar days. A swing must have made a minimum of a 5% price change for at least 21 CDs to be included.

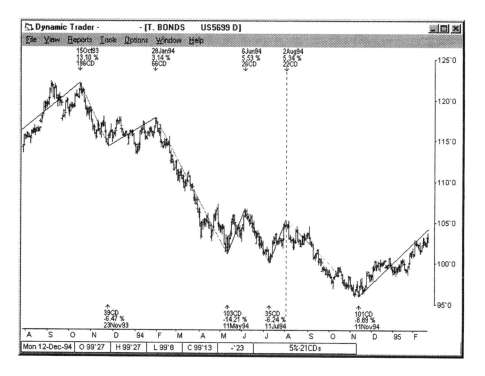

Bonds began a bear market in Oct. 1993. The swings shown on the chart above are a minimum of 5% price change and 21 calendar days. The dashed vertical line is placed at the Aug. 2, 1994 high.

The historical period to accumulate the timing data begins with the April 1986 bull market top. From that period through Aug. 1994, there were two complete bull and bear markets with an adequate number of 5%+ swings for our purposes. The chart below shows this period with the 5%/21 CD swings overlaid on the daily, close-only data.

During this period there were 15 low-to-low cycles. They were made in a very wide range of time from 61 to 302 calendar days. As you can see, once an *objective* criteria is applied to identify cycle pivots, the idea of cycles of fixed-length periodicity goes out the window with the flat-earth theory. If we eliminate the shortest and longest 10% of the cycles, the time range is reduced to 119 to 278 calendar days. In other words, 80% of the low-to-low cycles were made in the broad period between 119-278 calendar days from the prior low during the period from April 1986 to Aug. 1994. This is still too long of a period to be of much use to traders and investors, but we will see in a moment how additional data will provide a much shorter time-range target for a low.

The table below shows the time ranges and equivalent dates of the low-to-low cycles since the April 1986 high.

Time Rhythm Zone Detail							Dynamic Trader	✕
Primary Swing file: 5%-21CDs			All swings		**Project from:** 11July94 Low			
	Swing	**Type**	**#**	**Min**	**10**	**Median**	**90**	**Max**
Detail	Pri	L-L	11	10Sep94	7Nov94	9Feb95	15Apr95	9May95
				61	119	213	278	302

There were a total of 15 low-to-low swings in this data group. If the shortest and longest 10% of the swings are eliminated, there remains 11 swings. Ten percent of 15 equals 1.5. Rounding up to the next higher number eliminates the two shortest and two longest. The time range between 10%-90% of the low-to-low bond cycles ranged from 119 to 278 calendar days.

The time period of Nov. 7, 1994 to April 15, 1995 is the equivalent period if this time range is projected from the July 11, 1994 low. Ninety percent of the low-to-low cycles lasted at least 119 days (10% were shorter) and 90% terminated by 278 days (only 10% were longer).

80% Low-to-Low Time Rhythm

The chart below shows the 5%/21CD swings overlaying the continuous daily bar chart of bonds. The Nov. 23, 1993 low to Jan. 28, 1994 high shown in the chart below appears to be an exception to the swing criteria. The data below is the continuous futures data with no adjustments at contract rollover. The data rolled over between the Nov. low and Jan. high from the Dec. to the March contract causing a distortion in the continuous file. If just the March contract were shown, there would not be a lower-low between the Nov. low and Jan. high.

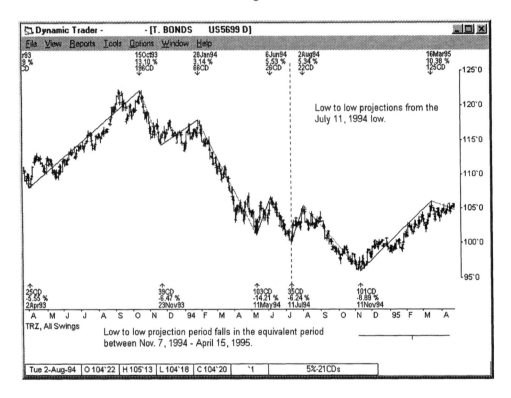

The horizontal bar in the indicator window below the bar chart represents the equivalent time range of 80% of the low-to-low swings since the April 1986 bull market top projected from the July 11, 1994 low. The equivalent period to anticipate the next low is the broad period from Nov. 7, 1994 through April 15, 1995. These dates are the 119 and 278 calendar day counts from the July 11, 1994 low.

Projecting the equivalent time for a low based solely on past low-to-low cycles will almost always result in a time period that is too broad to be of much use to traders and investors. There is an additional criteria that may be considered that will usually result in a more narrow range of time with a high reliability for a low to be made.

High-to-Low Time Rhythm

A *high-to-low* projection may be made in the same manner as the low-to-low projection. The *overlap* period of the high-to-low and low-to-low projected ranges will usually provide a relatively narrow and useful time period to anticipate when the next low should be made.

	Swing	Type	#	Min	10	Median	90	Max
Time Rhythm Zone Detail							Dynamic Trader	☒
Primary Swing file: 5%-21CDs			All swings			Project from: 2Aug94 High		
Detail	Pri	H-L	12	25Aug94 23	1Sep94 30	27Sep94 56	2Dec94 122	11Feb95 193
Detail	Pri	L-L	11	10Sep94 61	7Nov94 119	9Feb95 213	15Apr95 278	9May95 302
		Overlap:	7Nov94 - 2Dec94			97 - 122		

There were a total of 16 high-to-low swings in the 5%/21 CD data file from April 1986 through the Aug. 2, 1994 high. The time range of these 16 swings ran from just 23 calendar days to 193 days. As with the low-to-low cycles, this is far too wide a range to be of any use to traders and investors. If we eliminate the shortest and longest 10% of the swings, the remaining 80% time range runs from 30 to 122 days. Still too long to be of much use.

Time Rhythm Zone - 80% Overlap Period

What if we combine the low-to-low projections from the July 11, 1994 low and the high-to-low projections from the Aug. 2, 1994 high? We discover that the common or overlap period for these two time ranges is less than one month and runs from Nov. 7 to Dec. 2. The overlap period is a relatively narrow range of time that can be put to practical use by traders and investors.

The Time Rhythm Zone Detail table above shows both the low-to-low and high-to-low time ranges as well as the overlap period.

The indicator window below the bar chart below shows the time ranges of the low-to-low and high-to-low swings. The overlap period of these two periods is the fat bar which represents the period from Nov. 7 to Dec. 2. The tails extending from the overlap period represent the full range of time of H-L and L-L.

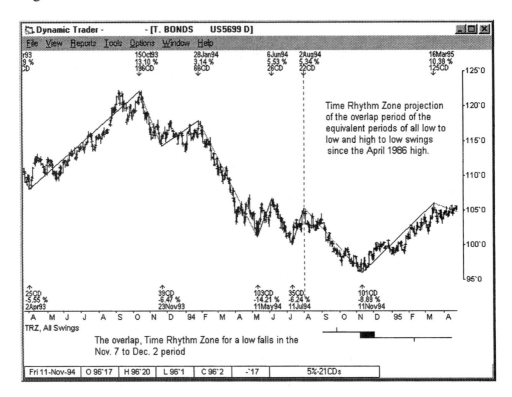

I have termed this method of projecting overlapping cycles, *Time Rhythm Zones (TRZ)*. The general concept of overlapping cycles is not new or original. It has been used and taught by Walt Bressert for many years.

However, there are critical differences between the old way of projecting overlapping cycles and Time Rhythm Zones. Time Rhythm Zones use the actual, recent market swings, not average length swings from historical data. In other words, the data for TRZs is market driven. Swing lengths may change as a market progresses and new swings are made.

Bull or Bear Rhythm?

A *high-to-low* (H-L) swing in a *bull market* is a *counter-trend* swing. A low in a bull market is the termination of the counter-trend and the beginning of a new trend swing. A *high-to-low* (H-L) swing in a *bear market* is a *trend swing*. A low in a bear market is the termination of a trend swing and the beginning of a counter-trend swing. If we are compiling data to project the probable low of a trend swing in a bear market, should we include the high-to-low, counter-trend swings that were part of bull markets? Probably not. Relevant statistical conclusions should be derived from data that compares like to like, not apples to oranges.

Trend and counter-trend swings should usually not be included in the same data series for purposes of statistical analysis. Swings from bull and bear markets should not be mixed together. If our analysis indicates that a market is in a bear trend and a trend swing decline is underway, we should only use high-to-low trend swings and low-to-low swings from prior *bear markets* to determine the Time Rhythm Zone for a low. If we included high-to-low counter-trend swings from bull markets, the projected TRZ would not accurately represent what we are looking to discover which is the high probability period for a trend-swing low in a bear market.

Trend swings are usually longer in time than counter-trend swings. This applies to both bull and bear markets. If the objective is to project a high-to-low trend swing low in a bear market but we include high-to-low counter trend swings from bull markets to determine the TRZ, the time range will probably be skewed to shorter term swings than are typical of high-to-low trend swings in bear markets. If there is not a confident opinion of the major trend direction, use all prior swings from bull, bear and trading range markets.

The previous bond example included all swings from the historical period without distinguishing swings from bull or bear markets. From the Oct. 1993 high, bonds had made consecutively lower-lows and lower-highs. Bonds were considered in a bear market as of the Aug. 1994 top. The objective was to project when the next low within a *bear market* would take place. Rather than use all 5%/21 CDs swings to make the TRZ projection for a low, we should only use those swings from prior bear markets.

The chart on the following page shows the intermediate (5%/21 CD) and major swing files together. The bar chart data has been removed so the swing files are easier to see. The dashed, vertical line is at the Aug. 2, 1994 high. As of Aug. 1994, there had been two completed bull and bear markets. Bonds were in a bear market as is evidenced by the consecutive lower-lows and lower-highs. If our objective is to project the high probability period for the next swing low in a bear market, we should only include data from prior bear markets to make the projections.

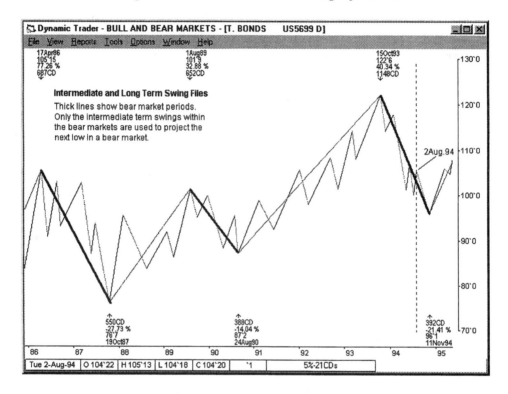

The Time Rhythm Zone Detail table below shows the results of only including swings from bear markets. While fewer swings are used than when both bull and bear trends were considered in the previous example, the output should be more reliable since only data from similar markets is included in the projections.

The new Time Rhythm Zone period (overlap of low-to-low and high-to-low time ranges) is Oct. 26, 1994 to Nov. 28, 1994. The Nov. 11, 1994 low was made right in the middle of this period.

Time Rhythm Zone Detail							Dynamic Trader	
Primary Swing file: 5%-21CDs			Bear		**Project from:** 2Aug94 High			
	Swing	**Type**	**#**	**Min**	**10**	**Median**	**90**	**Max**
Detail	Pri	H-L	8	25Aug94	1Sep94	23Sep94	28Nov94	8Dec94
				23	30	52	118	128
Detail	Pri	L-L	5	10Sep94	26Oct94	10Dec94	9Feb95	11Mar95
				61	107	152	213	243
	Primary Overlap:	26Oct94 - 28Nov94				85 - 118		

The Oct. 28-Nov. 28 TRZ was a product of the overlap period of the 80%-range of the prior H-L and L-L swings of bear markets only. Each TRZ should be identified by the percent of swings used. Throughout this book, a TRZ is always a TRZ-80% unless otherwise noted. If a TRZ is the product of other than 80% of the swings, it will be noted such as TRZ-70% or TRZ-90%.

Dynamic Trader	TRZ Low - Low Swings		☒
Swing file: 5%-21CDs	Bear	Scenario: BULL AND BEAR	

	Pivot Date	Pivot Date	Time CDs
1	May-11-94 (Wed)	Jul-11-94 (Mon)	61
2	Jun-04-86 (Wed)	Sep-19-86 (Fri)	107
3	Apr-27-90 (Fri)	Aug-24-90 (Fri)	119
4	May-20-87 (Wed)	Oct-19-87 (Mon)	152
5	Nov-23-93 (Tue)	May-11-94 (Wed)	169
6	Sep-26-89 (Tue)	Apr-27-90 (Fri)	213
7	Sep-19-86 (Fri)	May-20-87 (Wed)	243

| Sort Date | Sort Time | | Print | Close |

The table above shows the seven low-to-low swings made during the bear markets that were used to make the TRZ projection for the next low following the Aug. 2, 1994 high. The low-to-low periods have been sorted by time range. The range of time is from 61 to 243 calendar days. Note how the time ranges are fairly evenly spaced out from the shortest to the longest. This series of L-L swings is an excellent example of how an average period would provide very misleading information. The average period of the seven swings is 152 CDs. While one swing fell exactly at the average, the rest of the swings are not grouped tightly around the average.

If you were projecting a "cycle low" for bonds, would you be comfortable considering a target date of 152 days from the prior low as a relevant piece of information? You shouldn't! Averages are used by average traders and investors. Average traders and investors do not succeed in the long run!

The chart on the following page shows the Time Rhythm Zone of Oct. 26-Nov. 28 for the next low in the indicator window below the bar chart. This period only considered swings from bear markets. The Nov. 11, 1994 low fell right in the middle of this period.

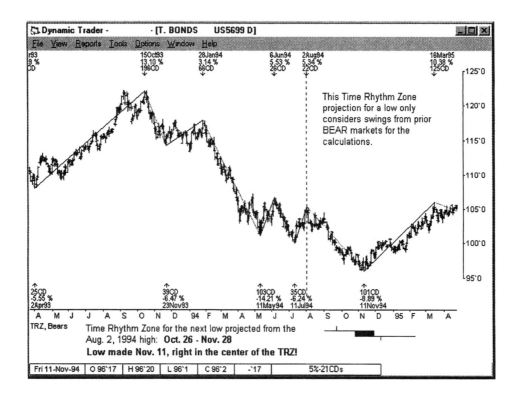

Let's review exactly what information we have when we do a Time Rhythm Zone calculation using the example above.

Based on the historic data since the April 1986 high and assuming the same market forces are in effect during the current period:

1. There is a 90% probability that bonds will not make a low prior to Oct. 26. Based on past history, 90% of the L-L cycles in bear markets were made at or later than the equivalent date of Oct. 26. As bonds decline, traders and investors should not be too anxious to consider long positions prior to the beginning of the overlap period of Oct. 26.

2. There is a 90% probability that bonds will complete the low by Nov. 28 followed by a rally of at least 5% price change and at least 21 calendar days. Based on past history, 90% of the H-L swings in bear markets were complete by the equivalent date of Nov. 28. If bonds are continuing to decline into late Nov. or so, traders and investors should be particularly alert to reversal signals as bonds are approaching the extreme time when a low should be made.

3. If bonds make a low followed by at least a 5% rally in 21 or more days outside of the Oct. 26-Nov. 28 period, it would be an unusual situation that should warn the analyst that the market forces may be changing. The analyst should be alert to other potential extreme price or pattern activity that may also signal a fundamental shift in market structure.

Multiple Degree Projections Provide The Most Reliable Signals

In all areas of technical analysis, we should consider at least two degrees of change in order to provide the most reliable trading information. This is also true with Time Rhythm Zone projections. The most reliable projections will result when the lesser degree projections overlap with the larger degree projections. An overlap of the lesser degree projections to the larger degree projections is signaling that the larger degree trend change should unfold within the period of the lesser degree time projection.

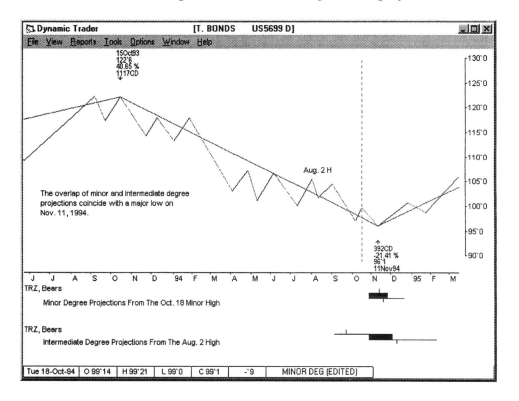

The chart above shows the minor degree swing file with the major degree (bull / bear trend) swings. The minor swing file includes swings of approximately 2%. The lower indicator window is the TRZ projection from the Aug. 2, 1994 high using the 5%/21CDs swing file shown earlier.

The top indicator window is the TRZ of minor degree swings. The minor degree TRZ overlaps the intermediate degree TRZ providing an even more confident outlook that a low will be made in this period. While the overlap periods of the two degrees are almost the same, the extreme period of the minor degree is much less than the extreme period of the intermediate degree as represented by the shorter "tails."

	Swing	Type	#	Min	10	Median	90	Max
Detail	Pri	H-L	12	27Oct94	29Oct94	13Nov94	26Nov94	23Dec94
				9	11	26	39	66
Detail		L-L	12	27Oct94	29Oct94	20Nov94	22Dec94	5Jan95
				20	22	44	76	90

Time Rhythm Zone Detail

Primary Swing file: MINOR DEG   Bear   Project from: 18Oct94 High

Primary Overlap: 29Oct94 - 26Nov94   11 - 39

The minor degree TRZ runs from <u>Oct. 29 to Nov. 26</u>. Most of this entire period overlaps with the intermediate TRZ which is <u>Oct. 26-Nov. 28</u>. Notice that the minor degree projection is more "tightly packed" as there are fewer extreme ranges as compared to the far out "tails" of the intermediate degree projections.

Time Rhythm Zones and Sample Size

TRZ projections will often be made with a relatively small sample size of past swings depending on the degree of change of the swing file, whether just bull or bear swings are used and the length of the historic period that is included. It is far more important to be concerned with constructing a representative swing file and only including the historic periods that are representative of current conditions than it is with having a minimum number of swings to work with.

In the examples above, there have been as few as five swings used for the 80% range. So be it. We must use the information at hand that is representative while being aware of the limitations of a small sample size. Even if only a small number of swings are used, the TRZ still accurately represents the range of time that trend changes have been made in the past for the period of time and degree of change under consideration. That is exactly what we want to know.

Time Rhythm Zones Are Adaptive

Time Rhythm Zones are adaptive to the market behavior. TRZ projections are a reflection of the actual swings for the historic period included in the statistical analysis. As a market progresses and new swings are made and included in the swing file, the most recent TRZ projections will adjust or adapt by including the new swings with the calculations. If the recent time rhythm is changing, it will be reflected in the new projections. New swings added to the statistical base will only change the range of a TRZ projection if a new swing is outside the old range.

Time Rhythm Zone Summary

1. Time Rhythm Zone projections provide a completely *objective* method for projecting high probability time zones from where a reversal of a minimum amount of price change should occur based on the actual historic precedents.

2. The high probability Time Rhythm Zone is the *overlap* of two time-range projections. In the case of a projected low, the overlap of the low-to-low (L-L) and high-to-low (H-L) projected time ranges provide the Time Rhythm Zone with a high probability of a low based on past market swings. The overlap of the H-H and L-H ranges provide the TRZ for a potential high.

3. The user has complete control over the historic period to use for the TRZ studies. If the current major trend of the market is known (bull or bear), only swings from similar markets in the past should be included in the TRZ projection calculations.

4. The user has complete control over the percentage of swings from the historical period to include in the TRZ projection. Generally, the projected time ranges eliminate the smallest and largest 10% of the periods leaving an 80% range. An 80% range implies that 90% of prior reversals were not made prior to the beginning of the 80% range and 90% were complete by the extreme of the 80% range. Unless otherwise noted, a TRZ is an overlap of two 80% ranges.

5. Time Rhythm Zones of two degrees will provide more reliable projections for the time of the termination of a trend if the smaller degree projection overlaps with the larger degree.

6. If the TRZ is a relatively broad period of time, it is still a valuable bit of information as it provides the most likely minimum and maximum extreme from where the next trend reversal should be made. Other time projection methods will provide the period within the TRZ when the actual reversal is most likely.

7. With statistical analysis, the greater the sample size the greater the reliability of the conclusions. Time Rhythm Zones often have a relatively few number of occurrences of past swings of a similar nature and degree of change. They still remain valuable, as they accurately represent the actual outcome of prior similar swings and provide a framework of what to anticipate for the current outcome.

TRZ For A Trend Swing High

This TRZ projection from the Aug. 15, 1995 low used all bull market swings from the Sept. 1981 low. The projection was a fairly broad, three month period. The Jan. 1996 top was made right within the TRZ zone for the top.

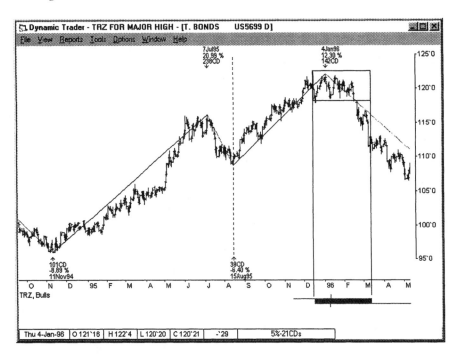

The TRZ Detail table below shows the range of L-H and H-H swings from bull markets since the Sept. 1981 bear market low. The TRZ overlap period is from Dec. 17, 1995 through March 12, 1996.

Time Rhythm Zone Detail								Dynamic Trader
Primary Swing file: 5%-21CDs			Bull		Project from: 15Aug95 Low			
	Swing	Type	#	Min	10	Median	90	Max
Detail	Pri	L-H	12	17Oct95	13Nov95	10Jan96	12Mar96	16Apr96
				63	90	148	210	245
Detail	Pri	H-H	9	10Nov95	17Dec95	9Jan96	3Jun96	28Jun96
				126	163	186	332	357
		Overlap:	17Dec95 - 12Mar96			124 - 210		

As bonds rallied and exceeded the July high, traders and investors would be alert to not anticipate a top prior to mid-Dec. The final top of Jan. 4, 1996 was made right within the projected TRZ for the top.

TRZ For A Counter-Trend Top In A Bear Market

The mark made a sharp rally off of the Sept. 15, 1995 low. Since the mark was making lower-lows and lower-highs, a bear market is assumed. A TRZ projection is made for a counter-trend high in a bear market. All bear market swings since the Dec. 1987 high are used. Since this is a relatively small number of swings, 100% of the swings are used to make the Time Rhythm Zone projection.

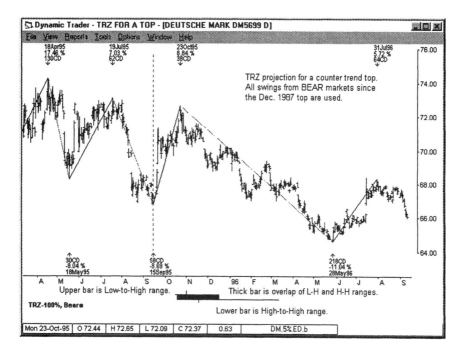

The TRZ Detail table below shows the range of all H-H and L-H swings from bear markets since the Dec. 1987 bull market top. There are relatively few swings because the mark often makes relentless bear trends with less than 5% counter-trend rallies. This is demonstrated by the fact that the H-H range is much more extensive than the L-H range. The table shows that 100% of the swings are used. The Oct. 23, 1995 top was made just a few days into the TRZ for a top.

	Swing	Type	#	Min	0	Median	100	Max
Time Rhythm Zone Detail						**Dynamic Trader**		
Primary Swing file: DM.5%.ED.b			Bear		**Project from:** 15Sep95 Low			
Detail	Pri	L-H	6	15Oct95	15Oct95	1Nov95	17Dec95	17Dec95
				30	30	47	93	93
Detail	Pri	H-H	6	19Oct95	19Oct95	18Nov95	11Mar96	11Mar96
				92	92	122	236	236
			Overlap:	19Oct95 - 17Dec95				

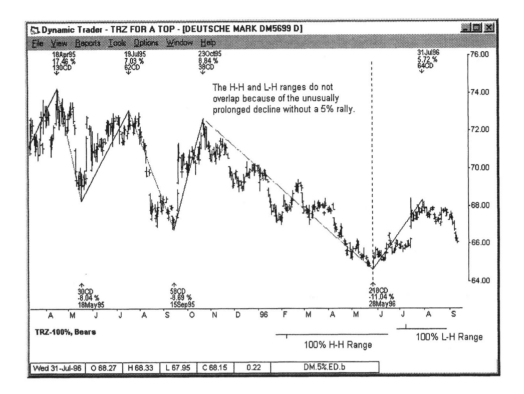

Another TRZ projection for a top is made from the May 28, 1996 low. The mark had not make a 5% rally since the Oct. 23, 1995 high. One-hundred percent of the swings from all bear markets since the Oct. 1987 high were used. Note that the time range of the Low-to-High and High-to-High swings do not overlap. This is a result of the prolonged, Oct.-May decline without an intervening high made by at least a 5% counter-trend rally. The mark made a top on July 31 which was right within the Low-to-High range of past bear market, counter-trend highs. However, the high was later than any prior High-to-High period making a new H-H extreme for bear markets.

Past Low-to-High swings in bear markets had lasted from 30 to 93 days. The July 31 high was made right within this time zone for a top.

Time Rhythm Zone Detail

Primary Swing file: DM.5%.ED.b   Bear   Project from: 28May96 Low

	Swing	Type	#	Min	0	Median	100	Max
Detail	Pri	L-H	7	27Jun96	27Jun96	9Jul96	29Aug96	29Aug96
				30	30	42	93	93
Detail	Pri	H-H	7	23Jan96	23Jan96	7Feb96	15Jun96	15Jun96
				92	92	107	236	236
		Overlap:						

Time Rhythm Zones Are Simple, Yet Effective

Time Rhythm Zone projections are one of the simplest yet most useful analytical procedures a trader or investor will employ. A narrow-range TRZ will provide a very high probability time zone for a trend change. A wide-range TRZ will at least provide the minimum and maximum dates likely for trend change which will alert the trader or investor if a market is nearing an extreme relative to past history.

If there is no overlap of the two time ranges, the trader or investor is alerted to the fact that the market is operating outside the range of past activity and extra care should be taken to consider the position of the market from other perspectives.

The best use of Time Rhythm Zones is in conjunction with other dynamic time factors that provide target dates for high probability trend change. When a Dynamic Time Projection falls within a TRZ, the odds increase for a trend change.

Combining Dynamic Time Projections and Time Rhythm Zones For High Probability Time Analysis

The highest probability time projections for trend change will occur when Dynamic Time Projections fall within an 80% or greater Time Rhythm Zone. The TRZ provides the relatively broad zone that indicates the probable minimum and maximum period where the trend change will take place while the Dynamic Time Projections (Projected Turning Point Periods) provide the relatively narrow time zones of usually just 2-4 trading days that target the specific dates for trend change.

Every change-in-trend will not take place at a coincidence of a Time Rhythm Zone and Dynamic Time Projection, but most will. When there is a coincidence of Time Rhythm Zone and Dynamic Time Projection, there is a very high probability for trend change.

DM - Time projections from the Sept. 15, 1995 low.

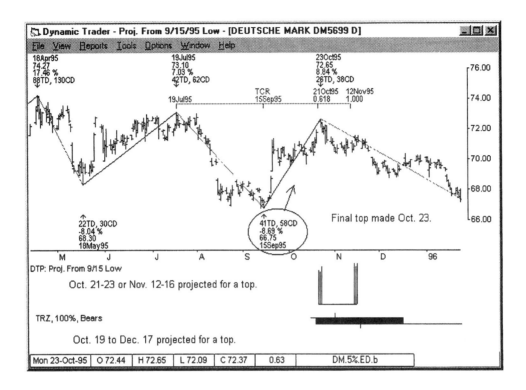

The *Time Rhythm Zone* (TRZ) projection from the Sept. 15 low shown in the indicator window above is the same one used as an example in the previous Time Rhythm Zone section. This TRZ used 100% of all rallies in bear markets since the Dec. 1987 high. The TRZ projected the two month period of Oct. 18-Dec. 17 for a counter-trend top. While this is a very broad period of time, it provides the minimum and maximum dates with a very high probability of completing a top.

Dynamic Time Projections which include Time Cycle Ratios and Time Counts indicated either <u>Oct. 21-23</u> or <u>Nov. 12-16</u> were the two periods within the TRZ with the highest probability of making a counter-trend top. The chart above shows only two TCRs which are the Time Retracements. The 62% and 100% Time Retracements fell on Oct. 21 and Nov. 12. The final top was made <u>Oct. 23</u>. The following charts show some of the other dynamic time factors that fell near the Oct. 23 high.

The chart below shows just five of the TCRs that fell in Oct. and Nov.

Oct. 19: 100% H-H Cycle TCR (4/18/95H-7/19/95H projected forward).
Oct. 21: 62% Time Retracement TCR (Time retracement of the 7/19H-
9/15L).
Oct. 23: 62% Alternate Time Projection (ATP) TCR (5/18/95L-7/19/95H
projected from the 9/15/95L)
Nov. 12: 100% Time Retracement TCR (Time retracement of the 7/19H-
9/15L).
Nov. 16: 100% ATP (5/18/95L-7/19/95H projected from the 9/15/95L)

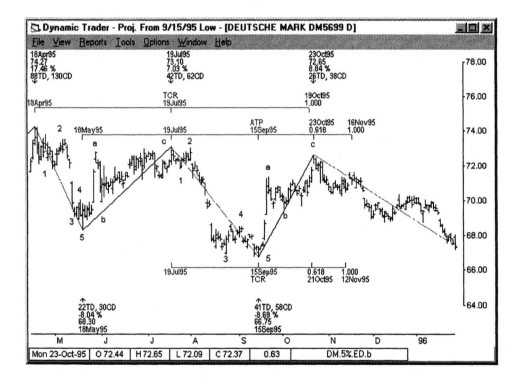

The mark had been making five wave declines and three wave (ABC) rallies implying the larger degree trend was bearish. The rally from the Sept. 15 low appeared to continue that pattern.

Oct. 23, 1995 Top Made At A Coincidence Of Projected Time and Price

A price resistance zone (71.74-72.52) was made by three price projections:

71.74: 78.6% retracement of the 7/19/95H - 9/15/95L.
72.46: 162% retracement of wave b (not shown on the chart below).
72.52: 62% Alternate Price Projection (App). Wave C = .618 Wave A.

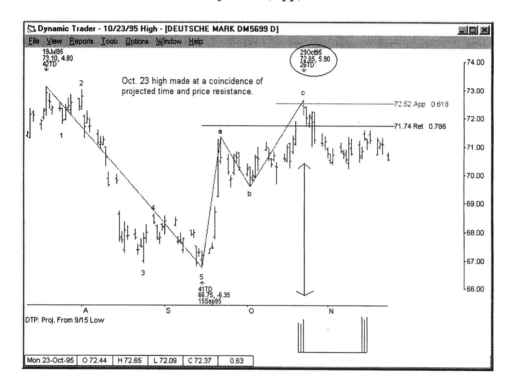

The mark rallied into the projected price resistance zone (71.74-72.52) in the projected time resistance period (Oct. 21-23) and an ABC rally was complete. The mark continued to decline to new lows from the Oct. 23 top.

On Oct. 23, the mark made a *gap signal day* which is one of the most reliable daily reversal signals. A *gap signal day* is made when a market gaps open followed by a new high and a close below the opening. The daily range leaves a gap from the previous day. When a *gap signal day* is made at a coincidence of projected time and price, trend reversal is just about inevitable.

DM - Projections from the May 28, 1996 low.

The TRZ projection shown below is also from an earlier example in the Time Rhythm Zone section. It includes 100% of the Low-to-High swings in bear markets for about the past 10 years. The relatively broad period of June 27-Aug. 29 had a very high probability of making a counter-trend top based on the past history.

The Dynamic Time Projections indicated that either July 15-18 or July 26-28 should complete the counter-trend rally. The DTPs fell right within the TRZ period resulting in a very high probability a top would be made in this time period.

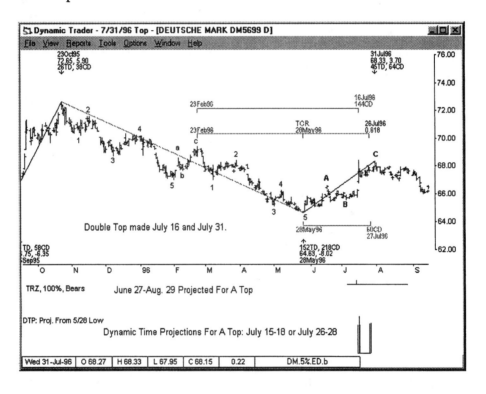

A double top was made on July 16 and July 31. The July 16 high was slightly higher. The chart above shows three of the time factors behind the Dynamic Time Projections:

July 16: 144 Calendar Days from the Feb. 23 H.

July 26: 62% Time Retracement (TCR) of the Feb. 23 high to May 28 L.

July 27: 60 Calendar Days (CD) from the May 28 low. 30, 60 and 90 CD counts are particularly significant in the currency markets.

The charts on the following pages show other time and price projections that fell near the double top.

More time factors at the July 16 / 31 double top:

July 14: 50% Time Retracement (TCR) of the Feb. 23 H to May 28 L.

July 16: 34 Trading Days (TD) from the May 28 L.

July 16: 144 CD from the Feb. 23 H.

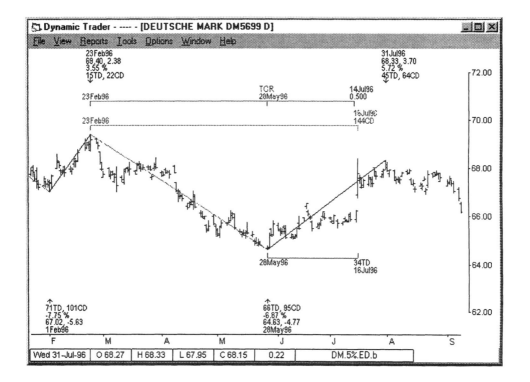

The chart below focuses in on just the ABC rally from the May 28 low.

July 26: 100% Alternate Time Projection (ATP); 5/28H-6/18L projected from the 7/5L. This projection fell three days prior to the July 31 high and coincided with several of the longer term time factors shown earlier.

Aug. 1: 162% Time Retracement of the B wave decline (6/187H-7/5L).

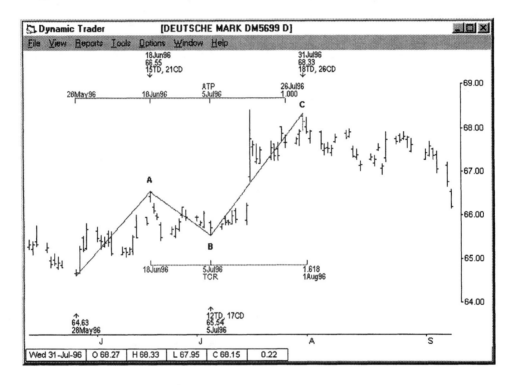

When short term time factors coincide with longer term time factors the probabilities increase for a trend change.

Price Projections At July Top

Price retracements and alternate price projections indicated two resistance zones where a counter-trend high was probable.

67.34-67.69: This zone included retracements from two prior highs and an alternate price projection

67.34: 100% Alternate Price Projection (Wave C = Wave A).
67.58: 62% Retracement (2/23H-5/28L)
67.69: 38% Retracement (10/23H-5/28L)

68.38-68.64: This zone included the all important 50% retracement of the major range as well as a variety of other important price factors.

68.38: 78.6% Retracement of the 2/23H-5/28L (not shown on chart).
68.38: 262% Retracement of Wave B.
65.53: 162% Alternate Price Projection (Wave C = 162% Wave A)
68.64: 50% Retracement of the 10/23H-5/28L.

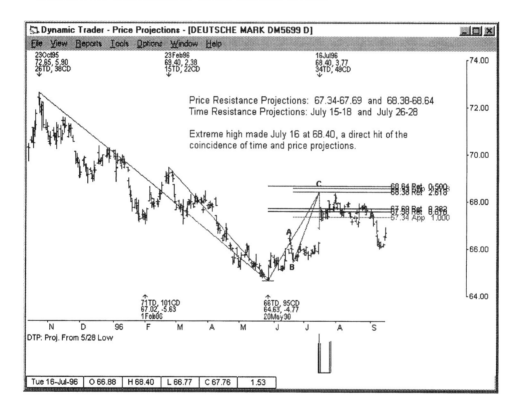

The extreme high of the rally was made July 16 at 68.40 right within the resistance zone of 68.38-68.64. The mark reached this upper resistance level right within the Dynamic Time Projection for a top of July 16-18. "When time and price coincide, change is inevitable."

Bonds: Nov. 11, 1994 Low

Bonds are one of the most consistently reliable markets that make nearly every significant trend reversal at direct hits of projected time and price targets. The Nov. 11, 1994 low was no exception. Time, price and pattern all came together to signal a major trend change was unfolding in Nov. 1994. The Time Rhythm Zone and Dynamic Time Projections shown below are made from the Aug. 2, 1994 high which is labeled as a wave 4.

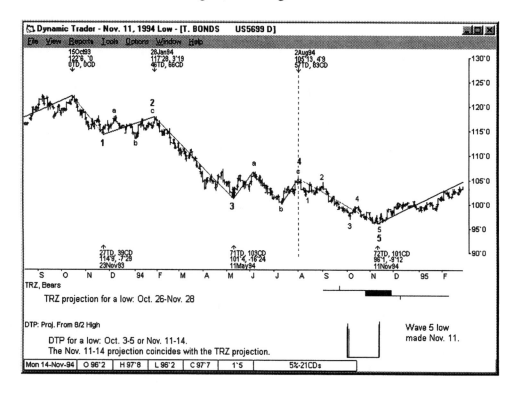

The TRZ projection for a low was the period of <u>Oct. 26-Nov. 28</u>. The Dynamic Time Projections for a low fell on <u>Oct. 3-5</u> and <u>Nov. 11-14</u>. The second period, Nov. 11-14, fell within the TRZ projection for a low.

The Nov. 11 low fell directly on the coincidence of the DTP and TRZ time projections for a low. Wouldn't it be nice if every trend change fell directly within the coincidence of each of these important time projection methods? Every trend change does not, but, many do. *All successful traders* have the patience to wait for the high probability trade set-ups that are made within the context of their analysis methodology and trading plan.

Alternate Time Projections Into Nov. Low

The chart below shows three different Alternate Time Projections that were targeted for Nov. 12 and 13. This was a Saturday and Sunday. The DTP target dates were expanded to Nov. 11-14 to include Friday and Monday. The final low was made Nov. 11.

Nov. 12: Wave 5=262% Wave 1 (10/15/93H-11/23/93L projected from 8/2/94L)

Nov. 13: Wave 5=100% Wave 3 (1/28/94H-5/11/94L projected from 8/2/94H)

Nov. 13: [C:C (Cycle:Cycle) projection]: 1/28/94H-8/2/94H projected from the 5/11/94L (Wave 3-4 = Wave 4-5).

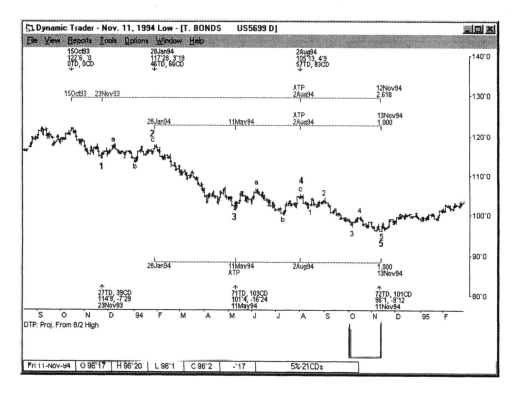

Price Projections At Nov. 11, 1994 Low

The Nov. 11 low was made at the price target of the three most frequent projections for a wave 5 low. These three are:

   Wave 5 = 100% Wave 1

   Wave 5 = 62% or 38% Waves 1-3

   Wave 5 = 127% or 162% Wave 4

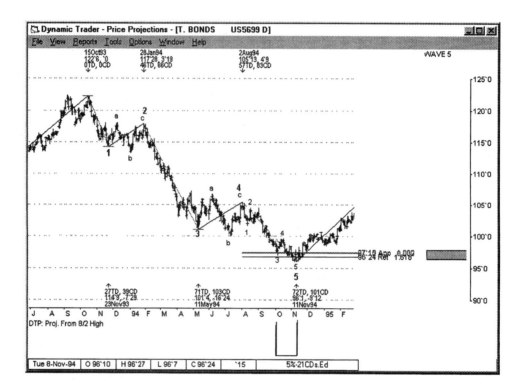

The **97.16-96.24** zone was targeted as the ideal price zone for a wave 5 low.

97.16: Wave 5 = 100% Wave 1

97.10: Wave 5 = 38% Waves 1-3

96.24: Wave 5 = 162% Wave 4

    As bonds made new lows going into Nov., the minor cycles are used to fine tune the larger degree price projections. The sub-divisions of wave 5 are shown on the chart on the following page.

Wave 5 sub-divided into a smaller degree five wave structure in text book Elliott wave manner. The ideal target for the end of wave 5:5 was the 96.14-95.11 price zone which fell just below the larger degree target of 97.16-96.24. Ideally, we like to see the price targets of two degrees overlap. *When they do not but are close to each other, the smaller degree target is preferred.*

Wave 5:5 Price Target: 94.14-95.11

96.14: Wave 5 = 38% Waves 1-3
95.31: Wave 5 = 100% Wave 1
95.11: Wave 5 = 162% Wave 4

Bonds made the Wave 5:5 low at 96.01 on Nov. 11, a direct hit of the coincidence of projected time and price for a high probability trend reversal. The pattern couldn't have been more perfect. It was an almost ideal five wave decline from the Oct. 1993 high. Wave 5 that began with the Aug. 2 high sub-divided into an ideal five wave structure.

The implications of identifying a completed five wave decline are significant for traders and investors: The subsequent rally should exceed in time and price all rallies since the Oct. 1993 high, offering a major opportunity for long position trades and investments.

Time and Price Into The Bond Top Of Jan. 4, 1996

Bonds rallied relentlessly from the wave five low of Nov. 11, 1994. In fact, they rallied beyond what was anticipated for a typical corrective rally to a five wave bear trend. However, when the top came, it was made on a direct hit of time projections for a top even though the price target was not as right on.

From the Aug. 15, 1995, wave B low, the TRZ projection for a top was the relatively broad period of Dec. 17-March 12. For further explanation of this TRZ, see the Time Rhythm Zone section which used this projection as an example. The Dynamic Time Projections pointed to two periods in Dec. and Jan. that had a high probability of making a trend change. These periods were Dec. 1-2 and Jan. 2-6. The Jan. 2-6 period overlapped with the TRZ period providing a high probability period for trend change.

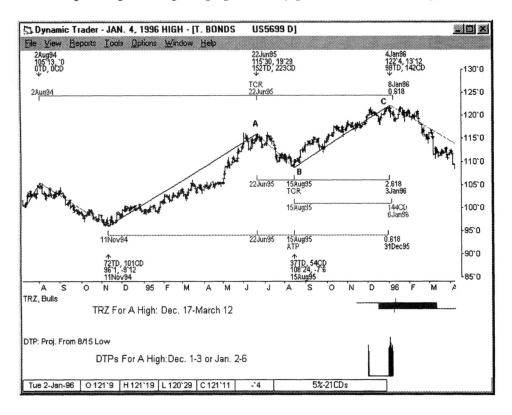

The chart above illustrates three of the TCRs that fell near the Jan. 2-6 PTPP for a top as well as the 144 calendar day count from the Aug. 15 low. Bonds made the final high on Jan. 4, directly within the coincidence of the PTPP for a top (Jan. 2-6) and the TRZ for a top (Dec. 17-March 12).

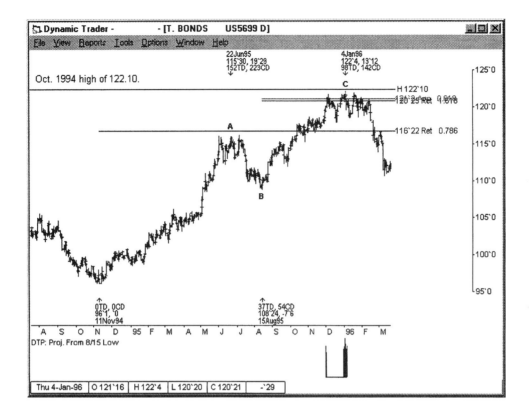

Typically, a *corrective* rally does not exceed a 78.6% retracement. Many end right at 78.6%. The June-July triple tops were made just below the 78.6% retracement. However, bonds subsequently continued to rally to new highs.

When the June-July highs were exceeded, new price projections for a top were made. Bonds made another triple top in Dec.-Jan. at the coincidence of the 62% Alternate Price Projection and 162% Price Retracement of Wave B. These two projections fell just below the Oct. 1994 high at 122.10. Unfortunately, the choppy pattern of the rally did not provide a wide variety of swings to make projections from. When high confidence price projections are not available, traders rely on pattern and time projections to signal the position of the market. In this case, the time projections accurately signaled the exact day of the high.

Price Projections At Jan. 4 Top

120.23: Wave C = 162% Wave B
121.02: Wave C = 61.8% Wave A

See the previous page for the time projections. *Note that the Jan. 4 top was made where Wave C equaled 61.8% of both the price <u>and</u> time of Wave A!*

Dynamic Time Analysis - An Important Key To Trading Success

Consistently reliable time analysis is a very important factor to the success of Dynamic Traders. If you will include Dynamic Time Projections and Time Rhythm Zone time analysis into your technical analysis trading plan, you should find immediate and significant results.

Chapter 6

Trade Strategies and Trade Management

It is not too difficult to make money in commodity trading.
The problem is to keep it.

Roy W. Longstreet

In the *Trade Strategies and Trade Management* chapter you

• Learn low-risk and low-capital exposure trade entry strategies including trend-reversal and trend-continuation entry techniques.

• Learn how and where to place the initial protective stop-loss on a position and strategies to adjust the stop-loss as a market progresses.

• Learn about short, intermediate and long term positions

• Learn how and when to take profits.

• Learn how to keep a trading log.

• Learn how to develop a trading plan.

Trading Strategies

There are many entry strategies available to enter a market. I suggest traders stick to the simple trend-reversal and trend-continuation strategies that have the highest probability of resulting in a profitable trade with the minimum amount of capital exposure. The following pages describe these entry strategies and the initial protective stop-loss placement. First, let's review what we are trying to accomplish and the basic assumptions for Dynamic Trading strategies.

1   *The objective of Dynamic Trading technical analysis is to identify opportunities <u>within the context of the analysis methods</u>*. The technical analysis methods will not accurately describe the position of every market, all of the time. That is not the purpose of technical analysis. The purpose of technical analysis is to identify markets that are in a position to allow a trade with relatively low risk and acceptable capital exposure.

2.   *Loss control or identifying the protective stop-loss level is the most important factor in trading*. It is the only factor that the trader has control over. The potential profit of any trade is always no more than guess work and can never be defined. I always get a kick out of trading, educational material that teaches a trade should not be taken unless there is a "3-to-1 risk/reward ratio." When ever you see this, you know the person probably has no successful trading experience. First of all, risk is the probability of an event occurring. It has absolutely nothing to do with a dollar amount. More importantly, you can never define the potential profit. You can only define the potential capital exposure by where the protective stop-loss is placed. This is not even a sure thing given a market can gap against you, beyond the stop-loss price.

3.   *The protective stop-loss level must always be determined within the context of the same methodology that determined the trade opportunity*. The same information that describes a trade opportunity must provide the exact market activity that voids that opportunity.

4.   *The protective stop-loss level must always be determined before a trade entry is initiated*. Before initiating a trade ask yourself: *"What is the market activity that invalidates the decision to make this trade."* That is your protective stop-loss.

   Once the protective stop-loss level is determined, the price level that is acceptable for a trade entry is precisely defined within the amount allowed for capital exposure on any one trade. If the market activity does not allow trade entry within the acceptable parameters for capital exposure, the trade cannot be initiated. For example, consider the following situation:

A. Your trading plan allows a maximum capital exposure on a gold trade of $500 per contract.

B. One of the entry strategies of your trading plan allows trade entries on the close of a daily reversal signal <u>and</u> the protective stop-loss must be placed one tick beyond the extreme of the daily reversal signal.

C. The technical analysis indicates that gold is approaching a target for major low.

D. Gold makes a wide-range *key reversal day* with a low at $370 and a close at $377.

E. According to the trading plan which allows a maximum $500 capital exposure per contract on a gold trade, the protective stop loss can be placed no lower than $372 which is $500 from the entry price at the close of $377. However, the trading plan also states that the protective stop-loss can be placed no nearer the close-only entry price than one tick beyond the daily extreme which is at $370 or at $369.9 which would be a $710 capital exposure.

F. What is the trading action in this case? *None!* A trader must follow his or her trading plan. The trade entry strategies require the stop to be placed outside the acceptable maximum capital exposure allowed, so the trader cannot take this trade on the close of the reversal day. The trader would have to wait for a set-up, such as a trend-continuation trade entry, where the capital exposure is within the limits of the trading plan.

5. *Generally, the Protective Stop Loss (PSL) on the initial trend-reversal trade entry should not be adjusted until the market activity has confirmed the trend reversal.* If a trade is entered at or near a suspected trend reversal, traders should not be too quick to bring the protective stop loss (PSL) close to the market. The PSL is adjusted each time the technical analysis describes a price level that should not be exceeded if the trend is to continue.

Consider this example:

A. Your analysis indicates that the market has made a bear market low, has reversed trend and is in the initial stages of a new bull trend.

B. Bull trends are described by a market making higher swing highs and higher swing lows.

C. Once the market exceeds the initial swing high, it must not exceed the prior swing low if it is in a new bull trend.

D. The *maximum* price level for the protective sell-stop for a long trade would be placed just below the prior swing low. It may be placed much closer, but this is the maximum protective stop-loss level.

E. This is a simple example of how to *think* in terms of protective stop-loss placement. The question to ask each day is: *"At what point will the market demonstrate within the context of my analysis techniques that it will not continue to trend in the trade direction."* That is always the *maximum* level where a protective stop loss is placed.

6. *There is more than one protective stop-loss technique that is a part of a trading plan.* The stop-loss technique implemented at any one time will depend on the position of the market relative to the analysis methods. The PSL technique in the initial stages of a trend should be different than in the latter stages of a trend. Dynamic Trading analysis will signal what stage the trend is in.

7. *Let the market take you out of a trade.* It is usually best to let the market stop out the trade rather than to take a profit at a price objective. If a market reaches a price objective or the analysis indicates that a trend is at or near completion, the protective stop-loss can be moved very close to the market such as just below the prior day's low or high or on any day a market closes below the open, etc. This prevents a trader from exiting a trade where the market may continue the trend beyond expectations, but still allows only a small amount of the unrealized profit to be given up if stopped out.

   The amount that will be gained by remaining in a market that continues to trend beyond expectations will more than offset the amount of potential profit that is given up in those cases where the market takes you out of the trade with less profit than may have been gained if exiting at a price objective. Allowing the market to take you out of a trade is dealing with things as they are. Taking a profit at an objective is speculating on the future when it is not necessary to do so.

   The exception to this plan is with multiple position trading. One position may be exited at a profit objective while the balance are not.

8. *Always consider if the protective stop-loss should also be a trigger to reverse position, in other words, a stop-and-reverse order.* Does the analysis indicate that if the protective stop-loss is hit, that the trend will continue in the opposite direction? This is often the case. Unfortunately, traders often become personally involved in their trading decision and find it very difficult to reverse position at some of

the most opportune times. Always remember: The business is trading, not predicting the future. The objective is to go with the market flow, not be right in any one particular trade. A stop-and-reverse order is only considered if the same order that is the stop-loss would also be a trade-entry order.

Entry Strategies and Initial Protective Stop-Loss Placement

The two types of entry strategies depending on the current market position are *trend-reversal* and *trend-continuation* strategies. Several of these entry strategies will be described in this section along with their initial protective stop-loss placement.

1. *The main concept for the initial protective stop-loss placement is as follows:* The same analytical methods and trading strategies that signal a trade entry opportunity must also signal if the analysis or entry strategy was invalid. The protective stop-loss is initially placed where the entry strategy is invalidated.

   The objective of the initial stop-loss placement is to immediately exit the position with a relatively small loss if the entry strategy or analysis is invalidated. Remember, the overriding requirement for long-term trading success is *capital preservation*. If capital is needlessly reduced by remaining in losing trades beyond the invalidation signal, capital will be less available for the trade signals that result in the profits necessary to remain in business.

   If the market moves in the anticipated direction following the trade-entry, the next objective is to remain in the trade for the majority of the trend.

2. *The main concept for the protective stop-loss adjustment as a trend progresses is as follows:* The protective stop-loss is kept relatively far from the current market activity in the initial stages of the trend until the new trend direction is confirmed. The protective stop-loss is brought relatively close to the market when the technical analysis signals that the market is near a position to complete the trend.

   In other words, different protective stop-loss strategies are used depending on the position of the market.

Trend-Reversal Entry Triggers

Trend-reversal entry strategies are designed to buy at or very near the bottom and sell at or very near the top. Most academic trading advisors and educators regurgitate the often repeated trading "rule" to never try to buy the bottom or sell the top. That is because their technical analysis studies are always lagging indicators. They do not have methods that project in advance the time and price zones for trend reversal and the pattern studies that signal trend termination.

Dynamic Traders are usually prepared in advance for the high-probability, specific time and price zones for trend reversal. Dynamic Traders are often able to buy the bottom and sell the top with very low capital exposure.

There are three reversal patterns that have a high probability of forming a pivot high or low if made at a time and/or price target. These are Reversal Day (RD), Signal Day (SD) and Snap-Back Reversal Day (SBRD). These will be described relative to an established bull trend and a short position trade-entry. Just substitute high for low, etc. for long position examples. The descriptive examples are daily bars. They may also be applied to intraday bars.

Reversal Day (RD) Entry Signal

A *reversal-day* top is made when a market makes a new daily high but closes below the prior day's close and the current day's open. The trend to new highs is not able to be sustained by the close of the day. Variations on the reversal day are the *key-reversal-day, outside-reversal- day* and *outside-key-reversal-day.*

> **Key Reversal Day (KRD):** The market opens below the prior day's close, makes a new high, but closes below the prior day's close and the current day's open. A KRD is a stronger reversal signal than a RD.
>
> **Outside Reversal and Key Reversal Day (OSRD, OSKRD):** These reversal days meet the criteria of a *reversal day* and are also an *outside day.* OSRDs are an even stronger reversal signal than a reversal day and an OSKRD is a stronger signal, yet.

Initial Protective Stop Loss: One tick above the high of the RD.

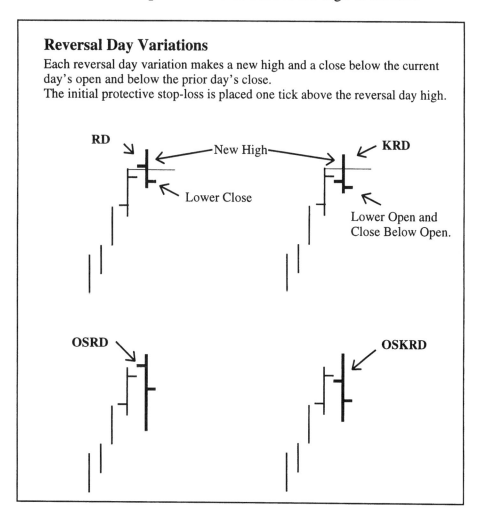

Reversal Day Variations

Each reversal day variation makes a new high and a close below the current day's open and below the prior day's close.
The initial protective stop-loss is placed one tick above the reversal day high.

Signal Day (SD) Entry Signal

The market opens above the prior day's close, makes a new high and the close is below the current day's open. The open must be in the top 1/3 of the daily range and the close must be in the bottom 1/3 to qualify as a valid *signal day*. Unlike a *reversal day*, the *signal day* close does not have to be below the prior day's close, only below the current day's open.

Gap Signal Day (GSD): A very strong daily reversal signal. The entire daily range of the *signal day* is above the prior day's range which leaves a gap at the end of the day. Analysts and traders who only consider closing prices would view a GSD reversal as a positive day because the market closed up.

Initial Protective Stop Loss: One tick above the high of the SD.

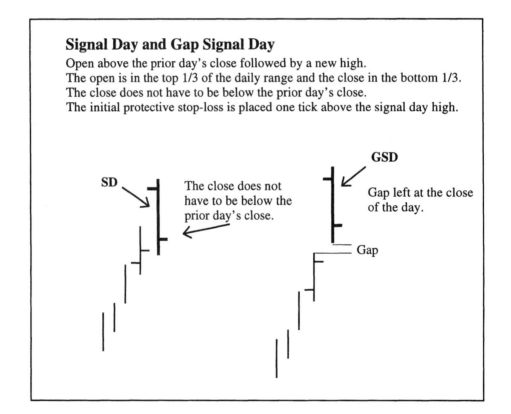

Signal Day and Gap Signal Day
Open above the prior day's close followed by a new high.
The open is in the top 1/3 of the daily range and the close in the bottom 1/3.
The close does not have to be below the prior day's close.
The initial protective stop-loss is placed one tick above the signal day high.

GSD

SD

The close does not have to be below the prior day's close.

Gap left at the close of the day.

Gap

Snap-Back Reversal Day (SBRD) Entry Signal

A two-day reversal signal.

<u>Day One</u>: The market makes a new high with an open in the lower 1/3 of the daily range and the high in the top 1/3 of the daily range. It appears to be a very bullish day.

<u>Day Two (snap-back day)</u>: The open is in the top 1/3 of the daily range and the close in the bottom 1/3 of the daily range. The second day does not have to reach new highs or lows compared to Day One. The wider the range of each day, the stronger the signal. A stronger SBRD would result if the second day's open was below the prior day's close with a new daily low and a close below the prior day's low.

Initial Protective Stop Loss: One tick above the higher of the two days.

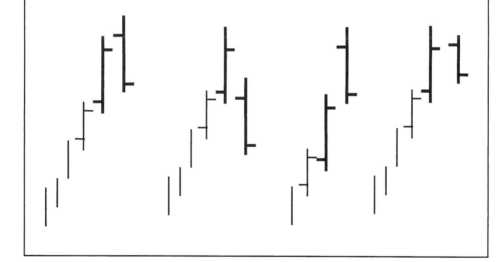

Snap Back Reversal Days (SBRD)

Day 1: New high and open in the lower 1/3 of the daily range and close in the upper 1/3.

Day 2: Open in the upper 1/3 of the daily range and close in the lower 1/3. The two days may be in any position to each other.

The initial protective stop-loss is placed one tick above the higher high of the two days.

Trend Reversal Signals Only Valid At Time, Price and Pattern Reversal Set-ups

These daily reversal signals are only valid as trend reversal signals when the technical analysis indicates the market is in a position for trend reversal. Ideally, time, price and pattern projections are all in a position for a trend reversal set-up. In other words, a daily reversal signal is only considered as a trade-entry trigger at the coincidence of a time and price objective for a reversal and at the completion of a trend-termination pattern such as wave 5 or wave C.

These daily reversal signals will frequently occur in a trending market and not result in trend change unless the market is in a time and price position for a trend change. Many studies have been done on the validity of trend change following daily reversal signals. All of those studies concluded that they were not reliable indicators of trend change. None of these studies have considered the position of the market when the reversal signal was made. If the market is not approaching a set-up for trend change, these daily reversal signals should be ignored.

For most markets, one of these three daily reversal signals will occur at 70%-80% of trend reversals of all degrees. *These three reversal signals are not triggered until the close of the day, as the signal is based on the position of the close.* If a market is trending up and makes a new high for the day, the criteria necessary for a *reversal day* is known - the prior day's high, today's open and today's high. The definition of a *reversal day* includes a close below the current day's open and prior day's close. A Stop-Close-Only (SCO) order may be entered at a price just below the lower of the prior day's close or the current day's open. If the market closes below the prior day's close and current day's open after having made a new high, it is a *reversal day.*

In the case of a *signal day* or *snap back reversal day,* we do not know if one of these signals will occur until near the close when we know the current day's range. If all of the criteria except the close has been met for one of these days, we wait until 5-10 minutes before the close and place the appropriate SCO order at a price that must be met on the close in order to satisfy the requirements for either of these reversal signals. If a trader is not able to collect the open and range price information, the entry may be made on the open of the following day.

Initial Protective Stop For Trend Reversal Entries

Where is the Protective Buy Stop (PBS) or Sell Stop (PSS) placed if one of these three daily reversal signals occurs? In the case of one of the *reversal days* or a *signal day*, the protective buy stop for a short sale is placed one tick above the high of the day as each of these signals involves having made a new high. If these are to result in a valid daily reversal signal, the high should not be exceeded. If the high is exceeded, it is no longer a valid daily reversal signal, and you want to immediately be out of the market and wait for the next trade set-up and reversal signal. In the case of a *snap back reversal day*, the stop-loss is placed one tick above the higher of the high of day one or day two.

One of these three daily reversal signals will not always occur at a trend reversal or the ideal coincidence of time, price and pattern. The trader has one of two choices in this case:

1. Do not take the trade at the time, price and pattern set-up unless one of these three reversal signals is made. You may miss entering trades at some important tops and bottoms, but, so what? If the conditions were not all in your favor at the trend reversal, a trade is not warranted. If you limit your entry trigger to one of these three signals, you may have fewer trades, but you should have a higher percentage of wining trades than if you broadened your acceptable entry techniques.

   Trading junkies may not like this recommendation, but their objective is not to maximize profits but to always be in the market regardless of the consequences. If your objective is to maximize profits, you will only enter with reliable signals that you have proven to yourself are valid. Remember, there is always another trade set-up approaching that will meet all of the criteria of your trading plan, whatever that criteria may be.

2. Include entry techniques other than these three trend-reversal signals. It is not necessary to enter a trade at the trend reversal. Other trading techniques provide entry strategies after a trend reversal has unfolded.

There are other entry techniques that may be considered at trend reversal projections. One of these is the Reversal Confirmation Day discussed next. The most important factor is to allow the market to provide at least some minor indication of the new trend direction.

Reversal-Confirmation Day (RCD) Entry Signal

Technically, the daily *reversal-confirmation* signal is not a trend-reversal signal. Because it is usually made within one-three days of the actual pivot high or low, I have included it with the trend-reversal signals and not the trend-continuation signals. The reversal confirmation signal is used if the market is suspected of having reversed at a projected trend-reversal zone but one of the three trend-reversal signals described above were not made at the pivot high or low. The description of the reversal-confirmation signal assumes the market has made a pivot high and the objective is to initiate a short position.

Reversal-Confirmation Day Entry Rules

1. A trend reversal is suspected of having taken place, but one of the three trend-reversal patterns were not made.

2. Sell on the close if the close is below the current day's open and prior day's close.

This is a minor trend-confirmation signal that does not have all of the special conditions of the three reversal signals described above. It does not consider the relationship of the daily range of the entry day, but does consider two important factors. The close below the prior day's close and current day's open shows at least a minor degree of trend direction.

A more reliable signal is to add the qualifier that the low of entry day must exceed the prior day's low. In other words, sell on the close if the market has exceeded the prior day's low and the close is below the current day's open and the prior day's close.

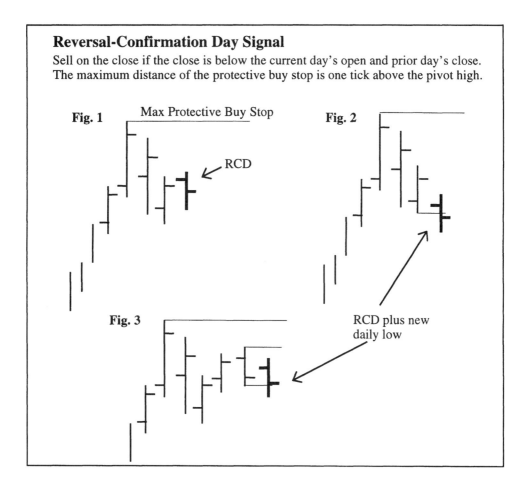

Reversal-Confirmation Day Signal

Sell on the close if the close is below the current day's open and prior day's close. The maximum distance of the protective buy stop is one tick above the pivot high.

In *figure 1* above, the pivot high was not made on one of the three daily reversal signals. While the first two days following the pivot high made lower closes and lower lows, each of these days closed above the open. The third day after the pivot high was a RCD where the market closed below the current day's open and prior day's close.

In *figure 2* above, the first two days following the high are the same as in figure 1. Day three is a RCD. The close was below the current day's open and prior day's close *plus* the day exceeded the prior day's low. This is a stronger trend direction signal, but also usually results in the protective stop-loss being further from the closing entry signal. There is usually a trade-off with any new qualification for an entry signal. In this case, the signal has a higher probability of being correct, but the initial capital exposure is usually greater.

In *figure 3*, day four following the high is a reversal-confirmation day while the fifth day is a RCD with a new low.

What is the logical protective stop placement for entries following a RCD signal? The market activity that would invalidate the outlook that a trend reversal has been made is if the market exceeds the pivot that is considered the trend reversal extreme. In other words, the protective stop-loss is placed *no further* than one tick beyond the last pivot. The only inviolate rule for stop loss placement with a RCD entry is the *maximum* stop-loss position, one tick beyond the pivot extreme. There may be a logical place to place the protective stop-loss that is closer than the pivot extreme. In the case of figure 3 above, the protective stop-loss may be placed above the minor swing high prior to the RCD entry signal.

Because a market may have moved away from the pivot price before making a RCD signal, the capital exposure on trade entries made on a RCD signal will often be more than if a daily reversal signal were made.

All traders must have a maximum acceptable capital exposure amount for any one trade that must be part of their trading plan. If the trade entry/protective stop-loss strategy calls for more capital exposure than acceptable to the trading plan, the trade simply cannot be taken.

The charts on the following pages illustrate many of these reversal signals at trend reversals. The purpose of the charts is only to point out the reversal patterns at highs and lows, not the reversal patterns that occurred within the trend. As you will see, almost every top or bottom was made on one of the three trend-reversal signals. If a trend reversal was not made on one of the three reversal patterns, a reversal-confirmation day followed the high or low within three days and only a few points away from the pivot high or low.

Trend-Reversal Entry Signals

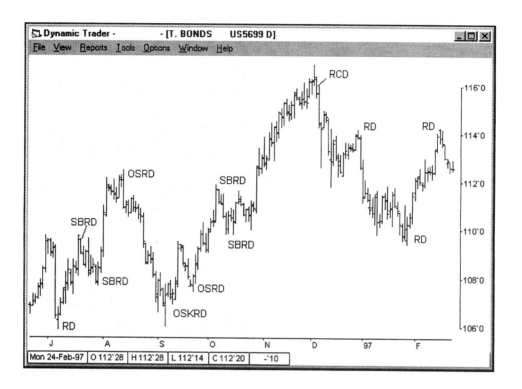

Almost every minor and intermediate degree trend change was made on one of the three trend-reversal signals. The high in early Dec. was not made on one of the three reversal signals but a reversal-confirmation day was made the day after the extreme high.

If you scan the chart day-by-day, you will find many of these daily reversal patterns that were not followed by a change in trend. The three trend-reversal patterns are not considered reversal signals unless the dynamic technical analysis signals a trend is at or near completion.

The reversal-confirmation-day entry-strategy is used if a market has reached a time and price zone anticipated for a trend change and a trend-reversal signal is not made. The reversal-confirmation signal will provide at least a minor confirmation a pivot has been made and allow the trader to enter with relatively small capital exposure.

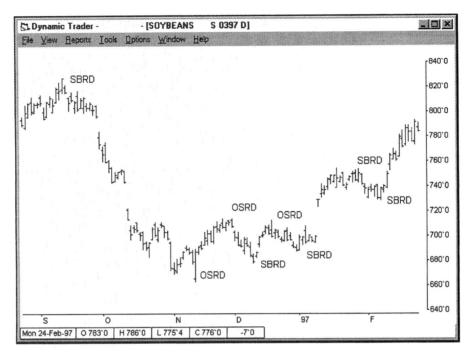

Eight out of eight trend changes in soybeans shown above were either Snap-Back-Reversal-Days (SBRD) or Outside-Reversal-Days (OSRD).

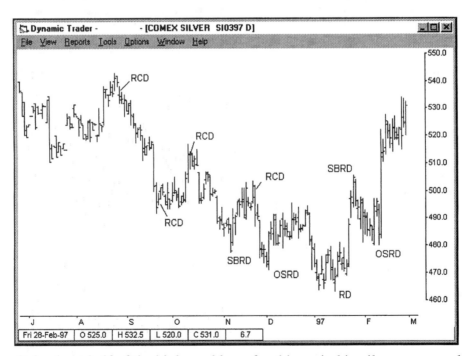

Only about half of the highs and lows for this period in silver were made on one of the three trend-reversal signals. A reversal-confirmation-day (RCD) was made within three days of the other pivots.

The two charts below show either one of the three trend-reversal signals at each pivot high or low or a reversal-confirmation-day within two days of the pivot.

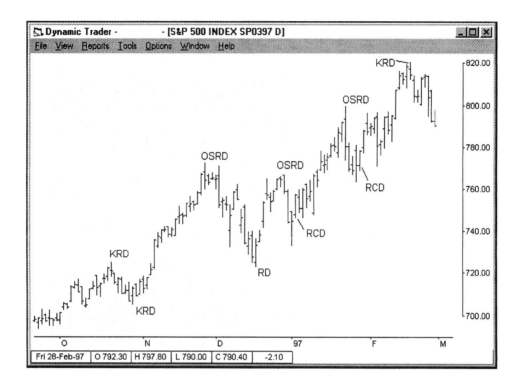

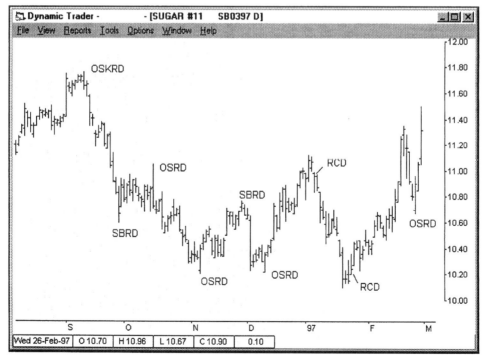

Trend-Continuation Entry Strategies

Many traders are under the illusion that trades cannot be entered with an acceptable capital exposure after the new trend is established. Of course this is not the case. While the trend-reversal entry strategies are designed to buy the bottom and sell the top, we must also have trading strategies that allow us to enter after the new trend is confirmed. Trend-continuation entry strategies do just that.

It is important to keep in mind that we are trading against a pivot reversal. The Dynamic Trading analysis factors of time, price and pattern are each designed to identify trend reversals as well as the probable extent in time and price of the new trend. There are several entry strategies with low-risk and low-capital exposure to use after the new trend is established.

Inside-Day Trade Set-ups

An *inside-day* is a day when the high of the day is lower than the high of the previous day and the low of the day is higher than the low of the previous day. In other words, the price range of an inside-day is *within* the price range of the previous day.

An inside-day is a day of indecision. It is a day when traders do not have a strong conviction as to the trend of the market. An inside-day often occurs after a wide-range day when the range exceeded the average range of the prior few days. Inside-days also often occur either after a trend-reversal when traders have not yet made the decision that the trend has reversed or after a fast move and represents a brief period when traders are catching their breath, so to speak.

Usually, the direction of the breakout from the inside-day is the direction that the trend will continue. Even more reliable, the direction of the breakout of the day *prior* to the inside-day is the direction that the trend will continue.

Because no single entry strategy is foolproof, each trading strategy must provide the trigger that tells us that the market is not going to go our way. In other words, the stop-loss strategy associated with a particular entry strategy must be formulated within the same context of market activity as the entry strategy. Traders must always keep in mind: *All market analysis and trading strategies are a matter of probabilities. Losses are inevitable and a cost of doing business. The trading plan must provide a stop-loss approach that minimizes losses when they occur.*

Inside-Day Trade Entry Set-Up Rules

1. Only enter in the direction of the trend. What is the direction of the trend? Against the last pivot reversal considered the beginning of the new trend as suggested by the time, price and pattern dynamic trading analysis.

2. To enter a long position, as long as the low of the day <u>prior</u> to the inside-day has not been exceeded, on the day <u>following</u> the inside-day, buy at one tick above the high of the day <u>prior</u> to the inside-day.

3. Place the initial protective sell stop one tick below the <u>lower</u> of the low of the inside-day or the low of the entry day.

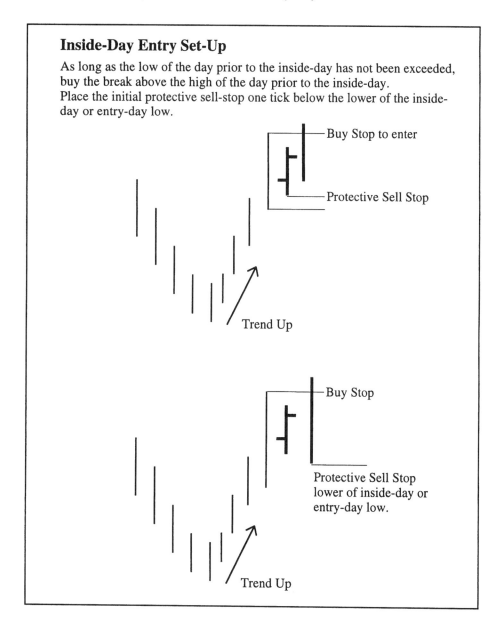

Inside-Day Entry Set-Up

As long as the low of the day prior to the inside-day has not been exceeded, buy the break above the high of the day prior to the inside-day.
Place the initial protective sell-stop one tick below the lower of the inside-day or entry-day low.

Buy Stop to enter

Protective Sell Stop

Trend Up

Buy Stop

Protective Sell Stop lower of inside-day or entry-day low.

Trend Up

Inside-Day Entry Strategy

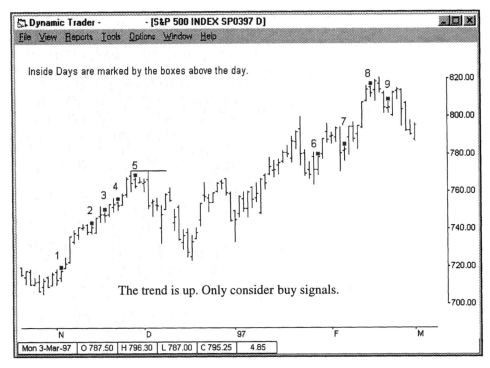

All of the inside-days (ISD) for the period shown for the S&P are marked by the software program with a small solid box above the inside-day. For these examples, we are considering the inside-days out of the context of any technical analysis and trend position. We will assume the technical analysis signals the trend is up throughout this period and only buy-signals would be considered.

ISDs #1-4: Each of these four inside-days were ideal trend-continuation trade set-ups. In each of these four set-ups, the day following the inside-day exceeded the high of the day preceding the inside-day and provided a buy signal.

ISD #5: A long trade was not elected as the high of the day prior to the inside-day was not exceeded prior to the sharp decline.

ISDs #6 and 7: Each were ideal trend-continuation trade set-ups where the trend continued higher.

ISD #8: The day following ISD #8 exceeded the low of the ISD but not the low of the day prior to the inside-day. A long trade was elected with the initial protective sell-stop one tick below the entry-day low.

ISD #9: The day following ISD #9 opened below the day prior to the inside-day voiding a buy entry signal.

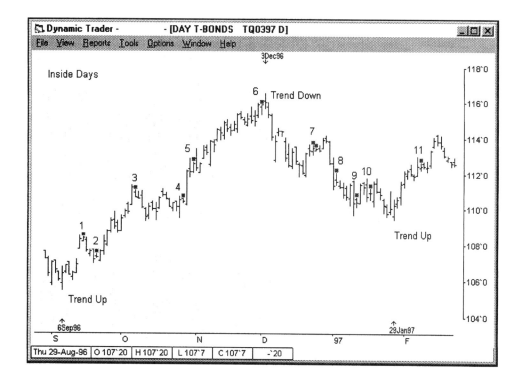

Assume the Dynamic Trading analysis signaled the trend was up from the Sept. 6 low, down from the Dec. 3 high and up again from the Jan. 29 low. Which inside-days would have been followed by a trade entry? Which would have been stopped out with a small loss?

Trend Up From Sept. 6 - Only Long Trades Considered

#1: No trade entry. The day following the inside-day did not exceed the high of the day preceding the inside-day.

#2: No trade entry. The day following the inside-day did not exceed the high of the day preceding the inside-day. However, as we will see in the next section, the day following the inside-day was an outside-day entry set-up.

#3: No trade entry.

#4: An ideal trade entry. The bullish trend continued without stopping out the inside-day entry strategy.

#5: Another successful trade entry. The trend continued up.

#6: The trade would have been stopped out on the second day following the inside-day. If the market was at or approaching a time and price target for a trend-reversal top in late Nov.-early Dec., the trade would not be taken.

Trend Down From Dec. 3 - Only Short Trades Considered

#7: Two consecutive inside-days. A short trade was not triggered.

#8: A short trade was not triggered. The day following the inside-day did not exceed the low of the day preceding the inside-day.

#9: No short trade was triggered.

#10: A short trade was triggered and stopped out the same day for a small loss.

Trend Up From Jan. 29 - Only Long Trades Considered

#11: A long trade was not triggered.

There were twelve inside-days during this five month period for bonds. Four inside-day trade set-ups were triggered. Two were profitable entry strategies as a consistent bull trend continued after the long position entries. Two were small losses.

While inside-days occur frequently, a trade was not triggered following each inside-day. Whether a trade is triggered depends on the trend direction and the price range following the inside-day.

In several of the cases with these two charts, the day following the inside-day did not exceed the range of the day preceding the inside-day and a trade was not triggered. The rules could be expanded to include a breakout in the trend direction of the day prior to the inside day at any time following the inside-day. If this rule were added, trade entries for the bond period shown above following ISDs numbers 2, 8 and 11 would have been successful entries.

Why haven't I broadened the rules to include a breakout of the range of the day prior to the inside-day at any time following the inside-day? Because I haven't thoroughly tested this broader rule on a wide variety of markets, and I only want to present to you those strategies that have been thoroughly tested which have the highest probability of success.

Outside-Day Trade Set-Ups

An *outside-day* is a period of range expansion. A market usually continues in the direction of the close of an outside-day. The outside-day entry set-up requires the market to be monitored during the day.

Outside-Day Trade Set-Up Entry Rules

1. Only enter in the direction of the trend.
2. For a buy set-up, if the market first exceeds the low of the prior day without having exceeded the high of the prior day, buy one tick above the high of the prior day.
3. Place the initial protective sell-stop one tick below the low of the entry day up to the time the trade is entered.
4. Exit the position on the close if the close is below the current day's open and prior day's close. The failure of the close to be in the anticipated trend direction is a negative signal and reason to exit the trade.

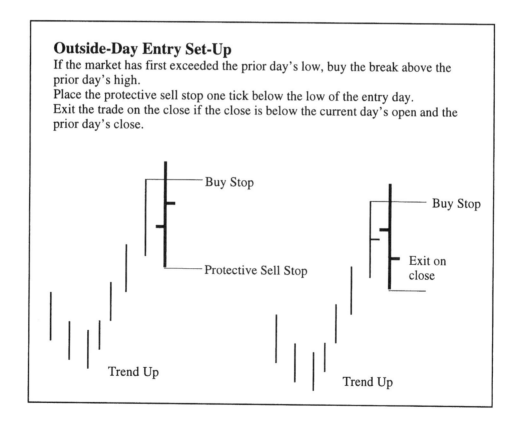

Outside-Day Entry Set-Up
If the market has first exceeded the prior day's low, buy the break above the prior day's high.
Place the protective sell stop one tick below the low of the entry day.
Exit the trade on the close if the close is below the current day's open and the prior day's close.

Outside-Day Plus Entry Strategy (OSD+)

The outside-day entry strategy described above requires the market to be monitored during the day. If this is not possible, enter on the break of the outside-day the following day if the break is in the direction of the trend. Also use this entry strategy even if the outside-day entry was exited on the close. Maintain the buy order until the market has broken out of the range of the outside-day.

Outside-Day Plus Entry Rules

1. Only trade in the direction of the trend.
2. For a bull trend, place a buy-stop one tick above the high of the outside-day. Maintain the buy-stop until the price range of the outside day is exceeded.
3. Place the initial protective sell-stop one tick below the low of the outside-day.

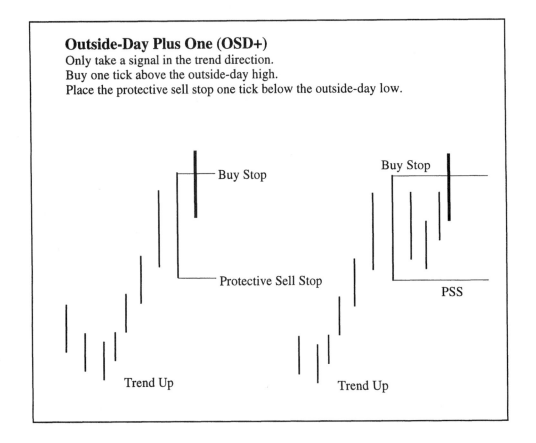

Outside-Day Plus One (OSD+)
Only take a signal in the trend direction.
Buy one tick above the outside-day high.
Place the protective sell stop one tick below the outside-day low.

Outside-Day Entry Strategies

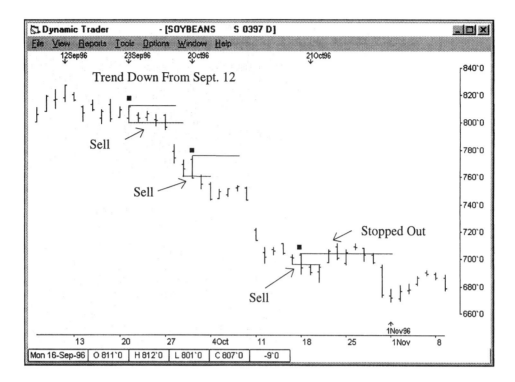

Trend Down - Only Consider Short Entries

Each outside-day for this period is marked by a the solid box above the day. A bear trend began Sept. 12. Only short position trade set-ups are considered. For short position set-ups, the high of the previous day must be exceeded during the day before the sell-stop below the previous day may be made.

Sept. 23: An outside-day was made, but the open was below the low of the prior day. A sell order was not considered as the low of the previous day was exceeded before the high. An *OSD+* may be possible the following day. As long as the high of the outside-day is not exceeded, maintain a sell-stop one tick below the low of the outside-day. Three days later, the sell order is elected. The protective buy-stop is placed one tick above the high of the outside day. It was never elected as the trend continued down.

Oct. 2: The open is above the prior day's high. Place the sell-stop one tick below the prior day's low. The sell order is elected later in the day. The close is below the current day's open and prior day's close. The protective buy-stop is placed one tick above the Oct. 2 high. Traders who didn't enter short on Oct. 2 may place a sell-stop one tick below the low of the outside day for an *OSD+1* sell strategy. This would have been elected the following day.

Oct. 21: Beans opened one tick above the prior day's high. A sell-stop is placed one tick below the prior day's low. It is elected later in the day. The short trade is not exited at the close of the outside-day because the close is below the current day's open and prior day's close. The protective buy-stop is placed one tick above the high of the outside-day. The short position is stopped out three days later.

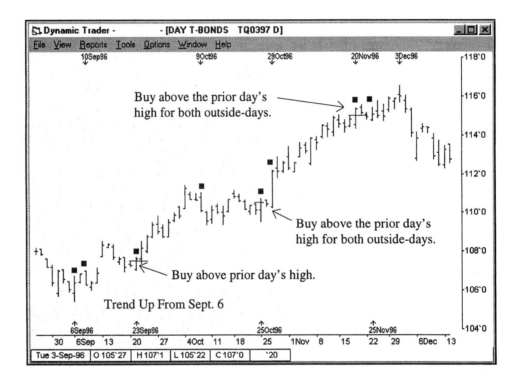

Trend Up - Only Consider Long Trade Entries

Sept. 6 was an outside-reversal-day which began the bull trend.

Sept. 10: Since the trend is up, only set-ups for long trades are considered. This outside-day did not meet the conditions for a long entry.

Sept. 23: Perfect outside-day entry set-up. Bonds opened below the prior day's low. Place a buy-stop one tick above the prior day's high. The buy-stop was elected later in the day and the close was above the current day's open and prior day's close. The protective sell-stop is placed one tick below the low of the outside-day. Bonds continued straight up.

Oct. 9: The set-up conditions for a long position were not made.

Oct. 25 and 29: These were both ideal outside-day trade set-ups for long positions. A buy was elected each of these days one tick above the high of the previous day.

Nov. 20 and 25: Both these days were also perfect outside-day trade set-ups for long positions. The protective sell-stops below the lows of the outside-days were not elected.

Of the seven outside-days during the Sept. 6 low - Dec. 3 high bull trend (9/6 reversal day not counted), five met the conditions for a long trade entry. Not one of the five was stopped out. The trend continued up in each case.

Outside Day Plus One: Each of the days above that made the outside-day trade entries also could have been entered on the day following the outside-day with the *OSD+1* entry strategy. The capital exposure would have been slightly higher for each of these entries as the buy price was slightly higher.

Outside-day trade entry strategies are very high probability with relatively low capital exposure. Like all trade entry strategies, they must be considered in the context of the trend direction and the position of the market within the trend. If the dynamic technical analysis is signaling a trend is near termination, new trade entries should not be considered except for very short-term trades of 1-3 days.

Gann Pull Back Trade Entry Set-Up (GPB)

The Gann Pull-Back entry strategy is based on W. D. Gann's observation that minor corrections in trending markets usually only last three days or so. This is a correct observation as anyone who has studied market trends is aware. The Gann Pull-Back trade set-up is designed to enter a trade on the *minor* corrections against the main trend.

<u>Gann Pull-Back Entry Rules</u>

1. Only enter in the direction of the trend.
2. For a sell set-up, the three most recent days must each have higher highs or any combination of two higher highs and an inside-day. Just the opposite for a buy set-up.
3. For a sell set-up, place a sell-stop one tick below the low of the prior day once the set-up conditions are met.
4. If the market makes a new high, adjust the sell-stop one tick below the low of the prior day.
5. Place the initial protective buy-stop one tick above the higher of the high of entry day or the day prior to entry.
6. Exit the position on the close of the entry day if the close is above the current day's open and the prior day's close.

Gann Pull-Back Trade Entry Set-Up

If the market has made at least a three day counter-trend, sell one tick below the prior day's low.

Place the initial protective buy-stop one tick above the high traded for the correction.

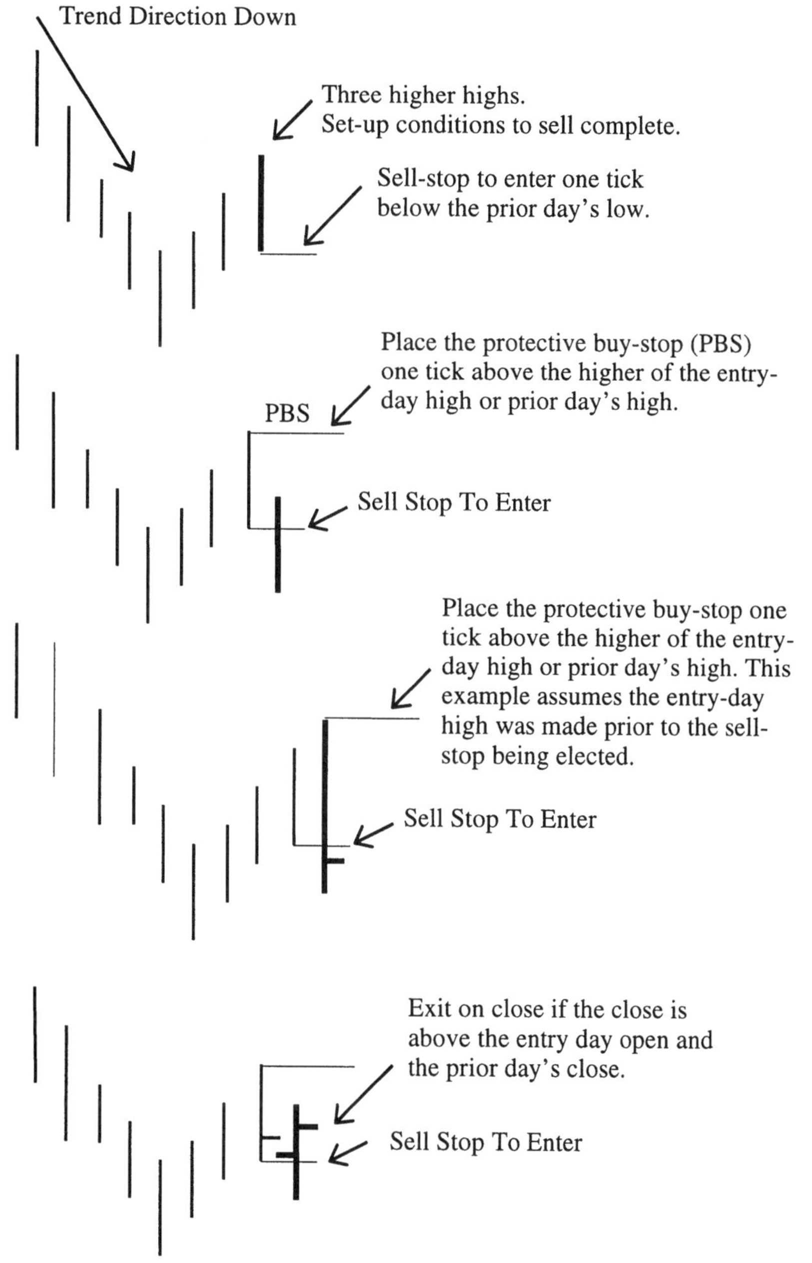

Trend Direction Down

Three higher highs.
Set-up conditions to sell complete.

Sell-stop to enter one tick below the prior day's low.

Place the protective buy-stop (PBS) one tick above the higher of the entry-day high or prior day's high.

PBS

Sell Stop To Enter

Place the protective buy-stop one tick above the higher of the entry-day high or prior day's high. This example assumes the entry-day high was made prior to the sell-stop being elected.

Sell Stop To Enter

Exit on close if the close is above the entry day open and the prior day's close.

Sell Stop To Enter

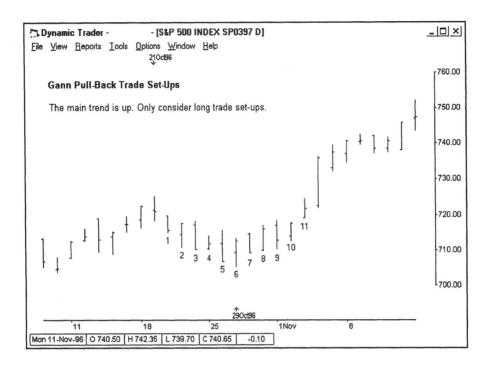

Trend Up - Only Consider Long Trade Set-ups

The S&P bull trend was well established in Oct. 1996. The Gann Pull-Back trade entry technique should only be used to initiate long positions. The days following the Oct. 21 high are numbered for reference.

Day 3: The set-up conditions have been met. The S&P had made three consecutive lower-lows on Day 3. A buy-stop is placed one tick above the Day 3 high.

Day 4: The buy-stop above the Day 3 high was not elected. A new low is made on Day 4. Adjust the buy-stop to one tick above the Day 4 high to enter a long position.

Day 5: The buy-stop was elected. The initial protective sell-stop is placed one tick below the low of Day 4. The low of Day 4 was one tick below the prior day's low. This protective sell-stop was hit later in the day for a small loss on the day. Because the market has made another consecutive, new low, a new buy-stop is placed one tick above the high of Day 5.

Day 6: A new low is made without electing the buy-stop one tick above the previous day's high.

Day 7: The buy-stop to enter a long position is adjusted to one tick above the Day 6 high. The buy-stop is elected. The trade is exited on the close for a loss as the close is below the current day's open and prior day's close.

The following day, the bull trend resumed. The Gann Pull-Back entry strategy has not placed the trader in a long position on the six day correction. The rule to exit the trade on the lower close on Day 7 took the trader out of a long position on the day prior to the resumption of the bull trend. Professional traders stick to the entry rules, even if the rules occasionally take you out of a trade.

Three days later on Day 10, the S&P made an inside-day trade set-up. The following day (Day 11) triggered a long position on the inside-day trade set-up and the S&P went straight up from there more than making up for the two small losses on the Gann Pull-Back trades.

I purposely chose an unsuccessful example first, so you would keep a firm grasp on reality and the principles of trading. Not all trading strategies are successful all of the time. The key is to follow the trading strategy rules which are designed to keep losses small. It is also important to have two or three trend-continuation entry strategies as part of the trading plan. When one fails, the other is likely to be successful.

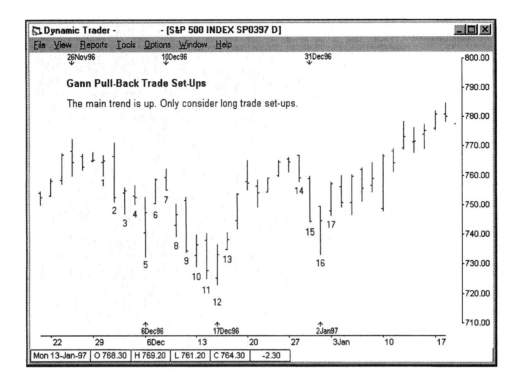

Trend Is Up - Only Consider Long Trade Set-Ups

The above chart shows the first correction that followed the Oct. 1996 correction on the previous chart. A high was made Nov. 26 followed by three days that traded within the range of Nov. 26. On the third trading day following the Nov. 26 high, the S&P made the first lower-low.

Day 3: The third lower-low. The set-up is complete. For a long trade entry on Day 4, place a buy-stop one tick above the Day 3 high.

Day 4: The buy-stop is elected to enter a long position. The initial protective sell-stop is placed one tick below the Day 3 low. However, the trade is exited on the close for a small loss. The close of entry day was below the current day's open and the prior day's close.

Day 5: At the end of Day 5, the set-up conditions of three lower-lows or two lower-lows and one inside-day are **not** met. The S&P has not made three **consecutively** lower-lows. The S&P rallies for two days (Days 6-7) followed by a resumption of the decline.

Day 10: A new set-up for a potential long trade is in place. The S&P has made three consecutively lower-lows at the completion of Day 10. A buy-stop to enter a long position is placed one tick above the Day 10 high.

Day 11: The buy-stop is elected as the Day 10 high is exceeded. The initial protective sell-stop is placed one tick below the Day 10 low. The sell-stop is elected later in the day for a loss. Even though the prior day's high was exceeded, the S&P is still making lower daily lows. A new buy-stop is placed one tick above the Day 11 high

Day 12: A new low is made and the buy-stop above the prior day's high is not reached. The buy-stop is adjusted to one tick above the Day 12 high.

Day 13: The buy-stop is elected for a long position. The initial protective sell-stop is placed one tick below the Day 12 low. The S&P rallies strongly. Within just a day or two, the gain from the long trade has more than off-set the losses from the first two attempts to position long. A minor high is made Dec. 31.

Day 16: The S&P has made three lower-lows for a Gann Pull-Back trade entry set-up. A buy-stop to enter a long position is placed one tick above the Day 16 high.

Day 17: The buy-stop is elected. The initial protective sell-stop is placed one tick below the Day 16 low. The bull trend continues to new highs.

As you can see from the set-ups and trades of these two charts, the Gann Pull-Back trade entry technique is designed to enter in the direction of the trend following minor corrections to the main trend. It may take two or three attempts to enter. The key is that unsuccessful trade entries only result in relatively small losses which should be quickly recovered by profits of the successful trade entry.

As with all trend-continuation entry techniques, it is critical to first determine the main trend direction and only take trades in the direction of the larger degree trend. It is also important to be alert if the Dynamic Trading analysis indicates a trend is nearing completion. If it appears to be nearing a zone with a high probability of completing the trend, trade entries should be avoided.

There are many other trend-reversal and trend-continuation entry strategies that are applicable to unique situations. Whole books have been written on short-term entry strategies such as Connor's and Raschke's *Street Smarts* and Cooper's *Hit and Run*, both of which are highly recommended. If incorporating other short-term entry strategies, keep in mind to only consider them within the context of the trend direction and market position.

Protective Stop-Loss Adjustment - Protecting Unrealized Profits

The prior sections described the initial trade-entry strategy and the initial stop-loss placement. If the trade-entry strategy is successful and the initial protective stop-loss is not elected prior to the trend continuing in the direction anticipated, the next objective is protecting the unrealized profits of the trade.

If a protective stop-loss is brought too close to the current position of the market, the trade may be stopped out on a short-term reaction prior to continuing the trend. If the protective stop-loss is kept too far from the current position of the market, a substantial portion of the unrealized profits may be "given back" if a trend reverses prior to an anticipated reversal.

While there is no perfect solution to this conundrum, Dynamic Trading analysis and trading strategies will help to limit losses and protect the majority of unrealized profits.

The Principles of Stop-Loss Placement

Dynamic Trading analysis methods help to identify how long in time and price a trend is likely to continue, the specific time and price zones with a high probability for trend reversal and the pattern that signals a trend termination.

1. The protective stop-loss should be kept relatively far from the current market position until the trend is confirmed.

2. The protective stop-loss should be brought relatively close to the market position when the Dynamic Trading analysis signals a trend has a high probability of terminating.

3. As a trend continues, traders must have a plan to adjust protective stops to either reduce the capital exposure for a loss or protect unrealized profits.

4. If a market approaches a set-up of projected time, price and pattern that signals the trend has a high probability of terminating, the protective stop-loss should be brought very close to the current market position.

There are many protective stop-loss strategies that may be utilized. The most effective and logical ones will be contingent on the market activity as it unfolds.

The initial protective stop strategies for trend reversal and trend continuation trade-entry have already been described. It is usually prudent to keep the initial stop away from the market in the initial stages of a trend until the market has confirmed that a new trend is underway. The initial stages of a trend can often be volatile with the market coming back to test the pivot extreme. What about when a trend is underway? How is the stop adjusted on a periodic basis as a market trend progresses?

Swing Stop-Loss

The simplest method for stop-loss placement is to place the protective stop-loss (PSL) just beyond the prior swing low or high. The definition of a bull market is the market that makes higher-highs and higher-lows. If the most recent low is exceeded, the bull trend is probably over. If the most recent high is exceeded, the trend is confirmed.

A strategy to adjust the protective stop-loss in a bull trend is to place it one tick below the prior swing low. As higher swing lows are made, the PSL is adjusted to the new low. Swing highs and lows must be objectively defined. What are the draw-backs to this simple but logical method of stop-loss placement?

1. In a strong trending market, price may move a great distance without making a new swing pivot. The PSL may remain a great distance from the current market position and a substantial unrealized profit may be greatly reduced before the PSL is elected.

2. If a market enters a prolonged, volatile trading range, the trader may be whipsawed to ruin prior to the trend getting underway. In the long run, net profits will only accrue from markets with large and consistent trends. Consistent losses will occur in trendless, choppy, trading-range markets. The relatively large profits that accrue from the major trends will often not overcome losses from high-volatility, trendless periods.

A swing high or low should only be considered as a *maximum* stop-loss position. The initial stages of a trend usually have larger reactions with greater volatility as the consensus of traders is not yet-one sided. In the latter stages of the trend, reactions against the trend are usually relatively short in price and time as the vast majority of traders are one-sided in their opinion of the market position.

Three-Day Low or High (3DL or H)

If a trend is valid, there should only be minor corrections to the trend. If you examine long histories of daily charts for many markets, you will find that once a trend is underway, the market will usually not retrace the range of the prior three days. The three-day high or low may be used to adjust the protective stop-loss as a market trend progresses.

A three-day low is the lowest price of the three days from the extreme high, inclusive of the high day. Inside-days are not counted. It is not the same as the low of the most recent three days.

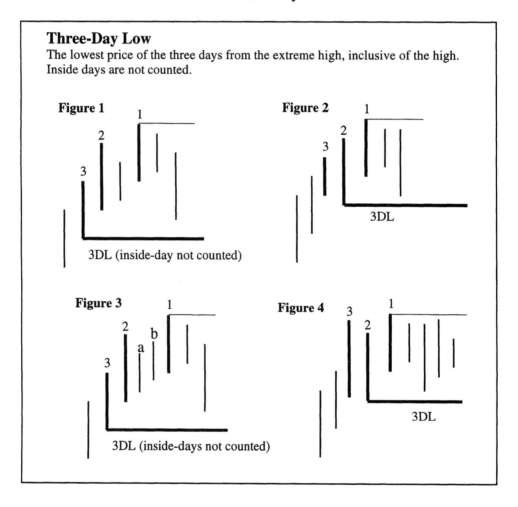

Three-Day Low
The lowest price of the three days from the extreme high, inclusive of the high. Inside days are not counted.

In the figures above, the three days used to determine the three-day low are labeled 1, 2 and 3. Day one is always the highest price of the immediate trend. In **figure one** above, the *inside-day* following day-two is not counted. In **figure two**, day-three is not an inside-day. In **figure three**, the two days following day-two both traded within the range of day-two. Neither day is counted for the 3DL. Day-a is an inside-day to day-two. While day-b is not normally considered an inside-day because it traded outside the range of the prior day, it did not trade outside the range of day two. The next day will not be counted until the range of day-two is exceeded. In **figure four**, the 3DL will not change until price moves outside the range of the high of day-one and the low of day-two. A three-day low is not the lowest price of the prior three days, but the lowest price of the three days from the extreme high inclusive of the high and exclusive of inside-days.

Adjusting Protective Stop-Losses To The 2DL and 1DL

Stop-losses placed one tick below the 3DL will usually keep you in the market through the majority of the trend. As a market nears a target with a high probability of completing the trend, the stop-loss should then be adjusted daily closer to the current market position to the two or one-day low.

The charts on the following pages illustrate when three-day lows and highs were exceeded for several markets. These chart illustrations are simply for you to be able to identify the position of the three-day highs and lows. Other analysis and trading factors are not considered.

Three-Day Lows

During the Dec. 17, 1996 to Feb. 19, 1997 rally, the S&P exceeded the 3DL three times as noted by the bold horizontal bars on the chart below. Daily reversal signals are also noted.

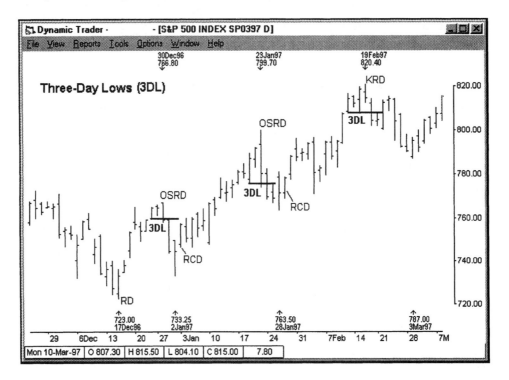

The main trend of the S&P was very bullish during this period. As you can see, the S&P remained above the 3DLs throughout this period right up to the minor tops prior to the corrections.

Only the 3DLs that were exceeded are marked by the bold horizontal lines on the chart. The dates of the swing highs and lows are noted. Follow the daily bars one day at a time beginning with the Dec. 17 low and note each new 3DL. Remember to not count the inside-days.

Three-Day Highs (3DH)

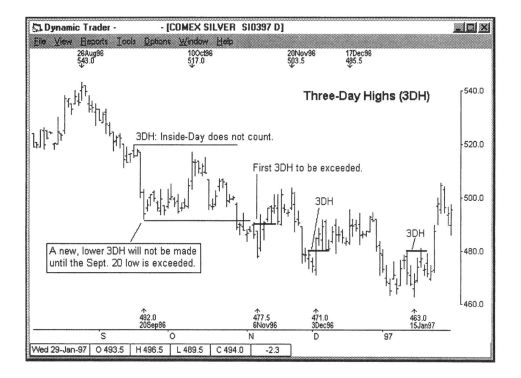

Silver was in a consistent bear trend from the Aug. 1996 high into the Jan. 1997 low. The first 3DH to be exceeded was the trading day following the Nov. 6 low.

Note that the 3DH in late Sept. was far above the market and was never exceeded during the three week correction that began from the Sept. 20 low.

Three-Day Highs (3DH)

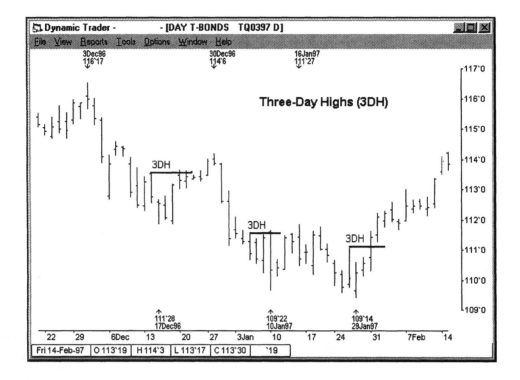

Bonds exceeded the 3DH just three times during the Dec. 3, 1996 to Jan. 29, 1997 decline. Remember that these examples are only to show the positions of the 3DHs without consideration to market position or trading strategies.

A 3DH or L would not be used as a protective stop-loss target if the time, price or pattern analysis signaled a trend was near termination. The stop-loss would be adjusted to the two or one-day high or low.

Multiple Contract Positions - Short and Intermediate Term Trades

Initial positions should be taken with two or three units. A unit is a specified number of contracts. For our discussion, we will consider one unit is one contract. If two contracts are traded, one contract should be considered a short-term position and one an intermediate-term position. If the market moves in the anticipated direction, the objective is to take profits on the short-term position relatively quickly and remain in the market with the intermediate-term position for the majority of the trend.

Why cover the short-term position relatively quickly? If the technical analysis of the markets was right-on all of the time, we would hold all positions to the ultimate trend objective. No analysis method is correct all of the time. The objective is to take profits on one unit relatively quickly in the event the market does not reach the trend objective.

Profit Objective For Short-Term Positions

What is the target for profit-taking on the short-term position? As with every aspect of trading, the first consideration is the philosophy or concept behind the trading guideline.

Short-Term Profit Objective

The *minimum* profit objective for the short-term position should be the minimum price target anticipated if the main trend is *not* in the direction anticipated but is only a correction.

For instance, if the trader believes that a new bull-trend is beginning, what would the price objective be if the rally was only a typical correction to the prior bear-trend. In other words, what is the minimum expectation of the rally if it is only a corrective rally to a bear trend and not a new bull trend? The short-term long position would be covered if the market reached the minimum price anticipated if the main trend had not turned and the rally was only a correction.

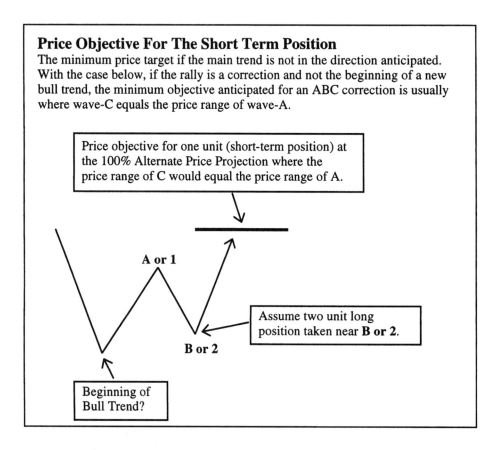

Price Objective For The Short Term Position
The minimum price target if the main trend is not in the direction anticipated. With the case below, if the rally is a correction and not the beginning of a new bull trend, the minimum objective anticipated for an ABC correction is usually where wave-C equals the price range of wave-A.

Price objective for one unit (short-term position) at the 100% Alternate Price Projection where the price range of C would equal the price range of A.

A or 1

Assume two unit long position taken near **B or 2**.

B or 2

Beginning of Bull Trend?

In the example above, profit should be taken on the short-term position either at or near the 100% Alternate Price Projection or the trailing protective sell-stop on the short-term position should be adjusted close to the market such as one tick below the prior day's low if the 100% APP is reached.

The examples of short-term profit objectives on the following pages do not attempt to show all of the possibilities. They only show the assumed major trend and where is the short-term profit objective. *They are designed to make you think.* If you know how to think in terms of your trading objective, you will be able to make a logical trading decision regardless of what ever market activity unfolds.

The examples on the following pages do not show how the market activity progress after the short-term profit objective was met. We are only concerned at this point in time with how to arrive at a profit objective for the short-term units of a multiple-unit position.

Short-Term Profit Objective

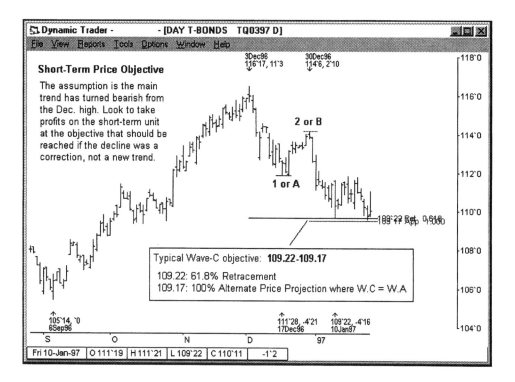

Let's assume that our analysis of the bond market concluded that the Dec. 3 high was the beginning of a bear trend that should continue to decline below the Sept. low. Where should the profit objective be for the short-term units of a short position?

The profit objective for the short-term position should be at the price target that would be anticipated if our outlook for a new major bear trend was incorrect and the decline from the Dec. 3 high was a correction to a bull trend and not the beginning of a new bear trend.

If a bear trend is underway, Dec. 17 should be a Wave-1 low and Dec. 30 should be a Wave-2 high. If the decline is a correction, Dec. 17 should be a wave-A low and Dec. 30 a wave-B high. The price zone of **109.22-109.17** would be the logical objective for a wave-C low if the decline is a correction. This price zone includes the 100% Alternate Price Projection where W.C = 100% W.A and the 61.8% retracement of the prior rally. On Jan. 10, bonds tagged this price zone. Either profits should be taken at this price or protective sell-stops brought very close to the market position on the short-term units.

It is important that you understand the line of thinking here. We are not concerned whether bonds continued lower or not. We are only concerned with the process of taking profits on a portion of the short position.

Short-Term Profit Objective

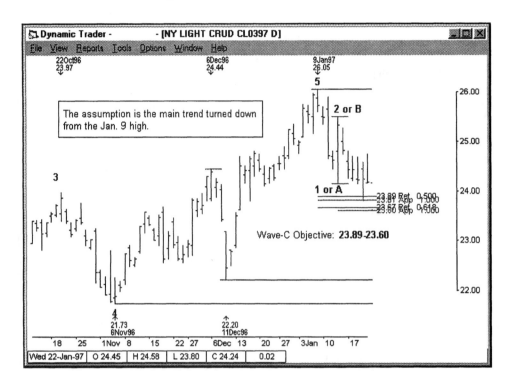

Crude made what appeared to be a wave-5 high on Jan. 9 on a *key reversal day*. Let's assume our analysis suggests a major bear trend began with the Jan. 9 high and we took a multiple short position at or near the Jan. 9 top. The initial sharp decline and rally is labeled **1 or A** and **2 or B** on the chart above. The same wide-range bar is both the low and high. The intraday chart (not included) shows that the low was made early in the day and the high near the end of the day.

If the decline were to be an ABC correction, the typical price objective for the wave-C would be the **23.89-23.60** price zone. This price zone includes where W.C = W.A, the 50% retracement from the Nov. 6 low, the 61.8% retracement from the Dec. 11 low and the 100% Alternate Price Projection of the Dec. 6 H-Dec. 11 L.

Crude reached this price zone in the second half of Jan. The short-term, profit-taking units of the short position should either be covered at this price zone or the protective stop-loss brought very close to the market such as trailed one tick above the one-day-high (1DH).

Short-Term Profit Objective

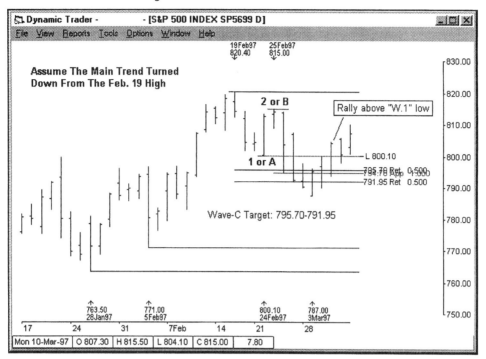

On Feb. 19, the S&P made a *reversal day* high. Let's assume we considered that top as the beginning of a major bear trend. The S&P declined to make a swing low and high that are labeled **1 or A** and **2 or B** on the chart above. If the decline were a correction and not the beginning of a major bear trend, the typical price objective for the correction would be **795.70-791.95**. This price zone includes where W.C = 100% W.A and the 50% retracements from the prior two lows (Jan. 28 and Feb. 5) prior the Feb. 19 high.

The S&P slightly exceeded this price zone and reversed sharply up. Profits on the short-term units of a short position would be taken when this price was reached or the protective stop-loss brought very close to the market.

On the chart above, I have shown a few days following the March 3 low. If a five-wave bear sequence had begun from the Feb. 19 top, the S&P should not trade above the wave-1 low prior to completing the five-wave sequence. Remember the Elliott Wave guideline that wave-4 should not trade into the price range of wave-1.

In early March, the S&P traded and closed into the range of wave-1, voiding a five-wave count. Where do you think the logical protective stop-loss price would be for the long-term units of a short position? If the S&P trades above the wave-1 low and closes above the wave-1 closing low, the five-wave, bearish impulse sequence is voided. All short positions would be abandoned when this occurred.

Intermediate-Term Profit Objective

Where is the objective for the second unit of a position? It is most important to first have a concept of what we are trying to accomplish and the practical application usually follows with little effort.

Intermediate Term Profit Objective

The intermediate-term profit objective is where time, price and pattern coincide to signal the termination of the trend.

In other words, the profit objective is defined by the market activity particular to any one situation. While this sounds very vague, it is firmly grounded in the reality that a market is dynamic and fixed rules for profit-taking are not based on the reality of a dynamic market. Dynamic Trading analysis methods will usually provide you with a firm opinion of the current position of a market and the high probability objectives of any trend or counter-trend.

We will take a look at just one example of how to be prepared for an intermediate-term position profit objective. The important lesson to learn from this example is how to think in terms of identifying a profit objective. The *Putting It All Together* chapter will provide a variety of examples.

Intermediate-Term Profit Objective

The chart example below of bonds declining into the Nov. 1994 low was shown in the chapters on time, price and pattern analysis. We will include all of the factors here to illustrated the objective for an intermediate-term position. The previous chapters provided more detail on the position of bonds going into the Nov. 1994 low.

As you will recall, Aug. 2, 1994 was a wave-4 high counting from the Oct. 1993 high. In early Oct. 1994, bonds declined to make a wide-range, reversal day up on Oct. 7, just two days following a Dynamic Time Projection with a potential for making a low. Two factors clearly indicated that the low was probably not complete on Oct. 7.

1. Clearly, a five-wave decline had not completed. The decline from the Aug. 2, 1994 high to the Oct. 7, 1994 low had all of the characteristics of the first three waves of a five-wave sequence.

2. The Time Rhythm Zone projection for a low did not begin until Oct. 26. The second Dynamic Time Projection of Nov. 11-14 fell right within the TRZ for a low.

These two factors, time and pattern, strongly suggested that bonds would continue lower to at least late Oct. before completing the decline from the Aug. 2 high. The time, price and pattern factors had not coincided to signal the trend was complete.

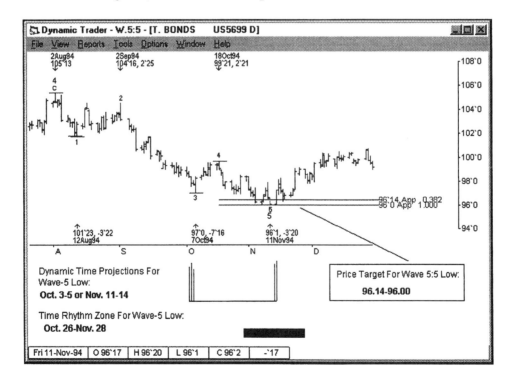

Following the Oct. 18, W.4:5 high, bonds continued to decline to new lows as anticipated. A price target for the W.5:5 low was 96.14-96.00. Bonds had declined to new lows into the Time Rhythm Zone for a low which began Oct. 26. On Nov. 11, right within the TRZ for a low and a Dynamic Time Projection for trend change (Nov. 11-14), bonds made a low of 96.01, precisely within the price target for the low.

Time, price and pattern had all coincided to signal the bear trend was at or near completion. The intermediate-term profit objective had been met. Bonds had now reached the ideal target to complete the bear trend. Protective buy-stops on short positions should be brought very close to the market such as one tick above the prior day's high. The following day, bonds completed a *snap-back-reversal day*. The bear trend was complete.

This is a real example of the power of Dynamic Trading analysis and trading strategies. Wouldn't it be nice if every market trend unfolded in textbook, symmetrical five-wave structures and completed every trend at the projected time and price targets? They don't, but that is not important for this discussion. What is important is that you understand the concept of trend and profit objectives. When you understand the concept, you will be able to judge from most market positions the logical objective for the trade.

> *A profit objective for the intermediate term position is when the dynamic technical analysis signals that a trend is at or near completion. That is when protective stops are brought very close to the market.*

Trading Log - An Important Key To Success

It is very important that all traders keep a trading log of one form or another, particularly in the early years of trading until good analysis and trading habits are formed. The trading log may be in a journal form with entries each day concerning the relevant information for each market that you intend to trade or in a chart / data format. It is less important how detailed is the trading log than whether it is consistently updated on a regular basis.

Consistently keeping a trading log will provide several benefits.

1. It will help ensure that you keep current on all relevant information needed to make a trading decision.

2. You will be prepared in advance for the market activity that provides an acceptable trade set up.

3. You will have written down in advance the trading strategies to implement including the specific entry and initial protective stop-loss orders.

4. It will facilitate the trader to keep assessed of the market position in order to manage the trade until closed out.

5. You will have a hard copy record of the trade for later review to discover if you have followed your trading plan and can improve on the analysis techniques, trading strategies, etc.

6. A consistently updated trading log will help you to define specific trading rules and strategies.

7. The trading log will be a permanent record of your thoughts, ideas and motivation for each trade which will help you to learn about yourself as a trader.

If the trading log is kept in a journal format, I suggest keeping a separate journal for each market or at least for each market group. That way it will be easier to follow the line of thought regarding the analysis and trading strategies for each market.

I use and recommend a chart / critical information format for several reasons. I know the key information that I need to develop an opinion of the position of a market and the necessary trade set-up to consider entering a trade. Since the categories of that information are always the same, it is easiest to develop a form where I will not forget to include the key information, and I can review the critical information quickly.

In the many years of teaching market analysis and trading strategies to hundreds of traders and prospective traders through my workshops, newsletter and home study course, almost every successful trader that I have talked to keeps a trading log of one form or another. And, they review the trading log on a regular basis for keys to avoid mistakes and improve trading performance in the future. Virtually none of the unsuccessful or prospective traders keep trading logs. That should tell you something.

A trading log should include the key information necessary to make a trading decision. It should also include a brief description of your opinion of the market, what will constitute a trade set-up and what are the specific triggers that will signal a trade.

One of the important benefits of a trading log is that it helps to employ the discipline that all of the decisions for trading are made in advance. Once the criteria for a trade are decided upon, it is simply a matter of waiting for the market to meet that criteria and the trader then automatically takes action.

The following pages include formats for a trading log that are helpful to prepare for and follow through on a trade. I like to keep all of the relevant information on one page which includes a current chart of the market. I use three different worksheets which are the *Trade Preparation and Initiation, Trade Management* and *Closed Trade Critique Worksheets*. The descriptions of the trading logs begin on the following page.

The *Putting It All Together Chapter* will include completed trading logs.

Trade Preparation and Initiation Worksheet

The purpose of this form is to ensure the trader is aware of all of the critical information necessary before making a trade. This form is completed as a market is approaching a set-up for a potential trade. The relevant technical information is included as well as the "set-up" that is required to initiate the trade and what trading action will be taken if a trade is initiated.

Trade #/Date: Assign a number to the trade and date the worksheet. If multiple worksheets are made relative to the one trade, they will be kept in order.

Objective: The objective is a short note of what to anticipate from the trade within the context of the analysis. It is often stated in terms of the pattern that is developing and may state the relative degree of the trade anticipated such as short, intermediate or long term.

Trend: Included are the three degrees of trend of the current market position. If your trading plan includes the restriction of never trading against the intermediate term trend, this will be a reminder in which direction you must trade. Always include the date of the pivot each trend began.

Time (PTPPs): The Projected Turning Point Periods projected from the past pivots. Include the date of the past pivot and the projected dates.

Price-Res. (Resistance) and Support: Shows the potential price support and resistance zones and the date of the pivots from where they are projected.

TCS (Trend Continuation Signal): Usually a price level that, if exceeded, indicates the continuation of the trend. Can also be a time objective. If the trend continues beyond the time objective it is a signal that the trend will continue.

TRS (Trend Reversal Signal): Usually a price level against the trend that, if exceeded, signals the current trend is exhausted and has reversed.

Pattern: The current position of the market relevant to pattern. Frequently includes an Elliott wave count. It may be as simple as a statement whether the market is in an impulsive or corrective position.

Set-Up: Briefly describes the market activity that is required for a trade set-up. This could be a reversal signal at a time and price coincidence, break-out of a prior swing pivot or any other criteria that is required before a trade is acceptable.

Action To Take: This is the trade that will be taken if the market meets all of the trade criteria. It includes the details of how many futures or option contracts will be purchased or sold.

Order: The order is the specific order given to the broker. It includes a space for the order number given by the brokerage company.

Filled (D/T/P)?: The date, time and price an order is filled.

Canceled (D/T)?: The date and time if the order is canceled prior to being filled.

Initial PS (Protective Stop): The initial protective stop-loss order including the brokerage firm's order number. A position is *never* open without an *open protective stop-loss* order in the market. If the "Filled" space is complete and there is no open protective stop, quit trading. No one in their right mind has an open position without an open protective stop-loss order.

Adjust PS (Units 1, 2 and 3): The market activity that will signal an adjustment of the protective stop-loss order. Space is provided if the initial trade was up to three units as the PS on each unit may be different depending on the objective of each unit.

Commentary (Include Date): It is not necessary to complete a new worksheet each day. Make a brief note each day or just when any relevant information changes as to the position of the market or any other information you might want to review at a later date.

Trade Preparation and Initiation Worksheet   Trade # / Date _____

Trade Objective _____   Market _____

Chart Goes Here

Trend:	Minor _____	Int. _____	Major _____	
Time (PTPPs):	From _____	_____		
	From _____	_____		
Resistance	From _____	Minor _____		
	From _____	Int. _____		
Support:	From _____	Minor _____		
	From _____	Int. _____		
TCS _____		**TRS** _____		
Pattern:	_____			
Set-Up	_____			
Action to Take	_____			

Entry Order	#	Filled? (D/T/P)	Canceled? (D/T)

Initial PS			

Adjust PS	Unit 1	_____
	Unit 2	_____
	Unit 3	_____

Commentary	_____	
Date:	_____	_____
Date:	_____	_____
Date:	_____	_____
Date:	_____	_____

Trade Management Worksheet

Use this worksheet to monitor a trade while it is in progress. It includes the same categories of technical information as the *Trade Preparation and Initiation Worksheet*. The time projections usually do not change. The price support and resistance projections may change as new pivots are made. The trend continuation (TCS) and reversal (TRS) signals may change as a market progresses.

Trade # & Date of Worksheet: The Trade # followed by the worksheet number relevant to this trade and the date the worksheet was first prepared.

Current Position: The current trade position including the market, contract and long or short.

PS-OO (Protective Stop-Open Order): The open protective stop-loss order and its brokerage firm number.

Add Position: Describes the market activity that will signal to add to the initial position.

Adjust PS (Units 1, 2 and 3): Describes the market activity that will signal an adjustment to the protective stop on each position.

ST-Obj (Short-Term Objective): The profit objective for the short-term units of a multiple unit position.

Commentary: Enter a brief any day that any additional relevant information develops. This section may include dates of reports that are relevant to this market.

Trade Management Worksheet   Trade # / Date _____

    Current Position _____   **PS-OO** ⬚⬚

Chart Goes Here

PTPPs	Fr _____			
Resistance	Fr _____	Minor		
	Fr _____	Int		
Support	Fr _____	Minor		
	Fr _____	Int		

Pattern _____

TCS _____   **TRS** _____

Add Position _____

Adj. PS - Unit 1 _____

    Unit 2 _____

    Unit 3 _____

ST Obj. _____

Commentary

Date: _____
Date: _____
Date: _____
Date: _____
Date: _____
Date: _____
Date: _____

Closed Trade Critique Worksheet

The *Closed Trade Critique Worksheet* is completed when all positions of a trade are closed out. A review of each completed trade will be one of the most important factors to help improve your trading performance.

The *Trade Critique Worksheet* includes space for the account information of the trade including entry and exit date and price, net profit or loss, etc. It also includes space for trade comments and, most importantly, lessons learned.

Trade # & Date of Worksheet: The Trade # followed by the worksheet number relevant to this trade and the date this worksheet was first prepared.

Unit: The trade position of each unit including long (L) or short (S), number of contracts, contract month and market. There is space for three units that may have been taken relative to the same trade.

Entry / Exit: The date and price of entry and exit of each trade position.

P/L (Profit or Loss): The number of ticks profit or loss *per contract* of each position.

 # Con. (contracts): The number of contracts of each position.

Unit Value: The dollar value of each tick for the contract traded.

Com. (commission): The commission and fees charged *per contract* traded.

Trade P/L: The net trade profit or loss for the position. This considers the number of contracts, profit or loss per contract and commission charged.

Total Trade P/L: The total trade profit or loss considers all positions for the trade.

These worksheets were designed on a spreadsheet. The trade data rows and columns described above were designed so the spreadsheet will automatically calculate the Trade P/L and Total Trade P/L.

Trade Comments: Include any comments you feel are necessary to review the trade.

Lessons Learned: This is a very important section. Review what you did right as well as what could have been done better to improve the trade. You want to both reinforce the correct actions taken so you will continue to take them in the future, as well as review if you did not follow your trading plan so you will improve in the future. The Lessons Learned section will be your key to review whether your trading plan is acceptable, and if you are following it.

Closed Trade Critique Worksheet   **Market** _____   **Trade # / Date** _____

Chart Goes Here

		Entry		Exit						
	Unit	Date	Price	Date	Price	P/L	# Con.	Tick Value	Com.	Trade P/L
1										
2										
3										

Total Trade P / L: [   ]

TRADE COMMENTS _____

_____

_____

_____

_____

LESSONS LEARNED _____

_____

_____

_____

_____

Success Is A Choice You Make

Preparing a series of trade worksheets may seem like a lot of work, but they will pay big dividends in the long run. They are really not that time consuming to initially prepare and keep up-to-date. In most cases, once the initial worksheet is prepared, only a brief note is made each day unless the market provides new information that requires an adjustment to the technical analysis position such as new time or price objectives.

The *Putting It All Together* chapter will include examples of completed worksheets.

The worksheet formats described above are only suggestions. You may design a format that you find more suitable. The important factor is that you have the critical information needed to make a trading decision *in writing*. You will have a permanent record of your line-of-thought, analysis factors and why you made the trading decision. You may not want to include a chart with each worksheet, but I find the chart a very valuable reference of the market position when the trade was considered.

Whether you use the formats described on the previous pages or one of your own design, one thing is certain, a trading log of some form is critically important to your success. You will only be able to improve upon your future trading activities by carefully reviewing your past trading activities and monitoring your current trading activities. This is a critical principle for the success of any business.

If you want to be a success in the business of trading, keep a trading log religiously and review it frequently. Remember to keep in mind:

> *Almost all consistently, successful traders keep a trading log or journal in one format or another. Most unsuccessful traders do not keep a trading log or journal.*

Do you want to develop the habits of the successful or unsuccessful traders? It is your choice! It is your money! If you are committed to success in the business of trading, you will keep a trading log.

Trading Philosophy, Trading Plan and Trading Rules

All successful businesses are driven by a specific objective which includes a plan of action; how to accomplish the objective. Most traders would say, "my objective is to make a profit." A profit is the *outcome* of a well thought out, well tested and implemented trading plan.

The *Trading Philosophy* is the general style and objectives of your trading business. The *Trading Philosophy* will describe just what you are trying to accomplish. The *Trading Plan* is the fundamental set of rules that guide your trading decisions. The *Trading Plan* will describe the basis of the strategies and tactics that will be the guide to the day-to-day activities. The *Trading Rules* are the specific guidelines which must be met before a trading action is initiated.

It is essential that the trading philosophy, plan and rules be well thought out and *in writing*. The business of trading is like any other business. Its success will not only be contingent on the knowledge of the individual, but how well the business is planned. It is a mistaken belief that most businesses fail in a relatively short period of time because of a lack of capital.

The Business of Speculation Is Like All Other Businesses

Most businesses fail primarily because of a *lack of planning* and a *lack of knowledge* of the business and how to manage the business. It is no different with the business of trading. Significant capital is probably the least necessary component.

Each individual trader must develop his or her own trading philosophy, plan and rules. *You will never be successful in the long run by adopting someone else's trading philosophy, plan and rules.*

Trading Philosophy

The trading philosophy should be in a narrative form and describe:

1. The trading time frame. Is the objective to trade short, intermediate or long-term trades? What is the general time frame considered for each of these periods?

2. The general parameters of the type of activity necessary to indicate a potential trade. Are you only looking to enter on trend-reversal set-ups or breakout trend-confirmation set-ups or both?

3. The general parameters of the capital exposure that is acceptable and the profit objectives.

Trading Philosophy Examples

Below are a couple examples of trading philosophies. They represent two completely different trading objectives and will each have a different trading plan and trading rules.

> The objective is to identify the trading condition set-ups for short to intermediate term trades. Those that will last from several days to several weeks. At least two units will be taken with most trades with the objective to take profits at the short-term objective on one unit and hold the second unit to the termination of the intermediate term trend.
>
> Trend-reversal trades will be entered when the time, price and pattern analysis factors indicate a trend reversal is probable and a daily reversal is made. Trend-continuation trades will be made following a trend reversal.
>
> The capital exposure for any one position will not exceed 3% of the account balance. All trades will be held until stopped out of the market by the protective stop-loss.

This trading philosophy will form the foundation of the trading plan and trading rules for short to intermediate term trading where a trade is held until stopped out. A completely different trading philosophy might be:

> The objective is to identify the main trend and only enter short-term trades of one to three days in the direction of the main trend. A protective stop-loss is trailed very close to the market and profits are taken at short-term price objectives.

This is a completely different trading philosophy with a short-term time frame and the objective to take relatively quick profits on successful trades.

As with most businesses, you have a better chance of success if you specialize. It is unlikely you will be successful by trying to be a short-term, scalp trader as well as looking to trade the long-term trends that last several weeks to several months. The analysis techniques and trading strategies of each are much different. Almost all successful traders specialize in one type of trading.

The trading philosophy will provide the objective of what style of trading you are trying to accomplish and the general parameters of how you will accomplish the objective. The trading philosophy examples above are just that, examples. It is important for you too think about what your own trading objectives should be and for you to develop your own trading philosophy. This isn't the time to develop paralysis of analysis. Don't get hung-up on the details but take the time to simply state what you are trying to accomplish in your trading business.

Trading Plan

We move from the very general *Trading Philosophy* to the more specific *Trading Plan*. The *Trading Plan* consists of the fundamental principles that guide your trading business. The *Trading Plan* does not include specific trade-action rules.

An example of a trading plan might include the following:

1. The first objective is to protect and preserve capital.
2. Only initiate a trend-reversal trade when at least two of the three factors of time, price and pattern signal a trend-reversal is probable <u>and</u> one of the four daily reversal signals is made.
3. Only initiate a trend-continuation trade when at least two of the three factors of time price and pattern have signaled a trend reversal and one of the three trend-continuation entry set-ups is made.
4. Every open trade must have an open protective stop-loss.
5. Trades are only exited by the election of a protective stop-loss, never at a specific price objective.
6. <u>Never</u> add to a losing position.

The first objective is to protect and preserve capital. It seems ludicrous that this rule would even have to be stated. Almost all unsuccessful traders focus on the idea of potential profits and ignore the potential for losses. Almost all successful traders are fanatical about limiting losses knowing that there is no possibility of being profitable or even staying in business over the long run if capital is not preserved.

It is often said, "take care of your losses, and your profits will take care of themselves." There is a lot of truth to this statement. If you don't take care of losses by limiting them, you will not have the capital to commit to the opportunities to realize profits. The specific guidelines to protect and preserve capital should be stated in the trading plan such as the maximum allowable capital exposure per trade.

An example is the initial capital exposure per trade shall never exceed 3% of the available account equity. In this case, a trade will never be entered if the stop-loss position is further from the entry position than the dollar amount equal to 3% of the available trading equity. The capital exposure rule may be a fixed dollar amount per contract such as $500. The important factor is that you have agreed upon some guideline to preserve capital by limiting losses. *Every* trading plan must include the guideline to preserve capital by limiting losses.

Only initiate a trend-reversal trade when at least two of the three factors of time, price and pattern signal a trend-reversal is probable <u>and</u> one of the four daily reversal signals is made. This trading plan principle considers the context of the analysis methodology taught in this book and recognizes that a market must meet certain technical conditions before a trend-reversal, trade-entry is considered. The trading rules will define the acceptable conditions. This trading plan principle also limits the initial trend-reversal, trade-entries to a specific reversal pattern. In other words, trades will never be taken at the coincidence of projected time and price targets, no matter how strong, without a reversal signal.

This part of the trading plan is specifically oriented to the trader buying bottoms and selling tops when the high probability conditions for a bottom or top are met. Almost every trading educator, publisher and advisor teaches to never try to buy the bottom or sell the top and only enter on an established trend. That is because they do not have the technical analysis methods to identify with a high probability the conditions when tops and bottoms are made. Dynamic Traders have this knowledge and an important part of their trading plan should be to take advantage of these unique technical analysis methods.

Only initiate a trend-continuation trade when at least two of the three factors of time, price and pattern have signaled a trend reversal and one of the three trend-continuation entry set-ups is made. This guideline is similar to the previous one except it addresses trade entries after a trend is established and limits the trend-continuation trade entries to specific trend-continuation set-ups.

Every open trade has an open protective stop-loss. If you *ever* have a trade position without an open protective stop-loss order in place with the broker, you are not a trader. You're an idiot. If there is a time in your life when you will be hit by a truck, have a heart attack or fall into a coma, it will be when you have an open position. What if the market moves relentlessly against your position as you are resisting going down that one-way tunnel toward the light? Do you want the first words you hear when you return to consciousness to be "honey, what's a margin call?"

Trades are only exited by the election of a protective stop-loss, never at a specific price objective. The trading plan must include the rule for how a position is exited. The exit rule as stated here, requires a trade to only be exited by electing a stop-loss. The specific trading rules will define the specific position of initial and trailing protective stop-losses. A different trading plan may accept profit taking objectives of a fixed dollar amount or percentage gain on the trade.

Never add to a losing position. Adding to a losing position could be one definition of insanity. Do two wrongs make a right?

A trading plan should clearly define the basic foundation of your business of trading and the fundamental and general rules that will guide your decisions. The trading plan described above is just an example. Yours may be more comprehensive. But beware of paralysis of analysis. If your trading plan covers page after page of rules and guidelines, you've probably missed the point that the trading plan is a firm guideline to the direction you are taking and the general, inviolate rules. It is not a plan that dictates every individual action.

Planning is a three stage process that begins from the very general and works its way to the specific. The *Trading Philosophy* is a very generalized narrative of the direction and objectives of the business. The *Trading Plan* is a bit more specific and definitely provides some limited parameters on what activities will be engaged in. Step three is the *Trading Rules*. The *Trading Rules* are even more specific and provide the conditions that must be met before taking a specific trading action.

Trading Rules

The trading rules are the specific qualifications that must be met before any trade action may be taken. All rules are limiting by nature. Rules always relate to a condition. The more rules, the fewer conditions acceptable for a trade action.

A mechanical, trading system consists of specific, mathematically defined and inviolate rules. Each decision is made by the "system" without input by the user. In chapter one, I expressed my less than positive opinion of trading "systems" and the absurdity of considering any business could be successful without the application of the knowledge and judgment of the business owner. So then what do I mean by trading rules?

Trading rules as used here are the minimum qualifications that must be met before a trade action may be taken whether it is a trade entry, protective-stop placement or trade exit. In other words, a decision will only be made if a market is in a position where the probabilities for success are in favor of the decision maker. Let's consider a couple of examples of trading rules.

A initial trade entry is never taken prior to the market making at least a 50% retracement from what is suspected as the extreme high or low. In Elliott wave terms, traders would only look to buy when either the wave-2 or wave-B has made at least a 50% price retracement of wave-1 or wave-A. W. D. Gann taught that the "safest time to enter a market is on the first correction to the high or low." What did he mean by "safest?" He meant the time with the greatest probability of being followed by a fast and prolonged trend. In Elliott wave terms this would be the wave-3.

This rule would preclude considering buying the bottom of a bear trend or selling the top of a bull trend. This rule would force the trader to wait for at least some minor confirmation a trend has reversed and to be prepared to buy on the initial correction to the suspected new trend.

This rule does not cause a trading action to be taken, but provides the minimum qualifications for a market position before a trade may be considered.

Another rule might be - *The protective stop-loss shall never be placed further than one tick beyond the three-day high or low once a market has exceeded the 100% alternate price projection.* This simple rule recognizes that a market that exceeds the 100% alternate price projection is probably in an impulse trend that should only have relatively minor corrections until the trend is at or near completion. This is the time to trail the protective-stop relatively close to the market.

A relatively short-term trader's trading-plan may include a rule such as - *The protective stop-loss will never be further than one tick beyond the prior day's extreme once a position has reached a $700 profit.* This is a simple rule that considers the protective stop-loss should be kept close to the market position as soon as a minimum, unrealized profit is achieved. For very short-term traders, the prior day's high or low may be a long way away. Their minimum protective stop-loss rule may be much closer. Another trading rule may require a position be closed at a specific profit objective, say $500, no matter what the outlook for the main trend.

As you can see from just these three examples, a trading rule may be very specific and limiting, or it may only provide a minimum qualification before a trade action may be taken.

Your Trading Rules Must Be *Your* Trading Rules

I am not going to provide an example of a series of trading rules as I provided examples with the trading philosophy and trading plan. It is critical to *your* success that you develop your own trading rules based on the objectives of your trading plan and the technical analysis methods you employ. Developing your own, specific trading rules will require you to think carefully about your trading objectives and the technical analysis methods you are going to use. I don't want you to even be under the illusion that someone can do this for you.

Some readers may think this is a cop-out on my part. I've presented analysis methods and trading strategies. Shouldn't I now provide you with a specific trading plan and trading rules? Don't other authors of trading books provide you with just this? Your trading business is unique. You will have goals and objectives different from other traders. But, there is one factor that is common to all *successful* traders.

All successful traders have created their own trading plans and trading rules. They know success cannot be bought. All successful traders have taken the time to develop their own trading plans and rules that guide their business of trading. The Dynamic Trading analysis techniques and trading strategies taught in this book provide you with a comprehensive framework of understanding market activity and the position of the market at any time. The trading strategies taught have provided you with simple low-risk and low-capital exposure trade set-ups.

The next chapter, *Putting It All Together*, will help demonstrate to you the practical application of all that you have learned up to this point. After completing the next chapter, you will be in a position to develop your own trading plan, rules and strategies based on your goals and objectives.

Dynamic Time and Price Projections, Energy Levels and the Atomic Particle Model

Most of us are familiar with the model of an atom as a mini solar system where the nucleus is the sun and the electrons are the orbiting planets. This is called the particle model of the atom as opposed to the wave model. In the solar system, the distance of the planets from the sun varies somewhat because their revolution about the sun is not a perfect circle, but an ellipse. However, in the particle model of the atom, the position of the orbits of the electrons are discrete energy levels. That is, the orbiting electrons are maintained within a definite and distinct energy level and do not waver in or out of the orbit position or distance from the nucleus.

Electrons may "jump" from one orbit or energy level to another, but will never occupy a position between the orbits. The electron makes the jump without ever passing through the space between the orbits. However, we cannot determine in advance when a particular electron is going to jump from one orbit to another or whether it will jump to the closest or a further away orbit.

Our market model may be similar to the solar-system, atomic-particle model. Let's consider projected Dynamic Time and Price zones as being similar to the discrete, electron orbit levels. The Dynamic Time and Price levels are like the orbit/energy levels of the electrons. In this model, if a market exceeds a Dynamic Time or Price level, it will most likely continue to the next "orbit" or Dynamic Time or Price level. They are different in that they are relatively narrow ranges or zones rather that a single, distinct level.

In the atomic model, an electron does not spend any time between orbits as it jumps from one orbit to another. In our market model, price must travel through the "space" between the time and price orbits or levels. In the atomic model, there are no exceptions to the distinct orbit levels and jumping from one orbit to another. In other words, the distinct orbits are the only acceptable levels for an electron to exist and the electron will never reside in the space between orbits.

In the market model, we are dealing with probabilities. The greatest probability is that the market will proceed to the next projected Dynamic Time or Price level once one is exceeded, but it is not a certainty. And of course, the market must travel in the space between the projected Dynamic Time and Price "orbits."

How is the atomic, particle-model of practical value for traders and investors? If a market exceeds a projected Dynamic Price level, the odds favor that the market will continue to at least the next projected level. In other words, we have a high probability outlook that the trend will continue to a defined objective. The same is true of time. If the market trends through a Dynamic Time projection (orbit), the odds favor that the trend will continue to the next time projection or "orbit."

Our analogy of market movement with the solar/atomic-model makes an important assumption. The trader or investor has a methodology that identifies time and price zones or "orbits" with consistent reliability. Dynamic Traders have just that. While the analogy of the market with the atomic model is not perfect, it provides an excellent model of how a market typically "jumps" from one Dynamic Time and Price level to another.

Notes

Chapter 7

Putting It All Together

The man who goes to the top as a commodity trader does not do as he pleases. He submits to controls, to discipline. He brings his desires into line by channeling his resources and strengths into the trades that have a high potential and a high degree of certainty.

Roy W. Longstreet

In the *Putting It All Together* chapter you

- Learn how to initially organize all of the information to clearly understand the position of a market.

- Learn how to develop trading plans and trading strategies.

- Learn how to organize and update the Dynamic Technical Analysis and trading strategies with Trading Log Worksheets.

- Learn how to maintain a structured, patient and disciplined approach to technical analysis and practical trading strategies.

- Learn a *Consistency of Approach* to trading.

It's Easier Than You Think

The previous chapters have presented a vast array of dynamic technical analysis techniques and trading strategies. It may seem overwhelming how to put it all into practice to make a trading decision. It's not as difficult as it may seem. This chapter will walk you through the process of what Dynamic Trading technical analysis information and trading strategies to consider to make the trading decision.

The next seventy pages or so will describe a series of bond trades over approximately a one year time period. Keep in mind that it would only take a few minutes a day to keep the information up-to-date. This chapter is quite extensive because of the detailed commentary for this relatively brief period for bonds.

One of the important objectives of this chapter is to help you develop a disciplined and consistent approach to your trading. As you study this chapter, keep aware of the *consistency of the approach* to trading. There is a consistency in the time, price and pattern technical analysis and trading strategies. Only the most basic time and price projections and trading strategies are considered a part of the trading plan for these examples. The downfall of many amateur traders is "paralysis of analysis." Keep trading relatively simple until the basics are mastered. While there may be fewer set-ups that meet your relatively limited acceptable conditions for a trade, the chance of long-term success is *greatly* enhanced by first mastering the basics.

Organizing The Dynamic Trading Technical Analysis Information

The first step is deciding what information is necessary to make the trading decision. The previous chapters have described three main factors of market information that are important: time, price and pattern. Each of these factors help to describe what is the position of a market including identifying the degree of the most recent trend reversal and how far in price and long in time the current trend or counter-trend is likely to last.

Below are some of the questions to ask to help determine the market position?

Pattern

Does the market appear to be unfolding in one of the specific Elliott wave patterns? If a specific Elliott wave pattern is not evident, is the market in a trend or counter-trend? What degree?

What is the position within the trend or counter-trend? Near the beginning, middle or end?

What is the typical outcome of the current pattern position? New trend in the opposite direction? Minor or major counter-trend?

Time

What is the time-range target (Time Rhythm Zone) with a high probability of completing the current trend or counter-trend based on the past trends of similar degree?

What are the specific dates (Dynamic Time Projection clusters also called Projected Turning Point Periods) in the future when the trend or counter-trend have the highest probability of completing? Do any of these Dynamic Time Projections fall within a Time Rhythm Zone?

Price

What is the price-range target with a high probability of completing the current trend or counter-trend?

If the market appears to be in one of the specific Elliott wave patterns, what are the support and resistance projections based on the typical Elliott wave price projections for that pattern position?

Are there support or resistance projection zones that include at least two degrees of projections?

Trading Strategies

If you have a firm idea of the market position, the next step is to determine the trading strategies. The trading strategies to consider will be dependent on the market position.

Trend Reversal Trading Strategies

If a market is believed to be nearing the termination of a trend or counter-trend, protective stop-losses will be brought relatively close to the market on open trade positions in order to protect unrealized profits and trend reversal trade-entries will be considered.

Trend Continuation Trading Strategies

If a market is believed to be in the midst of a trend or counter-trend, trend continuation trade-entry strategies will be considered to initiate a position.

Trading Log

A trading log like one described in the previous chapter will help to keep the information organized and help to prevent overlooking any critical analysis factor.

Trading Philosophy, Plan and Rules For Chapt. 7 Examples

We must develop a trading plan that provides a definite framework from where to make trading decisions for the Dynamic Trading examples that follow. The plan must be simple and easy to put to the test by following the activity of a market over time.

Trading Philosophy

The *Trading Philosophy* provides the general description of the trading objectives.

The trading objective is to enter trades in the direction of the major trend relative to daily data. Trend swings usually last two-eight weeks.

There are three general conditions needed to consider a trade entry: 1. At the coincidence of time, price and pattern which indicates a reversal of trend; 2. At the first correction against the new trend; 3. On a trend-continuation signal after the market has signaled the new trend is established.

The initial trade for trend-reversal trade set-up as described in 1 and 2 above will always be two-units. A trend-continuation trade set-up will only be one-unit. Profits will be taken on the short-term unit at the first price target. The long-term unit will be held to the time and/or price targets anticipated for the complete trend.

The initial capital exposure on any two-unit position will not exceed 5% of the available account equity. The initial capital exposure on a one-unit position will not exceed 2.5% of available account equity.

This *Trading Philosophy* provides the general objectives for the trading business. Only daily data is considered and the objective is to trade the major swings of intermediate term trends. There is a very limited number of set-up conditions that are acceptable before a trade may be considered. Capital exposure is limited for each trade-entry. Given these limitations of the Trading Philosophy, trade set-ups and entrys may be relatively infrequent but should have a high probability of success.

Trading Plan

The Trading Plan provides more specific trading parameters than the Trading Philosophy. Trade-entries are only considered on trend-reversal set-ups at anticipated trend reversal extremes or on the first correction against a new trend.

Trend-Reversal Trade-Entry

Only enter a trend-reversal trade when at least two of the three factors of time, price and pattern are clearly in a position for trend reversal. A trend reversal trade is only made on the close of one of the three daily reversal signals (reversal-day, signal-day, snap-back-reversal-day). A trend-reversal trade-entry may be either at the trend extreme or first correction against the new trend. Trend-reversal positions will always be two units.

As long as a market remains within the time, price and pattern zones for a trend reversal, trend-reversal trades are considered. Even if an initial trend-reversal trade is stopped out, new trend reversal trades will be made as long as the time and price zones anticipated for the reversal have not been exceeded.

Trend-Continuation Trade-Entry

Only initiate a trend-continuation trade-entry when the market has made at least an initial signal a new trend is established by trading beyond a prior lesser degree swing extreme or beyond the 100% Alternate Price Projection. Never take more than one trend-continuation trade-entry position for any trend swing. Trend-continuation positions will always be one unit. The trend-continuation unit will be treated as an intermediate term unit for stop-loss and profit taking considerations. The maximum units that may be held for any trend swing will be three: two trend-reversal and one trend-continuation.

Profit Taking and the Short-Term Unit

Profits will look to be secured on the short-term unit at or near the 100% Alternate Price Projection. Either a profit objective order will be placed at this projection or the protective stop-loss will be trailed at no further than one tick beyond the one-day-high or low once this first objective is met.

Profit Taking and the Intermediate-Term Unit

The protective stop-loss on the intermediate term units will be brought to no further than one tick beyond the three-day high or low once the new trend is established by exceeding a prior high or low or the 100% APP. The protective stop-loss will be trailed at the one-day high or low if the market reaches the coincidence of time, price and pattern projections that typically will complete the trend. The intermediate-term unit is never exited on a price profit objective.

Every open trade must have an open protective stop-loss order.

Never add to a losing position.

This *Trading Plan* is very specific as to the objectives and methods of trading. While the trader must still make trading decisions, the plan provides very well defined parameters for the context within which to make trading decisions. There will be a judgment to be made as to the importance of the time, price and pattern position. Any two traders who have studied the Dynamic Trading Time, Price and Pattern material in this book should come to about the same conclusions when viewing any market position. There is some judgment to be made as to when the trend is considered established and when the protective stop-loss strategy is adjusted or when trend-continuation trades are considered. Once again, any two traders who have studied this Dynamic Trading material will come to about the same conclusion at any point in time.

Since only daily data is used and there are a very limited number of trade set-ups that are considered acceptable, acceptable trade set-up conditions will be relatively infrequent. However, the chances of success should be high as only fairly ideal trade conditions are acceptable. It is unlikely that complete trend swings will be missed, as the trend-continuation trade-entry set-ups should place the trader in the market even after the trend is established.

Trading Rules

We have worked our way from the very general *Trading Philosophy* to the more specific *Trading Plan*. Now let's add a few very specific and objective *Trading Rules* that may not be violated at any time.

Trend-Reversal Trade-Entry

Trend-reversal trade-entries may only be made on the close of one of the three daily reversal signals: *reversal-day, signal-day and snap-back-reversal-day*. The initial protective stop-loss is always placed one tick beyond the extreme of the daily reversal signal.

Trend-Continuation Trade-Entry

Trend-continuation trade-entries are only made on *inside-day, outside-day* and *Gann pull-back* set-ups. The initial protective stop-loss is placed according to the rules of each set-up.

Protective Stop-Loss (PSL) Short-Term Unit

Once a market has traded to the 100% Alternate Price Projection, the PSL on the short-term unit is trailed at *no further* than one tick beyond the one-day-high or low (1DH-L).

Protective Stop-Loss (PSL) Intermediate-Term Unit

Once a market has closed beyond the 100% Alternate Price Projection, the PSL on the intermediate-term unit is trailed *no further* than one tick beyond the three-day-high or low (3DH-L).

Trend-Reversal Trade-Entry At The Initial Correction To A New Trend

The initial correction to a new trend is usually considered a Wave-2 or Wave-B. A trend-reversal trade-entry on the initial correction to a new trend may only be taken in the 50%-78.6% retracement zone.

These *Trading Rules* are very specific and completely objective. They do not provide a rule for every trading condition by any means. They do provide minimum and maximum conditions for trade-entries and stop-loss placement that may limit the number of trades but should increase the probabilities of success for the trade. For instance, for every trade and PSL position, the rules provide the *maximum* protective stop-loss by stating the *furthest* the PSL may be from the market position. Depending on market conditions, the trader may decide the PSL should be closer to the market than the maximum distance allowed. Now that we have developed a

Trading Philosophy, Plan and Rules, let's see how we put what we have learned about *Dynamic Trading* together in the real-world.

Putting It All Together In The Real-World

To demonstrate how to prepare the dynamic technical analysis and trading strategies, the balance of this chapter will follow a market for several months. It will view the market in relatively small periods of time with comments and chart examples.

Admittedly, this is a relatively short period of time with a limited number of trade set-ups. The objective is to demonstrate to the reader how to apply the principles, analysis methods and trading strategies as a market unfolds. Once the process is learned, it doesn't matter what is the market or particular market position. It is more important that you learn how to think from an analysts and traders point of view than it is to view dozens of out-of-context examples.

Bonds

Every trade begins with an assumption of the market position based on the dynamic technical analysis. The first few charts and comments will provide some background of the position of bonds going into the second half of 1994. We will then look at how specific trade decisions are made once the position of the market is understood.

What Is The Market Position?

Do not consider a trade until you have a firm opinion of the market position.

> Is the trend impulsive or corrective?
> What is the position of the market relative to the trend?
> Is the trend in the initial, middle or final stages?
> What are the time, price and pattern objectives for the market position?

The *pattern* of a market trend often provides a firm opinion of the market position. Bonds made a high in Oct. 1993 followed by a persistent decline into the summer of 1994. The chart on the opposite page shows a wave count that appears to indicate bonds made a Wave-5 low in July 1994.

Once an opinion is formed of the pattern position of the market, determine what pattern must unfold to confirm the market position.

The simplest corrective pattern to a five-wave impulse trend is an ABC, zigzag. An A-wave is usually a five-wave structure. Five-wave structures should be in the direction of the larger degree trend. A five-wave rally following the July 11 low would be an important pattern signal to confirm the July 11, 1994 low completed the bear trend.

What is the market activity to anticipate following the completion of a five-wave impulse trend?

Corrections usually reach at least a 38.2% price and time retracement of the prior five-wave trend. We would initially anticipate the same for a rally from the July 11 low, if that low completed a five-wave bear trend. Corrections to a five-wave trend are usually greater in time and price than the Wave 2 or 4 corrections within the trend. We would initially anticipate that a corrective rally from the July 11 low would exceed the price and time of the Wave 2 and 4 corrective rallies.

What is the market activity that will invalidate the market position?

The failure to complete a five-wave impulse rally would be a strong signal that the bearish impulse trend is not complete. This would also indicate that the rally from the July low may be either a correction itself or part of a complex, corrective structure.

Bond Major Low?

As of late July, it clearly looks as if bonds have completed a five-wave bear trend. A failure to make a five-wave rally would signal the bear trend may not be complete.

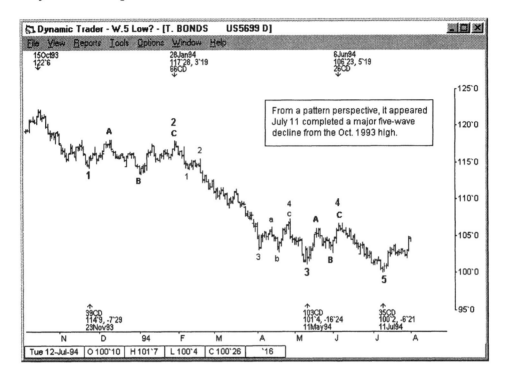

The chart above is daily continuous futures data, often called spot futures or first-month futures data. The contract data is rolled over on the last trading day to the next most active contract with no price adjustments made for the gap at roll-over. All continuous contracts provide certain problems, depending on how the data is used. Any continuous contract that adjusts data backward or forward to "normalize" the data is not suitable for Dynamic Trading analysis as actual prices are not used. All non-adjusted continuous contracts provide some continuity gaps at roll-over periods. In most cases, they are not a problem for long term analysis.

Spot Futures Data And The Wave-2 Correction

The chart on the top of the next page is a close-up of the daily continuous, spot-futures contract for the Nov. 1993 - Jan. 1994, Wave-2 correction. Wave-2s are usually a simple, ABC zigzag. On the spot futures data, the Wave-2 appears to be an ABC, irregular correction where the Wave-B exceeds the low of Wave-1.

If a trend change occurs near a roll-over of a continuous contract, the pattern may be distorted. The next page also shows the same period for Wave-2 on the March 1994 contract which was traded throughout this period.

March 1994 Contract And The Wave-2 Correction

The Nov. - Jan., Wave-2 on the March 1994 contract appears to be a more typical ABC correction. Wave-B does not exceed the low of Wave-1. Wave-C is higher than Wave-A.

Long term time, price and pattern analysis uses the spot-futures data and provides the long term pattern and the relatively broad time and price zones for support, resistance and trend change. Once the long term analysis is complete, traders look to the actual contract data that will be traded to update the market position and time and price targets for the tradable contract.

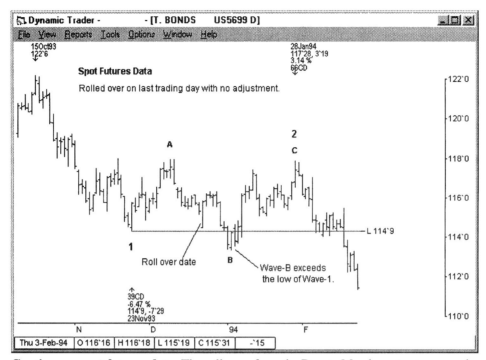

Continuous spot-futures data: The roll-over from the Dec. to March contract occurred a few days prior to the Wave-B low. Distant bond contracts trade at a discount to nearby contracts which distorted the form or pattern of the data near the Wave-B reversal.

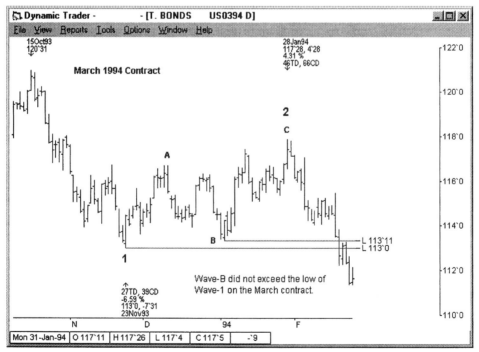

March contract: The March contract traded continuously through the roll-over period and shows price did not actually decline below the W.1 low. If a continuous data roll-over is made near a trend reversal which may distort the pattern, check the single contract month data for that period for the more accurate pattern.

**If A Market Doesn't Do What It Is "Supposed" To Do,
It Will Probably Do Just The Opposite**

The chart on the opposite page is a close-up of the activity immediately following the July 11 low which was initially considered the completion of a five-wave bear trend. Through Aug. 2, it appeared bonds had completed a textbook Wave-1 and Wave-2. Wave-1 (7/11L-7/20H) was clearly subdivided into five minor degree waves. Wave-2 was a perfect ABC correction making the low just three ticks below the 50% retracement. The sharp rally above the Wave-2 high signaled Wave-3 should be underway.

What is the market activity that validates the opinion of the market position?

If July 28 is a Wave-2 low, Wave-3 should reach a price range of approximately 162% of the price range of Wave-1. A decline below the low of Wave-2 would invalidate the outlook that a five-wave impulse trend began from the July 11 low.

Bonds made a top on Aug. 2 and declined to below what was considered the Wave-2 low. The decline below the Wave-2 low invalidated the outlook that an impulsive, five-wave rally began from the July 11 low. The rally to the Aug. 2 high must be considered corrective. Could it be a completed ABC correction of the five-wave bear trend from the Oct. 15, 1993 high to July 11, 1994 low? No. The rally lasted just 22 CDs while the bear trend had lasted over 200 CDs. This July-Aug. rally was probably part of the Wave-4 correction that was originally considered to be complete at the June 6 high.

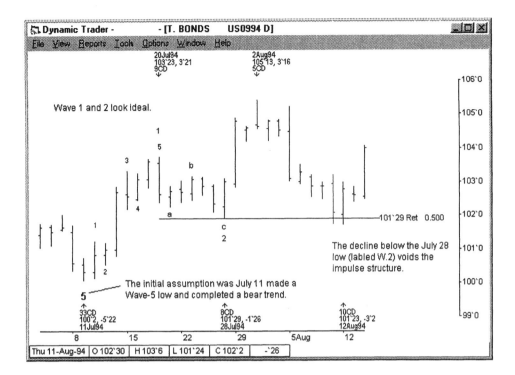

The market activity following the July 11, 1994 low did not unfold in an impulse trend. It was too short in time and price to be considered a completed ABC correction to the Oct. 1993 - July 1994 bear trend. The best alternative is that it was still a part of the Wave-4 correction.

If the rally was not impulsive, then it must be corrective. What does that imply? The bear trend should continue to new lows below the July 11, 1994 low.

Have an opinion on what the market should do, but don't decide what the market will do. - Bernard Baruch

Every decision is made from the basis of an opinion which is a result of our interpretation of the facts at hand. Never be afraid to form an opinion of a market position. But be very afraid of expecting the market to fulfill that opinion. One of the primary causes of failure is traders or investors who hold onto an opinion of the market position long after the market has invalidated the opinion. That is why no opinion should be considered out of context of the activity that will invalidate the opinion.

Trading Strategies Are Related To The Market Position

When you have developed a firm opinion of the market position, formulate trading strategies.

The chart on the next page shows the most probable adjusted wave count. It is assumed Aug. 2 completed a Wave-4 (irregular ABC) correction. The Aug. 2 high was made at the coincidence of the 78.6% retracement and 100% Alternate Price Projection where W.c:C:4 = 100% W.a:C:4. Aug. 2 was also the 61.8% Time Retracement of the prior decline and the 100% Alternate Time Projection where the time range of W.C:4 = 100% of the time range of W.A:4. The Aug. 2 reversal-day high was made at the coincidence of projected time and price.

Since we now have a confident opinion of the position of bonds through the Aug. 2 high, we can begin to consider trading strategies to trade what we believe will be Wave-5 and the final swing down from the Oct. 1993 high.

Only formulate a trading strategy and consider entering a trade once you have a confident opinion of the market position <u>and</u> have identified what market activity will invalidate that opinion.

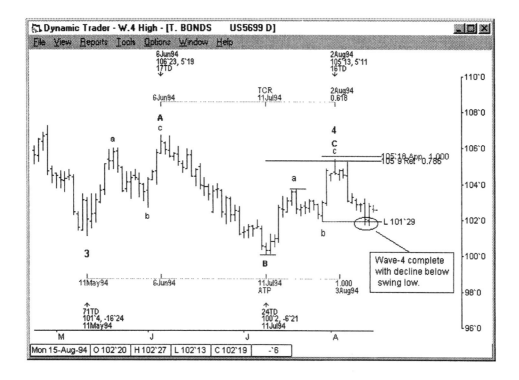

The Bond Market Position As Of Mid-Aug., 1994

1. The Aug. 2 high completed Wave-4 of a five wave count beginning with the Oct. 13, 1993 high. A Wave-5 decline should take bonds to a new low below the July 11 low without exceeding the Aug. 2 high.
2. If Aug. 2 is a completed Wave-4 high, trading strategies should prepare to enter either on the Wave 2:5 correction or on a trend-continuation signal following a confirmation the Wave-2:5 top is complete.
3. A Wave-2 usually retraces 50%-78.6% of Wave-1. A Wave-2 is usually an ABC, zigzag correction.
4. This bearish opinion of the market position is invalidated if the Aug. 2, 1994, Wave-4 high is exceeded.

What Is The Dynamic Trading Analysis That Is Relevant To The Market Position?

Now that we have a firm opinion of the market position including the market activity that will confirm or invalidate the opinion, it is time to identify the Dynamic Trading analysis factors that are relevant to the trading strategies.

Price: A corrective Wave-2 usually terminates in the 50%-78.6% retracement zone.

> 102.25-103.27: 50%-78.6% retracement of Wave-1, (8/2H-8/12L)

Time: There are two periods following the Aug. 12, Wave-2:5 low with clusters of Time Cycle Ratios.

> Aug. 23-24: Includes the 100% Time Retracement of W.1, 100% Second Minor Alternate Time Projection (7/11L-7/20H from 8/12L) and others.

> Sept. 1-5: Should be the maximum time period for W.2:5 correction. Includes the 100% Alternate Time Projection (7/11L-8/2H from 8/12L), 162% Time Retracement and others. See the chart on the opposite page.

Pattern: Ideally, a symmetrical ABC pattern would evolve. Even if the ideal corrective pattern does not evolve, trades should be considered as long as the market has not exceeded the extreme anticipated time and/or price projections for a corrective high.

Initial Trading Strategy: Enter on the close of a daily reversal signal if made within the 50%-78.6% price retracement. If a trend-reversal signal is not made, enter on the first trend-continuation signal following a decline below the Wave-1:5 low.

Trade Preparation and Initiation Worksheet

The worksheet and chart on the next page show the daily bond activity following the Aug. 2 high through Aug. 16, the day bonds rallied into the 50%-78.6% retracement zone.

The worksheet provides all of the relevant information regarding the current market position, time and price projections and signals that will confirm or invalidate the opinion of the market position.

Bonds completed the Wave-1:5 low on Aug. 12. Wave-1:5 subdivided into five minor waves. Three trading days later on Aug. 17, bonds made a minor high on a *signal-day* just below the 78.6% retracement. Since a 78.6% retracement is usually the maximum retracement anticipated for a Wave-2:5 correction, a two-unit, short position (short and intermediate term units) is taken on the close of the *signal-day* with a stop at 103.24, one tick above the high of the signal-day.

The chart on the *Trade Preparation and Initiation Worksheet* does not include the market activity after the date the worksheet was first prepared, Aug. 16. The *Closed Trade Critique Worksheet* will show all of the market activity for the period of the trade.

Review the *Trade Prep* worksheet on the next page and you will see how simply and concisely all of the relevant information is together in one place.

Trade Preparation and Initiation Worksheet

Trade # / Date #1 - 8/16/94

Trade Objective Enter on W.2:5 correction to trade W.3

Market Bonds, Dec. '94

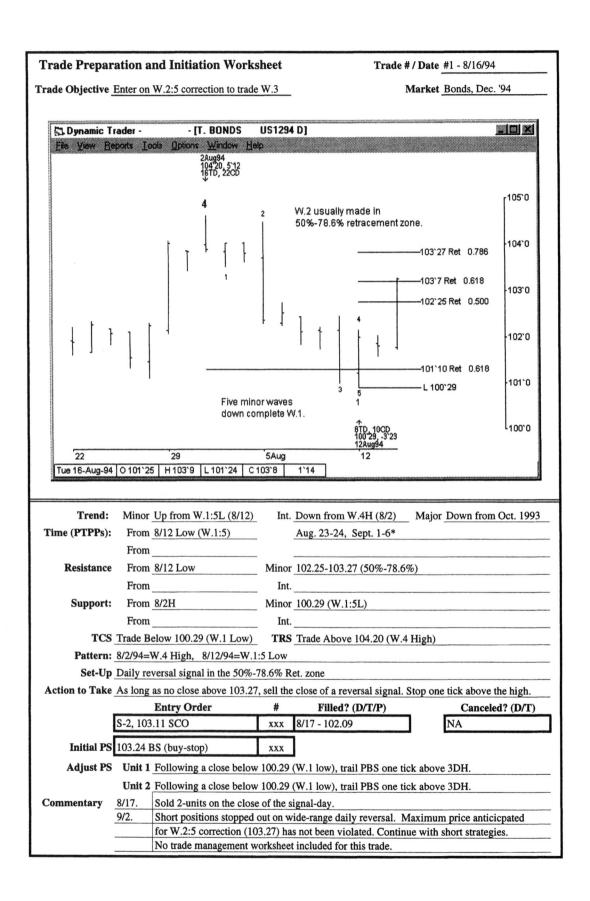

Trend:	Minor Up from W.1:5L (8/12)	Int. Down from W.4H (8/2)	Major Down from Oct. 1993	
Time (PTPPs):	From 8/12 Low (W.1:5)	Aug. 23-24, Sept. 1-6*		
	From			
Resistance	From 8/12 Low	Minor 102.25-103.27 (50%-78.6%)		
	From	Int.		
Support:	From 8/2H	Minor 100.29 (W.1:5L)		
	From	Int.		

TCS Trade Below 100.29 (W.1 Low)   **TRS** Trade Above 104.20 (W.4 High)

Pattern: 8/2/94=W.4 High, 8/12/94=W.1:5 Low

Set-Up Daily reversal signal in the 50%-78.6% Ret. zone

Action to Take As long as no close above 103.27, sell the close of a reversal signal. Stop one tick above the high.

Entry Order	#	Filled? (D/T/P)	Canceled? (D/T)
S-2, 103.11 SCO	xxx	8/17 - 102.09	NA

Initial PS

	#
103.24 BS (buy-stop)	xxx

Adjust PS   Unit 1 Following a close below 100.29 (W.1 low), trail PBS one tick above 3DH.

Unit 2 Following a close below 100.29 (W.1 low), trail PBS one tick above 3DH.

Commentary	8/17.	Sold 2-units on the close of the signal-day.
	9/2.	Short positions stopped out on wide-range daily reversal. Maximum price anticicpated
		for W.2:5 correction (103.27) has not been violated. Continue with short strategies.
		No trade management worksheet included for this trade.

Trade Summary (ST=Short Term, IT=Intermediate Term)

Bonds	Open	Price	Close	Price	P/L
Short (ST)	8/17/94	103.11	-	-	-
Short (IT)	8/17/94	103.11	-	-	-

The Wave-2:5 high would be confirmed as complete on a decline below the Wave-1:5 low. Bonds declined for four trading days and then began to slowly advance.

No *Trade Management Worksheet* was prepared for this trade, as the trade was stopped out relatively quickly before any new, relevant information was made.

Closed Trade Critique Worksheet

The 2-unit short position taken on the close Aug. 17 was stopped out on Sept. 2 when bonds elected the protective buy-stop by trading one tick above the high of the entry-day, Aug. 17.

Traders should not hesitate to include any information considered relevant in the *Trade Comments* and *Lessons Learned* section of the worksheet. These comments will be very valuable when reviewing past trading activity in the future.

Closed Trade Critique Worksheet   **Market** Bonds, Dec. 94   **Trade # / Date** #1, 9/2/94

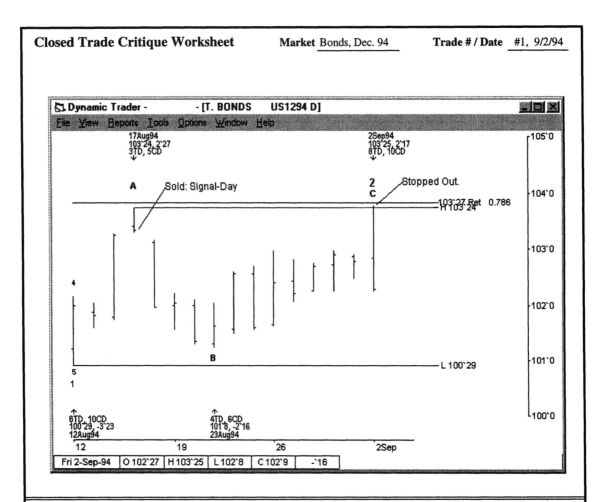

		Entry		**Exit**						
	Unit	Date	Price	Date	Price	P/L	# Con.	Tick Value	Com.	Trade P/L
1	Short (ST)	8/17	103.11	9/2	103.24	-13	1	31.25	35	-441.25
2	Short (IT)	8/17	103.11	9/2	103.24	-13	1	31.25	35	-441.25
3										

Total Trade P / L: -882.50

TRADE COMMENTS Short sale made prior to one of the two Projected Turning Point Periods for a high as price was near the maximum (78.6% Ret.-103.27) anticipated for a corrective W.2:5 high.

Even though stopped out, the larger degree trend remains bearish unless 8/2H exceeded.

LESSONS LEARNED While the trade was stopped out for a loss, the initial capital exposure per contract was relatively small (13 ticks, close to high on entry day).

Trade was well thought out and justified according to the bearish opinion of the market position (larger degree trend). However, a large open profit (over $2000) was given back because the protective buy-stop was not brought closer to the market prior to the W.2 low being exceeded.

Continue to take each trade signal as long as your opinion of the market position has not changed.

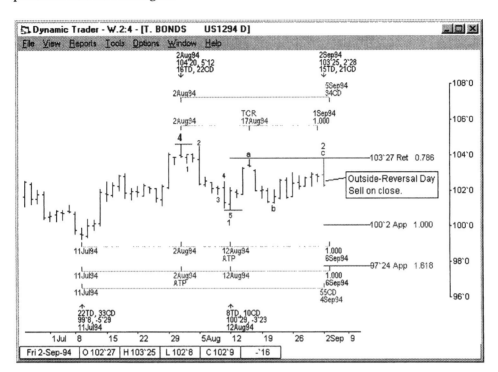

Five time factors are shown on the chart above that cluster in the three trading day period of <u>Sept. 1-5</u> (Thursday-Monday). The time factors for the Aug. 23-24 period are not shown for lack of chart space. If bonds continue to rally, Sept. 1-5 should be the maximum period to complete the Wave-2:5 correction.

On Sept. 2, right within the Sept. 1-5 Projected Turning Point Period, bonds made a wide-range *outside-reversal-day* with a high one tick above the previous high of Aug. 17. The short position was stopped out.

On the very day the short position was stopped out, the ideal conditions to complete an ABC corrective rally are made with the Sept. 2 *outside-reversal-day* high.

Time (Sept. 1-5), *price* (50%-78.6% retracement), *pattern* (Wave-2, ABC) and *daily reversal signal* (outside-reversal-day) coincided.

Another two-unit short position is taken on the close of Sept. 2 at 102.09. The protective buy-stop is placed at 103.26, one tick above the reversal-day high.

Trade Summary To Date, includes $35 Commission
(ST=Short Term, IT=Intermediate Term)

Bonds	Open	Price	Close	Price	P/L
Short (ST)	8/17	103.11	9/2	103.24	($441.25)
Short (IT)	8/17	103.11	9/2	103.24	($441.25)
Short (ST)	9/2	102.09	-	-	-
Short (IT)	9/2	102.09	-	-	-

Trade Management Worksheet

A *Trade Preparation and Initiation Worksheet* is not made for this second short position as the information included on the initial short trade was the same for this second short position.

The next page shows the *Trade Management Worksheet* that was completed a few days following the Sept. 2 entry date.

Trade Management Worksheet

Trade # / Date #2, 9/8/94

Current Position S-2 Dec. Bonds, 9/2, 102.09   **PS-OO** | xxx | B-2, 103.26 |

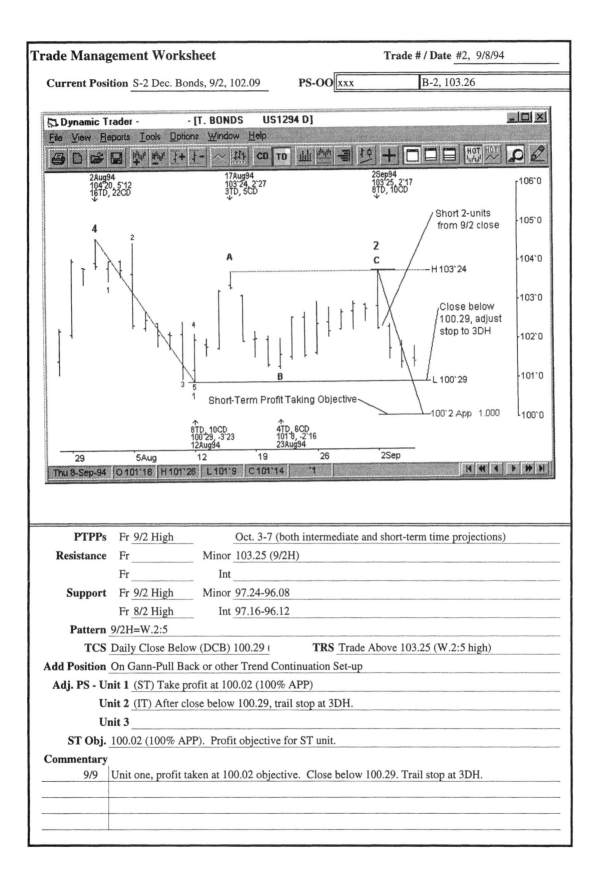

PTPPs	Fr 9/2 High	Oct. 3-7 (both intermediate and short-term time projections)
Resistance	Fr _____	Minor 103.25 (9/2H)
	Fr _____	Int _____
Support	Fr 9/2 High	Minor 97.24-96.08
	Fr 8/2 High	Int 97.16-96.12
Pattern	9/2H=W.2:5	
TCS	Daily Close Below (DCB) 100.29 (	**TRS** Trade Above 103.25 (W.2:5 high)
Add Position	On Gann-Pull Back or other Trend Continuation Set-up	
Adj. PS - Unit 1	(ST) Take profit at 100.02 (100% APP)	
Unit 2	(IT) After close below 100.29, trail stop at 3DH.	
Unit 3	_____	
ST Obj.	100.02 (100% APP). Profit objective for ST unit.	

Commentary

9/9	Unit one, profit taken at 100.02 objective. Close below 100.29. Trail stop at 3DH.

Intermediate Term Wave-5 Price and Time Objectives

Let's step back again for a new look at the larger degree picture. We consider that Aug. 2, 1994 completed a Wave-4 high counting from the Oct. 15, 1993 high. We also consider that bonds have completed Waves 1 and 2 of the larger degree Wave-5. Bonds should continue to decline to a new low before completing Wave-5.

As the chart on the top of the next page shows, the ideal price projection for the Wave-5 low is 97.16-97.12. This relatively narrow price zone includes where W.5 = 100% W.1 and 38.2% W.1-3, each typical W.5 projections. This price zone also included the 50% percentage change retracement of the Sept. 1990 low to the Oct. 1993 high.

These price projections for the bond Wave-5 low are also included as examples in the *Dynamic Price Analysis* chapter. Refer to that chapter for more detail. If bonds continued to decline as anticipated, the sub-divisions of Wave-5 should fine-tune the price projections. Ideally, we will find the price projections of the sub-divisions of Wave-5 would fall at or near the Wave-5 price projections.

The chart on the bottom of the opposite page is from the *Dynamic Time Analysis* chapter and shows the Time Rhythm Zone and Dynamic Time Projections for a Wave-5 low projected from the Aug. 2, 1994 Wave-4 high. The Time Rhythm Zone indicates the Wave-5 low should be made in the Oct. 26-Nov. 28 period. The Nov. 11-14 Dynamic Time Projection falls in the TRZ period. For more detail how these specific time projections were made, review the *Dynamic Time Analysis* chapter.

Wave-5 Minimum Price and Time Objectives

97.16: *Minimum* price objective for W.5
Oct. 26: *Minimum* time objective for W.5

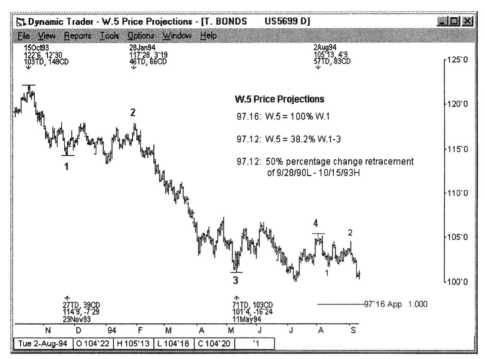

The minimum W.5 price objective is 97.16, the beginning of the ideal price range for W.5. Ideally, the price projections of the subdivisions of W.5 will fall at or near the W.5 projections.

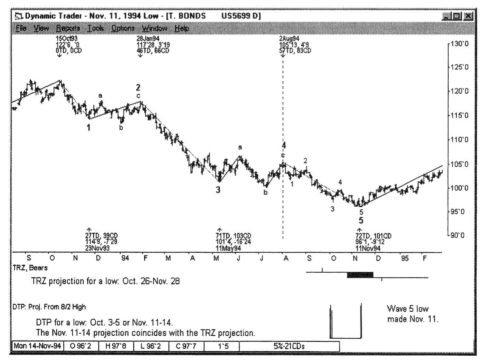

The minimum time objective for W.5 is Oct. 26, the beginning of the Time Rhythm Zone for the W.5 low. The ideal period to complete W.5 is Nov. 11-14, the Dynamic Time Projection which falls within the TRZ.

Trailing The Stop and Adding Positions

When the trend is confirmed, trail the protective stop-loss to protect open profits.

The W.3:5 trend is confirmed when the market trades below the W.1:5 low at 100.29. If this should occur, trail the protective buy-stop at one tick above the 3DH.

Add positions on a trend-continuation trade entry set-up.

A Wave-3 is usually the longest wave in a five-wave sequence. In the current case, W.3:5 should be greater in time and price than W.1:5. Once the trend is confirmed by making the *Trend Continuation Signal* of a trade below the W.1:5 low, consider trend-continuation trade entry set-ups to add a position.

What is the logical profit objective for the short-term position of a mult-unit trade?

Recall from the *Trading Strategies* chapter that the short-term trade objective should be the objective reached even if the trend was the opposite of what is anticipated. In other words, if an impulsive trend is anticipated, what would be the typical objective if the trend was corrective, not impulsive? In the current case with bonds, the 100% Alternate Price Projection where W.3:5 would equal W.1:5 is the minimum price objective anticipated even if the trend were not impulsive.

Bonds continued to decline to below the Wave-1:5 low confirming Sept. 2 completed Wave-2:5. On Sept. 9, bonds declined sharply to close below the Wave-1:5 low and hit the profit objective of 100.02 for the short-term position.

Trade Summary To Date , includes $35 commission
(ST = Short Term, IT = Intermediate Term)

Bonds	Open	Price	Close	Price	P/L
Short (ST)	8/17	103.11	9/2	103.24	($441.25)
Short (IT)	8/17	103.11	9/2	103.24	($441.25)
Short (ST)	9/2	102.09	9/9	100.02	$2183.75
Short (IT)	9/2	102.09	-	-	-

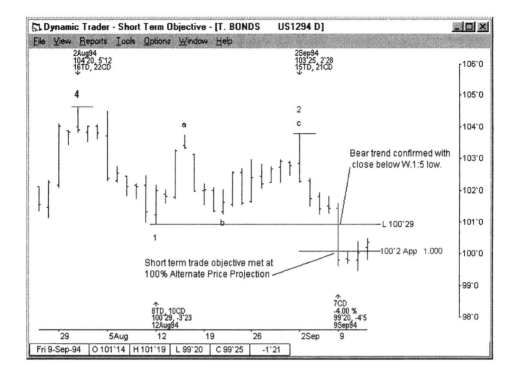

On Sept. 9, bonds made a sharp decline below the W.1:5 low confirming the W.2:5 high. Bonds also reached the profit-taking objective for the short-term unit of the two unit short position. No matter how confident we are of the position of a market, we never know in advance if a trend will continue. In the long run, it is most profitable to trade in two or three unit positions and take profits on one unit on a short-term objective. Even though we have taken profits on the short-term objective, we still anticipate a continued decline unless and until the market signals otherwise.

With the close below the W.1:5 low at 100.29, the protective-buy stop on the second, intermediate term position is trailed at one tick above the 3DH. If bonds reach a time and price support objective, the stop will be brought closer to the market.

Gann Pull-Back Trend Continuation Trade Set-Up

In the second week of Sept., bonds made a three day rally, setting up a *Gann-Pull Back* (GPB) trend-continuation trade set-up. The chart on the next page will show this set-up. Bonds were still near the 100% Alternate Price Projection. Lower prices were anticipated. As of Sept. 15, bonds had made three-higher highs for the GPB trade entry set-up. A sell-stop is placed one tick below the prior day's low. On Sept. 16, bonds declined below the prior day's low electing the sell-stop at 100.09, one tick below the prior day's low. The protective buy-stop for this new position is placed at 100.29, one tick above the higher of entry day or the prior day per the Gann Pull-Back trend-continuation initial stop-loss rules.

There are now two short positions. The intermediate-term unit taken from the Sept. 2 outside-reversal-day high and one taken Sept. 16 on the Gann Pull-Back, trend-continuation signal.

Protective Stops and Trend-Continuation Trade Entry

Each trend-continuation trade entry set-up includes an initial protective stop rule that is quite close to the trade-entry price. In the case of the GPB trade entry set-up, the protective sell-stop is placed one tick above the higher of the high of entry day or the high of the day prior to entry. (See Gann Pull-Back, *Trading Strategies* chapter.)

Even if an additional position is taken with a trend-continuation entry strategy, the protective stop on the open position should continue to follow the existing strategy.

In the current case with bonds, the protective buy-stop on the intermediate-term short position is one tick above the 3DH. This strategy should be maintained. Trend-continuation entry strategies are high probability and low capital exposure positions that are only maintained if the short-term trend immediately continues in favor of the trade. Immediately being stopped out of a trend-continuation trade is not a sign the larger degree trend has changed. It is only a signal that the immediate short-term trend may not continue.

If the trend immediately continues in favor of the trend-continuation trade, the protective sell stop for both open positions should soon be the same.

Short Position Added On Gann-Pull Back Set-Up

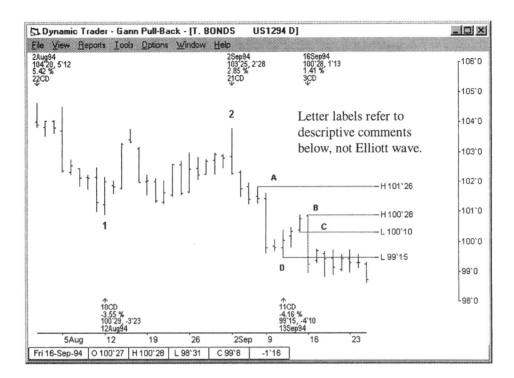

From the Sept. 13 low, bonds made three higher-highs making a Gann Pull-Back trend-continuation trade set-up. A sell-stop to enter a short position is placed one tick below the prior day's low each day.

On Sept. 16, bonds declined below the prior day's low (C, 100.10) for a GPB trade entry. The initial protective buy-stop is placed at 100.29 one tick above the high or 100.28 (B).

At the time of the GPB short sale, the 3DH was at 101.26 (A). The stop on the open intermediate term position remains one tick above the 3DH.

The wide-range down-day of Sept. 16 declined below the Sept. 13 low (D). The 3DH is now at 100.28. The protective buy-stop for both short positions is now the same at one tick above the 3DH.

Trade Summary To Date , includes $35 commission
(ST = Short Term, IT = Intermediate Term)

Bonds	Open	Price	Close	Price	P/L
Short (ST)	8/17	103.11	9/2	103.24	($441.25)
Short (IT)	8/17	103.11	9/2	103.24	($441.25)
Short (ST)	9/2	102.09	9/9	100.02	$2183.75
Short (IT)	9/2	102.09	-	-	-
Short (GPB)	9/16	100.09	-	-	-

Trade Management Worksheet

A new and updated *Trade Management Worksheet* is prepared after taking the new Gann Pull-Back short position.

The time and price targets are described on the pages following the worksheet.

Trade Management Worksheet

Trade # / Date #2 and #3, 9/16/94

Current Position S-2 Dec. Bonds   **PS-OO** xxx   B-2, 3DH

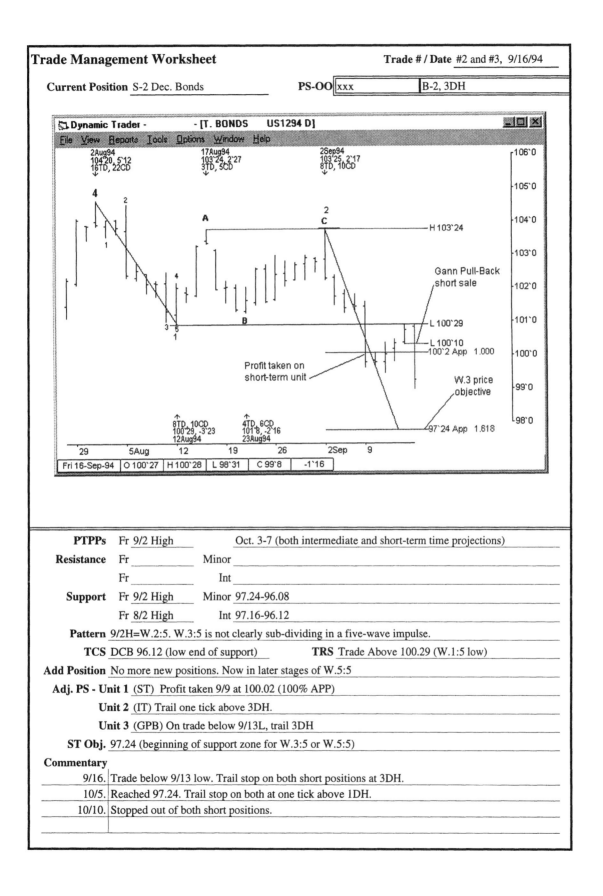

PTPPs	Fr 9/2 High		Oct. 3-7 (both intermediate and short-term time projections)
Resistance	Fr	Minor	
	Fr	Int	
Support	Fr 9/2 High	Minor	97.24-96.08
	Fr 8/2 High	Int	97.16-96.12
Pattern	9/2H=W.2:5. W.3:5 is not clearly sub-dividing in a five-wave impulse.		
TCS	DCB 96.12 (low end of support)	**TRS**	Trade Above 100.29 (W.1:5 low)
Add Position	No more new positions. Now in later stages of W.5:5		
Adj. PS - Unit 1	(ST) Profit taken 9/9 at 100.02 (100% APP)		
Unit 2	(IT) Trail one tick above 3DH.		
Unit 3	(GPB) On trade below 9/13L, trail 3DH		
ST Obj.	97.24 (beginning of support zone for W.3:5 or W.5:5)		

Commentary

9/16.	Trade below 9/13 low. Trail stop on both short positions at 3DH.
10/5.	Reached 97.24. Trail stop on both at one tick above 1DH.
10/10.	Stopped out of both short positions.

Time and Price Support Projections

Calculate in advance the time and price projections with the greatest probability of support or resistance and trend change. If an Elliott Wave pattern is evident, consider the high probability time and price projections that are typical for the wave in progress.

Wave-3 is in progress for bonds. What are the high probability time and price targets typical for a Wave-3?

Wave-3:5 Price Target: 97.24-96.08

97.24: W.3:5 = 162% W.1:5
96.08: W.3:5 = 262% W.2:5.

These projections fall in the same price area as the larger degree projections at 97.16-97.12 for the larger degree W.5 low shown earlier. Unfortunately, W.3:5 was not clearly subdividing into a five wave structure. There was no confident way to project the lesser degree sub-divisions.

Wave-3:5 Time Projection: Oct. 3-7

Oct. 5-7 included four minor-degree, time projections including the 162% Time Retracement where the time of Wave-3:5 would equal 162% of the time of Wave-1:5. See the chart on the opposite page.
Oct. 3-5 was a larger degree Dynamic Time Projection cluster made from the Aug. 2 high shown on the chart several pages ago.
Oct. 3-7 is the combination of both degrees of dynamic time projections.

Should these time and price support zones be considered targets to complete Wave-5 from the Aug. 2 high, not just Wave-3:5? Maybe. The time objectives do not fall within the minimum time projection of Oct. 26 for a W.5 low according to the TRZ. However, if the decline from the Aug. 2 high were clearly sub-dividing into a five wave structure into these time and price support projections, a final low may be anticipated. Otherwise, a low made in these support projections would probably only be a W.3:5. As bonds approached the Oct. 3-7 PTPP, they were not clearly completing a five-wave structure.

Adjust trading strategies as the market evolves.

As a market approaches time and price objectives for the current trend, stop-losses on open positions should be brought relatively close to the market. There are currently two open short positions. If bonds should reach the price support zone within the time support zone, protective stop losses on both positions should be adjusted daily to one tick above the 1DH.

Time Support: Oct. 3-7
Price Support: 97.24-96.08

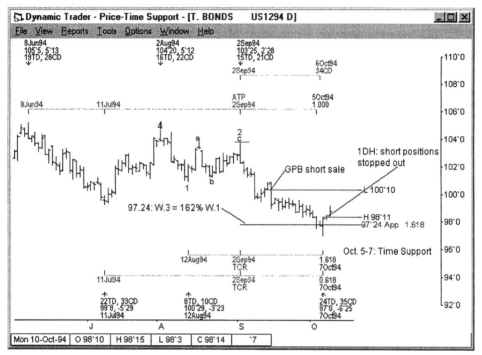

On <u>Oct. 5</u>, right within the Oct. 3-7 time support zone, bonds reached <u>97.24</u>, the beginning of the price support zone at 97.24-96.08. The protective buy-stop should now be adjusted daily to one tick above the one-day-high (1DH). Two day's later on Oct. 7, bonds made an *outside-reversal-day* (OSRD) precisely within the projected time and price support zones. The next trading day, Oct. 10, the two short positions were stopped out as bonds rallied above the 1DH. The short positions were not stopped out on the Oct. 7 OSRD because the previous day was an inside-day. Inside days are not counted for 1, 2 or 3 day highs.

Trade Summary To Date , includes $35 commission
(ST = Short Term, IT = Intermediate Term)

Bonds	Open	Price	Close	Price	P/L
Short (ST)	8/17	103.11	9/2	103.24	($441.25)
Short (IT)	8/17	103.11	9/2	103.24	($441.25)
Short (ST)	9/2	102.09	9/9	100.02	$2183.75
Short (IT)	9/2	102.09	10/10	98.12	$3871.25
Short (GPB)	9/16	100.09	10/10	98.12	1871.25

Closed Trade Critique Worksheet

The next page shows the *Closed Trade Critique Worksheet* that includes the intermediate-term and Gann Pull-Back short positions.

Closed Trade Critique Worksheet   **Market** Bonds, Dec. 94   **Trade # / Date** #2 & 3, 10/10

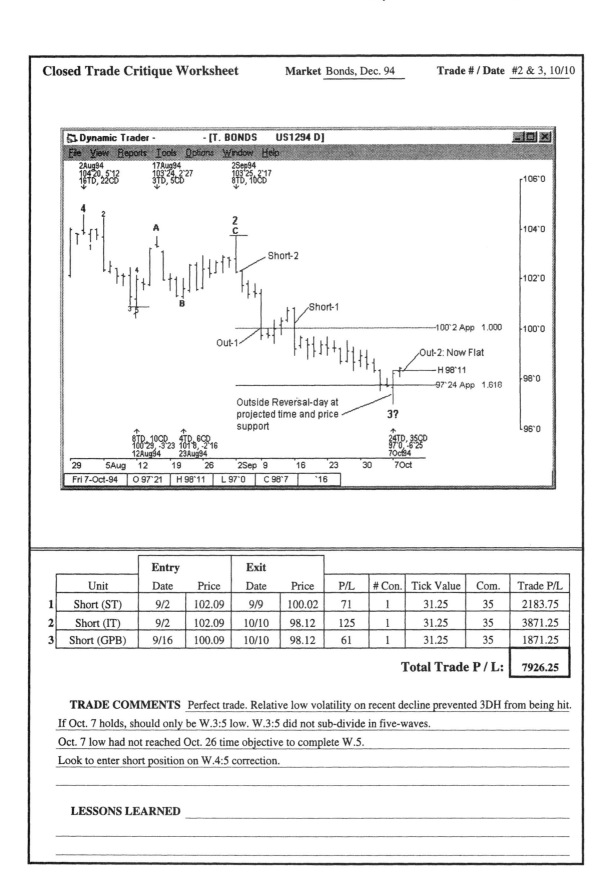

	Unit	Entry Date	Entry Price	Exit Date	Exit Price	P/L	# Con.	Tick Value	Com.	Trade P/L
1	Short (ST)	9/2	102.09	9/9	100.02	71	1	31.25	35	2183.75
2	Short (IT)	9/2	102.09	10/10	98.12	125	1	31.25	35	3871.25
3	Short (GPB)	9/16	100.09	10/10	98.12	61	1	31.25	35	1871.25

Total Trade P / L: 7926.25

TRADE COMMENTS Perfect trade. Relative low volatility on recent decline prevented 3DH from being hit.

If Oct. 7 holds, should only be W.3:5 low. W.3:5 did not sub-divide in five-waves.

Oct. 7 low had not reached Oct. 26 time objective to complete W.5.

Look to enter short position on W.4:5 correction.

LESSONS LEARNED

Trading Strategies Evolve As The Market Evolves

The Aug. 2 high to Oct. 7 low did not appear to be a complete five-wave structure. Bonds should still make a Wave-4:5 corrective rally followed by a further decline to a new low. Ideally, the final Wave 5:5 low would be made in the Oct. 26-Nov. 28 TRZ and at or near the Nov. 11-14 PTPP for a low.

The next trading objective is to look to enter a short position at or near a Wave-4:5 corrective top or on a confirmation that a Wave-4:5 corrective top is complete. A Wave-4:5 corrective top should be made in the broad price zone of 99.18-100.17.

Ideal Wave-4 Price Objective: 99.18-99.27 or 100.12-100.17

99.18: W.c = 162% W.b
99.19: 38.2% retracement, W.3
99.23: W.c = 61.8% W.a
99.27: W.4 = 100% W.2

100.12: 50% retracement
100.17: W.c = 100% W.a

Trading Strategy: Sell bonds on the close of a daily reversal signal if bonds have reached at least 99.18. Or, if a trend-reversal trade set-up is not made, sell bonds on a trend-continuation trade signal following a trade below the Wave-3:5 low.

On Oct. 18, bonds made an ABC corrective high at 99.21 on a *reversal-day*, right within the ideal price projection for a Wave-4:5 high at 99.18-99.27. The sell order is made at the close of 99.01 with a protective buy-stop at 99.22, one tick above the *reversal-day* high. Bonds continued to decline to below the Wave-b:4:5 low confirming the Wave-4:5 high.

Trade Summary To Date , includes $35 commission
(ST = Short Term, IT = Intermediate Term)

Bonds	Open	Price	Close	Price	P/L
Short (ST)	8/17	103.11	9/2	103.24	($441.25)
Short (IT)	8/17	103.11	9/2	103.24	($441.25)
Short (ST)	9/2	102.09	9/9	100.02	$2183.75
Short (IT)	9/2	102.09	10/10	98.12	$3871.25
Short (GPB)	9/16	100.09	10/10	98.12	1871.25
Short (ST)	10/18	99.01	-	-	-

Trade Preparation and Initiation Worksheet

Trade # / Date #4 - 10/13/94

Trade Objective Enter on W.4:5 correction for W.5:5 decline

Market Bonds, Dec. '94

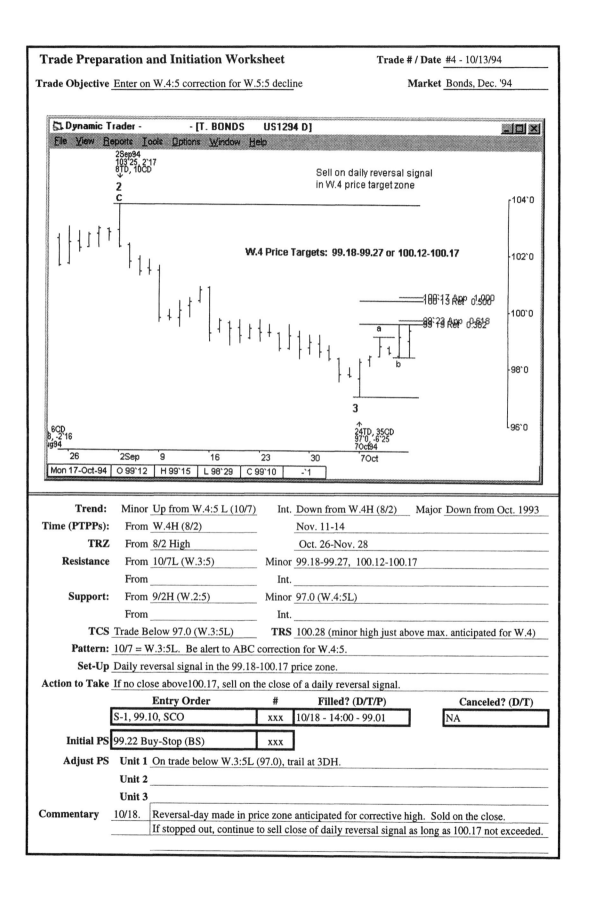

Trend:	Minor Up from W.4:5 L (10/7)	Int. Down from W.4H (8/2)	Major Down from Oct. 1993
Time (PTPPs):	From W.4H (8/2)	Nov. 11-14	
TRZ	From 8/2 High	Oct. 26-Nov. 28	
Resistance	From 10/7L (W.3:5)	Minor 99.18-99.27, 100.12-100.17	
	From	Int.	
Support:	From 9/2H (W.2:5)	Minor 97.0 (W.4:5L)	
	From	Int.	

TCS Trade Below 97.0 (W.3:5L)   **TRS** 100.28 (minor high just above max. anticipated for W.4)

Pattern: 10/7 = W.3:5L. Be alert to ABC correction for W.4:5.

Set-Up Daily reversal signal in the 99.18-100.17 price zone.

Action to Take If no close above100.17, sell on the close of a daily reversal signal.

	Entry Order	#	Filled? (D/T/P)	Canceled? (D/T)
	S-1, 99.10, SCO	xxx	10/18 - 14:00 - 99.01	NA
Initial PS	99.22 Buy-Stop (BS)	xxx		

Adjust PS   **Unit 1** On trade below W.3:5L (97.0), trail at 3DH.

        Unit 2

        Unit 3

Commentary   10/18. Reversal-day made in price zone anticipated for corrective high. Sold on the close.

If stopped out, continue to sell close of daily reversal signal as long as 100.17 not exceeded.

Wave 5:5 Price Objective

Bonds continued lower from the Oct. 18, Wave-4:5 high and continued to decline to below the Wave-3:5 low. At what price should the Wave-5:5 low be made?

The chart included with the *Trade Management Worksheet* on the next page shows that 95.30-94.30 is the ideal target for the Wave-5:5 low. This price zone included all typical Wave-5 price objectives.

Wave-5:5 Price Target: 95.30-94.30
95.30: W.5 = 100% W.1
95.11: W.5 = 162% W.4
94.30: W.5 = 61.8% W.1-3

As a market reaches the time and/or price targets with a high probability of terminating the trend, trail the protective buy-stop relatively close to the current market position.

Adjust the protective buy-stop: On a trade below 95.30, the beginning of the ideal price zone projected for the W.5:5 low, trail the protective buy-stop at one tick above the 1DH.

When Projected Time, Price and Pattern Coincide, Change Is Inevitable

In early Nov., bonds closed below the Wave-3 low. The protective buy-stop is trailed at the 3DH. Bonds were making new lows into the TRZ beginning Oct. 26 for a final bottom. Nov. 11 was approaching which began the Dynamic Time Projection for the W.5 low (Nov. 11-14). Bonds were nearing the time and price projections for a Wave-5:5 low. Ideally, the Wave-5:5 decline from the Oct. 18 high would sub-divide into five waves.

Bonds never reached the 95.30 price which would have changed the protective buy-stop strategy to the 1DH. On Nov. 10, bonds traded above the 3DH stopping out the short position.

The following two pages include the *Trade Management* and *Closed Trade Critique Worksheets* for this bond short trade.

Trade Management Worksheet

Trade # / Date #4, 11/3/94

Current Position S-1 Dec. Bond, 10/18, 99.01   **PS-OO** | xxx | Trail at 3DH

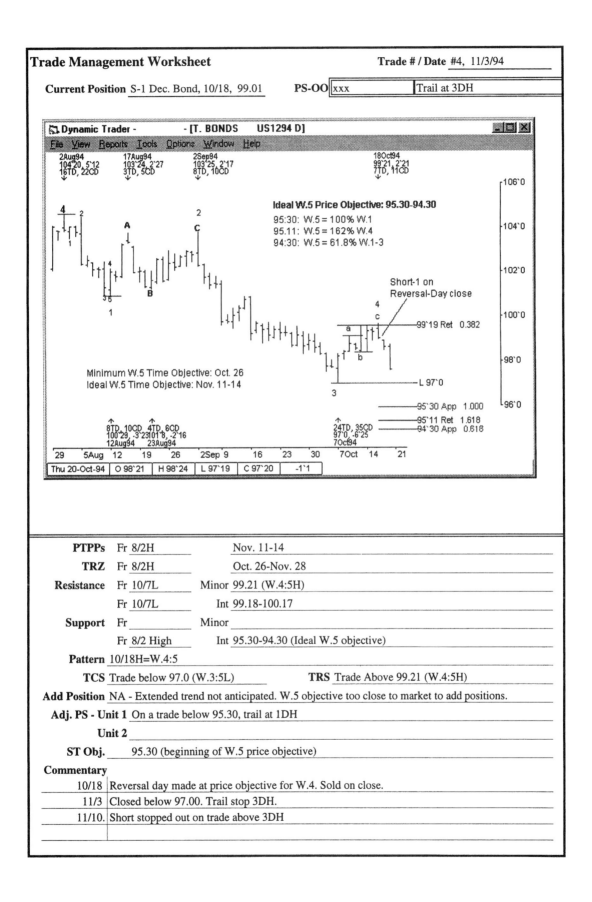

PTPPs	Fr 8/2H		Nov. 11-14
TRZ	Fr 8/2H		Oct. 26-Nov. 28
Resistance	Fr 10/7L	Minor	99.21 (W.4:5H)
	Fr 10/7L	Int	99.18-100.17
Support	Fr	Minor	
	Fr 8/2 High	Int	95.30-94.30 (Ideal W.5 objective)
Pattern	10/18H=W.4:5		

TCS Trade below 97.0 (W.3:5L)   **TRS** Trade Above 99.21 (W.4:5H)

Add Position NA - Extended trend not anticipated. W.5 objective too close to market to add positions.

Adj. PS - Unit 1 On a trade below 95.30, trail at 1DH

Unit 2

ST Obj. 95.30 (beginning of W.5 price objective)

Commentary

10/18	Reversal day made at price objective for W.4. Sold on close.
11/3	Closed below 97.00. Trail stop 3DH.
11/10.	Short stopped out on trade above 3DH

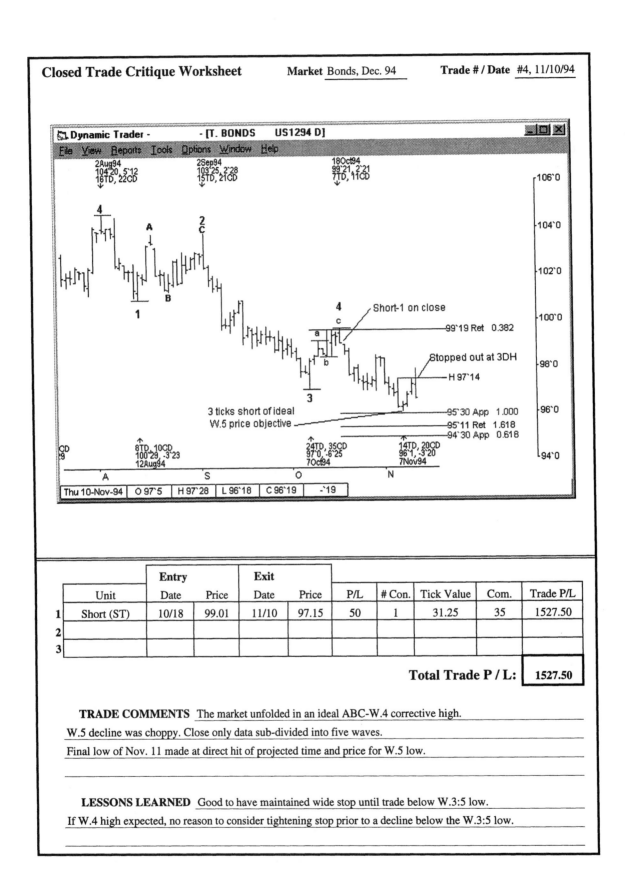

	Unit	Entry		Exit		P/L	# Con.	Tick Value	Com.	Trade P/L
		Date	Price	Date	Price					
1	Short (ST)	10/18	99.01	11/10	97.15	50	1	31.25	35	1527.50
2										
3										

Total Trade P / L: **1527.50**

TRADE COMMENTS The market unfolded in an ideal ABC-W.4 corrective high.

W.5 decline was choppy. Close only data sub-divided into five waves.

Final low of Nov. 11 made at direct hit of projected time and price for W.5 low.

LESSONS LEARNED Good to have maintained wide stop until trade below W.3:5 low.

If W.4 high expected, no reason to consider tightening stop prior to a decline below the W.3:5 low.

When Time, Price and Pattern Coincide, Change Is Inevitable

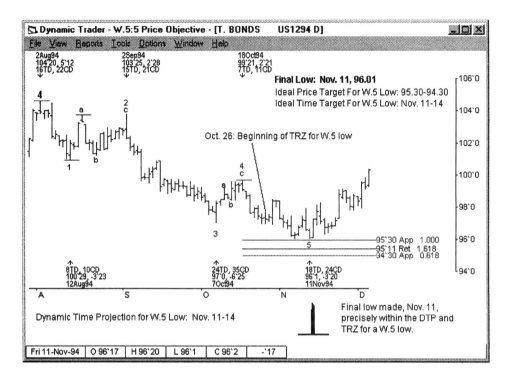

The final Wave-5:5 low was made <u>Nov. 11</u> at <u>96.01</u> precisely within the time projection for a low and just three ticks short of the ideal price projection.

Time (Oct. 26-Nov. 28 TRZ and Nov. 11-14 PTPP), *Price* (95.30-94.30, W.5:5 projections) and *Pattern* (W.5 from Oct. 1993 high) had all coincided to form a major low. The only missing factor was Wave-5:5 did not appear to sub-divide in an ideal, five-wave impulse structure. However, if you look at a close-only chart (not shown), you will find the Nov. 11 closing low completed an ideal five minor waves from the Oct. 18 high.

Trade Summary: Dec. 1994 Bond Trades: 8/17/94 - 11/10/94

Below is a table of the summary of all of the trades described with a chart showing each buy and sell signal.

Trade Summary To Date , includes $35 commission
(ST = Short Term, IT = Intermediate Term)

Bonds	Open	Price	Close	Price	P/L
Short (ST)	8/17	103.11	9/2	103.24	($441.25)
Short (IT)	8/17	103.11	9/2	103.24	($441.25)
Short (ST)	9/2	102.09	9/9	100.02	$2183.75
Short (IT)	9/2	102.09	10/10	98.12	$3871.25
Short (GPB)	9/16	100.09	10/10	98.12	1871.25
Short (ST)	10/18	99.01	11/10	97.15	$1527.50

Net Profit / Loss $8571.25

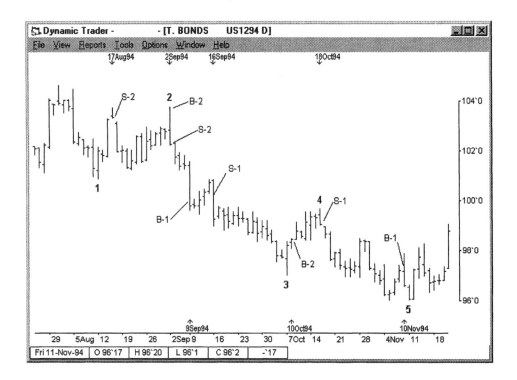

It Really Is Easier Than You Think

It has taken over 30 pages to describe in detail the approach, analysis and trading strategies that were a part of just these four trades that took place over a three month period. In actual practice, it takes only a few minutes per day to update the analysis, review the market position and prepare the trading strategies.

If you review this section again, note how few price and time calculations were actually made as the market unfolded over this period. Most important, review the *consistency of approach*.

1. The market position (major trend and position in the trend) is first considered.
2. The time and price projections anticipated to put the market in a low-risk, low-capital exposure trade set-up are calculated and noted on the worksheet.
3. Trades were only entered on a daily trend-reversal or trend-continuation signal when the market was in the appropriate time, price and pattern position.
4. Early in the trend sequence, two-unit positions were taken. Profits were taken on one unit at a short-term price objective. The second unit was held in the event the anticipated price projections were met.
5. Early in the trend sequence, additional units were added on low-risk, low-capital exposure trend-continuation signals.
6. The initial protective stop-loss was not adjusted until the market action confirmed the trend direction.
7. The protective stop-loss was trailed fairly far from the current market activity (3DH) until the market reached either the minimum or ideal price projection.
8. The protective stop-loss was then brought close to the market (1DH).

Consistency Of Approach Is A Key Factor To Trading Success

Bonds declined from the Aug. 2, 1994, Wave-4 high in a five-wave structure. While each of the waves did not sub-divide ideally, they each made their highs and lows at typical price and time projections for that particular wave. Do market trends always unfold in almost ideal five-wave structures at direct hits of projected time and price? Of course not. But they often do! If you stick to a trading plan, you will take advantage of the opportunity each time they do. When they don't, your Dynamic Trading analysis and trading strategies should help to capture relatively small profits and keep losses relatively small while you remain in a position to take advantage of a trend swing.

Do all corrections unfold in nice symmetrical ABC, zigzags? Of course not. But many of them do! You can *never* know how a market will unfold. But you must have the discipline to wait and be prepared to take advantage of high probability market positions when they do unfold.

Bonds Following The Nov. 11, 1994, Wave-Five Low

Let's continue to follow the bond activity and implement trading strategies for the months that followed the Nov. 1994 low. The following pages will not provide as much descriptive and commentary detail as the prior pages. We will rely more on the trading log worksheets for the necessary information. Most importantly, the approach will remain consistent.

Bonds made a five-wave bear trend of just over a year from the Oct. 1993 high to the Nov. 1994 low. Since the five-wave decline began from historic high levels for bond futures, we may consider it Wave-1 of a long-term, five-wave sequence. Long term Elliott wave analysis is not particularly reliable, so let's not make a long-term analysis just yet.

We should anticipate that a corrective trend would reach the broad zones of 38.2%-61.8% price and time retracements and should not exceed the 78.6% price retracement. These are very broad ranges, but at least initially provide us with minimum and maximum time and price targets to anticipate. The dynamic time and pattern analysis as the market unfolds as well as the price projections of lesser degree should help to pinpoint the important targets to complete the corrective rally.

Minimum Time and Price Objectives For The Correction

The assumption is Nov. 11, 1994 completed a major five-wave decline from the Oct. 1993 high. A corrective rally from the Nov. low should be of greater "degree" than any of the corrective rallies that were sub-divisions of the bear trend. A corrective rally should "overbalance" the corrective rallies within the five-wave decline. In other words, the time and price of the corrective advance should exceed the largest time and price of the Wave 2 and 4 corrective rallies.

The largest corrective price rally was Wave-A of Wave-4. The alternate price projection of W.A:4 projected from the Nov. 11, 1994 low is at 101.20. A corrective rally from the Nov. 11 low should exceed 101.20.

Recall from the previous section that the continuous spot futures chart distorted the Wave-2 rally at roll-over to appear like an irregular-ABC. The March 1994 contract showed that Wave-B did not actually trade below the Wave-1 low. The Wave-2 correction lasted 66 CDs. Sixty-six calendar days from the Nov. 11, 1994 low is Jan. 16, 1995. A corrective rally from the Nov. 11 low should continue beyond Jan. 16, 1995.

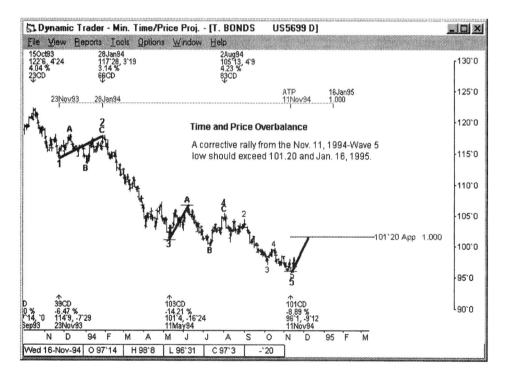

Jan. 16 and 101.20 are only the very minimum time and price ranges anticipated for the corrective rally. Being aware of the minimum ranges helps the trader keep a perspective on a trend or counter-trend and avoid taking a position against the trend too early. Other Dynamic Trading factors will provide the high probability targets for support, resistance and trend reversal.

Typical Time and Price Objectives For The Correction

The typical correction falls in the 38.2%-61.8% time and price retracement zones. From an Elliott wave perspective, corrections very often conclude in the price range of the previous Wave-4 and usually at the extreme of Wave-4. The Wave-4 high fell at 106.23 just above the 38.2% retracement. This provides a strong confirmation that the corrective rally should reach 106.01 or higher.

The 38.2% time retracement is April 13, 1995. There is a high probability that a corrective rally will not be complete prior to April 13, 1995.

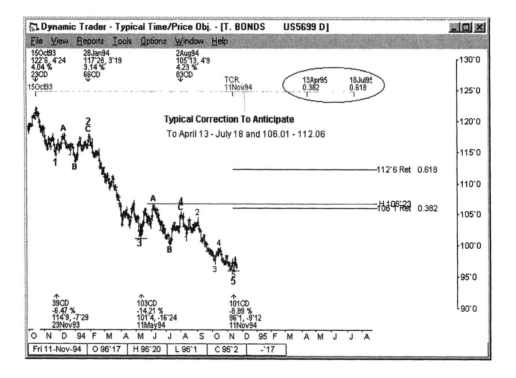

The minimum and typical time and price targets for the corrective rally provide us with important yardsticks to judge the position of a correction. We should anticipate the corrective rally will exceed the minimum objectives and reach the typical objectives unless the Dynamic Trading technical position of the correction provides a compelling reason to think otherwise.

Buy Bottoms, Sell Tops

When the Dynamic Trading analysis provides overwhelming evidence of a trend reversal, trading strategies should be oriented to entering a position on the first opportunity rather than waiting for the market to confirm the new trend.

In the current case with bonds, each factor of time, price and pattern strongly signals that Nov. 11, 1994 completed the bear market. A five-wave sequence should always be in the direction of the larger degree trend. If the larger degree trend has turned bullish, a five-wave advance should follow the Nov. 11 low.

A Wave-2 usually retraces at least 50% and usually not more than 78.6% of the Wave-1. The trading strategy is to look to buy bonds on a daily reversal signal in the 50%-78.6% retracement of the initial minor rally. If bonds enter the 50%-78.6% retracement zone, a long position should also be taken on a trend-continuation signal.

The next page is the *Trade Preparation and Initiation Worksheet* to prepare to enter a bond long position.

Trade Preparation and Initiation Worksheet Trade # / Date #5 - 11/16/94

Trade Objective Enter on W.2 correction   Market Bonds, March '95

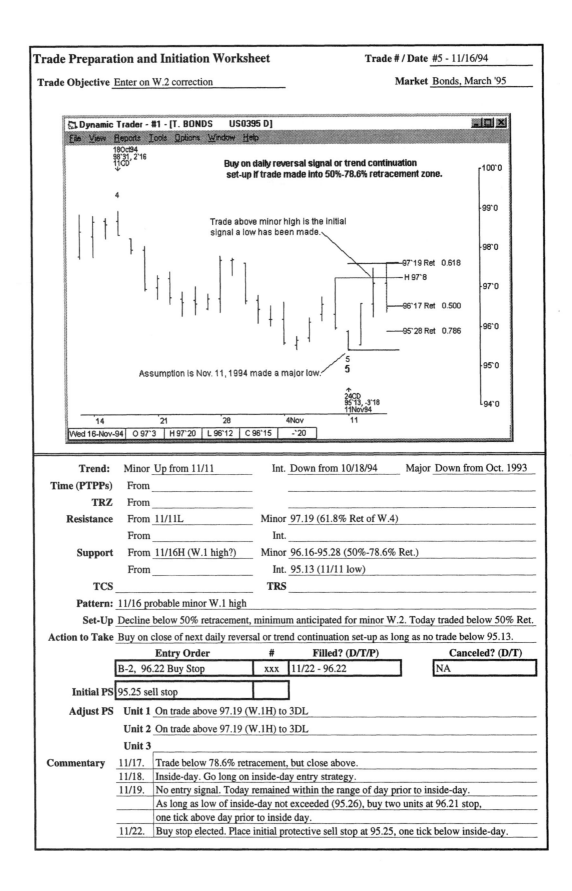

Trend:	Minor Up from 11/11	Int. Down from 10/18/94	Major Down from Oct. 1993
Time (PTPPs)	From		
TRZ	From		
Resistance	From 11/11L	Minor 97.19 (61.8% Ret of W.4)	
	From	Int.	
Support	From 11/16H (W.1 high?)	Minor 96.16-95.28 (50%-78.6% Ret.)	
	From	Int. 95.13 (11/11 low)	
TCS		TRS	

Pattern: 11/16 probable minor W.1 high

Set-Up Decline below 50% retracement, minimum anticipated for minor W.2. Today traded below 50% Ret.

Action to Take Buy on close of next daily reversal or trend continuation set-up as long as no trade below 95.13.

	Entry Order	#	Filled? (D/T/P)	Canceled? (D/T)
	B-2, 96.22 Buy Stop	xxx	11/22 - 96.22	NA
Initial PS	95.25 sell stop			
Adjust PS	Unit 1 On trade above 97.19 (W.1H) to 3DL			
	Unit 2 On trade above 97.19 (W.1H) to 3DL			
	Unit 3			
Commentary	11/17.	Trade below 78.6% retracement, but close above.		
	11/18.	Inside-day. Go long on inside-day entry strategy.		
	11/19.	No entry signal. Today remained within the range of day prior to inside-day.		
		As long as low of inside-day not exceeded (95.26), buy two units at 96.21 stop, one tick above day prior to inside day.		
	11/22.	Buy stop elected. Place initial protective sell stop at 95.25, one tick below inside-day.		

Trade Management

Bonds did not make a daily reversal signal after having declined below the 50% retracement. An *inside-day* was made Nov. 18 which provided an inside-day trade-entry set-up. A buy-stop to enter a long position is placed one tick above the high of the day prior to the inside-day. The day following the inside-day did not trade out of the range of the day prior to the inside-day and did not trade below the low of the inside-day. The buy-stop was held for the next day.

On Nov. 22, the buy-stop was elected for a two-unit long position. The protective sell-stop was placed one tick below the low of the inside-day.

A profit objective for the short-term unit is 97.29, the 100% Alternate Price Projection.

On a trade above 97.20, the W.1 high, the protective stop-loss should be trailed at the 3DL for both units.

Trade Management Worksheet   Trade # / Date #5 - 11/22/94

Current Position L-2, 11/22-96.22   PS-OO xxx   95.25 Sell-stop

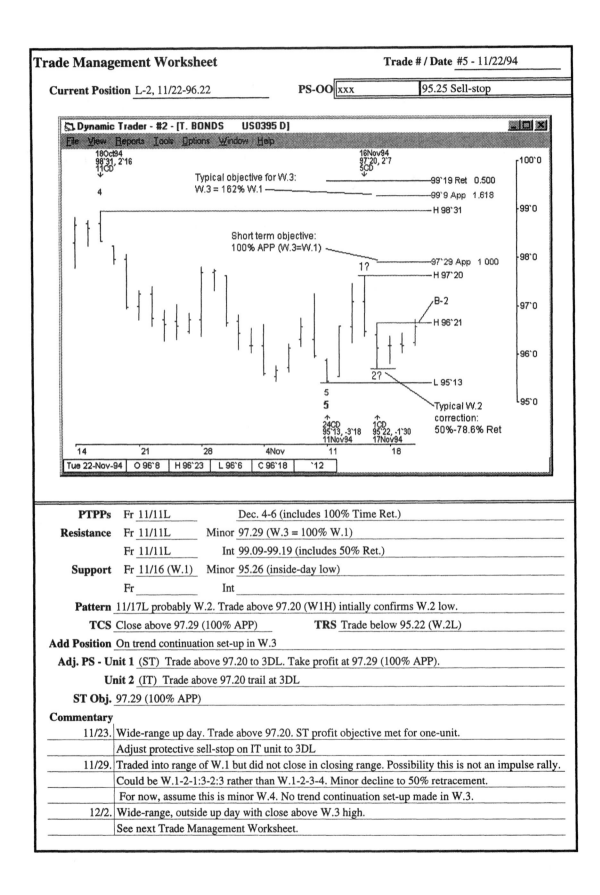

PTPPs	Fr 11/11L		Dec. 4-6 (includes 100% Time Ret.)
Resistance	Fr 11/11L	Minor	97.29 (W.3 = 100% W.1)
	Fr 11/11L	Int	99.09-99.19 (includes 50% Ret.)
Support	Fr 11/16 (W.1)	Minor	95.26 (inside-day low)
	Fr	Int	

Pattern 11/17L probably W.2. Trade above 97.20 (W1H) intially confirms W.2 low.

TCS Close above 97.29 (100% APP)   **TRS** Trade below 95.22 (W.2L)

Add Position On trend continuation set-up in W.3

Adj. PS - Unit 1 (ST) Trade above 97.20 to 3DL. Take profit at 97.29 (100% APP).

Unit 2 (IT) Trade above 97.20 trail at 3DL

ST Obj. 97.29 (100% APP)

Commentary

11/23.	Wide-range up day. Trade above 97.20. ST profit objective met for one-unit.
	Adjust protective sell-stop on IT unit to 3DL
11/29.	Traded into range of W.1 but did not close in closing range. Possibility this is not an impulse rally.
	Could be W.1-2-1:3-2:3 rather than W.1-2-3-4. Minor decline to 50% retracement.
	For now, assume this is minor W.4. No trend continuation set-up made in W.3.
12/2.	Wide-range, outside up day with close above W.3 high.
	See next Trade Management Worksheet.

Trade Management #2

The chart on the next *Trade Management Worksheet* on the next page is up-to-date through Dec. 2, the last comment entry on the prior worksheet.

The entry on the previous worksheet for Nov. 29 noted that bonds made a minor decline into the price range of W.1. An Elliott wave "rule" (guideline) is W.4 should not trade into the range of W.1 although with close-only data, a daily close had not been made in the closing range of W.1. Unless both daily range and closing data violate a "rule", I usually continue under the assumption the most obvious pattern is correct. In this case, a note was made that the pattern may be a W.1-2 and followed by W.1-2 of W.3. Bonds would have to accelerate the bull trend above the W.5 price objective (99.08-99.19) to alter the assumed wave count to W.1-2-1:3-2:3.

The next worksheet is dated Dec. 2 1994 and continues with this bond trade where the last worksheet ended.

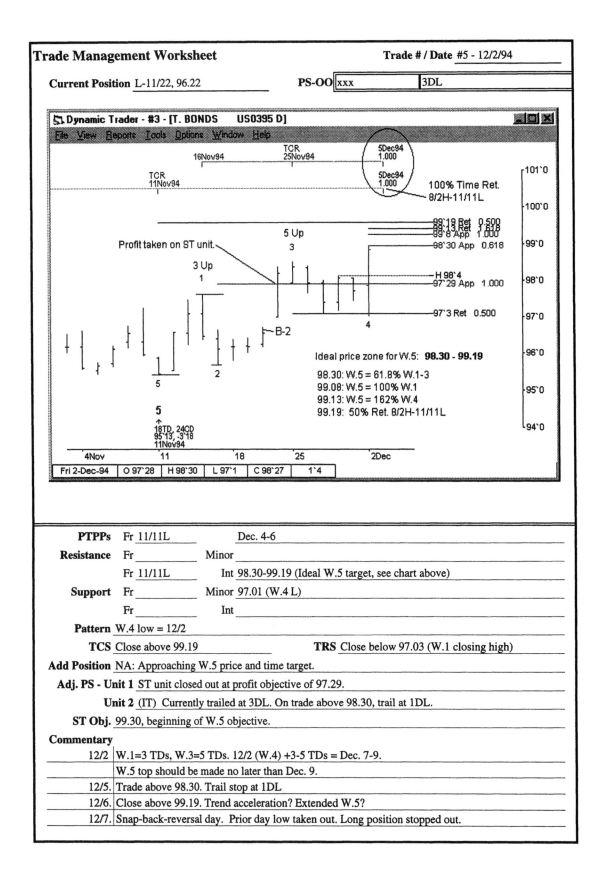

Trade Management Worksheet Trade # / Date #5 - 12/2/94

Current Position L-11/22, 96.22 **PS-OO** xxx 3DL

PTPPs	Fr 11/11L	Dec. 4-6
Resistance	Fr _____	Minor _____
	Fr 11/11L	Int 98.30-99.19 (Ideal W.5 target, see chart above)
Support	Fr _____	Minor 97.01 (W.4 L)
	Fr _____	Int _____
Pattern	W.4 low = 12/2	
TCS	Close above 99.19	**TRS** Close below 97.03 (W.1 closing high)
Add Position	NA: Approaching W.5 price and time target.	
Adj. PS - Unit 1	ST unit closed out at profit objective of 97.29.	
Unit 2	(IT) Currently trailed at 3DL. On trade above 98.30, trail at 1DL.	
ST Obj.	99.30, beginning of W.5 objective.	

Commentary

12/2	W.1=3 TDs, W.3=5 TDs. 12/2 (W.4) +3-5 TDs = Dec. 7-9.
	W.5 top should be made no later than Dec. 9.
12/5.	Trade above 98.30. Trail stop at 1DL
12/6.	Close above 99.19. Trend acceleration? Extended W.5?
12/7.	Snap-back-reversal day. Prior day low taken out. Long position stopped out.

Closed Trade Critique Worksheet

The intermediate term position was stopped out on Dec. 7 when the 1DL (one-day-low) was taken out. The Dec. 6-7 *snap-back-reversal* was made at the coincidence of time, price and pattern. Each of these factors were in place for the completion of a minor five wave advance.

Note that the *consistency of approach* to this trade was exactly the same as the prior trades for the Wave-5 decline into the Nov. 11 low. The same entry signals (trend-reversal or trend-continuation) were employed as well as the same protective stop-loss strategies.

We would anticipate that this minor five-wave advance was either a Wave-A of a correction or just Wave-1 of Wave-A. At this point in time there is no reason to guess. We can let the market continue to unfold and provide us with more information.

The important factor is that it appears bonds have made at least a minor five-wave advance which signals Nov. 11 is indeed the completion of the major decline and a major correction is in the initial stages. Bonds should eventually exceed the Dec. high without declining below the Nov. 11 low. This factor itself is important information for traders as well as investors who are concerned with the intermediate trend of interest rates.

What should be anticipated following a five-wave advance? At least an ABC correction. If an ABC correction appeared to unfold, we would have the ideal set-up to enter long for a W.C or W.3:A.

We can now assume that the major trend has turned from bearish to bullish. We would wait for some sort of correction to the minor five-wave advance to unfold to consider taking another long position.

Closed Trade Critique Worksheet **Market** Bonds, March '95 **Trade # / Date** #5 - 12/7/94

```
Dynamic Trader - #4 - [T. BONDS    US0395 D]
File  View  Reports  Tools  Options  Window  Help
```

2Aug94
103`25, 5`5
5.23 %
16TD

18Oct94
98`31, 2`16
11CD

6Dec94
99`24, 4`11
16TD, 25CD

Second long unit stopped out Dec. 7.
Wave-5 top made at the coincidence of projected time and
price which coincided with the parallel channel line.

TCR
18Oct94   11Nov94   5Dec94
1.000

99`19 Ret 0.500
99`8 Alt   1.618
98`30 App 0.618

66CD
96`15, -7`10
7Oct94

24CD
95`13, -3`18
11Nov94

| Wed 7-Dec-94 | O 99`23 | H 99`23 | L 98`17 | C 98`29 | -`26 |

	Unit	Entry		Exit		P/L	# Con.	Tick Value	Com.	Trade P/L
		Date	Price	Date	Price					
1	Long (ST)	11/22	96.22	11/23	97.29	39.00	1	31.25	35.00	1183.75
2	Long (IT)	11/22	96.22	12/7	98.18	60.00	1	31.25	35.00	1840.00
3										

Total Trade P / L: 3023.75

TRADE COMMENTS Not an ideal five-wave rally. W.4 traded into range of W.1 but did not close into the closing range of W.1. Possibility this was a complex correction of some sort (ABCDE?). A continued rally and close above 99.24 (high-to-date, 12/6) signals trend continuation.

LESSONS LEARNED Dec. 2 wide-range outside-reversal was a very high probability set-up for a short-term long position. Considering probably in W.4 at the time and very near W.5 price objectives, good to have passed up this trend-continuation trade entry set-up.

Prepare To Enter Long Positions On Correction

A W.2:A or W.B correction would typically make a low in the 50%-78.6% retracement zone. If bonds declined into this zone, a trading strategy for a long position would be made.

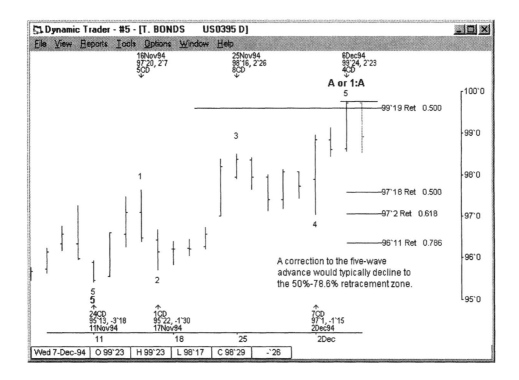

The next page shows the bond chart that includes the data following the Dec. 6 top. Bonds did not make a correction from the Dec. 6 high as anticipated. Bonds drifted sideways then up to the 61.8% retracement (8/2/94H-11/11/94L) and declined into a low on Jan. 6 labeled Wave-A as shown on the chart on the next page.

Bonds did not make the low-risk corrective set-up anticipated and no trade was considered.

Until you have a firm opinion based on market action of the position of the market, a trade is not considered.

Bonds continued essentially sideways to complete an ABC-flat correction at the Wave-C low on Jan. 25. We can clearly see the diagonal-fifth-wave and ABC-flat correction after-the-fact, but, as it was unfolding, there was no way to determine how this market activity would play out. Take a sheet of paper. Place it just to the right of the Dec. 6 bar which was originally considered a Wave-5 high. Move it to the right one day at a time to the last break-out bar. Can you honestly say the market pattern provided a strong signal in advance of what was to come?

The Jan. 25, outside-reversal-day low was made one day prior to the coincidence of two important time factors: 61.8% Time Retracement and 100% Alternate Time Projection.

Only after the Jan. 27 wide-range breakout day to a new high did the market provide a strong signal of its position. Bonds appeared to have completed a five wave advance and ABC-flat correction. Because bonds had not provided a set-up for a trend-reversal trade entry in a support zone, we now must consider a trend-continuation trade entry.

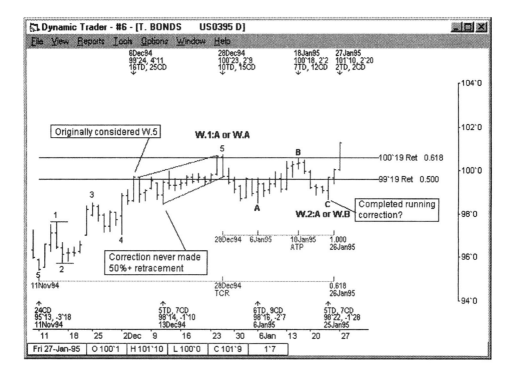

1. When the long position was stopped out on Dec. 7 at the projected time and price for a W.5 high, Dec. 6 was assumed to be a completed minor five-wave advance which would be followed by a correction to the 50% retracement or lower.

2. Instead, bonds drifted to a new high making a top Dec. 28 at the 61.8% retracement in what appears to be a diagonal-fifth-wave. Diagonal-fifth-waves are usually followed by a greater than typical correction. Not this time.

3. The Wave-A low was made just two ticks above the 61.8% retracement (not shown) of Wave-5.

4. Wave-B tested the Wave-5 high. Wave-C was made just above the Wave-A low to complete an ABC-flat correction.

5. It was not until the breakout day of Jan. 27 that the market position made sense. Until the market itself provides a strong signal of the position and most probable direction, a trade should not be considered. *Trade market behavior, not the forecast. When in doubt, stay out.*

6. No trades were considered for over six weeks after being stopped out of the long position on Dec. 7. Bonds had also advanced less than two points in this period of time. Trading junkies would not have the patience to wait six weeks for a low-risk, low-capital exposure trade set-up. Successful traders all have the patience to wait for the market to set-up according to their trading plan.

Trade Preparation Worksheet

Bonds are now in a position to consider a long trade. Since the bond activity did not provide a trend-reversal trade entry set-up, we must wait for a trend-continuation set-up unless and until bonds make a correction.

Readers may wonder why a long trade was not entered on the breakout of the double-top. We have not discussed breakout strategies in this book. Only strategies described in the book will be considered. Breakout strategies have not been considered because they do not provide highly objective trade set-up and stop placement rules. Breakout strategies can be very worthwhile strategies to consider, but require a lot of experience and judgment on the part of the trader before entry is considered. Or, they require a very wide stop.

The safer strategy is to consider a trend-continuation trade or entry on the initial correction following a breakout.

Before completing the *Trade Preparation and Initiation Worksheet*, let's determine the Dynamic Time and Price resistance projections.

Price Resistance Zones

The assumption is the Jan. 25, 1995 low is the completion of an ABC-flat correction and that this correction was the B-Wave of a larger degree corrective rally from the Nov. 11, 1994 low which will be labeled (A)-(B)-(C). The chart below is the weekly, spot futures chart from the Oct. 1993 high. This chart shows the 38.2%, 50% and 61.8% retracements.

A correction to a five-wave advance or decline often terminates at or near the extreme of the prior Wave-4. In this case, the prior Wave-4 price high was 106.23 which falls just above the 38.2% retracement of the five-wave bear trend.

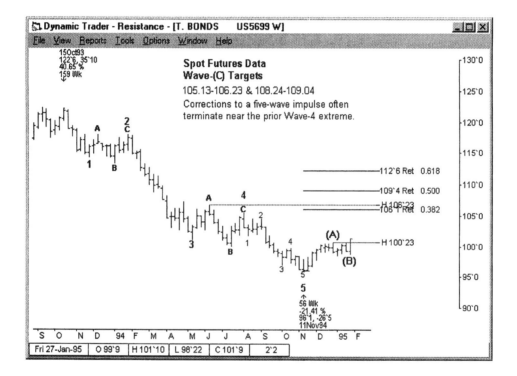

A C-wave is often equal to either 61.8% or 100% of the price range of the A-wave and/or 162% or 262% of the B-wave. These projections are shown on the March contract chart on the following page.

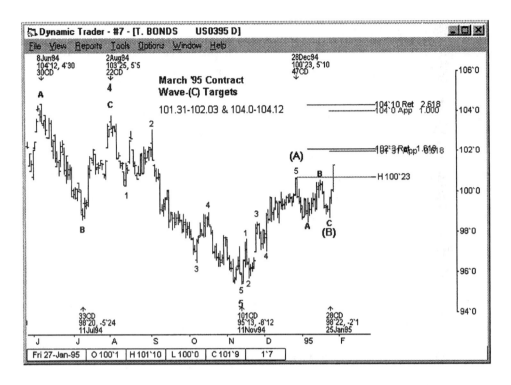

If we combine the longer term retracements from the weekly, spot futures data and the shorter term projections from the March contract, we have the price zones shown below. Projections followed by an asterisk are usually the most important to consider

Ideal Price Targets For Wave-(C)

101.31: W.(C) = 61.8% W.(A) (March)
102.03: W.(C) = 162% W.(B) (March)

104.00: W.(C) = 100% W.(A) (March)*
104.10: W.(C) = 262% W. (B) (March)
105.13: 8/2/94H (spot futures)
106.01: 38.2% Ret. (spot futures)*
106.10: 50% Ret.-percentage change (spot futures)
106.23: 6/6/94H-W.A:4 (spot futures, high price of Wave-4)*

108.24: 61.8% Ret.-percentage change (spot futures)
109.04: 50% Ret. (spot futures)

The broad price zone of <u>104.00-106.23</u> should be the ideal price target to complete Wave-(C) and the corrective rally. This price zone includes the most frequent C-wave targets including where W.C = 100% W.A, a major retracement (38.2%) and the extreme of the prior Wave-4. If the corrective rally continues to unfold as anticipated, the minor degree sub-divisions should focus in on a much narrower cluster of price targets.

Time Resistance Zones For Wave-(C)

Let's take a look at the Time Rhythm Zones and Dynamic Time Projections from the Nov. 11, 1994 low to determine the time resistance projections for a potential corrective high.

Time Rhythm Zone (TRZ): Feb. 28-June 9
The TRZ shows that the corrective rally from the Nov. 11, 1994 low should not complete prior to Feb. 28, 1995 but should complete by June 9, 1995. The minimum Dynamic Time Projections anticipated for a Wave-(C) high and shown on the next page is the Feb. 28-March 10 period which falls at the very beginning of the TRZ. If bonds make new highs after June 9, the odds are bonds are either making a much larger degree correction than anticipated or the rally is a bull trend that will eventually exceed the Oct. 1993 high.

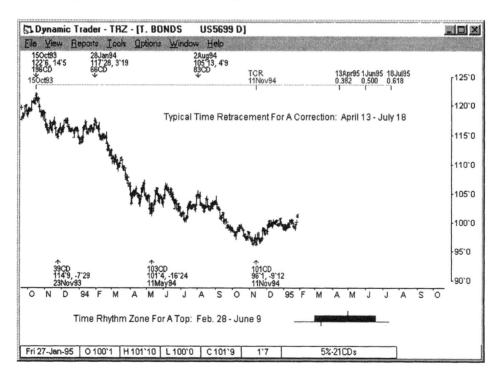

Projected Turning Point Periods: Feb. 28-March 10 and April 8-11

Feb. 28: 100% Time Retracement (8/2/94H-11/11/94L)*
March 8: W.(C) = 162% W.(B)
March 10: W.(C) = 100% W.(A)*
March 10: W.(A)-(B) = 100% W.(B)-(C) (11/11/94L-1/25/95L projected
from 12/28/94H)

April 8: W.(C) = 262% W.(B)
April 11: W.(C) = 162% W.(A)*
April 13: 38.2% Time Retracement (10/93H-11/94L)*

If bonds make a new high after April 13, the odds are a typical ABC
corrective rally is not being made. April 11 is the time projection where
the time of Wave-C would be equal to 162% of the time range of Wave-A.
This is usually the maximum time projection of a Wave-C. If bonds make
a new high after April 13, the rally is probably only Wave-(A) and the
correction will be much greater in time and price than anticipated.

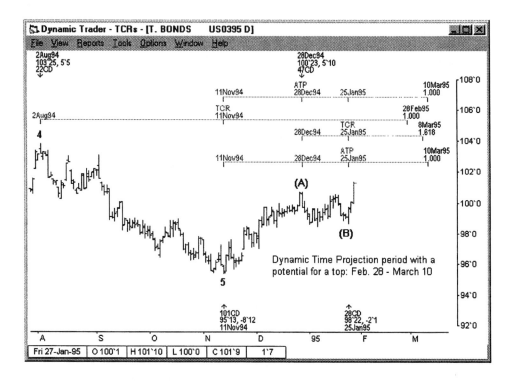

The following page includes the *Trade Preparation and Initiation
Worksheet* that includes the time and price projections described in the
previous pages.

Trade Preparation and Initiation Worksheet ...... Trade # / Date #6 - 1/27/95

Trade Objective W.3:A or W.C trend ...... Market Bonds, March '95

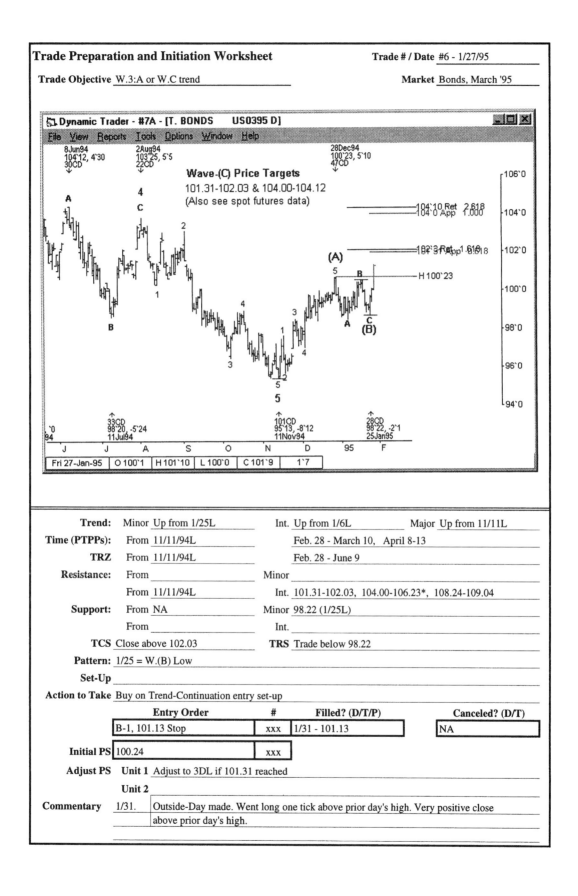

Trend:	Minor Up from 1/25L	Int. Up from 1/6L	Major Up from 11/11L
Time (PTPPs):	From 11/11/94L	Feb. 28 - March 10, April 8-13	
TRZ	From 11/11/94L	Feb. 28 - June 9	
Resistance:	From	Minor	
	From 11/11/94L	Int. 101.31-102.03, 104.00-106.23*, 108.24-109.04	
Support:	From NA	Minor 98.22 (1/25L)	
	From	Int.	
TCS	Close above 102.03	**TRS** Trade below 98.22	
Pattern:	1/25 = W.(B) Low		
Set-Up			
Action to Take	Buy on Trend-Continuation entry set-up		

Entry Order	#	Filled? (D/T/P)	Canceled? (D/T)
B-1, 101.13 Stop	xxx	1/31 - 101.13	NA

Initial PS	100.24	xxx	
Adjust PS	**Unit 1** Adjust to 3DL if 101.31 reached		
	Unit 2		
Commentary	1/31.	Outside-Day made. Went long one tick above prior day's high. Very positive close above prior day's high.	

Trade Management Worksheet Trade # / Date #6 - 1/31/95

Current Position US H5: L-1, 1/31/95, 101.13   PS-OO xxx   Initial Sell Stop -100.24

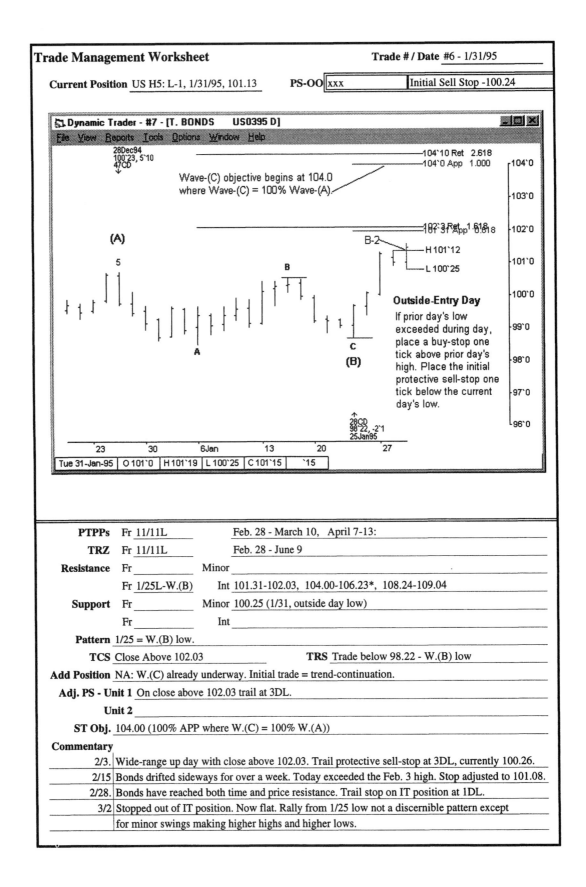

PTPPs	Fr 11/11L		Feb. 28 - March 10, April 7-13:	
TRZ	Fr 11/11L		Feb. 28 - June 9	
Resistance	Fr	Minor		
	Fr 1/25L-W.(B)	Int	101.31-102.03, 104.00-106.23*, 108.24-109.04	
Support	Fr	Minor	100.25 (1/31, outside day low)	
	Fr	Int		
Pattern	1/25 = W.(B) low.			

TCS Close Above 102.03   **TRS** Trade below 98.22 - W.(B) low

Add Position NA: W.(C) already underway. Initial trade = trend-continuation.

Adj. PS - Unit 1 On close above 102.03 trail at 3DL.

Unit 2

ST Obj. 104.00 (100% APP where W.(C) = 100% W.(A))

Commentary

2/3.	Wide-range up day with close above 102.03. Trail protective sell-stop at 3DL, currently 100.26.
2/15	Bonds drifted sideways for over a week. Today exceeded the Feb. 3 high. Stop adjusted to 101.08.
2/28	Bonds have reached both time and price resistance. Trail stop on IT position at 1DL.
3/2	Stopped out of IT position. Now flat. Rally from 1/25 low not a discernible pattern except
	for minor swings making higher highs and higher lows.

The chart on the *Trade Management Worksheet* on the preceding page was current though the date of entry of the trade. A journal of commentary is made at the bottom of the worksheet. A new *Trade Management Worksheet* is usually not completed unless the critical data such as the time and price projections are changed or a chart pattern that is critical to the analysis develops.

In the current case with bonds, nothing critical or dramatic unfolded with the analysis, trading strategies or chart pattern as bonds continued to advance and the long position was stopped out March 2. The chart below shows the data following the date the prior worksheet was begun. The dates of the commentary found in the worksheet are noted so you can compare the chart activity as the comments were made.

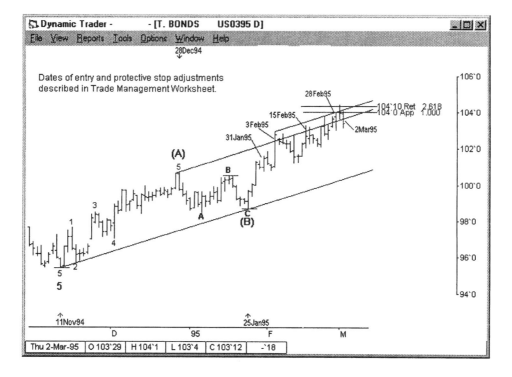

The next page includes the *Trade Critique Worksheet* with comments regarding the questionable position of bonds at this point in time.

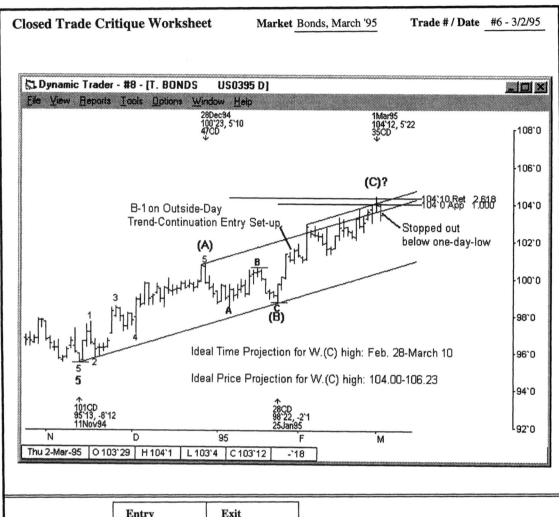

Closed Trade Critique Worksheet   **Market** Bonds, March '95   **Trade # / Date** #6 - 3/2/95

	Unit	Entry		Exit		P/L	# Con.	Tick Value	Com.	Trade P/L
		Date	Price	Date	Price					
1	Long	1/31	101.13	3/2	103.19	60.00	1	31.25	35.00	1840.00
2										
3										

Total Trade P / L: 1840.00

TRADE COMMENTS March 1 high made at direct hit of projected time and price resistance.

While Feb. 28 is minimum date of TRZ for top, corrective top not expected to be made prior to

April 13 (38.2% Time Retracement of bear trend). Pattern of W.(C) did not sub-divide nicely into

five wave structure. I am not highly confident this is the final corrective high. Maximum PTPP for a typical

ABC, corrective high should be April 8-13. Major resistance zone for ABC, corrective high

extends from 104.00 to 106.23.

LESSONS LEARNED

Corrective Top Complete?

Did March 1, 1995 complete a major corrective top to the Oct. 1993 - Nov. 1994 bear trend? The broad time and price zones anticipated to complete the corrective high are:

Time
Time Rhythm Zone: *Feb. 28 - June 9*
Dynamic Time Projections: *Feb. 28 - March 10, April 7 - 13*

Price (March contract): *104.00-106.23*

The **March 1** high was made at **104.12** directly within the time and price projections for a corrective high. There is still almost two points of price range (to 106.23) and another time period (April 7-13) from where a corrective high may be anticipated to complete.

Trading Strategies For A Short Position

If bonds have rallied into the broad time and price zones anticipated for a major, corrective high, our trading strategy is to look for low-risk and low-capital exposure trade set-ups to take a short position.

The chart below shows the position of June bonds a few days following the March 1 high. We are now considering June bonds as the March contract expires in the later half of March. At the contract roll-over, June bonds will become the spot-futures contract month.

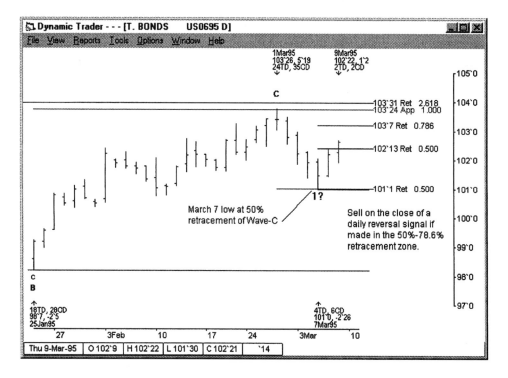

A low was made March 7 at 101.00, just one tick below the 50% retracement. We will consider this a potential Wave-1 low. We use the same trade-entry strategy as before by looking to take a short position in the typical retracement range for a Wave-2.

Short Position Trading Strategy: Sell June bonds in the *102.13-103.07* (50%-78.6% retracement zone) on the close of a *daily reversal signal*.

The chart below shows June bonds following the March 7 low. Bonds continued to rally to above the March 1 high without making a daily reversal signal in the retracement zone. No short trade was signaled.

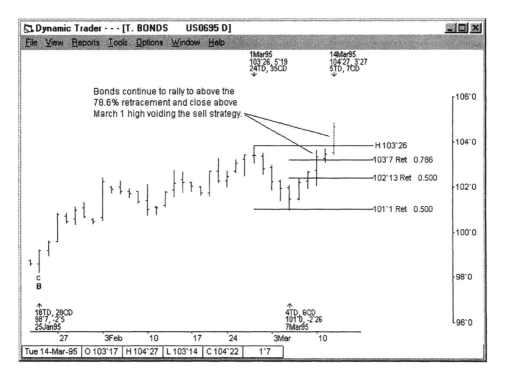

Bonds are still in the broad price zone for a major corrective high (103.24-106.23) which has been adjusted to begin at 103.24 to reflect the June contract price projections. Another Projected Turning Point Period for a high is *April 7-13*. The chart on the following page with the *Trade Preparation and Initiation Worksheet* dated April 6, 1995 shows bonds through April 6, the day prior to the Projected Turning Point Period.

The new trading strategy to take advantage of an anticipated corrective high in the current time and price zone is to sell on the close of a daily reversal signal or sell on a trend continuation signal if bonds decline to below the recent minor swing low of 103.00.

Trade Preparation and Initiation Worksheet   Trade # / Date #7 - 4/6/95

Trade Objective Go short on completion of corrective rally   Market Bonds, June

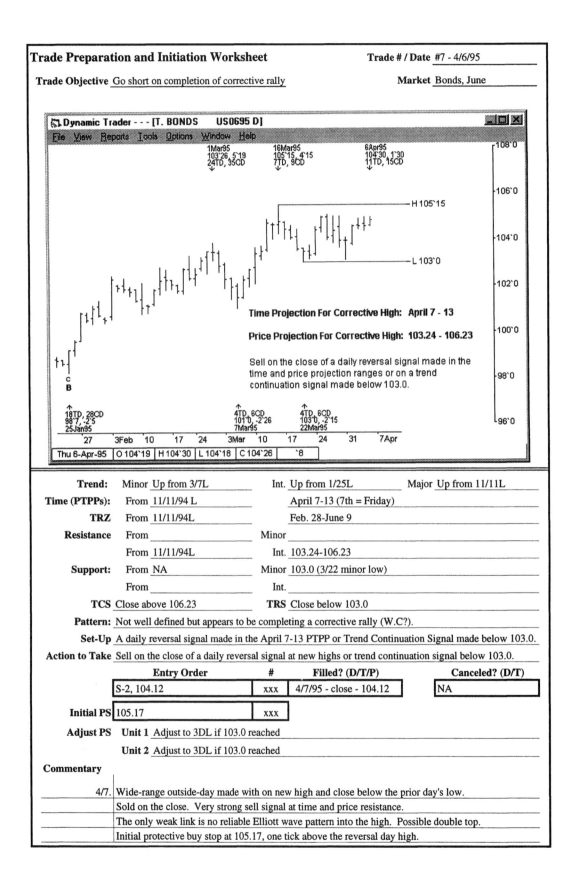

Trend:	Minor Up from 3/7L	Int. Up from 1/25L	Major Up from 11/11L
Time (PTPPs):	From 11/11/94 L	April 7-13 (7th = Friday)	
TRZ	From 11/11/94L	Feb. 28-June 9	
Resistance	From	Minor	
	From 11/11/94L	Int. 103.24-106.23	
Support:	From NA	Minor 103.0 (3/22 minor low)	
	From	Int.	
TCS	Close above 106.23	TRS Close below 103.0	

Pattern: Not well defined but appears to be completing a corrective rally (W.C?).

Set-Up A daily reversal signal made in the April 7-13 PTPP or Trend Continuation Signal made below 103.0.

Action to Take Sell on the close of a daily reversal signal at new highs or trend continuation signal below 103.0.

	Entry Order	#	Filled? (D/T/P)	Canceled? (D/T)
	S-2, 104.12	xxx	4/7/95 - close - 104.12	NA
Initial PS	105.17	xxx		

Adjust PS Unit 1 Adjust to 3DL if 103.0 reached

  Unit 2 Adjust to 3DL if 103.0 reached

Commentary

4/7.	Wide-range outside-day made with on new high and close below the prior day's low.
	Sold on the close. Very strong sell signal at time and price resistance.
	The only weak link is no reliable Elliott wave pattern into the high. Possible double top.
	Initial protective buy stop at 105.17, one tick above the reversal day high.

Short Position Stopped Out

On April 7, bonds made an *outside-reversal-day*. A two-unit short position is taken on the close at 104.12. The initial protective buy-stop is placed at 105.17, one tick above the April 7, entry-day high. Five trading days later on April 17, bonds made another new high on another *outside-reversal-day*. The short position taken April 7 is stopped out for a loss and another short-position is taken the same day on the close at 104.18.

I have not included the *Trade Management Worksheet* for this trade because it was short-term and no new information was made prior to the protective buy-stop being hit on April 17.

The following page is the *Closed Trade Critique Worksheet* for the stopped-out short position.

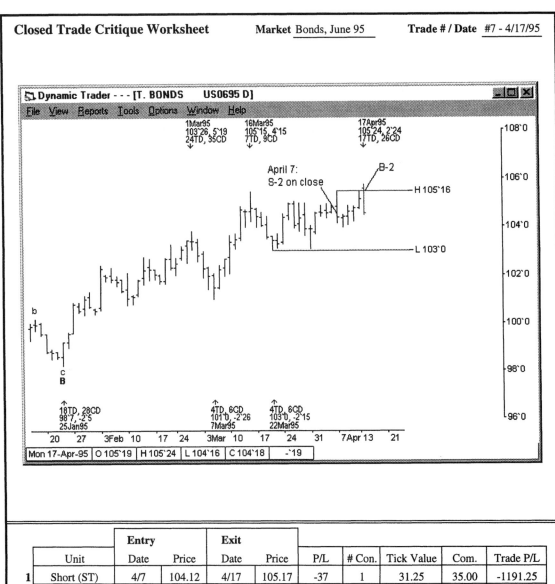

| Closed Trade Critique Worksheet | Market Bonds, June 95 | Trade # / Date #7 - 4/17/95 |

		Entry		Exit						
	Unit	Date	Price	Date	Price	P/L	# Con.	Tick Value	Com.	Trade P/L
1	Short (ST)	4/7	104.12	4/17	105.17	-37	1	31.25	35.00	-1191.25
2	Short (IT)	4/7	104.12	4/17	105.17	-37	1	31.25	35.00	-1191.25
3										

Total Trade P / L: -2382.50

TRADE COMMENTS The wide-range, outside-reversal-day required a wide stop at one tick above the high of the day.

LESSONS LEARNED Wed., April 12 was an inside-day with a close above the day's open and prior day's close. Could have considered lowering stop and limiting exposure to one tick above the high prior to the inside-day.

As long as the conditions remain for a top, the short-sale trading strategy is maintained.

On April 17, the same day the April 7 short position was stopped out, bonds made another new high on a wide-range *outside-reversal-day* with a close below the prior day's low. Another short position is taken on the close of 104.18. April 17 was a Monday and just one trading day past the Projected Turning Point Period of *April 7-13* that was a high probability projection for a high. April 13 was a Thursday. April 14 was a non-trading day holiday. The April 7-13 time period was considered the maximum time period to anticipate a corrective high. New daily and closing highs after April 13 indicated bonds should continue to rally to at least the next projected time and price zones. The April 7-13 period fell in the middle of the Feb. 28-June Time Rhythm Zone for a high. Bonds were still in the broad price zone anticipated for a corrective high.

The next page is the *Trade Management Worksheet* for the new short position. The commentary on this worksheet begins with April 17 when the second two-unit short position was taken. Note the May 1 comments when the protective buy-stop was changed to a *stop-and-reverse* order.

The *Trade Management Worksheet* is followed by the *Closed Trade Critique Worksheet.*

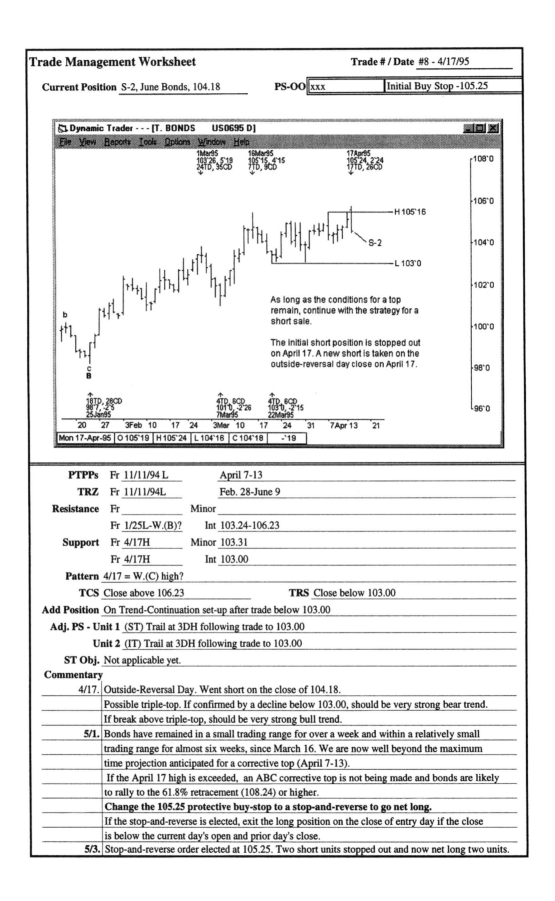

Trade Management Worksheet   Trade # / Date #8 - 4/17/95

Current Position S-2, June Bonds, 104.18   PS-OO | xxx | Initial Buy Stop -105.25

As long as the conditions for a top remain, continue with the strategy for a short sale.

The initial short position is stopped out on April 17. A new short is taken on the outside-reversal day close on April 17.

PTPPs	Fr	11/11/94 L		April 7-13
TRZ	Fr	11/11/94L		Feb. 28-June 9
Resistance	Fr		Minor	
	Fr	1/25L-W.(B)?	Int	103.24-106.23
Support	Fr	4/17H	Minor	103.31
	Fr	4/17H	Int	103.00
Pattern	4/17 = W.(C) high?			

TCS Close above 106.23   **TRS** Close below 103.00

Add Position On Trend-Continuation set-up after trade below 103.00

Adj. PS - Unit 1 (ST) Trail at 3DH following trade to 103.00

Unit 2 (IT) Trail at 3DH following trade to 103.00

ST Obj. Not applicable yet.

Commentary

4/17. Outside-Reversal Day. Went short on the close of 104.18.

Possible triple-top. If confirmed by a decline below 103.00, should be very strong bear trend.

If break above triple-top, should be very strong bull trend.

5/1. Bonds have remained in a small trading range for over a week and within a relatively small trading range for almost six weeks, since March 16. We are now well beyond the maximum time projection anticipated for a corrective top (April 7-13).

If the April 17 high is exceeded, an ABC corrective top is not being made and bonds are likely to rally to the 61.8% retracement (108.24) or higher.

Change the 105.25 protective buy-stop to a stop-and-reverse to go net long.

If the stop-and-reverse is elected, exit the long position on the close of entry day if the close is below the current day's open and prior day's close.

5/3. Stop-and-reverse order elected at 105.25. Two short units stopped out and now net long two units.

Closed Trade Critique Worksheet   **Market** Bonds, June 95   **Trade # / Date** #8 - 5/3/95

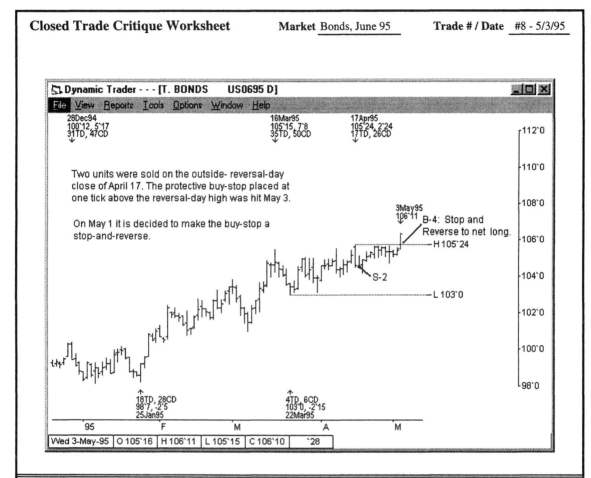

	Unit	Entry		Exit		P/L	# Con.	Tick Value	Com.	Trade P/L
		Date	Price	Date	Price					
1	Short (ST)	4/17	104.18	5/3	105.25	-39	1	31.25	35.00	-1253.75
2	Short (IT)	4/17	104.18	5/3	105.25	-39	1	31.25	35.00	-1253.75
3										

Total Trade P / L: **-2507.50**

TRADE COMMENTS The pattern from the Nov. low is not providing a clear indication of the market position. The April 17 reversal-day high was made one trading day past the anticipated maximum time period for a corrective (ABC) high. The April 17 short position was taken at an almost ideal time and price position for a corrective high.

LESSONS LEARNED Always keep very alert to a market that is not performing according to expectations. Be prepared to reverse position when a coincidence of projected time and price is exceeded. This is an important indication of an unusually strong market.

When A Market Doesn't Do What It Is Supposed To Do, It Will Probably Do Just The Opposite

The April 17 reversal-day high at 105.24 was less than one point from the maximum price projection anticipated for an ABC-corrective high (106.23) and one trading day after the April 7-13 Projected Turning Point Period anticipated for an ABC-corrective high. If these time and price targets were exceeded, the bond market has signaled that either a more complex and longer term corrective trend is underway or possibly an impulse bull trend. In either case, bonds should continue to rally to a much higher price level.

Because of these factors, the protective buy-stop order was changed to a stop-and-reverse (S&R) order. Four units were bought when the S&R order was hit which resulted in a two-units net long position.

Dynamic Time and Price Projections

In early May, bonds have continued to rally above the price zone anticipated for a corrective high and beyond the time zone anticipated for a corrective high. Let's take a look at the next price and time targets that should be reached.

Time Rhythm Zone Projection

The chart below shows the Time Rhythm Zone that was shown earlier. The overlap period extends to June 9. Recall that this TRZ was projected from 5%/21CDs swings and the overlap period considers 80% of the swings. What this translates to is based on the swing statistics, bonds have a 90% probability of making a top by June 9 that will be followed by at least a 5% price decline that will last at least 21 CDs.

The chart also shows that June 1 is the 50% Time Retracement of the bear trend.

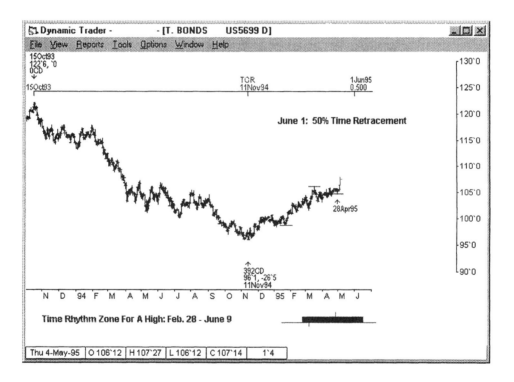

Dynamic Time Projections

The chart below shows three important Dynamic Time Projections that fall in June. From the top of the chart they are:

June 13: The two prior rally swings lasted 47 CDs and 50 CDs. June 13 is the 100% Alternate Time Projection of the shorter, 47 CDs swing

June 16: The 100% Alternate Time Projection of the 50 CDs rally (not shown).

June 1: The 100% Time Cycle Ratio of the previous High-to-High (A-C). Note from the previous page that June 1 is also the 50% Time Retracement of the major bear trend.

June 12: The 100% Time Retracement of the C-D trading range.

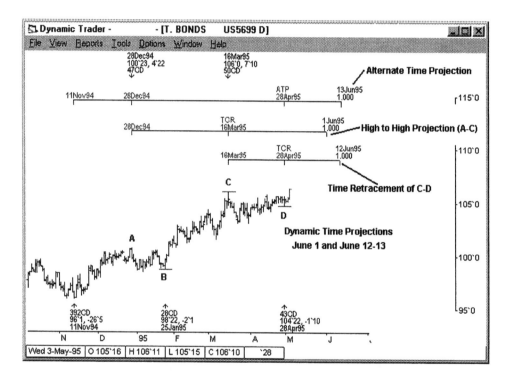

The two June 1 dates fall within the extreme range of the 80%-TRZ which ends June 9. The June 12-13 dates are just a few days following the TRZ. With both the extreme TRZ and Dynamic Time Projections falling in the first half of June, the probabilities are very high that a top will be made in the first half of June, ideally near June 1 or June 12-16.

Price Retracements

The two charts on the next page show the major price retracements by both price range and percentage change. Note how closely the retracement targets from these two methods cluster.

106.01-106.10: 38.2% range retracement and 50% percentage change retracement

108.24-109.04: 50% range retracement and 61.8% percentage change retracement

112.06: 61.8% range retracement and 78.6% percentage change retracement

116.19: 78.6% range retracement and 100% percentage change retracement

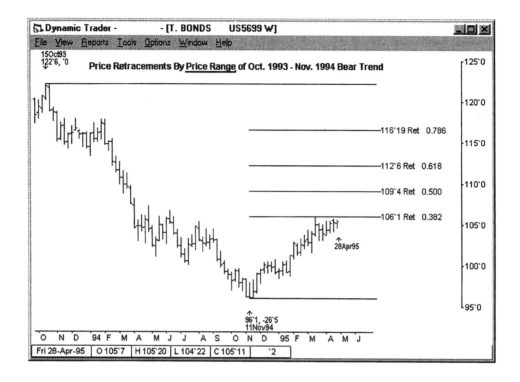

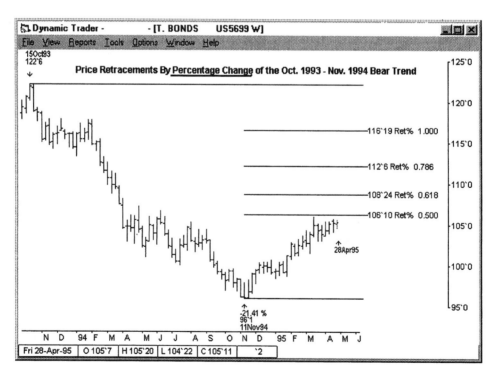

Dynamic Price Projections

The chart below is also the continuous spot futures data and shows the two 100% Alternate Price Projections where W.E = 100% W.A at 109.12 and 100% W.C at 112.0. These two projections fall near the retracement projections shown on the previous page.

The horizontal bars along the price scale represent the clusters of retracement and alternate price projections which are the high probability resistance zones.

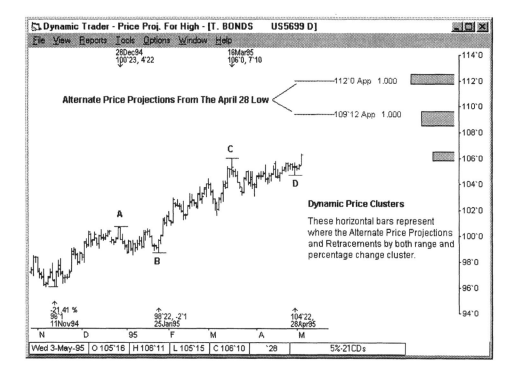

We now have the high probability time and price projections for a top and can complete a *Trade Management Worksheet* for the long position taken on the break above the recent time and price resistance zones. The *Trade Management Worksheet* is followed by the *Trade Critique Worksheet*. These two worksheets provide all of the data and commentary necessary to describe this trade.

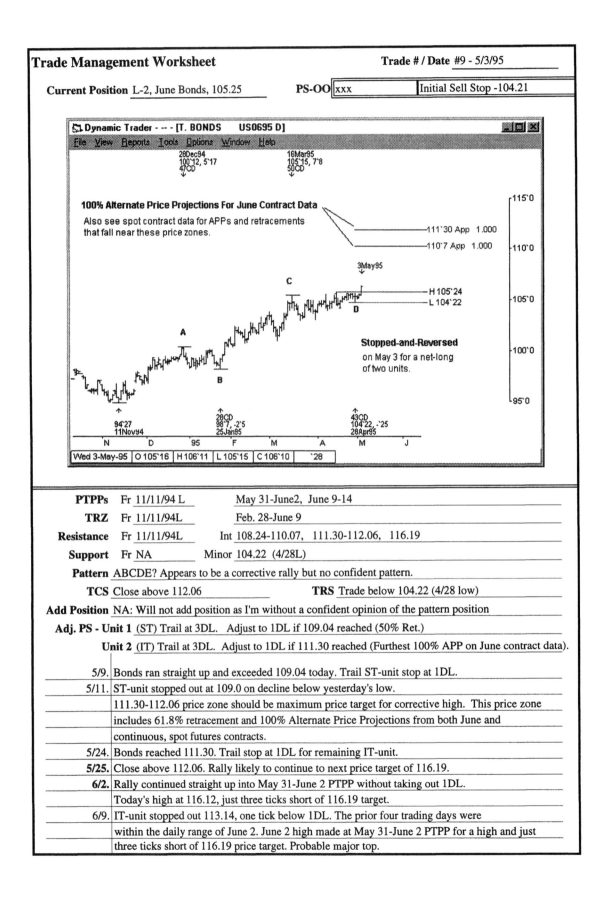

Trade Management Worksheet　　　　　　　**Trade # / Date** #9 - 5/3/95

Current Position L-2, June Bonds, 105.25　　　**PS-OO** xxx　　　**Initial Sell Stop** -104.21

PTPPs	Fr 11/11/94 L	May 31-June2, June 9-14	
TRZ	Fr 11/11/94L	Feb. 28-June 9	
Resistance	Fr 11/11/94L	Int 108.24-110.07, 111.30-112.06, 116.19	
Support	Fr NA	Minor 104.22 (4/28L)	
Pattern	ABCDE? Appears to be a corrective rally but no confident pattern.		
TCS	Close above 112.06	**TRS** Trade below 104.22 (4/28 low)	
Add Position	NA: Will not add position as I'm without a confident opinion of the pattern position		
Adj. PS - Unit 1	(ST) Trail at 3DL. Adjust to 1DL if 109.04 reached (50% Ret.)		
Unit 2	(IT) Trail at 3DL. Adjust to 1DL if 111.30 reached (Furthest 100% APP on June contract data).		

5/9.	Bonds ran straight up and exceeded 109.04 today. Trail ST-unit stop at 1DL.
5/11.	ST-unit stopped out at 109.0 on decline below yesterday's low.
	111.30-112.06 price zone should be maximum price target for corrective high. This price zone
	includes 61.8% retracement and 100% Alternate Price Projections from both June and
	continuous, spot futures contracts.
5/24.	Bonds reached 111.30. Trail stop at 1DL for remaining IT-unit.
5/25.	Close above 112.06. Rally likely to continue to next price target of 116.19.
6/2.	Rally continued straight up into May 31-June 2 PTPP without taking out 1DL.
	Today's high at 116.12, just three ticks short of 116.19 target.
6/9.	IT-unit stopped out 113.14, one tick below 1DL. The prior four trading days were
	within the daily range of June 2. June 2 high made at May 31-June 2 PTPP for a high and just
	three ticks short of 116.19 price target. Probable major top.

Closed Trade Critique Worksheet   Market <u>Bonds, June 95</u>   Trade # / Date   <u>#9 - 6/9/95</u>

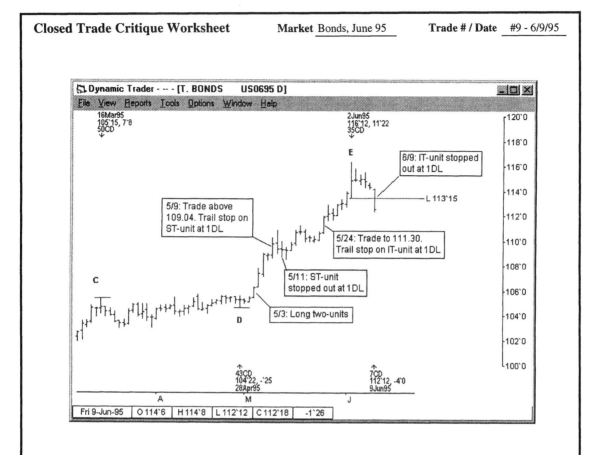

		Entry		Exit						
	Unit	Date	Price	Date	Price	P/L	# Con.	Tick Value	Com.	Trade P/L
1	Long (ST)	5/3	105.25	5/11	109.00	103.00	1	31.25	35.00	3,183.75
2	Long (IT)	5/3	105.25	6/9	113.14	245.00	1	31.25	35.00	7,621.25
3										

Total Trade P / L: **10,805.00**

TRADE COMMENTS June 2 top made just three ticks short of extreme price target and precisely within Dynamic Time Projection for a high which included the 50% Time Retracement of the prior bear trend. During the entire rally from the 4/28 low to 6/2 high, the 3DL was not taken out. The June 2 high was made just one week from the extreme TRZ overlap period of June 9. The June 2 high has probably completed a major corrective rally.

LESSONS LEARNED How to be wrong and make money. From the Nov. 1994 low, I was anticipating a more readily defined corrective pattern that would ideally top in the March - April time frame. The Dynamic Time and Price Projections and simple Trading Strategies kept me on the right side of the market for the unexpected bull swing into the June high.

The table below is a summary of the bond trades described on the previous pages.

Trade Summary: Bond Trades: 8/17/94 - 6/9/95

Bonds	Open	Price	Close	Price	Com.	P/L
Short (ST)	8/17	103.11	9/2	103.24	35	(441.25)
Short (IT)	8/17	103.11	9/2	103.24	35	(441.25)
Short (ST)	9/2	102.09	9/9	100.02	35	2183.75
Short (IT)	9/2	102.09	10/10	98.12	35	3871.25
Short (GPB)	9/16	100.09	10/10	98.12	35	1871.25
Short (ST)	10/18	99.01	11/10	97.15	35	1527.50
Long (ST)	11/22	96.22	11/23	98.18	35	1183.75
Long (IT)	11/22	96.22	12/7	98.12	35	1840.00
Long (IT)	1/31	101.13	3/2	103.19	35	1840.00
Short (ST)	4/7	104.12	4/17	105.17	35	(1191.25)
Short (IT)	4/7	104.12	4/17	105.17	35	(1191.25)
Short (ST)	4/17	104.18	5/23	105.25	35	(1253.75)
Short (IT)	4/17	104.18	5/23	105.25	35	(1253.75)
Long (ST)	5/3	105.25	5/11	109.00	35	3183.75
Long (IT)	5/3	105.25	6/9	113.14	35	7621.25
15 Trades (units)	9 Winners	6 Losers	Ave. Win 1,508.60	Ave. Loss 962.00	Ave Profit Per Trade $1,290.00	Net Profit $19,350.00

Many other trading opportunities were available during this period if the parameters for accepting a trade were broadened from those in the Trading Plan described early in the chapter. Review the charts for this period. Note how many trend-continuation trade set-ups there were during this period. If part of your trading plan is to include short-term trend-continuation set-ups for 1-3 day trades, many other opportunities were available.

Many other low-risk, low-capital exposure opportunities were available if intraday data such as 30 or 60 minute charts were incorporated into the analysis and trading plan.

June 2, 1995 did not complete a major corrective high in bonds as anticipated in early June. Bonds made a slightly higher high later in June followed by a decline greater than 5% and longer than 21 days just as anticipated. Following a mid-Aug. low, bonds continued to rally making a final top in Jan. 1996. The Dynamic Time and Price chapters describe the Dynamic Time Projections, Time Rhythm Zone and Dynamic Price Projections into the Jan. 1996 high.

Remember, we trade the market, not the forecast. The March 1995 high was also anticipated to be an important top followed by a continued bear trend to new lows. Yet, the long position trades that followed later in May were the most profitable of the past year. Once the June-July 1994 highs were exceeded, bonds signaled another major advance was underway.

Trading results for the period following the June-July, 1995 highs through the Jan. 1996 high are similar to the April-June 1995 period. Two or three relatively small losses followed by two or three sizable gains as bonds eventually advanced to make a top on a direct hit of projected time and price in Jan. 1996. If you have the bond data for this period, follow the same trading plan as the examples above and identify the trades for the period following the June 1995 high through the Jan. 1996 high.

How To Learn Dynamic Trading

The best way to learn Dynamic Trading, or any approach to trading for that matter, is to do what we have just done in this chapter. Develop a specific trading plan and trading rules. Choose a period of time from the past for a market and follow it day by day as if it were a current market unfolding each day.

Prepare all of the necessary time and price projections, complete the trading worksheets, follow the plan and "paper trade." Better yet, choose two or three diverse markets such as bonds, beans and silver. Update the current charts and projections each day as the markets unfold for at least a six month period. "Paper trade" them as they unfold. You will not only come to understand and appreciate the power of Dynamic Trading, but will acquire the closest thing to actual trading experience.

Notes

Chapter 8

The Real World Of Dynamic Trading

The real difference between winners and losers is not so much native ability as it is the discipline exercised in avoiding mistakes. What separates the amateur from the old pro is that the pro makes fewer mistakes.

Roy W. Longstreet

In This Chapter, You Learn To

Trade Market Behavior, Not Forecasts

I have published an advisory letter since 1986. The following pages include excerpts of the analysis and trade recommendations from recent issues up to the time this book was completed. This may be the most important chapter of this book. There is nothing theoretical about this chapter. It demonstrates the real-time application of what has been taught in this book.

The excerpts are from my monthly *Dynamic Traders Analysis Report* and *Dynamic Traders Weekly Fax Report*. It is easy for a trading or investing teacher to show historical examples of their methods that always seem to work out perfectly. My advisory reports are a track record of the value of the Dynamic Trading analysis and trading strategies taught in this book. These examples have been included because they are "real-time, real-world." They are a matter of record. They were published in advance of the market outcome and trading action taken. They provide a unique opportunity to show how the Dynamic Trading approach is put into practice day-by-day.

These are only a few recent examples. Each monthly report is over 20 pages, not counting the trading tutorials or special research reports included each month. Each weekly report is 8-12 pages. That adds up to a lot of analysis and over 800 pages of material each year! All of the forecasts or projections did not work out as planned. All of the trading recommendations were not profitable. But they all provide an important practical lesson to be learned.

Each example includes follow-up comments, often including a chart of the subsequent market activity. There is not an attempt to explain in detail how all of the time and price projections were determined. The methods used have all been described in the preceding chapters. Each report is educational in itself. You will learn a great deal by studying these reports and their comments. You will become convinced that the Dynamic Trading analysis and trading strategies hold great practical value.

One of the most important principles of successful trading you will learn from this chapter is that you *trade market behavior, not forecasts.* This theme is repeated throughout the follow-up comments. Dynamic Trading technical analysis is meant for the trader and investor to form an opinion of the market position and the most likely outcome of the current position. The analysis techniques identify trend reversals and the high probability time and price targets of the trend or counter-trend. While these projections are forecasts, traders must never fail to identify what market activity will invalidate the projections or forecast and never fail to take action if the forecast is invalidated. A trader or investor who fails to exit a market when the market position has been invalidated by the market activity will not succeed in the business of trading.

Trade Market Behavior, Not Forecasts

By studying all of the material in this book and applying it to your own analysis and trading strategies, **you** will also be able to put it into practical application on a day-to-day basis just as illustrated in these real-world examples.

The page lay-out of this chapter is wider than the previous chapters in order to accommodate the format of the excerpts from the reports. The excerpts shown are just as they appeared in their respective reports. The headings in this chapter are the headings from the respective reports.

More examples from the weekly fax report are included than from the monthly report. This is because the weekly fax report is more timely and often able to provide specific trade recommendations and protective stop-loss levels which is usually not possible with a monthly report. The monthly report provides the intermediate to long-term position of a market. This is critical information as the shorter-term trading strategies

The Real World Of Dynamic Trading

are always taken within the context of the larger degree trend position. All subscribers receiving the weekly fax report have also received the monthly report and are aware of the larger degree position of the market.

Study these examples in light of what you have learned, and I know you too will become a confident *Dynamic Trader*. First, let's take a look at the format of the reports so you will derive the most benefit from studying them.

Report Format

Each section of the report often provides commentary and explanations. One of the important objectives of each report is to educate the subscriber. The more knowledgeable the subscriber, the more confident he or she will be in the analysis and conclusions. More importantly, subscribers may then formulate their own trading strategies in light of their understanding of market position.

Comments: This section provides a brief commentary of the market activity since the last report.

Major Trend: Bullish or Bearish and from which prior pivot. Both the Bearish or Bullish Reversal and Continuation Signals must have been elected to signal the direction of the major trend.

Intermediate Trend: Bullish or Bearish and from which prior pivot. The election of the Bearish or Bullish Reversal Signal indicates the direction of the intermediate trend.

Support and Resistance: Shows the price support and resistance zones and which contract or index they relate to. There are often explanatory comments showing how the price zones were calculated. The price zones underlined are the most significant.

Time Analysis: Shows the Projected Turning Point Periods (PTTP) and Time Rhythm Zones (TRZ). Those underlined are usually the most significant with a potential for an intermediate or major trend change.

Pattern: Provides comments regarding the Elliott wave structure of the market position and other pattern comments.

Bearish or Bullish Reversal Signal: Price and/or time targets that, if elected, signal an intermediate degree trend change. The reversal signals are not completely objective or 100% mechanical, but based on the time, price and pattern position of the market.

Bearish or Bullish Continuation Signal: Price and/or time targets that, if elected, signal the direction of the major trend.

Minimum Time or Price Objectives: Often provides the minimum time and/or price objectives for the current trend.

General Trading Strategies: Usually summarizes the current market position and anticipated minimum, time or price targets for the current trend. Provides the general trading strategies to consider given the market position.

Last Week's Trading Activities: Only included in the weekly report. Describes any recommended trades entered or stopped out since the last report and/or adjustments to the protective stop-loss recommendations.

Specific Trading Recommendations: Only included in the weekly report. Most recommendations assume a two unit position is taken, short and intermediate term. The initial protective stop-loss is always provided with the trade entry recommendation. Recommendations for stop-loss adjustments are made until the trade is stopped out. Only general, not specific, trade recommendations are made for the stock indexes due to the limitations of a weekly report associated with the high volatility of the stock indexes.

The specific trading strategies recommended in the weekly report are limited due to the limitations of a weekly report. Subscribers may develop other strategies during the week to take advantage of the analysis and outlook provided. As you study these reports, consider trading strategies you may have incorporated other than the specific trade recommendations described in the reports.

While the Specific Trade Recommendations section is an important part of the report and any advisory service, some of the balance of the report, including the General Trading Recommendations, often provides the most valuable information. There are limitations to specific trade recommendations that can be made in a weekly report. Traders often formulate many trading strategies around the general trade recommendations.

Options: Provides the important considerations for option positions. Because there are many option strategies that may be implemented for any one option position, specific option recommendations are only occasionally made in the weekly report.

Mutual Fund Switchers / Investors: Recommendations are made when to enter or exit stock, bond or precious metals mutual funds.

Current and Recent Trading Recommendations Table: The weekly report provides a profit/loss summary table of the recent, specific trade recommendations. IT represents intermediate term trades and ST is for short term trades. Each table only includes the activity of a specific market. The table follows the commentary for that market.

We'll start by looking at the S&P from July 1996 through the time this chapter is completed, March 1997, and see how the Dynamic Trading analysis and trading strategies taught in this book were successfully applied in the real world.

S&P - Position Summary as of July 13, 1996 (Chart on Page 2)

Comments		The S&P made the Intermediate Term Bearish Price Reversal Signal with the Friday, July 5 close below 662.00. Futures and option traders and investors were out of long positions during last week's sharp decline. A comprehensive Stock Market Research Report will be mailed with the July monthly report on Monday, July 15. You will not only find a wealth of information in this report, but startling conclusions.
Major Trend	Bullish	From Nov. 1994 Low.
Inter. Trend	Bearish	From 5/23 High. The close below 662.00 on July 5 (Bearish Reversal Signal) turned the intermediate degree trend bearish.
Support (Sept.)	5/23 H	643.40-636.60, 617.00-608.95
Resistance (Sept.)	NA	662.10-664.30
Time Analysis		The election and decennial cycles and Dynamic Time Projections still indicate the S&P should make a new high in 1996 above the May high and Dec. will close higher than the May close!. The 1996 high should not be made prior to Oct.
	PTPP	From the 5/23H: **July 11-17**, July 31-Aug. 5
Pattern		The Wave 2 (8/94H-11/94L) correction was an ABC which implies Wave 4 should be "complex" which is exactly what appears to be unfolding. Complex corrections may take any shape imaginable. It is a hopeless job to try to predict their completion from a pattern standpoint. It is better to rely on price and time projections to anticipate the completion of the correction.
Minimum Bull Market Objectives	Price	691, **probable to 730** or higher.
	Time	Oct.: While the intermediate degree trend has turned down, the major trend objectives to new highs should come later in the year even though the S&P could be sideways to down into as late as Nov.
Bearish Reversal	Price	DCB 662.00 (Sept.). This was met Friday, July 5.
Bearish Continuation	Price	2CLDCB 608.95 (2 Consecutively Lower Daily Closes Below). Note that this long term Bearish Continuation Signal has been adjusted much lower than the one shown last week. If this signal is elected, it means that the outlook for new highs later in 1996 is voided and the bear trend from the May high should continue for many months. I do not anticipate this signal being elected.
Bullish Reversal	Price	DCA 664.3
General Trading Strategies		While the S&P is not unfolding in the ideal bullish scenario anticipated in recent weeks, the major bull trend from the April 1994 low is not yet voided and new highs later in the year are strongly anticipated. While a corrective low could come as late as Nov., the odds favor it being made by the end of Aug. and ideally in either the current PTPP of **July 11-17** or the upcoming July 31-Aug. 5 period. The ideal price zone for a corrective low is 643.4-636.60. The maximum anticipated decline is to the **617.00-608.95** support zone.
Options		Traders should be flat as of the July 5 close. No new recommendations.
Investors / Mutual Fund Switchers		Investors should be flat as of the July 5 close. No new recommendations.

Follow-up comments to the July 13, 1996 report: The chart above was included with the July 13, 1996 report. How did this outlook for a corrective low followed by a continued bull trend to new highs turn out? See the following pages.

S&P - Position Summary as of July 20, 1996 (Chart on Page 2)

Comments		Nothing has changed for the long term S&P outlook. **The July 16 low was made dead on the <u>617.00-609.96</u> support zone and the <u>July 11-17</u> PTPP for a low.**
Major Trend	Bullish	From Nov. 1994 Low.
Inter. Trend	Bearish	From 5/23 High. The close below 662.00 (bearish reversal signal) on July 5 turned the intermediate degree trend bearish.
Support (Sept.)	5/23 H	<u>617.00-608.95</u>
Resistance (Sept.)	NA	<u>645.85-654.25</u>, 666.20
Time Analysis		**July 16 should be the corrective low prior to a new high.** Note that this low was made 54 CDs from the May 23 high. Check your chart history for the large number of short term panic declines that were 55 CDs +/- a couple days!
	PTPP	From the 5/23H: <u>July 11-17</u>
Pattern		There is no confident wave structure interpretation at this point in time from my point of view other than a wave-four complex correction is at or near completion. If the July 16 low is exceeded, we must accept that the decline from May 23 high is a five wave pattern and probably the beginning of a larger degree bear market. <u>I don't expect the July 16 low to be exceeded without the S&P first making new highs.</u>
		The July 16 low was made dead on the <u>Andrew's support line</u> shown on last Saturday's report. When a market is making nice well defined swings, Andrew's support, resistance and median lines are often at least temporary support and resistance.
Minimum Bull Market Objectives	Price	<u>708</u>, probable to 730 or higher. *(These are <u>minimum</u> projections.)*
	Time	<u>Oct.</u>: While the intermediate degree trend has turned down, the major trend objectives to new highs should come later in the year even though the S&P could be sideways to down into as late as Nov. *Oct. is the <u>minimum</u> time projection for a top.*
Bearish Reversal	Price	<u>DCB 622.00 (Sept.)</u>. This was met Friday, July 5.
Bearish Continuation	Price	<u>2CLDCB 608.95</u> (2 Consecutively Lower Daily Closes Below).
Bullish Reversal	Price	<u>DCA 666.20</u>
General Trading Strategies		**The working assumption at this time is that the S&P made a corrective low at the direct hit of time and price support on July 16.** The S&P should exceed the May 23 high without exceeding the July 16 low although a trending rally probably won't begin prior to early Aug. Traders should only consider buying strategies unless the Bearish Continuation Signal is made.
Options		Put premiums are high. Option traders should consider selling out-of-the-money puts given the working assumption that the July 16 low will not be exceeded for some time. Needless to say, short puts must only be hedged in the event of another panic decline.
Investors / Mutual Fund Switchers		Investors should be flat as of the July 5 close. Enter long on a DCA 666.20, the Bullish Reversal Signal.

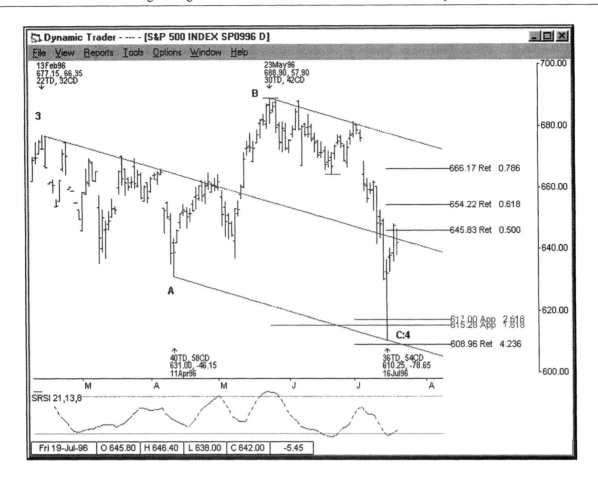

Follow-Up Comments To The July 13 and July 20, 1996 Weekly Reports

The dynamic time, price and pattern analysis for the July 16, 1996 corrective low shown in these two reports was dead-on. The S&P continued to rally to new highs as anticipated. You may recall that right at this time, a very well publicized "guru" sent out tens of thousands of promotional letters for her investment newsletter that said something like "sell everything now, a bear market has begun." I'll bet you were on a mailing list that received this "warning." Traders and investors using Dynamic Trading techniques knew just the opposite was likely to happen. Not a bear market, but the resumption of the bull market to new highs.

The "Minimum Bull Market Objectives" shown in the July 20 report are just that, minimum objectives. As of that period of time in late July when the S&P was at 642.00, the bull market was anticipated to reach *at least 708* and *probably 730 or higher* and not make a top prior to Oct. The bull trend continued as anticipated and the S&P reached 718.00 in Oct. As new swings were made, new price and time projections were also made which pointed to even higher prices in the months ahead.

S&P - Position Summary as of Aug. 31, 1996 (Chart on Page 2)

Comments	The sharp decline of the last two days does not void the long term outlook for new highs before year-end.	
Major Trend	Bullish	From Nov. 1994 Low. This bull trend should not complete prior to Oct.
Inter. Trend	Bullish	From the July 16 low. Only a close below Bearish Reversal Signal of 623.55 would turn the Intermediate degree trend bearish.
Support (Sept.)	8/22H	**646.30-640.05**, 634.05, 623.60-620.00 646.30: 50% Ret. 7/24L-8/22H 644.65: 100% APP 641.40: 50% Ret. 7/16L-8/22H 640.05: 61.8% Ret. 7/24L-8/22H
Resistance (Sept.)	7/16 L	666.20-672.10, 678.40-681.95
Time Analysis	PTPP	From the 8/22H: **Sept. 4-6**, Sept. 13-16 The decline from the 8/22 high should complete no later than the Sept. 13-16 PTPP followed by a continued rally to new highs.
Pattern	Bullish	Aug. 22 completed an oddball top. Check your charts to find another top made on a 2-3 week narrow range pattern. You'll have a hard time. The 7/16L-8/22H rally does not fit a well-defined and predictable pattern. At best, it appears to be a sloppy five wave impulse pattern. Given the larger degree outlook for new highs, this is the best interpretation.
Minimum Bull Market Objectives	Price	708, probable to 730 or higher.
	Time	Oct.
Bearish Reversal	Price	DCB 623.55
Bullish Cont.	Price	2CHDCA 672.55
General Trading Strategies	*The current decline is considered corrective and should provide an excellent entry opportunity for the anticipated advance to new highs later in the year.* The ideal time and price targets for a corrective low are **Sept. 4-6** and **646.30-640.05**. The decline should complete no later than Sept. 16 and should not close below 623.60.	
Options	No change. Option strategies should consider that the S&P should exceed the May high in the fourth quarter of the year without first making the Bearish Reversal Signal. Put premiums are relatively high. *Option traders should consider selling out-of-the-money puts given the working assumption that the Bearish Reversal Signal will not be exceeded for some time.* Needless to say, short puts must be hedged in the event of another panic decline.	
Investors / Mutual Fund Switchers	**Investors should be long as of the Aug. 2** close when the Bullish Reversal Signal was made. Exit long positions if the Bearish Reversal Signal is made.	

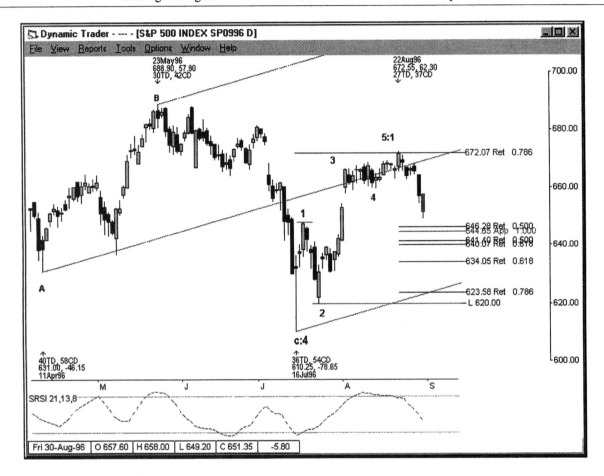

Follow-up Comments To The Aug. 31, 1996 Report

How did the projection for a corrective low <u>no later</u> than Sept. 16 followed by a continued rally to new highs turn out? See the follow-up chart on the next page. The Aug. 31, 1996 report also projected that the <u>minimum</u> bull market price objective was 708 and the S&P would probably reach 730 or higher.

On Sept. 3, one day before the Sept. 4-6 PTPP (Projected Turning Point Period) for a low, the S&P made a corrective low as anticipated at 642.70, precisely within the 646.30-640.05 projected support zone.

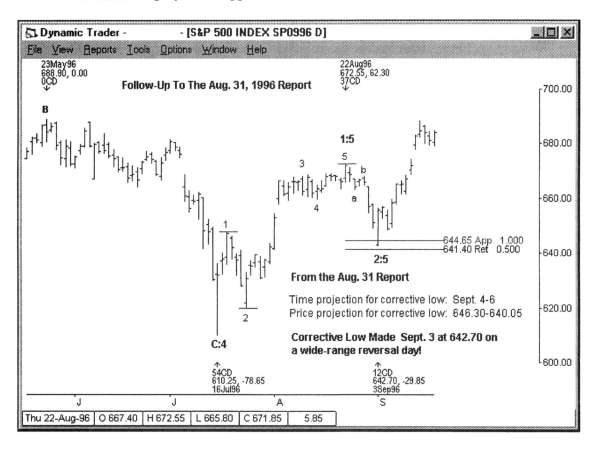

The S&P continued to rally to new highs as anticipated. Note above that the Aug. high was considered a Wave-1 and the Sept. low a Wave-2. This implies that Waves 3-5 to new highs should still unfold.

The Aug. 31, 1996 report projected that the minimum bull-market price objective was 708 with a probable objective of 730 or higher.

How did this outlook turn out? Let's move ahead to the Nov. 21, 1996 report to find out.

S&P - Position Summary as of Nov. 21, 1996

Comments		While the S&P has reached the broad price zone anticipated for a major top, time projections indicate a top was not made at the Nov. 20 high.
Major Trend	Bullish	From April 1994 Low. The S&P has met the minimum time and price objectives for the present trend. It will take a Bearish Reversal Signal to provide an indication that the trend is complete.
Inter. Trend	Bullish	From the July 16 low: Time projections indicate the trend from the July 16 low should complete by Dec. 15.
Support (Dec.)	NA	730.40: Calculate Fib. retracements if top confirmed by a close below 730.40.
Resistance (Dec.)	7/16 L	Broad price zone for major top: 738.00-761.25 743.90-744.70, 750.90-753.55, 761.25, 774.60-783.10 The high to date on Nov. 20 is 749.80. Given the upper end of the major resistance zone is at 761.25, it appears the S&P is near a major top in price. The S&P should still make at least marginal new highs to 750.90 or higher.
Time Analysis	PTPP	From the 7/16L: **Nov. 22-26**, Dec. 5-15: The rally from the July 16 low should complete by Dec. 15; ideally in either of the PTPPs shown above.
	TRZ	From the April 1994 Low: Dec. 5-March 25. (The TRZ is the broad time zone with a high probability of making a major bull market top.)
Pattern	Bullish	Pattern indicates the entire bull trend may be at or near completion. Oct. 29 is considered wave four from the July 16 low. The July 16 low is considered wave four from the April 1994 low. The daily chart on page 3 shows that the S&P may be at or near completion of a minor five wave sequence from the Oct. 29 low.
Minimum Bull Market Objectives	Price	S&P (Dec.) 726.55 (met Nov. 6), probable to 738.00 or higher (met Nov. 14.).
	Time	Oct. 31: Has been met. New daily and closing highs after Nov. 11 signal the advance should continue to **Nov. 22** or later.
Bullish Continuation	Price	S&P (Dec.): 2CHDCA 761.25 and (SPX) 2CHDCA 767.35. If these signals are made, which is very unlikely, look out above!
Bearish Reversal	Price	S&P (Dec.) DCB (Daily Close Below) 730.40
General Trading Strategies		While the S&P should make at least marginal new highs above the Nov. 20 high, keep in mind the S&P is near the extreme time and price projections for a major top. There is no reason not to be long as long as the trend is up, but stops on positions should be fairly close to the market.
Options		Initiate bearish option strategies if the Bearish Reversal is made.
Investors / Mutual Fund Switchers		Investors should be long as of the Aug. 2 close when the Bullish Reversal Signal was made. Exit long positions if the Bearish Reversal Signal is made.

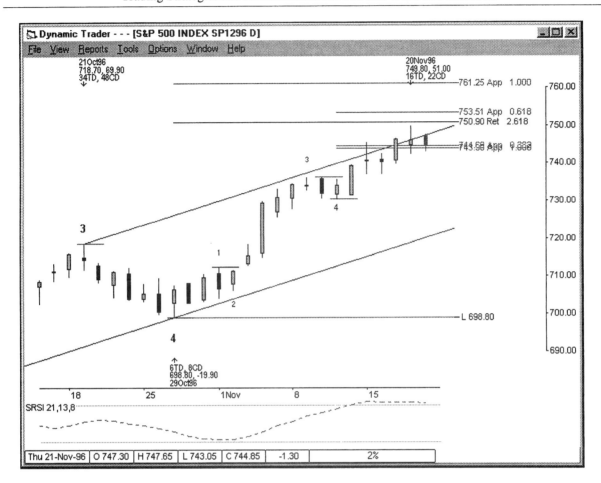

Follow-up comments to the Nov. 21, 1996 Report: The chart above, included with the Nov. 21, 1996 report, showed Oct. 29 as a Wave-4 low counting from the July low. It appeared minor Waves-1-4 of Wave-5 were also complete, implying the five wave advance from the July low was near completion.

The Nov. 21 report projected that the S&P had a high probability of completing the bull trend in either the <u>Nov. 22-26</u> or <u>Dec. 5-15</u> PTPP for a high. Time, price and pattern each seemed to be pointing to a major top.

On Nov. 26, precisely within the time zone for a high, the S&P made a reversal-day high followed by the sharpest decline since the July low. All of the factors seemed to be in place to signal the completion of a bull market and the beginning of a bear trend.

How did it turn out? Let's move ahead to the Dec. 14 report.

S&P - Position Summary as of Dec. 14, 1996

Comments	The S&P has continued lower as anticipated. It will not take much more of a decline to confirm the larger degree trend has turned bearish.	
Major Trend	Bullish	From April 1994 Low. Both the Bearish Reversal and Bearish Continuation Signals must be made to signal the major trend has turned bearish.
Inter. Trend	Bullish	From the July 16 low: While the Nov. 26 high has been made on a direct hit of projected time and price, the Bearish Reversal Signal (DCB 730.90) has not been elected to signal the trend has turned bearish.
Support (March)	11/26H	732.20-730.95, **722.20-718.20**, 705.30-697.50, 684.75
		722.20-718.20 is now the key support zone. This zone includes the 100% alternate price projection (W.3=W.1 counting from the Nov. 26 high), 78.6% retracement of W.5 and 38.2% retracement of W.1-5. Closing below this price zone is a high probability signal that the larger degree trend is bearish.
Resistance	7/16 L	(spot futures): Broad price zone for major top: 738.00-772.00
	12/15L	(March): 752.50-755.0. This zone should not be closed above if the larger degree trend has turned bearish. A close above 755.0 should be followed by a continued rally to new highs. Calculate Fib. retracements if low made.
Time Analysis	PTPP	Dec. 19 (potential for minor low).
Pattern	?	The working assumption is that Nov. 26 completed wave 5:5. Dec. 10 has either completed waves 1-2 or A-B. The assumption is waves 1-2 are complete. If this is the case, the S&P should currently be in a wave three decline which implies there is a high probability of continued volatility and relatively wide-range down days.
Minimum LT Bull Market Objectives	Price	Met
	Time	Met
Bullish Continuation	Price	S&P (Spot futures): 2CHDCA 767.25 and (SPX) 2CHDCA 772. If these Bullish Continuation Signals are met, the S&P should be in a panic buying frenzy with the next price objectives much higher.
Bearish Reversal	Price	S&P (March) DCB 730.90. The S&P has bounced off of this target but has not closed below 730.90. Only a close below 730.90 will signal a trend change.
Bearish Continuation	Price	S&P (March) 2CLDCB 718.20
		If the Bearish Continuation Signal is made, it implies an impulsive wave series began with the Nov. 26 top and the larger degree trend has probably turned bearish.
General Trading Strategies	The current trading assumption is that a major top was made Nov. 26 and the S&P should continue a bear trend to below the July 16 low without exceeding the Nov. 26 high. A close above 755.00 is the initial indication that this outlook is incorrect. A close below 730.90 is the initial confirmation of a top. Trading strategies should be oriented to the short side unless the S&P closes above 755.00.	
Options	Initiate bearish option strategies on a March contract close below 730.90.	
Investors / Mutual Fund Switchers	Investors should be long as of the Aug. 2 close when the Bullish Reversal Signal was made. Exit long positions if the Bearish Reversal Signal is made (DCB 730.90).	

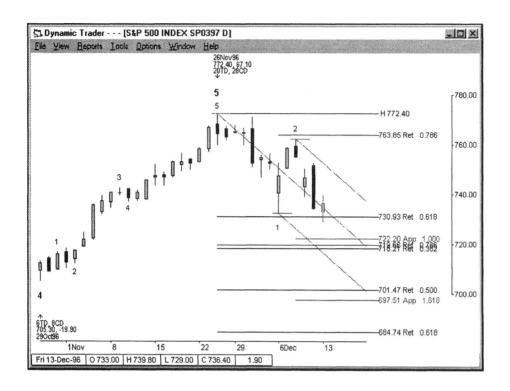

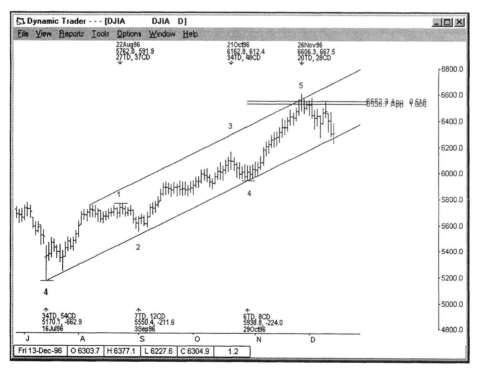

Follow-up Comments To The Dec. 14, 1996 Report

The March S&P and DJIA charts on the previous page that were included with the Dec. 14 report clearly showed what appeared to be the completion of a five wave rally into the Nov. 26 high. The assumption was Nov. 26 completed a bull-market. The initial decline from the Nov. 26 high was labeled assuming Waves 1 and 2 were complete (see the S&P chart on the previous page). If the 722.20-718.20 support zone was exceeded, the bear market would be confirmed. This support zone included typical corrective price targets (see the Price Support comments in the Dec. 14 report). If they were exceeded, the odds were the decline was not a correction, but an impulse.

Don't forget that we trade market behavior, not forecasts, no matter how confident the technical analysis appears. The objective is to always consider what market activity will confirm or invalidate your opinion of the market.

Within two weeks, the market signaled that a major top was probably *not* complete and the stock indexes would continue to rally to new highs. The market had quickly signaled that not only was the immediate bearish outlook probably incorrect, but new highs should unfold soon.

Let's skip ahead to the Jan. 18, 1997 report for an update.

S&P - Position Summary as of Jan. 18, 1997

Comments		The S&P has made new highs after Jan. 14 which signals the advance should continue at least into Jan. 23 if not longer.
Major Trend	Bullish	From April 1994 Low. Both the Bearish Reversal and Bearish Continuation Signals must be made to signal the major trend has turned bearish.
Inter. Trend	Bullish	From the July 16 low: **With the election of the Bullish Reversal Signal on Dec. 24**, the intermediate degree trend must be considered bullish unless the Bearish Reversal Signal is made.
Support (March)	NA	747.90, 733.25
Resistance (March)	12/17L	802.90-821.10: This is the critical resistance zone if the wave count shown on the daily chart (12/17 = W.4 L) is correct. At this price zone, W.5=61.8% W.1-3 and 162% W.1, W.5=162% W.4 and W.3-5:5=262% W.2:5. If the S&P exceeds this zone, the wave count shown last week (12/17L=W.2:5 counting from the 7/16L) is probably correct which would project much higher prices. The long term report which will be mailed Tuesday includes 40 pages of S&P and DJIA analysis and projections. Long term projections show 813.00-822.00 as a critical long-term resistance zone.
Time Analysis	PTPP	From the July 16 Low: Jan. 9-14, Jan. 23-24, **Feb. 5-11**. New highs have been made after Jan. 14 which implies the S&P should be sideways to up to at least Jan. 23 and probably to Feb. 5 or later.
Pattern	7/16L	After spending the last two weeks preparing the long term analysis and evaluating the various potential patterns, the current position of the market is best considered with the Dec. 17 low as wave 4:(5). Time and price projections confirm that this is a better outlook than the Dec. 17 low as wave 2:(5). The most important factor is there is no way to look at the July 16 low as other than a Wave (4) which implies however the final wave (5) will unfold, it will complete a long term bull trend.
Minimum LT Bull Market Objectives	Price	Met. While the long term objective has been met, the recent pattern analysis suggests the March S&P should reach at lest 802.90 before completing W.(5).
Bearish Reversal	Price	S&P (March) DCB 733.25.
Bullish Reversal	Price	S&P (March) Close above 758.80 (met Dec. 24)
Bullish Continuation	Price	S&P (March): 2CHDCA 772.40. Met week ending Jan. 17. Next minimum objective is 802.90.
General Trading Strategies		The S&P should be sideways to up at least to Jan. 23 and should reach at least 802.90. These are minimum objectives.
Options		There are no specific recommendations at this time.
Investors / Mutual Fund Switchers		Investors and mutual fund switchers exited the market on Dec. 16. Only re-enter long positions if the new Bullish Continuation Signal described above is made.

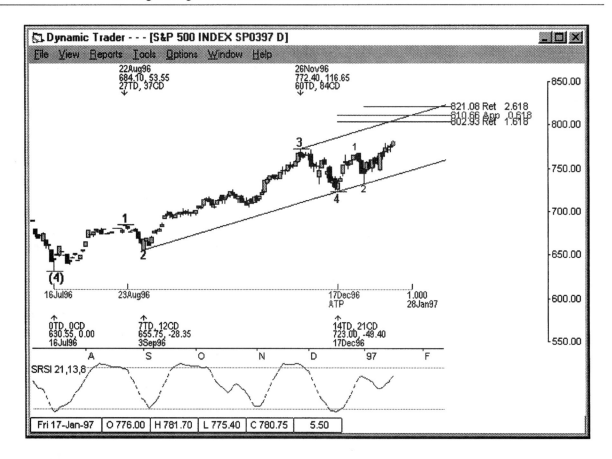

Follow-up Comments To The Jan. 18, 1997 Report

The chart above, included with the Jan. 18 report, illustrated the revised wave count which now considered the Nov. 26 high a Wave-3, not a Wave-5. The market behavior itself quickly invalidated the opinion that Nov. 26 was a Wave-5 high and provided new time and price projections for the bull trend.

Note that the Jan. 18 report projected the Feb. 5-11 period as having the greatest probability of making a top at the projected price zone of 813.00-822.00 where short, intermediate and long-term price projections coincided. The projection in mid-Jan. was for at least another three weeks and 20+ points of rally.

The S&P continued to rally to new highs as anticipated. Let's jump forward a few weeks for an update.

S&P - Position Summary as of Feb. 15, 1997

Comments		The S&P has continued to advance as anticipated in Wednesday's update report. Time, price and pattern projections are each nearing the extremes from where a major top should be made.
Major Trend	Bullish	From April 1994 Low. With the election of the Bullish Continuation Signal Jan. 17, the major trend must be considered bullish. Both the Bearish Reversal and Bearish Continuation Signals must be made to signal the major trend has turned bearish.
Inter. Trend	Bullish	From the July 16 low: The intermediate degree trend must be considered bullish unless the Bearish Reversal Signal is made.
Pattern	7/16L	Feb. 5 is considered the W.4:4, running-correction low. If this is correct, the completion of a minor five wave advance from Feb. 5 will complete five-wave structures of several degrees as outlined in the monthly report. A "running correction" is an ABC correction where the wave-c low is at a higher price than the wave-a low. It implies that the next impulse wave, in this case wave-5, has a high probability of extending beyond the typical price targets for a wave-5.

Feb. 13 is probably a minor W.3 high which implies there should only be a few more days to complete the minor five wave structure beginning from the Feb. 5 low. A decline below the wave-1 high (796.95) signals the minor five-wave advance should be complete.

In viewing the minor and intermediate degree wave patterns, I look for a wave pattern that is a strong candidate as an "alternate." I simply don't see a strong candidate at this time. |
| **Support** (March) | 1/23H | 796.96, 782.90, 771.00

Calculate Fib retracements if high confirmed.

A decline below 782.90 (W.2:5) is the first signal the advance is complete given the assumed wave pattern. A decline below 771.00 (W.4 low) confirms the advance is complete. |
| **Resistance** (March) | 12/17L | 810.66-824.90 (**818.40-824.90**), 841.85-850.85

The **810.66-824.90** price zone includes at least seven price projections from three degrees that are typical price targets for a wave five. This price zone falls at the area of parallel channel resistance of two degrees.

If the wave count from the Dec. 14 low is correct, the maximum price target should be 841.85-850.85. This considers W.4:5 is a running correction as described in the pattern section and W.5 that began Feb. 5 will exceed 100% of W.1 (probably to 162% W.1). |
| **Time Analysis** | PTPP | From the July 16 Low: Feb. 17-26 (**17-19**)

Time analysis is performed in the same manner as price and pattern analysis. From the top (larger degree) down. The long and intermediate term cycles pointed to a high probability top in the Feb. 5-11 period. *The recent short-term cycles extend the period through Feb. 26 with a concentration in the* **Feb. 17-19** *period.* |
Minimum LT Bull Market Objectives	Price	Met. While the long term objective has been met, Wednesday's report projected the recent short-term swings projected a continuation to at least 810.40 and a **probable objective of 821.00 or higher**. The minimum objective has been met.
Bearish Reversal	Price	S&P (March) DCB 771.00. A close below the minor wave four low (Feb. 5) signals the bull trend is complete.
Bullish Reversal	Price	S&P (March) Close above 758.80 (met Dec. 24).

Bullish Continuation	Price	S&P (March): 2CHDCA 772.40. Met Jan. 17.
General Trading Strategies		All factors of time, price and pattern signal the high probability of a major top no later than Feb. 26 and no higher than 850.85. These are <u>maximum</u> objectives anticipated. **The greater probability is for a top to be complete by next Wednesday, Feb. 19, with 824.90 as the probable maximum target.**
Options		Initiate bearish option strategies if the Bearish Reversal Signal is made.
Investors / Mutual Fund Switchers		Investors and mutual fund switchers entered long on the Bullish Continuation Signal made Jan. 17. Exit long positions if the Bearish Reversal Signal is made.

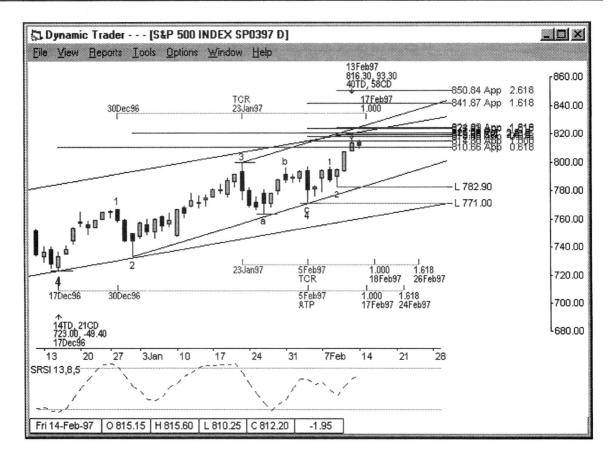

Follow-up Comments To The Feb. 15, 1997 Report

The March S&P made a *key-reversal-day* on <u>Feb. 19</u>, precisely within the <u>Feb. 17-19</u> PTPP for the final Wave-5 high. The top was <u>820.40</u>, precisely within the ideal objective for Wave-5 of <u>818.40-824.90</u>!

As of mid-March 1997 when this chapter is being completed, the S&P has only declined about 6% from the Feb. 19 high and has not yet confirmed whether the Feb. 19 high completed a major bull market. But, the time, price and pattern factors that would confirm or invalidate if the top is complete have been clearly identified. Remember, we will trade the market, not the forecast.

The Real World Of Dynamic Trading

S&P 500; July 1996 - March 1997

The daily S&P chart below includes the period since the July 1996 low described in the previous reports. Except for a brief period in Dec. when it appeared a Wave 5:5 had completed, the Dynamic Trading analysis and trading strategies continued to project higher prices as the market moved up from one price objective to the next.

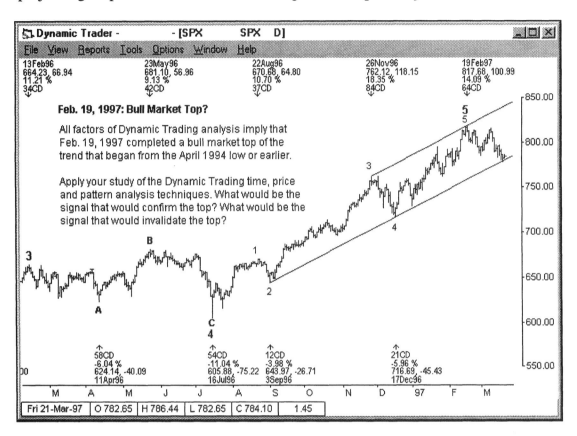

If you review these S&P reports again, the importance of Dynamic Trading analysis should become obvious.

1. Dynamic Price Analysis is much more than obvious support and resistance levels. Comprehensive Dynamic Price Analysis often provides the minimum price target anticipated for the market position. Dynamic Price Analysis also often provides the specific price levels that should not be exceeded if the opinion of the market position is valid.

2. Dynamic Time Analysis provides the specific time periods with a very high probability of trend reversal. Almost every intermediate-term high and low shown on the chart above was made within one trading day of a time projection. Dynamic Time Analysis also provides the trader and investor with the minimum time objectives probable for any degree swing.

3. Practical Elliott wave analysis often provides a very confident opinion of market position. When Elliott wave pattern analysis is combined with dynamic time and price analysis, high probability time and price projections are possible. The failure of many Elliott wave analysts is they trade their forecasts, not the market behavior. Any market will usually confirm or invalidate an Elliott wave forecast very quickly. To fail to recognize the confirmation or invalidation of the Elliott wave opinion is to fail to understand the practical application and true value of Elliott wave analysis.

By applying Dynamic Trading analysis methods you have learned in this book, you will be prepared for the highest probability market activity in the same manner shown in these reports.

Now, let's move on to examples from other markets.

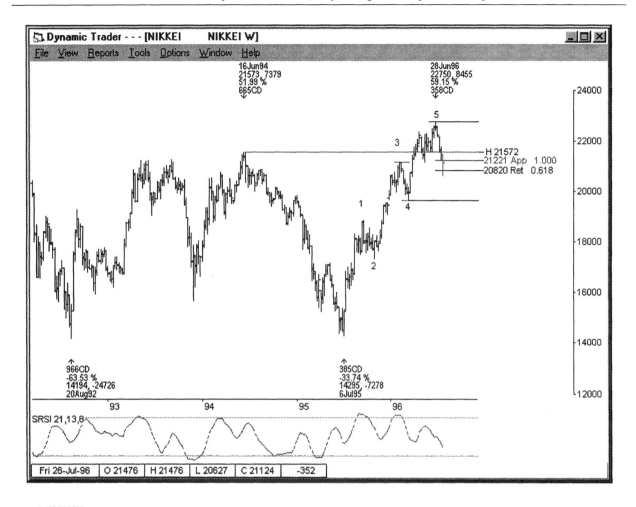

NIKKEI: The Nikkei has probably completed a major top in June. Summer time is an important period for seasonal change in the Nikkei. Note on the weekly chart that the last three major trend changes took place in Aug., June and July. The decline from the June 1996 high has exceeded the 100% Alternate Price Projection and reached the 61.8% retracement of wave five. While the long term trend remains unclear in the Nikkei, it appears June has began a decline that should at least correct the entire rally from the July 1995 low.

The following page shows the outcome of the Nikkei from the June 1996 high.

Follow-up Comments To The Nikkei In The Aug. 1996 Report

The Nikkei has declined over 25% from the June 1996 high through March 1997. A simple analysis of wave structure and the time of prior highs and lows signaled the high probability outcome from the June high.

The chart below shows the Nikkei through March 1997. Do you think the bear trend from the June 1996 high through the Jan. 1997 low is a correction or the beginning of an impulse trend to new lows? What is your rationale?

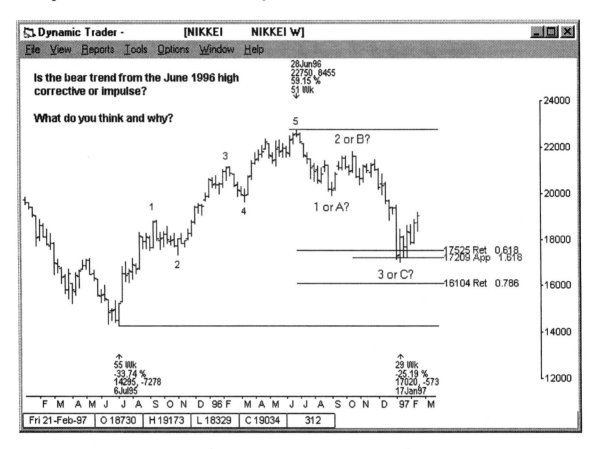

The Jan low was made at the coincidence of the 61.8% retracement and 162% Alternate Price Projection. Based on simple price projection analysis and wave form, the odds are high the Jan. low was not the completion of a corrective low. The odds are the Jan. low was a Wave-3 not a Wave-C of an ABC correction. The C-Wave is more often equal to 100% of the A-Wave, not 162%. A Wave-3 is often equal to or greater than 162% of the Wave-1.

If we consider the Jan. 1997 low the end of Wave-3, what would be the pattern factor that would invalidate this idea? A Wave-4 should not trade into the price range of Wave-1. If the Nikkei rallied above what is shown as the Wave-1 low, the bearish outlook for the Jan. low to be exceeded is at least questionable.

Strait Times (Weekly): *The Feb. top should not be exceeded for years.* The ST should complete a five wave decline within the relatively broad support zone of <u>2032-1948</u> which includes the 78.6% retracement, W.5=100% W.1, W.5=61.8% W.1-3 and W.5=162% W.4.

The following page shows the outcome of the Strait Times Index following the comments from the Nov. 1996 report.

Follow-up Comments To The Strait Times Index In The Nov. 1996 Report

The Wave-5 low of 2035.0 was made just three points short of the ideal price projection for Wave-5 of 2032-1948.

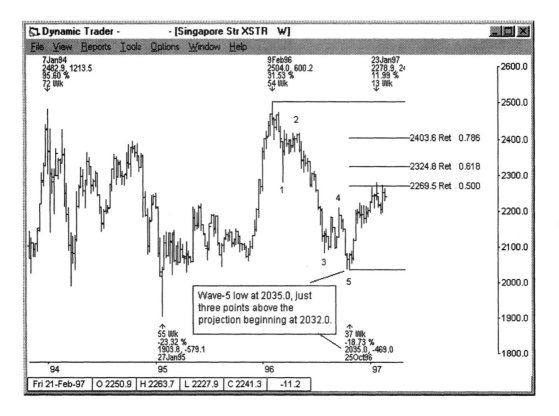

Elliott wave analysis and Dynamic Price Analysis prepared traders and investors for a major low that was followed by the largest rally in almost a year.

Cattle (Feb.)

<u>Resistance</u>: <u>65.20-65.54</u>

<u>Support (11/14H)</u>: <u>64.45-64.21</u>, 63.96-63.88, <u>63.61-63.45</u>, 63,11

The sell order was not elected last week. Cattle made a five-wave decline into the Oct. 25 low. Cattle have rallied to what should be the maximum objective if the rally is <u>corrective</u>. The Nov. 14 high appears to have completed an ABC correction at the <u>65.20-65.54</u> resistance zone which includes the 78.6% retracement, wave-four high, 100% alternate price projection (W.C=W.A) and 262% retracement of W.B (W.C=262% W.B). A close over 65.54 signals the rally is probably not corrective but should continue to rally and exceed the Aug. high. Seasonally, Feb. cattle have a high probability to be down from Nov. into Jan. or Feb. We should continue to initiate short position strategies as long as cattle have not closed above 65.54.

<u>Short and Intermediate Term Traders</u>: As long as cattle have not closed above 65.54, sell cattle at three ticks below the prior day's low. Adjust the protective buy-stop daily to one tick above the 3DH (three-day-high).

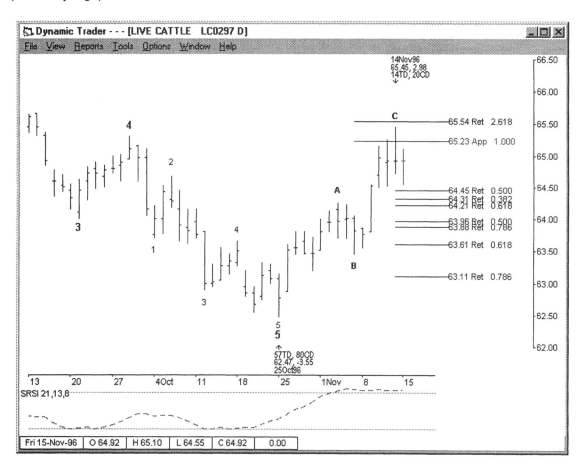

Follow-up Comments To Cattle In The Nov. 16, 1996 Report

For markets other than the S&P, the weekly report often provides specific trade recommendations. Specific trade recommendations are not provided for the S&P because of the enormous volatility that can occur during the week, making it impossible to provide judicious protective stops with trade recommendations from a weekly report.

The Nov. 14 high was made at the ideal price projection for a Wave-C corrective high. While the Dynamic Trading book has not discussed seasonal tendencies in markets, many of the agricultural markets have very reliable seasonal tendencies that traders should be aware of.

Note that the recommended sell strategy was to wait for a prior daily low to be exceeded before entering the short position. In other words, a minor confirmation of a bear trend. The sell strategy was voided if cattle closed over the upper extreme of the resistance zone. If cattle exceeded the extreme resistance zone typical for an ABC correction, the odds are the rally was impulsive, not corrective, and new highs would eventually be made.

The following page shows the next week's report and how the analysis and trading strategies worked out.

Cattle (Feb.)

Resistance: Calculate Fib. retracements if low confirmed

Support (11/14H): 63.61-63.45, 63.11, 62.47-62.39, 61.41

The sell order was elected on Monday, Nov. 18 at 64.52, three ticks below the prior day's low. Cattle completed an ABC correction at the Nov. 14 top as described last week. Cattle should continue to eventually decline to below the Oct. 25 low.

Short Term Traders (S-11/18, 64.52): Adjust the protective buy stop to 64.01. Take profits at 62.90.

Intermediate Term Traders (S-11/18, 64.52): Adjust the protective buy stop to 64.01.

Current and	Cattle	Opened	Price	Closed	Price	P/L	O/C
Recent Trading	Short Feb. (ST)	11/18	64.52	-	-	$488	O
Recommendations	Short Feb. (IT)	11/18	64.52	-	-	$488	O

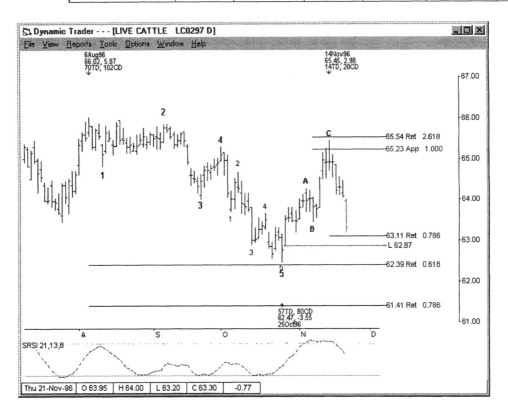

Follow-up Comments For Cattle To The Nov. 21, 1996 Report

Cattle declined sharply, electing the sell-stop for a short position as anticipated.

Dynamic Trading analysis prepared traders to take advantage of a low-risk and low-capital exposure trade. What ever your trading time frame, short, intermediate or long-term, you must have the patience to wait for the best opportunities.

Gold - Position Summary as of Oct. 29, 1996

Comments		Gold has exceeded a 20 year historical extreme for the time range of a decline without having made a 5% rally. Last month projected that at least a minor low should be made by Oct. 4 (Sept. 25-Oct. 4 PTPP). The low was made Oct. 1 at 379.8, just 70¢ below the projected support zone for the low of 382.6-380.5.
Major Trend	Trading Range	With the decline below the June-July low, the odds are equal for a break below or above the trading range.
Intermediate Trend	Bearish	Gold must make the Bullish Reversal Signal which is now 2CHDCA 386.5 to turn the trend bullish.
Support (Dec.)	8/5 H	381.6, 378.0-376.5
Resistance (Dec.)	NA	386.5, 388.0
Time Analysis	PTPP	From the Oct. 22 high: Nov. 4-6, Nov. 11-13
Pattern	8/5H	Oct. 22 is probably a wave-four high which implies gold should make another drive to new lows, ideally to the 378.0-376.5 support zone which is an ideal target for a wave five low. Only a close above the Oct. 22 high will void this outlook.
Minimum Trend Objective		There are no trend objectives until gold provides a trend direction signal. The larger degree position is a trading range. Gold must make a bearish or bullish continuation signal before trend objectives will be given.
Bullish Reversal	Price	DCA 386.5
Bearish Continuation	Price	DCB 376.4. A close below 381.6 will be an initial indication of a continued decline at least to 378.0.
General Trading Strategies		If the Bullish Reversal Signal is elected, gold should only be in the initial stages of a bull trend and should continue to rally above the long term trading range highs.
		If the Bearish Continuation Signal is made, gold should continue to decline to at least 355.
Options		No specific recommendations at this time.
PM Mutual Funds		Go long on a Dec. contract close above 386.5.

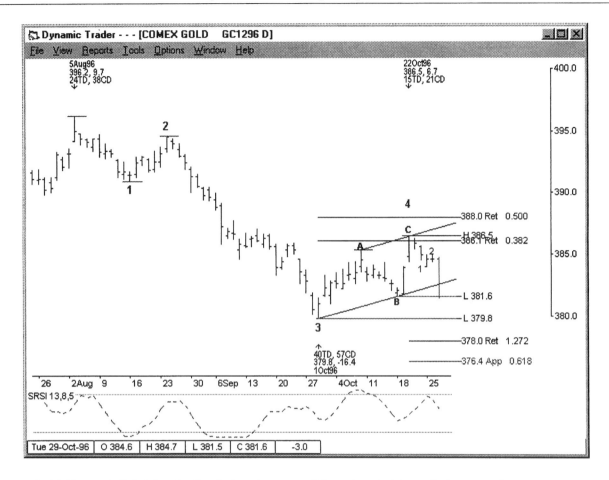

Gold (Dec., daily): The decline below the wave-B low signaled the rally from the Oct. 1 low is probably corrective and not impulsive. The odds favor a continued decline to the 378.0-376.4 support zone. Only a close above 386.5 (10/22H) will void this immediate bearish outlook.

Follow-up Comments For Gold To The Nov. 1996 Report

Why was a new low below the Oct. 1 low anticipated? Gold had declined below the Wave-B low signaling the rally to the Oct. 22 high and 38.2% retracement was an ABC correction, not the beginning of an impulsive trend. If the Oct. 22 high was a Wave-4, the ideal price projection for a Wave-5 low was 378.0-376.5. Nov. 4-6 was projected as the ideal time for a Wave-5 low.

Did gold make a Wave-5 low in the time and price targets as anticipated? The next page shows what transpired in the following weeks.

Gold continued to decline to a new low just as anticipated. On Nov. 1, one trading day prior to the Nov. 4-6 PTPP for a low, gold made a reversal-day low at 377.8, precisely within the price zone projected for a Wave-5 low. Time, price and pattern plus a daily reversal signal seemed to coincide for an important low. Gold rallied $8 and then fell out of bed and continued to decline to new lows.

The time and price projections were right on for a low, but not a major low as anticipated by the Elliott wave interpretation that considered the Nov. 1 low the completion of a five wave decline.

Dynamic Trading analysis and trading strategies will not project the market position correctly all of the time. No method of analysis is capable of doing that. The time, price and pattern position of the Nov. 1 low provided the trader and investor with a definitive, maximum protective stop-loss for long positions of one tick below the Nov. 1 reversal-day low.

When the Nov. 1 low was exceeded, traders could hold no bull market illusions, at least for the time being. The market itself had invalidated Nov. 1 as a major low and signaled the bear trend would continue.

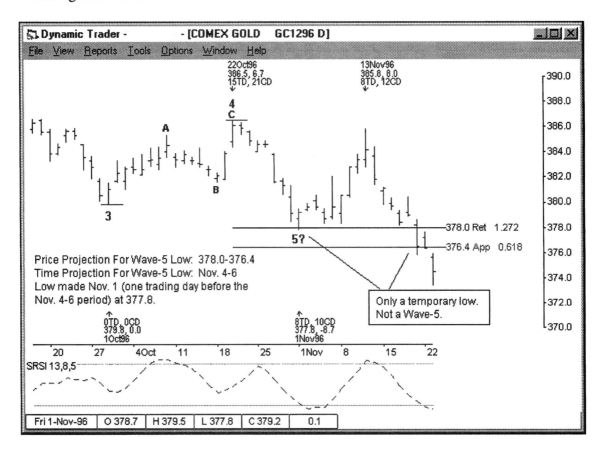

Trade market behavior, not forecasts. Always identify the market activity that will invalidate your opinion of the market position and do not fail to act when the market tells you in no uncertain terms that you are wrong.

The Real World Of Dynamic Trading

Bonds - Position Summary as of Sept. 7, 1996 (Chart on Page 2)

Comments		Bonds did not make the Bearish Price Reversal last week (2CLDCB 106.23) but did trade below the extreme time and price support targets anticipated to complete the decline from the Aug. 13 high. Friday's wide-range, *outside-reversal-day* has probably completed the steep decline and a corrective rally should now take place.
Major Trend	Bearish	From the Jan. 4 high: Bonds should eventually continue lower and exceed the Nov. 1994 low without having exceeded the Jan. 1996 high. The recent five wave decline suggests the Aug. 13 high will not be exceeded.
Inter. Trend	Bearish	From the Aug. 13 high: Bonds appear to have completed a five wave decline on Friday which implies the larger degree trend is now down.
Support (Dec.)	8/13 H	**105.23-105.11**, 104.31, 103.31 105.23-105.11 is the support zone where W.5=W.1 and W.5=.382 W.1-3 if Sept. 4 is considered the wave-4 high.
Resistance (Dec.)	9/6L	107.17-107.25, 108.18-109.10 A corrective rally should reach **at least 108.18**.
Time Analysis	PTPP	If bonds continue sideways to up as anticipated, **a corrective top should not be made prior to Sept. 19.**
Pattern	8/13H	Last week assumed Aug. 28 was a wave-four high. The continued declined has altered the count to a textbook five wave decline with wave-three subdivided into five minor waves. **Friday's low (Sept. 6) was made at the ideal price zone for a wave five low**. See the support price section above. The five wave decline implies that Aug. 13 was a major corrective high and bonds should exceed the June low without having exceeded the Aug. high.
Minimum Bear Trend Objectives		These will not be considered unless or until the June 13 low is exceeded and there is a confirmed bearish pattern to work off of.
Bearish Reversal	Price	DCB 107.24. This was made Aug. 30.
Bearish Continuation	Price	2CLDCB 106.23 (Sept.), 106.14 (Dec.). This was not made last week.
General Trading Strategies		All factors signal that Sept. 6 completed the swing down from the Aug. 13 high *and a corrective rally should continue into at least Sept. 19 and reach at least 108.18*. These are the minimum time and price objectives.
Last Week		The buy-on-close signal was elected Tuesday on the close of 107.12. The long position was stopped out on Friday 106.01.
Specific Trading Recommendations		Short and Intermediate Term Traders: Buy bonds at 106.13 or better, or 107.05 on a stop, OCO. Place the protective sell-stop at 105.19. While not a specific recommendation, subscribers who bought near the close Friday, use the 105.19 protective sell-stop.
Options		Option strategies should consider that bonds should remain within the extremes of the June low and Aug. high at least through Oct. Option traders should consider selling Dec. 106 puts and Dec. 112 calls on a futures buy signal.
Mutual Fund		The sell signal to liquidate for bond mutual funds was made Friday on the Bearish Reversal Signal.

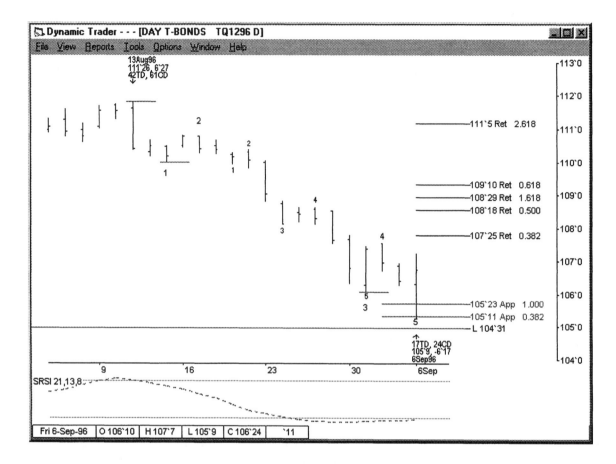

Follow-up Comments For Bonds To The Sept. 7, 1996 Report

Although the larger degree pattern position is not shown in the limited period of the chart above that was included with the Sept. 7 report, the Aug. 13 high was considered a major Wave-2 high. If it was indeed a Wave-2, it was not anticipated to be exceeded prior to a continued decline to new lows. The rally from the Sept. 6 low was anticipated to be a correction to the five wave decline from Aug. 13 to Sept. 6.

How did it turn out? See the next page for a follow-up chart and more comments.

The Real World Of Dynamic Trading

The chart below shows the bond activity following the Sept. 7 report. Bonds continued to rally from the Sept. 6 low just as anticipated. The buy-stop to enter a long position was elected the following trading day, Monday, Sept. 9. Bonds rallied almost straight up from there. The minimum price objective for the rally was 108.18 (50% retracement) and was reached within a few days.

The "correction" was projected to last at least to Sept. 19. The rally continued to Sept. 19 as anticipated, and beyond.

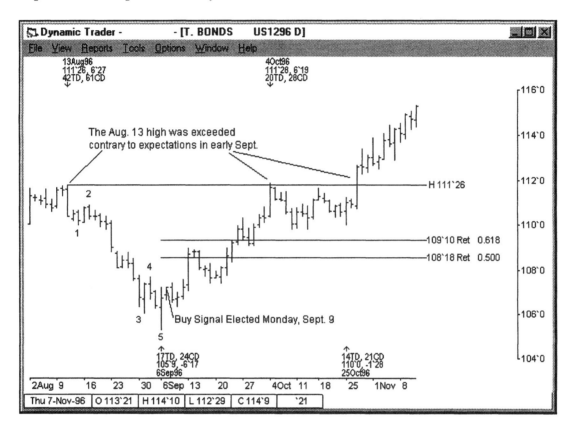

How To Be Wrong And Still Make Money!

Bonds eventually exceeded the Aug. 13 high, contrary to expectations. As it turned out, the rally from the Sept. 6 low was more than a correction to the Aug. - Sept. decline. It was part of a larger degree correction begun from the June 1996 low. You don't have to be right to make money trading. But you do have to quickly respond to the market, which is always right.

The excerpts from subsequent reports on the following pages follow-up on the bond position and trades.

Bonds (Dec.): Bonds also made a wide-range reversal today, with a close near the high. Today's low was made in the 61.8%-78.6% retracement zone and should be a wave 2 of 5 low. Unless bonds exceed today's low of 110.11, the odds favor a continued rally to test or exceed the Oct. 4 high.

<u>Short Term Traders</u>: Buy a break above the first hour's trading tomorrow. Place a buy stop one tick above the first hour's trading. Place the sell stop one tick below the first hour's trading; OR, buy at 110.23 OB. Place the protective sell stop at 110.10.

Update Comments

No charts were included with the mid-week update report. The daily chart below shows bonds from the Sept. low through Oct. 23, the date of the mid-week report.

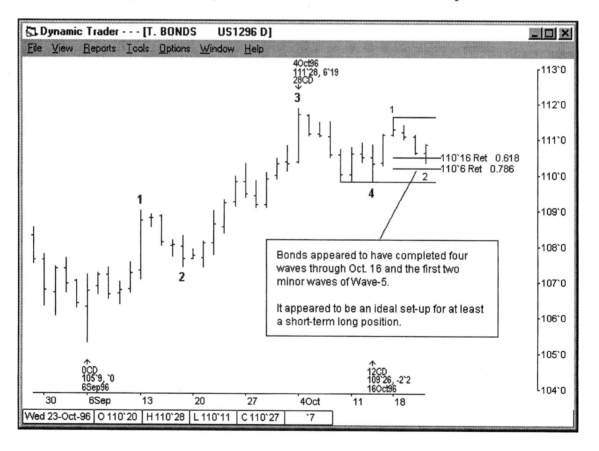

Bonds appeared to have completed a minor wave 2 of 5 low on Oct. 23, the day of the report.

Bonds - Position Summary as of Oct. 26, 1996

Comments	The outlook remains that bonds should make a new high before completing the advance from the Sept. 6 low. Last week's decline is considered a correction in a larger degree bull trend.	
Major Trend	Bearish	From the Jan. 4 high: The Jan. 4 high should not be exceeded prior to a continued decline below the Sept. low.
Inter. Trend	Bullish	From the Sept. 6 low. The wave pattern suggests the bull trend should have at least one more minor swing to new highs to complete Wave-5.
Support (Dec.)	10/4 H	109.26. Calculate Fib retracements from both 9/6 and 9/19 lows if high confirmed.
Resistance (Dec.)	9/6L	111.26-111.31, 113.05-113.28, 115.29-116.23 The ideal price objective for Wave-5 is 113.05-113.28 where W.5 = 100% W.1, 61.8% W.1-3 and 162% W.4.
Time Analysis	PTPP	From the Sept. 6 low: Nov. 1-6 Nov. 1-6 is the ideal period for this corrective rally to complete.
Pattern	9/6 L	The assumption is Oct. 16 completed a wave four low and Friday's outside-reversal-day completed wave 2:5. A decline below 109.26 (W.4 low) voids this wave sequence and signals Oct. 4 probably completed an ABC correction.
Bullish Reversal	Price	2CHDCA 113.28: If the current rally is corrective, the Bullish Reversal should not be made.
General Trading Strategies	The outlook remains that bonds will reach at least 113.05 without having exceeded 109.26.	
Last Week's Trading Activities	The 110.23 OB recommendation from Wednesday's update was elected Thursday. The 110.10 protective sell stop was elected shortly after the open on Friday.	
Specific Trading Recommendations	It is still anticipated bonds will make a wave five rally to reach at least 113.05. Buy bonds on a break above the first 30 minutes range any day next week as long as bonds have not traded below 110.0. Place the protective sell stop at 109.31	
Options	No recommendations at this time.	
Investors / Mutual Fund Switchers	There is no position in bond mutual funds at this time.	

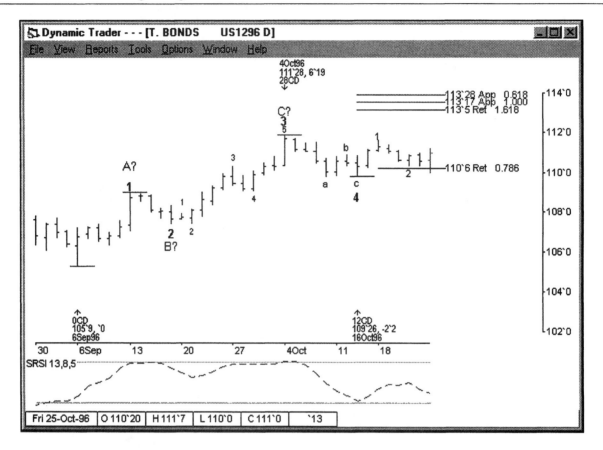

Follow-up Comments

The 110.23 OB buy order was elected on Thursday, Oct., 24 and stopped out the following day, Friday. Friday made a wide-range *outside-reversal-day*. The Oct. 16, Wave-4 low had still not been violated nor had the outlook for a continued rally to 113.05 or higher.

The trade resulted in a minor loss but the market had not violated the outlook for a continued rally. The stop on the trade was placed below the previous low. It could have been placed below the Oct. 16 low of 109.26, but that would have resulted in almost a $1000 capital exposure from the 110.23 OB entry. The Oct. 26 report considered new trade entry strategies on the long side as long as the Oct. 25 reversal-day low was not exceeded.

Let's take a look at the following week's report to see how it turned out.

Bonds - Position Summary as of Nov. 2, 1996

Comments		Friday's (Nov. 1) wide-range *reversal-day* high was made on a coincidence of both time and price projections for a W.5 high.
Major Trend	Bearish	<u>From the Jan. 4 high</u>: The Jan. 4 high should not be exceeded prior to a continued decline below the Sept. low.
Inter. Trend	Bullish	<u>From the Sept. 6 low</u>. The intermediate degree trend from Sept. 6 should complete by the end of next week.
Support (Dec.)	11/1 H	<u>112.13-111.20</u>: This key support zone includes the 38.1%-50%, wave-three retracements as well as the high of wave-one. If the wave count shown on the chart is correct (Nov. 1 = W.3:5 high), bonds should not decline below 111.20 before completing waves 4 and 5.
Resistance (Dec.)	9/6L	<u>113.05-113.28 (Ideal projection for W.5 high)</u>, 115.29-116.23 Friday's high of 113.28 reached the upper extreme of the ideal price zone for a top.
Time Analysis	PTPP	<u>From the Sept. 6 low</u>: <u>Nov. 1-6</u> Nov. 1-6 is the ideal period for this corrective rally to complete. Friday's high (Nov. 1) was made in the ideal time zone for a W.5 top.
Pattern	9/6 L	The assumption is that Friday's high (Nov. 1) is wave 3 of 5. If this is the case, bonds should make a wave four low above 111.20 and a wave five at least marginally above Friday's high. An alternate pattern considers Oct. 25 as the completion of an ABC, wave-four correction and Nov. 1 as the completion of the five minor waves of wave-five.
Bullish Reversal	Price	<u>2CHDCA 113.28</u>: If the current rally is corrective, the Bullish Reversal should not be made.
General Trading Strategies		The bulk of the rally should be over. The Nov. 1 high should be either wave 3:5 or wave 5. At best, only marginal new highs should be made. However, it is usually profitable to try to position on a wave four low for a potential wave five rally. Wave four of five should be complete by late next week.
Last Week's Trading Activities		Because bonds were advancing into the time and price zone anticipated for the W.5 high, Wednesday's update report recommended adjusting the protective sell-stop on the long position daily to one tick below the low of the first hour. The short and intermediate term positions were stopped out on Thursday at 112.17 as bonds traded below the range of the first hour.
Specific Trading Recommendations		<u>Short and Intermediate Term Traders</u>: Wed.-Friday only: As long as bonds have traded to at least 112.13 but have not closed below 111.20, buy bonds on the close if the close is above the prior day's close and the current day's open. Place the protective sell stop one tick below the low traded since the Nov. 1 high.
Options		No recommendations at this time.

Current and Recent Trading Recommendations	Bonds	Opened	Price	Closed	Price	P/L	O/C
	Long Dec. (ST)	9/9	107.05	9/17	108.07	$1063	C
	Long Dec. (IT)	9/9	107.05	9/19	107.23	$563	C
	Long Dec. (ST)	9/23	107.31	9/27	109.27	$1875	C
	Long Dec. (IT)	9/23	107.31	9/30	109.04	$1156	C
	Short Dec. (ST)	10/8	111.02	10/17	110.30	$125	C
	Long Dec. (ST)	10/24	110.23	10/25	110.10	($406)	C
	Long Dec. (ST)	10/29	111.04	11/31	112.17	$1406	C
	Long Dec. (IT)	10/29	111.04	11/31	112.17	$1406	C

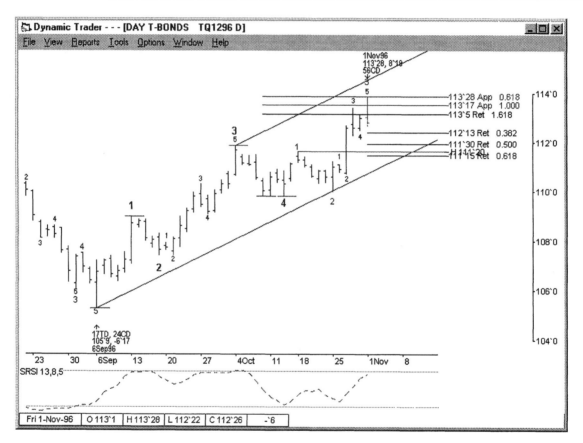

Follow-up Comments

While the Oct. 24 long trade resulted in a loss, the Oct. 29 trade was a winner. Even if a trade is stopped out, there is no reason to abandon the market if the market activity has not invalidated the longer term outlook, in this case, for higher prices.

The profit/loss trade recommendation table shown above includes the recent bond trades up to the time of the report. Did the bond market complete the wave-five for a top as anticipated? I reported in the Nov. 6 mid-week update report the trend was about to reverse.

Bonds (Dec.): Cancel the buy set-up recommendation from last Saturday's report. Minor cycles expand the upper end of the resistance zone to 114.09. 2CHDCA 114.09 signal a continued advance to 115.29 or higher. We are now in the ideal time period of Nov. 1-6 for a corrective top. Bonds have made at least a marginal new high as anticipated in last Saturday's report. Although the pattern is not ideally formed to signal a final top, a short strategy is recommended on the strength of the time and price projections.

Short and Intermediate Term Traders: Sell Dec. bonds tomorrow at 113.07 on a stop. Place the protective buy stop at 113.24.

Follow-up Comments To The Nov. 6 Update Report

Everything seemed to be in place for bonds to complete a five wave advance. The sell-stop order was a few ticks below the low of Nov. 6 (chart not included with the update report).

Bonds - Position Summary as of Nov. 7, 1996

Comments	Bonds are at a critical time and price juncture for a potential, corrective top.	
Major Trend	Bearish	From the Jan. 4 high: The Jan. 4 high should not be exceeded prior to a continued decline below the Sept. low.
Inter. Trend	Bullish	From the Sept. 6 low. Bonds have rallied to a coincidence of time and price resistance from where either the trend should terminate or continue to the next price and time level.
Support (Dec.)	NA	112.29: Calculate Fib retracements and alternate price projections if top confirmed.
Resistance (Dec.)	9/6L	113.05-114.18, 115.29-117.05 The upper end of the resistance zone is extended to 114.18, not 114.09 as stated in last night's update. There are 9 or 10 different price projections of three degrees that fall in the relatively broad zone of 113.05-114.18. **There is not a single price projection between 114.18 until 115.29 that I can find**. If bonds exceed 114.18, they should continue to rally to 115.29 or higher.
Time Analysis	PTPP	From the Sept. 6 low: Nov. 1-6, Nov. 20-21 Today's new daily and closing high after Nov. 6 is a bullish signal.
Pattern	9/6 L	Wave five has not ideally sub-divided into five minor waves. The pattern is sloppy and does not provide a confident opinion from my point of view if the minor trend from the wave four, Oct. 16 low, has completed or not. We will focus on time and price with the assumption that the pattern is probably completing. Bonds often make at least minor tops following a wide-range up-day to new highs. See the Sept. 13 (W.1) and Oct. 4 (W.3) tops as reference. This is not a predication that a top will be made now, in that manner, only to be aware that this kind of top often occurs and not to necessarily consider today's sharp up day as bullish.
Bullish Continuation	Price	**DCA 114.18** While a top is anticipated in the current time and price zone, a close above 114.18 voids this immediate bearish outlook and signals a continued rally.
General Trading Strategies	Trading strategies must let the market signal if the trend has reversed or will continued to the next time and price objective.	
Last Week's Trading Activities	A short position was taken today at 113.07 per the recommendation of last night's update. The short position was stopped out at 113.24.	
Specific Trading Recommendations	Trading strategies should take advantage of the critical price position of bonds. Either a corrective top should be made in the present price zone or a trend continuation signal should be made. Short and Intermediate Term Traders: As long as Dec. bonds have not closed above 114.18, sell bonds on a close below 113.20. Place a stop and reverse at 114.08, OR, buy bonds on a stop of 114.23 or 114.19 SCO, OCO. Place the protective sell stop at 113.24.	
Options	Buy a March 110 put on a futures sell signal with a stop at the stop-and-reverse signal for futures. Don't reverse the option position. The upside potential is more limited in both time and price than the downside.	
Investors / Mutual Fund Switchers	There is no position in bond mutual funds at this time.	

The Real World Of Dynamic Trading

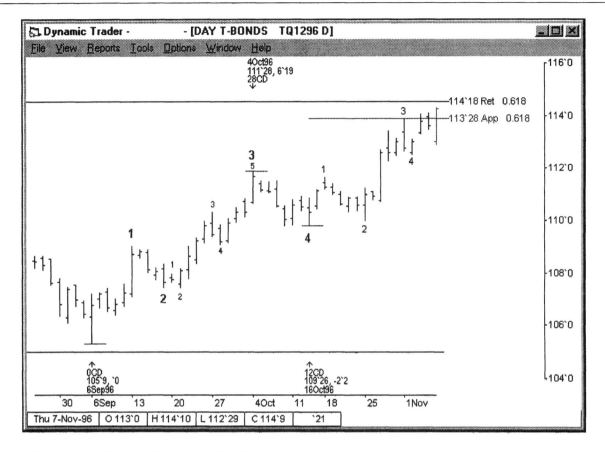

Follow-up To The Nov. 7, 1996 Report

The short position was elected on Nov. 7 per the Nov. 6 update report but was stopped out the same day on the wide-range outside-day for a small loss. Even though this trade was not successful, bonds had still not exceeded the maximum time and price zone for a corrective high.

There is an important analysis and trading strategies lesson to be learned from the Nov. 7 report. Bonds were at the extreme projections of time and price for a corrective top. The trading strategy was to sell if a minor low was exceeded or buy if the price resistance zone were exceeded. Note that the Resistance section commented that there were no price projections between 114.18 to 115.29. In other words, if a top was not made as anticipated and bonds continued to rally, they would probably continue to at least 115.29. Trading strategies would place the trader in a position no matter which direction bonds took. *Trade market behavior, not forecasts.*

Bonds - Position Summary as of Nov. 16, 1996

Comments	Last week, bonds exceeded both the time and price targets anticipated for a corrective top by closing over 114.18 and making new highs after Nov. 6. A continued advance to 115.29 or higher is now anticipated.	
Major Trend	Bearish	From the Jan. 4 high: The Jan. 4 high should not be exceeded prior to a continued decline below the Sept. low.
Inter. Trend	Bullish	From the Sept. 6 low. The rally from the Sept. low is considered a major correction to the decline from the Jan. high.
Support (Dec.)	NA	114.08, 112.29: Calculate Fib retracements from the Oct. 25 and Sept. 6 lows and alternate price projections if a top is confirmed by a close below 114.08.
Resistance (Dec.)	9/6L	113.05-114.18, 115.29-117.05 (115.29-116.13) Bonds have closed above 114.18 which signals the rally should continue to 115.29 or higher before completing the rally from the Sept. 6 low. The 115.29-117.05 price zone includes the 61.8% retracement (spot futures) and 78.6% retracement (Dec.) as well as several minor alternate price projections. If the current rally is corrective, this price zone should not be exceeded.
Time Analysis	PTPP	From the Sept. 6 low: Nov. 1-6, Nov. 20-21 Having rallied to new highs beyond the Nov. 1-6 PTPP, the current rally should not complete prior to Nov. 20.
Pattern	9/6 L	The pattern does not provide a confident opinion of the market position other than the rally from Sept. 6 should be part of a major correction. We will continue to focus on the more objective and reliable time and price projections for clues to trend termination and reversal.
Bullish Continuation	Price	DCA 114.18 (met Nov. 12) Current Bullish Continuation: DCA 117.05
Bearish Reversal	Price	DCB 111.28
General Trading Strategies	Bonds should continue to rally to 115.29 or higher and should not make a top prior to Nov. 20. However, a close below 111.28 signals the corrective rally is complete and bonds should then continue to decline below the Sept. low.	
Last Week's Trading Activities	A long position was taken at the 114.23 buy-stop on Tuesday, Nov. 12. The protective sell-stop was placed at 113.24.	
Specific Trading Recommendations	Short and Intermediate Term Traders (L-11/12, 114.29): Adjust the protective sell stop to 114.05. Take profits on the short-term position at 115.25.	
Options	No recommendations at this time. Bonds are at or near a position from where we will consider bearish option strategies.	
Investors / Mutual Fund Switchers	There is no position in bond mutual funds at this time.	

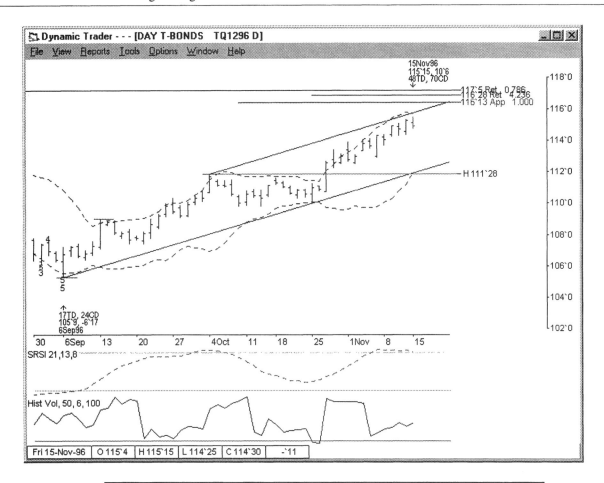

Current and	Bonds	Opened	Price	Closed	Price	P/L	O/C
Recent Trading	Long Dec. (ST)	9/9	107.05	9/17	108.07	$1063	C
Recommendations	Long Dec. (IT)	9/9	107.05	9/19	107.23	$563	C
	Long Dec. (ST)	9/23	107.31	9/27	109.27	$1875	C
	Long Dec. (IT)	9/23	107.31	9/30	109.04	$1156	C
	Short Dec. (ST)	10/8	111.02	10/17	110.30	$125	C
	Long Dec. (ST)	10/23	110.23	10/22	110.10	($406)	C
	Long Dec. (ST)	10/29	111.04	11/31	112.17	$1406	C
	Long Dec. (IT)	10/29	111.04	11/31	112.17	$1406	C
	Short Dec. (ST&IT)	11/7	103.07	11/7	103.24	($531)	C
	Long Dec. (ST&IT)	11/12	114.23	-	-	$219	O

Bonds - Position Summary as of Nov. 27, 1996

Comments		Bonds made a *reversal day* Tuesday, Nov. 26 at both projected time and price resistance.
Major Trend	Bearish	From the Jan. 4 high: The Jan. 4 high should not be exceeded prior to a continued decline below the Sept. low.
Inter. Trend	Bullish	From the Sept. 6 low. The odds are high that Nov. 26 completed the intermediate degree bull trend.
Support (Dec.)	11/26H	114.23, 113.25, 113.03-112.11, 111.10
Resistance (Dec.)	9/6L	115.29-117.05 (**115.29-116.19**) The Nov. 26 high was 116.05, right within the ideal price zone for a major corrective top.
Time Analysis	PTPP	From the Sept. 6 low: **Nov. 20-26, Dec. 4-6** The Nov. 26 *reversal day* high was made at the Nov. 20-26 PTPP for a top. *If bonds continue higher, the final top is likely to be made by Dec. 6.*
Pattern	9/6 L	The pattern does not provide a confident opinion of the market position other than the rally from Sept. 6 should be part of a major correction. We will continue to focus on the more objective and reliable time and price projections for clues to trend termination and reversal.
Bullish Continuation	Price	DCA 117.05
Bearish Reversal	Price	2CLDCB 114.18: Two Consecutively Lower Daily Closes Below 114.18.
General Trading Strategies		Bonds have probably completed a major corrective top at the Nov. 26 reversal day high. If the Bearish Reversal Signal is elected, the top is confirmed. If the Bullish Continuation Signal is elected, a major bull trend may be underway.
Last Week's Trading Activities		The stop-and-reverse order at five ticks below the first hour's trading was elected Tuesday, Nov. 26 at 115.12.
Specific Trading Recommendations		Intermediate and Short Term Traders (S-11/27-115.12): The protective buy-stop is at 116.05, one tick above the Nov. 26 high.

	Bonds	Opened	Price	Closed	Price	P/L	O/C
Current and	Long Dec. (ST)	9/9	107.05	9/17	108.07	$1063	C
Recent Trading	Long Dec. (IT)	9/9	107.05	9/19	107.23	$563	C
Recommendations	Long Dec. (ST)	9/23	107.31	9/27	109.27	$1875	C
For Bonds	Long Dec. (IT)	9/23	107.31	9/30	109.04	$1156	C
	Short Dec. (ST)	10/8	111.02	10/17	110.30	$125	C
	Long Dec. (ST)	10/23	110.23	10/22	110.10	($406)	C
	Long Dec. (ST)	10/29	111.04	11/31	112.17	$1406	C
	Long Dec. (IT)	10/29	111.04	11/31	112.17	$1406	C
	Short Dec. (ST&IT)	11/7	103.07	11/7	103.24	($531)	C
	Long Dec. (ST)	11/12	114.23	11/20	115.25	$1063	C
	Long Dec. (IT)	11/12	114.23	11/26	115.12	$656	C
	Short Dec. (IT&ST)	11/26	115.12	-	-	$63	O

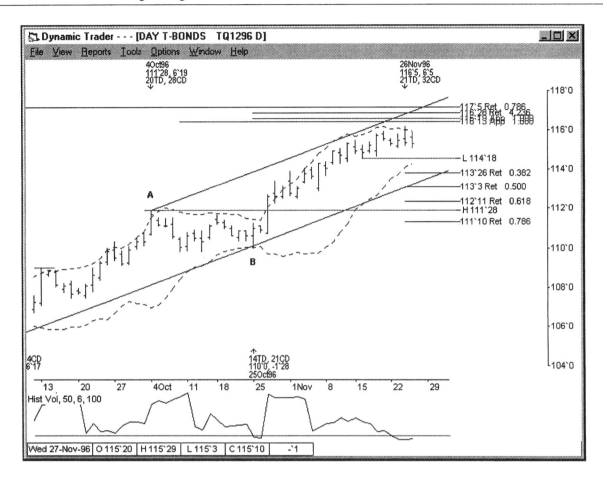

Follow-up Comments For Bonds To The Nov. 16 and 27, 1996 Reports

As you can see from the *Trading Recommendation Profit and Loss Table For Bonds*, the Dynamic Trading analysis and trading strategies had nailed the bond market for several months. There were two relatively small losses and a number of significant profits during this period.

The outlook for a corrective top to be made below the Aug. 13, 1996 high was dead wrong, yet the trading continued to be profitable. *Trade market behavior, not forecasts*. The important lesson is there was a consistent application of the Dynamic Trading analysis methods and trading strategies. While small losses were incurred, the net result was profitable.

The Nov. 27 report stated the Nov. 26 reversal-day high, which was made at a direct hit of projected time and price for a major corrective high, was probably the completion of a corrective top. The report also stated that if bonds made a new high, the final top should be complete by Dec. 6 (Dec. 4-6 PTPP). A stop-and-reversal from a long to short position was taken on the break below the first hour's range on Nov. 26, the day of the high.

How did this short position turn out? An Update Report was issued on Dec. 4. The comments from this report are shown on the following page. No chart was included with the update report.

Robert Miner's *DYNAMIC TRADER WEEKLY FAX REPORT* - Dec. 4, 1996 - Page 1 of 1
Mid-Week Update

Bonds (Dec.)

Bonds exceeded the high of Nov. 26 and elected the protective buy-stop on the short position on the gap opening at 116.15, Tuesday, Dec. 3. Tuesday's high probably completed the corrective rally one day prior to the <u>Dec. 4-6</u> PTPP for a top.

<u>Short and Intermediate Term Traders</u>: As long as bonds have not traded above 116.12, sell bonds on a stop one tick below the low of the first 30 minutes trading. Exit on the close of entry day if the close is above the current day's open. If not stopped out on entry day, place the initial protective buy-stop at 116.13.

Follow-up comments to the Update Report

Although the short position taken Nov. 26 was stopped out, bonds were still in the time and price zone for a major corrective high. As long as a market is in the time and price zone for a trend change, traders should take every opportunity to enter the trade. The Dec. 3 high did not qualify as one of the daily reversal signals even though the close was in the lower half of the daily range and below the day's open. The recommended sell signal was a decline below the trading range of the first 30 minutes, a minor signal of bearish trend.

The sell signal was only valid if bonds had not traded above 116.12, minor resistance on the intraday chart (not shown) that should not have been exceeded if the bear trend was to continue.

How did the Dynamic Trading analysis and trading strategies work out for this short position in bonds? The chart on the following page shows the outcome.

The sell signal of the break below the range of the first 30-minutes was made the following day, Dec. 5. Bonds continued straight down without electing the initial protective buy-stop at 116.13 recommended in the Dec. 4 Update Report. The chart below is the March contract in order to show the bond trend through Jan. which was past the Dec. contract roll-over.

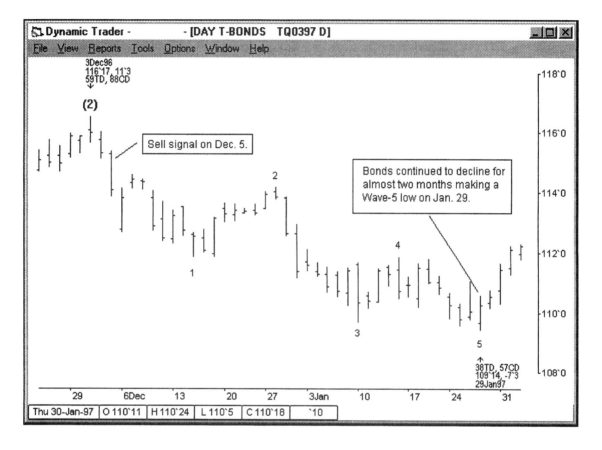

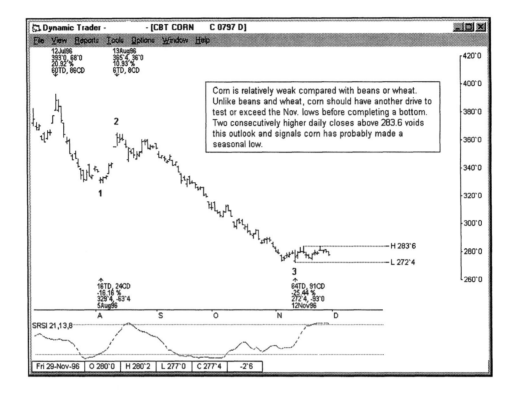

Corn is relatively weak compared with beans or wheat. Unlike beans and wheat, corn should have another drive to test or exceed the Nov. lows before completing a bottom. Two consecutively higher daily closes above 283.6 voids this outlook and signals corn has probably made a seasonal low.

How did it turn out?

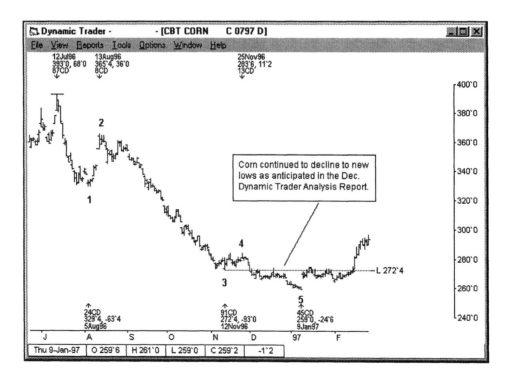

Corn continued to decline to new lows as anticipated in the Dec. Dynamic Trader Analysis Report.

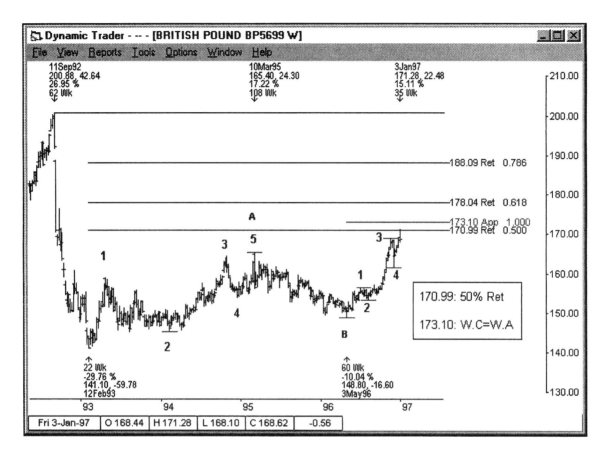

British Pound (weekly): The pound has reached the important resistance zone of 170.99-178.04 described in last month's report. The pound is at or near a wave-five top. The ideal price zones for a wave five high are either 170.90-171.10 or 173.65-174.40. The Dec. 31 high at 171.28 was just a few ticks above the first zone. Dec. 31 appears to be a wave-three high which implies the pound should make one more minor swing to a new high. If this should unfold, the top should be made no later than Jan. 14. A close below 167.25 signals wave-five is complete and a greater decline in time and price than any since the May low should unfold.

How did it turn out?

Follow-up To The British Pound Analysis From The Jan. 1997 Report

Simple price and pattern analysis prepared traders and investors for the largest decline in price in over a year. Take another look at the chart of the BP from the Jan. 1997 report on the prior page. What does it imply for the long term position of the BP? If the wave count is correct, the Jan. high was the completion of a long term correction which should eventually be followed by a decline below the May 1996 low without having exceeded the Jan. 1997 high.

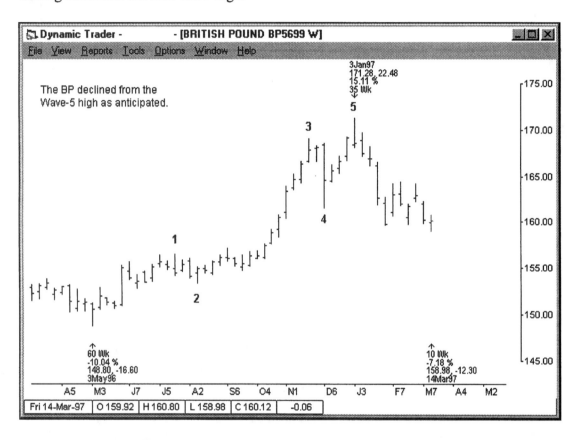

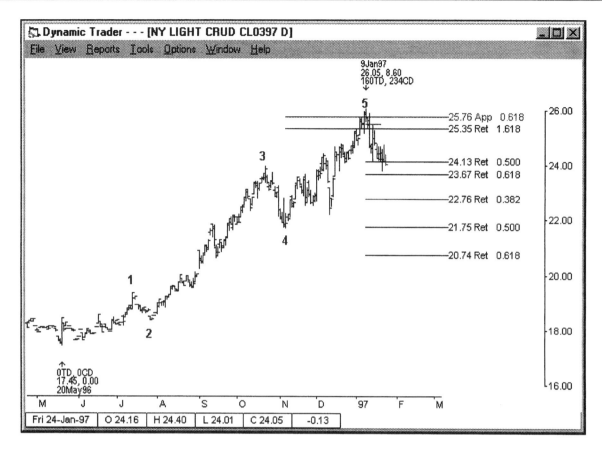

Crude (March)

Resistance (5/20L): 25.35-25.76

   25.35: W.5 = 162% W.4

   25.76: W.5 = 61.8% W.1-3

Support (1/9H): 23.67, 22.76, 21.80-21.70, 20.74

Jan. 9 probably completed a wave-five top. The minimum objective for the decline from the Jan. 9 high is the 21.80-21.70 zone which includes the 50% retracement of the five wave advance and the low of wave-four.

Did March crude reach the 21.80-21.70 support zone as anticipated?

Follow-up To The Crude Analysis Of The Feb. 1997 Report

Two months later, crude reached 21.50, just a few ticks beyond the minimum projection for a corrective decline to the five wave advance.

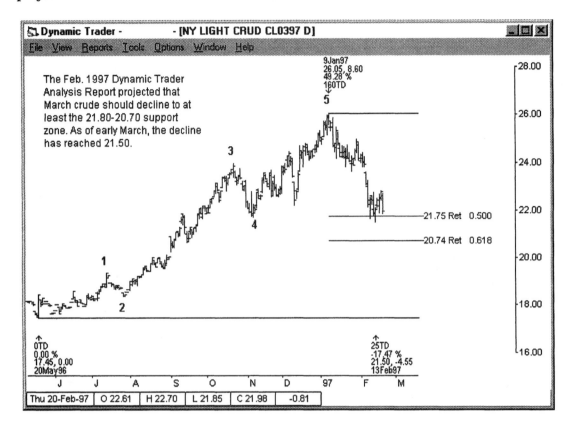

Why was the projection made for a decline to at least the 21.80-20.70 support zone? Corrections to five wave advances (declines) usually reach at or near the prior Wave-4 low (high). Corrections to five wave advances (declines) usually reach at least the 38.2%-50% retracement of the five wave advance (decline). In the case of crude, the 50% retracement coincided with the Wave-4 low.

While crude may continue lower, the important factor is that in early Feb., with crude at 24.00, the price and pattern position strongly indicated a continued decline to at least 21.80. That's information traders can take advantage of.

The Real World Of Dynamic Trading

Orange Juice, Nov. - No Chart: Aug. 26 appears to be the completion of wave-3 of a potential five wave advance from the July 23 low. The current decline should not exceed a close below 116.60 (Sept.) or 111.30 (Nov.) if the larger degree trend is bullish as anticipated. The protective sell-stop on the long position of 118.15 (Sept. contract) adjusted in the Thursday mid-week report was elected Friday, stopping out the long position for a $405 profit.

Intermediate Term Traders: As long as Nov. OJ has not closed below 111.30 (116.60, Sept.), buy Nov. OJ any day next week on the close if the close is above the current day's open and the prior day's close. Place the initial protective sell-stop at 111.20.

Current and Recent Trading Recommendations	OJ	Opened	Price	Closed	Price	P/L	O/C
	Long Sept.	7/29	115.45	8/30	118.15	$405	C

The Aug. 31, 1996 issue of the weekly report included a potential trade set-up for OJ. No chart was included with the commentary. The table shows the most recent trade recommendation for OJ at the time of the report.

Below is a chart for this period. Why was the trade set-up for a long position voided with a close below 116.60 (Sept. contract)? That would be a close below the Wave-1 closing high which would void the impulsive wave count as shown below. Two days after the report, OJ closed below 116.60 on the Sept. contract and 111.30 on the Nov. contract which voided the trade-entry strategy. Trade market behavior, not forecasts.

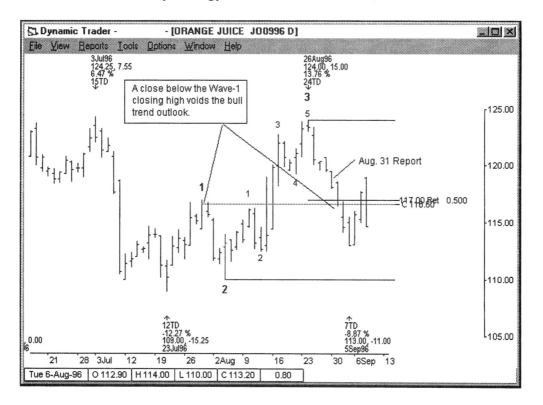

Copper (March)

Resistance (9/12L): 106.00-110.50

Support (2/13H): 106.11-104.14

Thursday's *signal-day* reversal appears to have completed the final minor five-wave advance needed to complete the larger degree five-wave advances. While a new intraday high was made, a new closing high was not. Thursday's high also tagged the parallel channel resistance line projected from the W.3 high.

Short and Intermediate Term Traders: As long as copper has not traded above 110.20 (Feb. 13 high), sell copper on the close if the close is below the current day's open and prior day's close. Place the protective buy stop at 110.25.

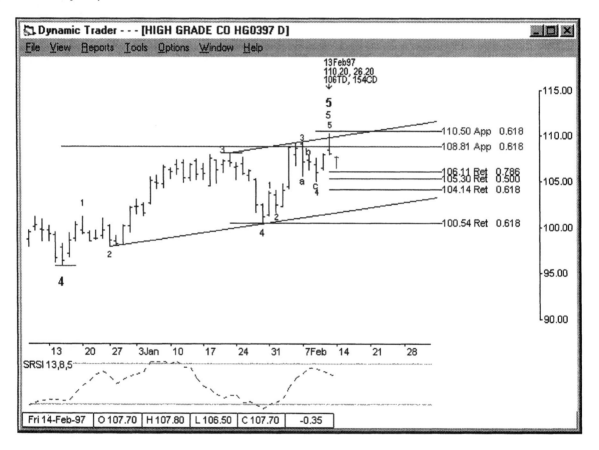

In Feb. 1997, copper appeared to be completing a major five wave advance from the June 1996 low. The outlook in the Feb. 15, 1997 weekly report shown above was that Feb. 13 completed the final, minor five wave advance. Everything seemed to be in place for a major top and a great short trade opportunity.

Follow-up On Copper To The Feb. 15, 1997 Report

The Feb. 13 signal-day high looked like a perfect set-up to prepare for a short trade. The copper market did not agree. It immediately gapped up to new highs and continued to rally. The short trade recommendation was never filled as copper did not make a close below the open prior to rallying above the 110.20 high. Trading strategies prevented a losing trade.

   If a short trade had been taken on the close of the Feb. 13 signal-day, the stop would have been placed at one tick above the Feb. 13 high. The short position would have been stopped out three trading days later on the gap opening for a lose. Losses can never be eliminated, but they can be minimized by logical protective stop-loss placement. In this case, the gap-signal-day reversal was invalidated as soon as the high of the day was exceeded.

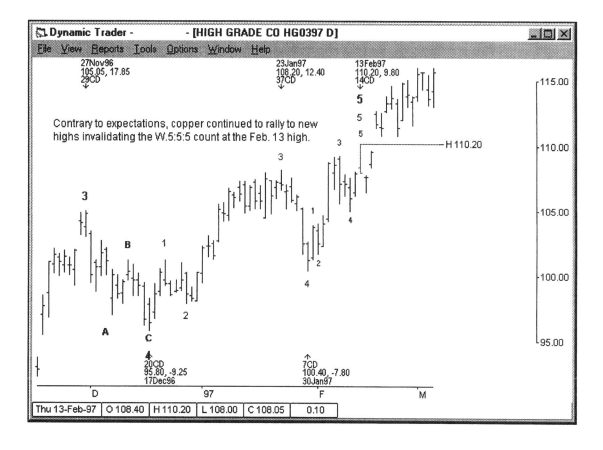

Gold (April)

Support (2/28H): 358.7

Resistance (2/12L): **364.4-365.6,** 370.4, 379.0

Gold has provided another signal of a major trend change to bullish by closing above the prior swing high of 359.7. The current rally appears to be completing a minor W.5 signaling a minor top is due soon followed by a correction to the advance from Feb. 12. The current rally has reached the ideal price objective for a minor wave-five of **364.4-365.6** where W.5=100% W.1 and 61.8% W.1-3. This price zone also includes the 50% retracement from the Nov. high.

The ideal time to initiate intermediate term positions is on the correction to an initial advance. It appears gold should be near the top of an initial advance. If a 38%+ correction follows, it will be the ideal opportunity to initiate intermediate term long positions.

Last Week's Trading Activity: No new trades last week.

Short Term Traders (L-345.30, 2/13): Adjust the protective sell stop to 359.7 one tick below Friday's low. Almost all of Friday's advance took place in the last 30 minutes of trading. A lack of follow through to this buying spree signals a temporary top and the completion of the minor five wave advance is probably complete.

	Gold	Opened	Price	Closed	Price	P/L	O/C
Current and Recent Trading Recommendations	Long (April)	2/13	345.30	-	-	$1980	O

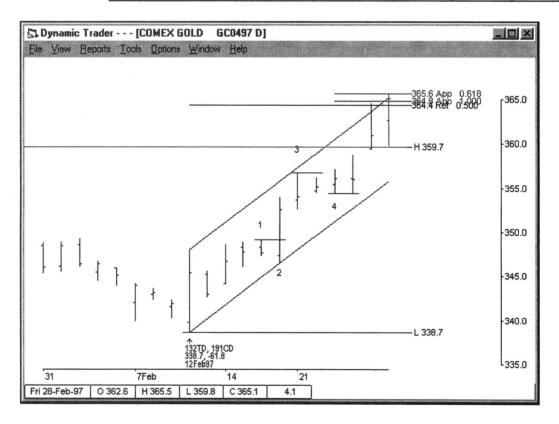

The Real World Of Dynamic Trading

Follow-up Comments On Gold To The March 1, 1997 Report

A long trade recommendation from a prior report was filled on Feb. 13, one day following the wide-range, outside-day low. Gold rallied straight up to the ideal price projection to complete a minor five wave advance. The protective sell-stop on the long position was adjusted to one tick below the low of the last bar shown on the chart on the previous page (Feb. 28 low).

The next trading day, March 3, was a *key-reversal-day*. This was an ideal signal for a stop-and-reverse to a short position. The nature of a weekly report could not take advantage of this timely signal. The protective sell-stop at 359.7, one tick below the Feb. 28 low, was elected two days later on the gap-down open of 357.6 for a profit of $1230.

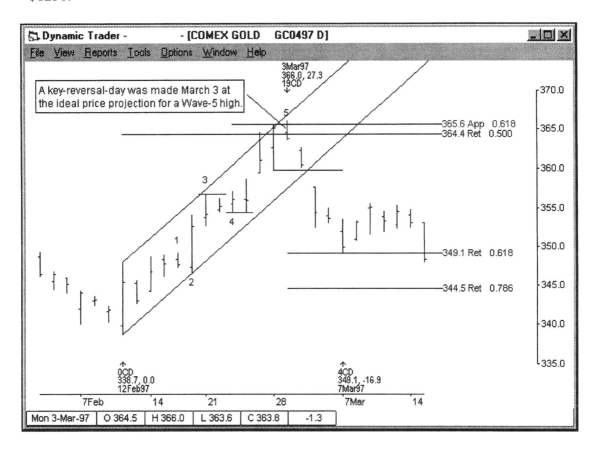

Free Trade Recommendations At
www.dynamictraders.com

Every week on our Web site we include a free current trade recommendation which is an excerpt from the *Dynamic Trader Weekly Report*. Far more important than just providing high probability trade alerts, the weekly trade recommendations serve as an ongoing trading education for the Dynamic Trading approach to technical analysis and trading strategies.

The *Dynamic Trader Weekly Report* is probably the only regularly published report with the purpose of educating its subscribers. Each report is 10-20 pages. Every month one or two special research reports or traders education tutorials are included. For less than the price of most weekend workshops, an annual subscription to the weekly report provides an ongoing and comprehensive trading education.

Appendix

Dynamic Trading Analysis and Trading Guidelines

The following pages put together the guidelines for the time, price and pattern conditions for each trend and counter-trend swing in a completed five wave, impulse sequence and the A, B and C components of corrections. These are *guidelines*, not definitive rules or projections of what must occur. By considering these guidelines, the trader puts the odds in his or her favor for a successful trade.

The *Guideline Tables* include three sections of comments for each wave.

Guidelines

This section provides the typical parameters of time, price and pattern for each wave. When there are typical minimum and maximum price and time parameters for a wave, they are included. These guidelines keep the trader on track as to what to normally anticipate with any swing, as well as the extremes that are usually not exceeded.

Trading Implications

This section includes the practical parameters for taking trading action related to the guidelines. There is frequently a definite consequence to many of the wave structures and time or price objectives. When this is he case, it is a cause for traders to take action. That action may be to either enter or avoid a trade or to adjust a protective-stop depending on the position of the market.

Potential Trading Rules

These are possible trading rules you may develop that will be a consequence of the position of the market described. At the very least, you must develop *minimum* conditions that must be met before considering a trade. This will keep you out of the really foolish trades that are not warranted by the position of the market.

These guidelines are described within the context of Elliott Wave structures. As you learned in the *Pattern* chapter, markets frequently do not unfold in text book Elliott wave patterns. This is irrelevant. *If* a market appears to be in a recognizable Elliott wave structure, assume that it will unfold according to the guidelines and rules for Elliott wave structures and violations of the rules will invalidate your opinion of the market's position.

These guidelines and trading strategies are applicable for all trend and counter-trend swings regardless of the ultimate outcome of the "wave" pattern. They will guide you to the best opportunities for trade entry, stop-loss protection and stop-loss adjustment to protect accumulated profits. Use these guidelines to develop your own trading plan in accordance with your own objectives.

Wave One Guidelines

Since Wave One is the initial wave of a five wave sequence, there are no waves of similar degree *within* the sequence for comparison projections. Wave Ones should sub-divide in a five wave sequence of lesser degree. The guidelines for projecting a wave five apply to the lesser degree swings within the suspected Wave One. The other comparisons that are made are related to the past trend that is counter to the new, suspected Wave One.

In most cases, projections for the termination of Wave One are not highly relevant. Traders who enter a move in the very early stages of Wave One will normally want to stay with the trend through the Wave Two correction and into the Wave Three swing. More important is to recognize a Wave One for what it is and recognize when it has terminated in order to prepare to enter or add to positions on the Wave Two correction.

It is always nice when a market provides an ideal set-up for a trend-reversal trade-entry at the very beginning of Wave One. When you are fortunate enough to catch that entry, do not be too anxious to exit the trade. The biggest profits are usually not made in the initial, Wave One impulse. There are usually made in the Wave Three or Wave Five impulse waves.

Wave One Guidelines Table

Most of the guidelines for Wave One are for the purpose of identifying the Wave One after it has unfolded. Trading strategies concentrate on either entering at the trend reversal that begins Wave One or at the projected termination of Wave Two.

Wave One	Guideline	Trading Implication	Potential Trading Rules
Pattern	A W.1 should sub-divide into a five wave impulse sequence of lesser degree. This will not always be identifiable on a daily chart.	A W.1 and a W.A may often appear almost exactly alike.	
	A W.1 may follow either a completed five-wave trend sequence or a completed corrective sequence.	Unless you have a firm opinion of the wave pattern that preceded the assumed W.1, go under the assumption if could be a W.1 or W.A. Trading strategies are about the same for either.	
	A W.1 that follows a completed five-wave trend sequence should be W.1:A. A W.1 that follows a completed corrective sequence should be W.1 of a five-wave sequence.		
Price	W.1 will usually overbalance in price the prior counter-trend swing such as a wave B or D.		
	W.1 will usually terminate at a dynamic retracement of the prior intermediate or major degree trend.		Sell on any reversal signal if W.1 appears to have clearly subdivided into five-waves and has reached the W.5 price target.
	Use the internal waves of lesser degree to project the price target for the end of W.1.	If the End-of-Wave 5 of 1 price targets coincide with the larger degree retracement, look to enter against the completion of W.5:1.	
Time	W.1 will usually overbalance in time the prior counter-trend swing.		

Wave Two Guidelines

The safest time to enter a market is on the first reaction against a new trend.

W. D. Gann

Wave Two may also be called the *initial counter -trend* of a new impulsive, trend sequence. We assume that we have identified with confidence the trend reversal pivot that began Wave One and the new trend. As Wave Three is usually the extended wave of the five wave sequence, the objective is to enter the position either in the terminal stages of Wave Two or the initial stages of Wave Three. The *maximum* bail out point (maximum protective stop-loss) is always a trade beyond the beginning of Wave One. If the market trades beyond the beginning of Wave One, the analysis that identified that pivot as the trend reversal is invalidated and, more than likely, the trend will continue in the direction prior to that pivot.

The minimum guidelines of Wave Two help to keep us from entering the market prematurely, before the Wave Two would typically have completed. If the trader has not entered the market at the pivot trend reversal (beginning of Wave 1) and the market has moved away from the reversal further than the trader's capital exposure rules allow for entry, the trader can take comfort in knowing there will *always* be a Wave Two counter-trend that will provide another opportunity for trade entry.

Indeed, many traders *never* attempt to enter on a trend-reversal trade at the beginning of a suspected Wave One. Their trading plan demands that the market must provide at least an initial indication that the trend reversal has unfolded by completing at least the minimum parameters of a Wave One. They then look to enter on the inevitable Wave Two correction.

Because Wave Twos have fairly reliable minimum parameters of time and price and typical form, a Wave Two entry trade opportunity will usually unfold with a minimum amount of capital exposure.

All trend reversals do not unfold at an ideal trade set-up of the coincidence of time, price and pattern. Traders, particularly novice traders, should limit trend reversal trades to ideal reversal set-ups. If a trend reversal is suspected but did not have all of the elements to warrant a trend reversal trade *and* the market provides a signal that a Wave One has probably been made, the next best opportunity to enter the market with minimum risk and capital exposure is in Wave Two.

Wave Two Guidelines Table

Wave Two trade entry strategies are usually the ideal combination of low risk with a well defined capital exposure level. The market has already defined the reversal pivot (beginning of Wave One) which is the maximum stop-loss level. Ideally, Wave One will be a well defined five wave sequence evident on the daily chart. If a trader will have the patience to wait for the minimum conditions to be present for a Wave Two trade entry, the trader will usually be in the market for the Wave Three fast moves.

Wave Two	Guideline	Trading Implication	Potential Trading Rules
Pattern	Usually, a simple ABC-zigzag correction.	Never enter on first minor counter-trend following a completed W.1, as it will usually just be the Wave A. Only enter on suspected the Wave C.	A Wave B must complete implying that a C Wave is underway before entry is considered. See minimum requirements for a Wave B.
Price	**W2:W1** A. 50% or greater retracement of W1. B. Usually, does not exceed a 78.6% retracement of W1.	A. Only look to enter a position if W2 has retraced a minimum of 50% of W1. B. Do not enter a position if W2 has exceeded a 78.6% retracement.	Only enter on a W2 correction in the 50%-78.6% retracement zone of W1. If W2 has retraced more than 78.6% of W1 but has not exceeded the beginning of W1, only enter on a trend-continuation entry strategy.
	W2:W1 Should not exceed the beginning of W1 (retrace more than 100% of W1). With futures data, W2 may briefly and by a small amount exceed the beginning of W1. With cash data, this "rule" should not be violated.	If the market trades beyond the beginning of W1, the impulsive trend outlook and reversal pivot is very questionable. More than likely, the market will continue in the direction of the trend prior to the pivot.	The Protective Stop Loss on a W2 entry must be no further than one tick beyond the beginning of W1.
Time	**W2:W1** Rarely, less than 50% of W1.	Never look to enter if W2 is not at least 50% of the time of W1.	W2 must be a minimum of 50% of the time of W1 before a W2 entry is considered.
	W2:W1 Usually, between 62% and 162% of W1.	Be particularly alert to the Pattern and Price position during this window of time.	Enter on a daily reversal signal any time a market has met the minimum criteria of time, price and pattern.

Wave Three Guidelines

The third wave of an impulse sequence is usually the longest and strongest wave. It usually unfolds at a greater rate of change than the initial impulse wave, Wave One. The third wave frequently has relatively wide range days and often gap days left unfilled. Wave 3:3 is usually the most powerful section of the entire sequence.

The trader's objective is to be positioned in the market prior to the potentially strongest section of a Wave Three (W.3:3). Once a strong trend develops, it is much more difficult to enter the market with a logical protective stop-loss that complies with the maximum stop-loss allowed in the trading plan.

The time, price and pattern guidelines for Wave Three provide the trader with two important pieces of information relative to the position of the market:

1. The parameters that confirm or invalidate that the market is probably in a Wave Three.

2. The parameters that will project the typical minimum length of Wave Three and the typical maximum length of Wave Three.

If the suspected Wave Three invalidates the parameters for a Wave Three, more than likely it is a Wave C of a correction.

The objective of the trading strategies should be to capture as much of a Wave Three trend as possible and usually be out of the market for the Wave Four which is often a prolonged correction. As a market approaches the pattern and time and price objectives that are typical of the termination of Wave Three, protective stop-losses should be brought closer to the market. Let the market take you out of the trade. You never know when a market will extend beyond expectations, and you want to have every opportunity possible to capture the explosive, extended moves if they should develop.

Wave Three Guidelines Table

Wave Threes are usually the longest and strongest waves of a five wave impulse sequence. One of the main objectives of any trading plan should be to be positioned for the wave three trend. Once positioned, the next objective is to be alert to confirmations that a wave three is underway and, most importantly, to recognize the conditions when a wave three will typically terminate. The most important purpose of monitoring a wave three is to adjust the protective stop loss as a wave three nears projections that would typically terminate the trend.

Wave Three	Guideline	Trading Implication	Potential Trading Rules
Pattern	W3 should sub-divide in a five wave sequence of lesser degree. This lesser degree pattern is not always discernible on a daily chart.	Time and price projections for the termination of the W5:3 will usually coincide with the time and price projections of the larger degree W3.	
	The initial confirmation that the W2 low has been made is when W3 exceeds the extreme of W1. In a bull market, when the markets break above the high of W1, W3 is confirmed as underway.	A. Once a W3 is confirmed, the market should not come back and trade beyond the beginning of W2. B. If W2:3 is identified, the market should not come back and trade beyond the beginning of W2:3. When the lesser degree waves are identified, they allow for closer protective stop-losses within the rules and guidelines for wave structure. Intraday data often helps to identify the sub-divisions of a wave.	A. Adjust the protective stop loss to <u>no</u> <u>further</u> than one tick beyond the W2 extreme when the W1 extreme is exceeded. B. If W2:3 is clearly identified, adjust the protective stop loss to <u>no further</u> than one tick beyond the extreme of W2:3 once the market trades beyond the extreme of W1:3.

Wave Three Guidelines (Con't)

Price		
W3:W1 W3 is usually greater than W1 (W3>W1). W3 should not be the shortest impulse wave of the five-wave sequence.	The minimum anticipated target of W3 is 100% of W1. If the suspected W3 completes a five wave structure and is less in price range than W1, there is a strong probability that it is a C Wave of a correction and the market is not in an impulsive trend.	A. Advance protective stop-loss (PSL) once W3 exceeds 100% of W1. Trail PSL at 3DL or similar relative wide stop.
W3:W1 W3 is usually 162%-262% of W1.	A. Once W3 exceeds 100% of W1 which implies that an impulsive sequence is probably underway, the typical <u>minimum</u> target would be of 162% of W1. B. If W3 exceeds 162% of W1, more than likely W3 is the extended impulsive wave and W5 will be near equality of W1. C. If W3 is approaching 262% of W1, the probabilities are that W3 is nearing its termination.	B. Advance protective stop loss once W3 exceeds 162% of W1. Trail PSL closer to the market. C. Advance protective stop loss once W3 exceeds 262% of W1. Trail PSL very close to the market such as the 1DL.
W3:W1 Expansion Wave Three is often related to the Wave One Expansion by 100%, 162%, 200% or 262%.		
W3:W2 Wave Three is frequently related to Wave Two by 162%, 200% or 262%. Wave Three will rarely exceed 424% of Wave Two.	Be very aware of other price projections that fall near where W.3 = 262% or 424% of W.2. The PSL should be brought relatively close to the market if these price objectives are reached.	

Wave Three Guidelines (Con't)

Time		
W3:W1 W3 is almost always longer in time than W1.	Unless the internal structure of W3 (five waves of lesser degree) is clearly evident and reaching a projected termination of Wave 5:3, anticipate that the W3 trend swing will continue at least as long in time as the W1 trend swing.	
W3:W1-2 W3 is usually as long as the range in time of Waves one and two combined.	Unless the internal structure of W3 is clearly evident and reaching a projected Termination of Wave 5:3, anticipate that W3 will last as long as the time of W1-2.	

Wave Four Guidelines

If Wave Two was an simple ABC-zigzag correction, Wave Four will generally be a relatively flat correction or one of the "complex" corrections that are impossible to predict the outcome (principle of alternation). Traders should avoid considering trading a Wave Four as they are often relatively prolonged choppy, trading ranges. The primary objective of traders should be to trade into the Wave Three termination, take profits and then prepare to enter again at the end of Wave Four for a Wave Five, impulse trade.

If the Wave Four becomes a complex correction, the price extreme will usually not be the time extreme of the correction. An example is a contracting triangle. The first counter-trend swing from the Wave Three extreme is the price extreme of the fourth wave. The Wave Four would then continue to make a series of highs and lows within the boundaries of the first counter trend swing. The final minor counter-trend swing would be within the bounds of the first swing. *The termination of the complex correction should fall at a dynamic time relationship of either Wave 3 or Waves 1-3*. Time projections will help provide the trader with the con ditions to enter the market at the termination of the Wave Four.

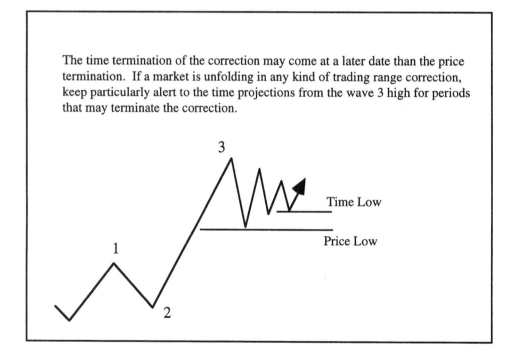

The time termination of the correction may come at a later date than the price termination. If a market is unfolding in any kind of trading range correction, keep particularly alert to the time projections from the wave 3 high for periods that may terminate the correction.

An important objective of many trader's trading plan is *not* to trade the Wave Three, but wait to enter a trade near the termination of Wave Four for a Wave Five trend trade. Why? A Wave Three is usually easy to identify once it is complete. If so, a Wave Five is *inevitable* whereas the Wave Three development was an educated guess in its initial stages. While the Wave Five swing will usually not be as great in price, therefore offering less profit potential, the *risk* of making the Wave Five trade is less as its outcome is more assured.

Keep in mind that risk is the probability of an event happening. The probability of identifying that a swing is a Wave Three is not high until the swing is well underway. In the early stages, many wave threes have the same appearance and structure as a C wave.

If Waves 1-3 have met all of the minimum criteria for their respective waves and, ideally, Wave Three was an extended wave, a Wave Five is inevitable following the completion of the Wave Four. That is why traders should have all of their time and price information up-to-date and carefully monitor a suspected Wave Four as it unfolds in order to prepare to position for the Wave Five.

Wave Four Guidelines Table

An important objective of any trading plan is to recognize the termination of Wave Four for the purpose of entering a Wave Five trend trade. Wave Fours are frequently complex corrections. While they almost always terminate right on a price and time projection from the Wave Three extreme, the time extreme of the Wave Four may not coincide with the price extreme.

Wave Four	Guideline	Trading Implications	Potential Trading Rules
Pattern	Alternation Guideline: If W2 was an ABC-zigzag, W4 will usually be a "complex" correction (other than an ABC) or at the least, an ABC other than a zigzag. If W2 was a "complex" correction, W4 will usually be an ABC-zigzag.	If W4 should be a complex correction, there is no reason to look to trade the W4. Remain out of the market and prepare to identify the termination of the W4 for a W5 trade.	
	Whatever shape is anticipated for a W4, always anticipate a minimum of an ABC where Wave C will test or exceed the extreme of Wave A.	Do not consider entering on the W4 for the W5 trend swing until at least a three wave correction appears complete.	
	W4 should not trade into the price zone of W1. More importantly, particularly with futures data, W4 should not close into the closing range of W1.	If the suspected W4 closes into the closing price zone of W1, the five wave impulse count is invalidated. Do not look to enter a trade for a W5.	The maximum protective stop loss on any W4 entry for a W5 trend trade is a close below the closing extreme of W1.
Price	**W4:W3** W4 is usually a lesser percentage retracement to W3 than W2 was to W1. (W4:W3<W2:W1)		
	W4:W3 W4 is usually a 38.2% - 50% retracement of W3	Avoid entering on W4 for a W5 trend trade at less than a 38% retracement of W3 unless the internal structure of W4 appears complete.	

Wave Four Guidelines Table (con't)

Price (con't)		
	W4:W2 W4 is usually between 62% and 162% of the price range of W2. Frequently, 100% of the price range of W2.	Don't be over anxious to enter at W4 for a W5 trend trade unless W4 has met the minimum parameters of what is a typical W4.
	W4:W1-3 W4 is usually a 23.6% - 50% retracement of Waves 1-3.	Avoid entering on W4 for a W5 trend trade at less than a 23.6% retracement of W.1-3 unless the internal structure of W4 appears complete.
Time	W4 time termination will often come later than the price extreme.	If price reaches a strong price projection, the W4 is probably not complete if the internal correction structure does not appear complete.
	W4:W2 While the price range of W4 compared to W2 is usually very near 62%, 100% or 162%, W4 time will often be much longer than the W2 time, particularly in the case of a W4 complex correction.	
	W4:W3 and W1-3 W4 time will usually terminate at the coincidence of dynamic time ratios of the time of both W3 and W1-3. In many cases, W4 can last longer than the total time of W3 or W1-3.	Do not be over anxious to consider the end of W4 from a time perspective unless the wave structure of W4 appears complete.
		Never enter counter to the W4 trend unless W4 has reached a minimum price range of 62% of W2.

Wave Five Guidelines

Wave Five is the final wave in a five wave, impulse sequence. It is the final wave in the trend. It is critical to be alert to the conditions that signal the termination of Wave Five for two reasons:

1. To protect profits accumulated by the trend trade,
2. To prepare to trade the counter trend to the completed five wave sequence.

Generally, the trader should not look to trade a Wave Two or Four counter-trend. These trades would be against the larger degree trend. Surprises and fast moves will almost always be in the direction of the larger degree trend. However, once the five wave sequence is complete, a correction that is larger in time and price than any correction prior to the beginning of the trend sequence should unfold. Traders want to be prepared to take advantage of the trading opportunities offered by a correction to a five wave sequence.

Because the internal structure of the impulse trend has already completed four waves, there are many typical time and price relationships that will be projected for the time and price targets of the end of Wave Five.

Wave Fives have the highest probability of reliably consistent trend termination projections because of the many swings of similar degree that have made up the whole impulse trend up to that time.

This is why a key component of many traders' trading plans is to identify the conditions for the termination of Wave Five in order to trade the larger degree counter-trend that follows Wave Five. While the profit potential of trading the correction to a five wave sequence is usually less than the profit potential of trading the five wave sequence, the risk is less given the time and price of a Wave Five termination is usually much easier to identify than the termination of any other wave.

An important consideration to keep in mind is that Wave Five should sub-divide into a five wave sequence of lesser degree. *When this five wave sequence of lesser degree is clearly evident and the lesser degree time and price projections coincide with the larger degree projections, traders will frequently recognize the termination of Wave Five the very day it occurs.*

A trading plan that ignores attempting to trade impulse trends and only looks to trade against the completion of five wave sequences is a very viable trading plan. While fewer potential trades will be generated, the risk should be much less and trades should be made with a high degree of confidence.

Wave Five Price Projections

Keep in mind that the most valid price projections for the termination of Wave Five will be a clusters of several projections of the sub-divisions that made up the five wave sequence. The price projection clusters will usually, easily stand out as two, three or more projections from prior waves fall near each other. I usually find that there are two distinct Wave Five price projection clusters once it has been confirmed that Wave Four is complete.

Always consider price projections of one larger and one smaller degree to project the high probability price target to complete Wave Five. The end of Wave Five will almost always be made at the coincidence of price projections from at least two degrees.

Wave Five Guidelines Table

Wave Five may be the most critical wave to identify the conditions for its completion. The end of Wave Five implies both the end of a five wave impulse sequence and the beginning of the largest correction since the beginning of the impulse sequence.

Wave Five	Guideline	Trading Implications	Potential Trading Rules
Pattern	W5 should subdivide into a five wave sequence of lesser degree. This lesser degree sequence is not always evident on the daily charts.	A. If the waves of lesser degree within the W5 are identified, use the same guidelines and trading rules described for each impulse wave to adjust protective stop losses.	A. If Waves 1 and 2 of 5 are identified, adjust protective stop-loss to just beyond the extreme of W2:5 once W3:5 exceeds 100% of W1:5.
	When the sub-divisions of W5 are clearly identifiable, be very alert to the time and price projections of the sub-divisions that fall in the same zones as the larger degree projections.	B. If W5:5 is identified, know that the end of the larger degree sequence is near and prepare to adjust the protective stop loss very close to the market.	B. If W4:5 is identified, adjust protective stop loss to just below W4:5.
	A. If W4 exceeded a 50% retracement of W1-3, W5 will often fail to exceed the extreme of W3 (Fifth Wave Failure).	Do not have unrealistic expectations of the extent of W5 if W4 was greater than a 50% retracement of W1-3.	Adjust the protective stop-loss closer to the market when W5 exceeds the extreme of W3.
	B. If W4 is less than a 50% retracement of W1-3, more than likely W5 will exceed the extreme of W3.		

Wave Five Guidelines Table (Con't)

Price		
W5:W1		
A. If W3 meets the minimum criteria for an extended impulse wave (greater than 162% of W1), W5 will frequently be near equality with W1.	Give strong consideration to the 62%, 100% and 162% price projections of W5:W1 if W3 appeared to be the extended impulse wave.	
B. W5 will usually not be greater than 162% of W1 unless neither W1 or W3 were extended impulse waves.		
W5:W3		
A: If W3 is less than W1, W5 should be less than W3 (W3 should not be the shortest impulse wave).	If W3 is shorter than W1, advance protective stop-loss once W5 is greater than 62% of W3.	
B If W3 meets the minimum criteria for the extended impulse wave (W3 > 162% of W1), W5 will usually not be greater than W3.		
W5:W1-3		
If W3 is extended, W5 will frequently be 62% or 38% of the price range of W1-3.	W5 is probably near termination if it approaches 62% of W1-3.	
W5:W4		
If W3 is an extended wave, the most common W5:W4 relationships are 127% or 162%.	W5 is probably near termination if it approaches 162% of W4.	
W3-5:W2		
W5 frequently terminates near a 162%, 262% or 424% external retracement of W2. In other words, the range of Waves 3-5 are frequently related to W2 by these ratios.	If the 424% objective of W3-5:W2 is above the W3 extreme, it is very likely near the extreme that W5 will reach.	If W5 has exceeded the extreme of W3, adjust the stop-loss to near the market if W5 reaches the projection of 424% R of W2.
W5 Terminus verses W1 Expansion		
Most frequent ratios of a W1 expansion that project the termination of W5 are 100%, 162%, 200%, 262%, 300% and 424%.		

Wave Five Guidelines Table (con't)

Time		
The most important time projections for W5 will come from comparisons with W4 and the alternate cycles (waves 1, 3 and 1-3).		
W5 will usually be of longer duration than W4 if W4 was a simple ABC-zigzag.		
W5 will usually be of shorter duration than W4 if W4 was a complex correction.		
The end of the W5 is the end of a five wave sequence of larger degree. Compare prior larger degree swings for the potential termination of the current five wave sequence.	Be very alert to the price and pattern position of the market if W5 is trending into a PTPP which includes time projections and counts of two or more degrees.	
Time projections that coincide from these two degrees of swings will almost always provide the period when the trend should terminate.		

Correction Guidelines

Correction guidelines are important as the trading plan should include the objective of entering a trade on the initial correction to a suspected new trend (W.2 or W.B).

We always go under the assumption that corrections will make a *minimum* of an ABC pattern. The C wave usually tests or exceeds the extreme of the A wave. This is the critical piece of information that pro

vides the minimum conditions for considering to enter a trade at the projected termination of a correction. We would never look to enter a trade on the correction until we have identified the A and B waves! There will *always* be a C wave following the A and B waves.

Wave Two corrections are usually simple ABC-zigzags and the most symmetrical in time and price and, therefore, the best corrective opportunities to position for the larger degree impulse. Wave Twos and Fours have been previously discussed. Here we will look at the internal structure and time and price guidelines for corrections.

Corrections Guidelines Table

The guidelines below are for the A, B and C components of a corrective structure. Also see the guidelines for Wave Two and Wave Four for guidelines for the completed corrective structure.

Wave A	Guideline	Trading Implications	Potential Trading Rules
Pattern	May be 3 or 5 wave structure.	If a three wave decline is made, do not be too hasty to assume it is a completed ABC correction. Consider the time and price position. It may only be W.A of an ABC.	
	Usually 5 waves.	If a five wave decline is made, assume it is only W.A of an ABC.	
Price	Usually a 38.2% - 50% retracement of the prior impulse wave.	A-waves have a broad range of potential retracement objectives. The termination of the A wave will usually only be projected with confidence if the internal waves of lesser degree are identified.	
Time	There is no consistent time relationship of the A wave to prior waves.		

Corrections Guidelines Table (Con't)

Wave B	Guideline	Trading Implications	Potential Trading Rules
Pattern	A B wave is a correction to the corrective trend. B waves should be three wave structures. They are usually ABC corrections to the larger degree correction.	Always look to enter against the trend direction of the B-Wave when the B-wave is in a position to complete.	If a B-wave has reached the minimum time and price targets and the B-wave has clearly subdivided into at least three waves (Waves abc where W.c has exceeded the extreme of W.a), look to enter on a reversal signal.
Price	B waves usually terminate in the 50%-78.6% retracement zone of the A wave.	Don't consider entering a trade against the trend of the B wave prior to a 50% correction of the A wave.	
Time	B waves usually terminate within 50%-100% of the time range of the A wave. This is particularly the case if the B wave appears to be unfolding in an ABC zigzag.		
WAVE C	**GUIDELINE**	**TRADING IMPLICATIONS**	**POTENTIAL TRADING RULES**
Pattern	C waves should be five wave structures. If the B wave has not exceeded the extreme of the beginning of the A wave (irregular zigzag), the C wave will normally test or exceed the A wave extreme.		

Corrections Guidelines Table (con't)

Wave C Price (con't)			
	WC:WA	Wave C will usually be at or very near 62%, 100% or 162% of Wave A. The most frequent is for W.C = W.A.	If the C wave exceeds 162% of the A wave, the labeling is probably wrong and an impulsive structure is underway. In this case, it they are probably 1-2-3.	Adjust the protective stop-loss closer to the market on a C wave trend trade once the C wave reaches 100% of the A wave. Adjust the stop even closer if W.C reaches the 162% APP of W.A.
	WC:WB	Wave C will frequently be 127% or 162% and usually not more than 200% or 262% of Wave B. If the suspected W.C exceeded a 262% retracement of W.B, it is probably not a W.C.		
	WC:W1-5	If Wave C has exceeded the extreme of Wave A and reached at or near 100% of Wave A, more than likely the correction will terminate on an ABC zigzag.		
		See the guidelines for Waves 2 and 4 for the most important price criteria for the termination of the entire corrective trend.		
Time		W.C is usually near 62%, 100% or 162% of the time of W.A.		
Beyond ABC Corrections		There are so many variations beyond the ABC corrections that it is not constructive to try to list all of the guidelines and exceptions.		

Dynamic Trading Glossary / Index
Chapter-Page numbers are where the term was first used.

Alternate Counts, 3-56 If a market does not unfold within the Elliott wave guidelines as anticipated according to the "preferred" count, an alternate count may be valid. Alternate counts are a result of "what if" scenarios. An alternate count should be considered in the early stages of the wave-structure and not just made up after-the-fact to explain what you weren't prepared for.

Alternate Price Projections (APP), 4-20 The proportion of a past swing that moved in the same direction as the current trend. Trend swings are compared with prior trend swings and counter-trend swings are compared with prior counter-trend swings.

Alternate Time Projection (ATP), 5-18 ATPs are calculated in the same manner as alternate price projections except units of time are used rather than price. The time range of trend swings is compared with prior trend swings and counter-trend swings are compared with prior counter-trend swings.

Alternation, Principle of, 3-42 A wave-four usually alternates in complexity with the preceding wave-two. If wave-two was a simple, ABC, zigzag, wave-four will often be a more "complex" correction.

Anniversary Dates, 5-44 Markets often make a trend change at or very near the date of prior trend changes. Traders should keep an anniversary date file for each market traded.

Coincidence of Time, Price and Pattern, 2-3 When a market trades into a projected time and price zone and is completing a pattern, trend change is highly probable.

Corrective Waves, 3-10 Market movement made against the larger degree trend. Also called counter-trend waves. Waves two and four within the five-wave impulse sequence are corrective waves.

Dynamic Price Projections™, 4-59 The coincidence of several price projections within a relatively narrow price zone.

Dynamic Time Cycles, 5-6 Time cycles that expand and contract by the dynamic growth ratios. A current cycle length will usually be related to several past cycle lengths by one of the dynamic ratios.

Dynamic Time Projections™, 5-61 Time targets that result from a cluster of several time factors. Used interchangeably with the term Projected Turning Point Periods.

Elliott Wave Pattern Analysis, 3-1 Based upon the idea that markets represent the process of mass psychology which grows and contracts in fairly predictable and identifiable patterns.

Fibonacci Counts, 2-10 A additive series of numbers where each adjacent number is related to its neighbor by 1.618.

Fibonacci Ratios, 2-10 A series of ratios related to the root ratio of 1.618 also called the Golden Mean or Divine Proportion. The most prevalent ratios found in all forms of natural growth processes including the process of mass psychology. One series of dynamic ratios.

Gann-Pull-Back Trade Entry Set-Up, 6-28 A trend-continuation entry set-up designed to enter a trade on the minor corrections against the main trend.

Impulse Waves, 3-10 Usually a five-wave sequence made in the direction of the larger degree trend. Waves one, three and five within the larger degree sequence are themselves impulse waves of a lesser degree.

Insane Trader, 1-3 A trader who continues to do the same thing but expects different results.

Inside-Day Trade Set-Ups, 6-18 A trend-continuation entry set-up. A market usually continues in the direction of the breakout of the day preceding the inside-day.

Outside-Day Trade Set-Ups, 6-23 A trend-continuation entry set-up. A market usually continues in the direction of the close of the outside day.

Price Expansions (Exp), 4-31 The expansion of the price range of a swing. The most frequent use of price expansions is the expansion of the initial impulse wave (wave-one or A).

Price Overbalance, 4-55 When the price range or percentage change of a correction exceeds the price range or percentage change of the prior corrections. A price overbalance is an alert that a larger degree trend change may be underway.

Probability, 2-9 A key concept all successful traders and investors understand. All consistently successful investors and traders know that every trading and investing decision only has a probability of success, never a certainty. That is why they are concerned with identifying the market action that will invalidate their trading decision in order to limit losses on unsuccessful trades.

Projected Turning Point Periods™, 5-61 Time targets, usually 1-3 trading days, with a high probability of making a trend reversal. Can also be considered as time support and resistance.

Protective Stop-Loss, 6-34 The order that protects the open position and "stops the loss" if the market moves against the position. The *initial* protective stop-loss is placed when the position is first entered. The protective stop-loss is adjusted as a market trends to protect the unrealized profits of an open position.

Retracements, Price (Ret), 4-7 Retracements are the percentage of the price range of the prior swing that the market moves counter to the direction of the prior swing. Internal price retracements are less than 100%. External price retracement are greater than 100%.

Retracements, Time, 5-10 The same as a price retracement except in time units. It is the amount of time that a market moves counter to the prior trend compared to the time of the prior trend. Time retracements are expressed in percentage terms.

Reversal-Confirmation Day (RCD) Entry Signal, 6-12 Assuming a trend reversal high is suspected of being complete, the RCD is made if the close is below the current day's open and the prior day's close.

Reversal Day (RD), 6-7 A trend-reversal entry trigger. A reversal-day high is made if the market makes a new high but closes below the close of the prior day. Variations are the key-reversal-day and outside-reversal-day.

Signal Day (SD), 6-8 For a signal-day top, the market opens above the prior day's close, makes a new high and the close is below the current day's open. The open must be in the top 1/3 of the daily range and the close in the bottom 1/3. Unlike a reversal day, the signal-day close does not have to be below the prior day's close, only below the current day's open.

Snap-Back Reversal-Day (SBRD), 6-9 A two day reversal signal. For a top reversal, on day-one, the open is in the lower 1/3 of the daily range and the close in the upper 1/3. On day-two, the open is in the upper 1/3 of the daily range and the close in the lower 1/3.

Static Time Cycles, 5-5 Time cycles of fixed-length periodicity. There are no cycles of fixed-length periodicity that are consistently evident in any market over a prolonged period of time. Short-term static cycles are some times evident for relatively brief periods of time.

Technical Analysis, Objective, 2-3 The objective of technical analysis is to identify those market conditions and the specific trading strategies that have a high probability of success. The objective of technical analysis is not to be a market prophet.

Time Counts, 5-44 Calendar or trading day counts from prior pivot highs or lows. The time counts are usually numbers in either the Fib sequence or one of the Gann sequences.

Time Cycle Ratios™ (TCR), 5-9 The general term for proportioning the time range of prior cycles and projecting those proportions forward in time.

Time Overbalance, 5-55 When the time of a correction exceeds the time of the prior corrections. A time overbalance is an alert that a larger degree trend change may be underway.

Time Rhythm Zones™ (TRZ), 5-6 A time range that represents the corresponding time ranges when trends of similar degree and character have terminated in the past. The Time Rhythm Zone provides what the minimum and maximum time targets should be for a trend.

Three-Day Low or High (3DL or H), 6-36 A three-day low is the lowest price of the three day's from the extreme high, inclusive of the high day. Inside-days are not counted.

Trading Log, 6-49 A very important key to success. The trading log may be in a journal form with entries each day or a data/chart format. The important thing to consider is that all successful traders keep a trading log of one form or another. Most unsuccessful traders do not.

Trend-Continuation Entry Strategies, 6-18 Trade entry strategies that are initiated after the trend is underway. Three trend-continuation entry strategies are described in this book: Inside-day, outside-day and Gann pull-back.

Trend-Reversal Entry Triggers, 6-6 Designed to buy the bottom and sell the top. They include Reversal-Day, Signal-Day and Snap-Back Reversal-Day entry signals. These reversal signals are only valid if made at a time and/or price projection or when an Elliott wave pattern appears to be terminating.

Trend Vibration™, 5-38 The time range of the initial cycle (low-to-low in the case of a new bull trend or high-to-high in the case of a new bear trend) proportioned by the dynamic ratios and projected forward. Subsequent highs and lows are often made on the projections of the initial cycle.

Waves of Similar Degree, 2-12 Similar degree waves are those that are similar in time and price within the context of the trend. Waves are also called swings in this book.

Bibliography

I am often asked what books I recommend to help learn technical analysis. While many books have an idea here and there that is useful, most are written by academics or inexperienced traders and are often more mis-leading than valuable. I guess that's why I finally prepared this book which I intend for you to find valuable from cover to cover.

I highly recommend the books listed below. They each provide solid information for the trader or investor from cover to cover. Each of these books is currently in print and easily available. There are other valuable books that are no longer in print and are not included for this reason. Many of the books below do not teach specific technical analysis methods. Many are not directly related to the material presented in *Dynamic Trading*, but each provides invaluable insights for the serious trader and investor.

Reminiscences of a Stock Operator, Edwin Leferve, Traders Library

Viewpoints of a Commodity Trader, Roy W. Longstreet, Traders Press, Inc.

Filtered Waves - Basic Theory, Arthur A. Merrill, Analysis Press

Behavior of Prices On Wall Street, Arthur A. Merrill, Analysis Press

How To Make Profits in Commodities, 45 Years In Wall Street, Wall Street Stock Selector and *Truth of the Stock Tape*, W. D. Gann, Lambert-Gann Publishing Co., Inc.

Commodity Futures Trading Orders and *Commodity Futures Trading With Stops*, J. R. Maxwell, Sr., Traders Press, Inc.

Hit and Run Trading, Jeff Cooper, M. Gordon Publishing Group

Street Smarts, Laurence Connors and Linda Bradford-Raschke, M. Gordon Publishing Group

The Major Works of R. N. Elliott and *R. N. Elliott's Market Letters (1938-1946)*, Edited by Robert R. Prechter, Jr., New Classics Library

Elliott Wave Principle Applied To The Foreign Exchange Markets, Robert Balen, BBS Financial Publications

The New Options Advantage, David L. Caplan, Probus Publishing

Techniques of a Professional Commodity Chart Analyst, Arthur Sklarew, Commodity Research Bureau, Inc.

Charting Commodity Market Price Behavior, L. Dee Belveal, Dow Jones Irwin

The Disciplined Trader, Mark Douglas, New York Institute of Finance

Why You Win or Lose, The Psychology of Speculation, Fred Kelly, Fraser Publishing Company

What I Learned Losing A Million Dollars, Jim Paul and Brendan Moynihan, Infrared Press

The Psychology of Technical Analysis (formerly called Forecasting Financial Markets), Tony Plummer, Kogan Page Press

A Short History of Financial Euphoria, John Kenneth Galbraith, Whittle Books

The Greatest Bull Market In History, Volumes 1 & 2, Martin A. Armstrong, Princeton Economics

Market Wizards and *New Market Wizards*, Jack Schwager, New York Institute of Finance

Investment Biker, Jim Rogers, Random House

Sacred Geometry, Robert Lawlor, Crossroad Press

The Geometry of Art and Life, Matila Ghyka, Dover Press

The Power of Limits, Gyorgy Doczi, Shambahla Publications

Booksellers

Fraser Publishing
P. O. Box 494, Burlington, VT 05402
802-658-0324 or FAX 802-658-0260
Fraser Publishing offers an outstanding collection of books of interest to traders and investors including many formerly out-of-print books that they have re-published.

Traders Press
P. O. Box 6206
Greenville, SC 29606
864-298-0222 or FAX 864-298-0221

Traders Press carries a complete line of more recent books of interest to traders and investors.

Dynamic Traders Group, Inc.

Providing Comprehensive Analysis Reports, Trading Education
and Unique Technical Analysis Software For The Serious Trader and
Investor

Within this ancient symbol lies coded the structure of life -
and the markets themselves.

For those interested in expanding upon and furthering their proficiency in the Dynamic Trading analysis techniques and trading strategies taught in this book, Robert Miner's Dynamic Traders Group, Inc. offers the products and services described on the following pages.

For complete information on our products and services, go to our Web site at www.dynamictraders.com.

Introducing Robert Miner's

Dynamic Trader Software
And Trading Course

A Powerful Combination Of Trading Education and
Unique Technical Analysis Software

We Offer The Most Comprehensive Technical Analysis and Trading Education Package Available To The Public!

Dynamic Trader Software - The most unique and comprehensive technical analysis software for time, price, pattern, trend and chart analysis.

Dynamic Trader Trading Course - The DT Trading Course begins where the Dynamic Trading book ends. The DT Trading Course teaches you how to make the best use of all of the unique reports, routines and charting capabilities of the Dynamic Trader software.

Dynamic Trader Weekly Report - A three-month subscription to the Dynamic Trader Weekly Report is included with the purchase of the DT Software and Trading Course. This ongoing education ensures the DT owner they will quickly get up to speed with the whole Dynamic Trading approach and make the most of the Dynamic Trader Software.

Think of what you would pay for this knowledge by going to weekend workshops and seminars. Thousands of dollars. Consider the value of your time. Now you can have all of this information in a step-by-step learning experience with the unique technical analysis software included. I am so sure you will find the *Dynamic Trader Software and Trading Course* package to be invaluable to you that I offer an unconditional money back guarantee.

Unconditional Money Back Guarantee - The *Dynamic Trader Software and Trading Course* is offered with a 30-day unconditional money back guarantee. If for any reason you are not happy with this package, you may return it for a complete refund.

The following pages provide just a brief description of some of the unique features of the *Dynamic Trader* software. For a comprehensive review of this unique software program and trading course, go to the Download page on our Web site at www.dynamictraders.com where you can download a 36-page booklet that describes all of the unique features of the Dynamic Trader Software.

Dynamic Trader's Comprehensive Dynamic Price Analysis

Some software programs allow the user to make simple price retracements. Dynamic Trader goes way beyond simple price retracements. Dynamic Trader provides the user with comprehensive and totally flexible price projection routines not found in any other program.

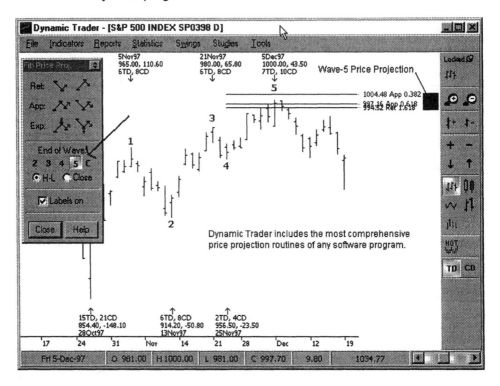

No Other Software Program Offers The User The Ease of Use
and
Flexibility of Dynamic Trader

➢ Project and display any price retracement, alternate price projection or price expansion.

➢ Chose a specific End-of-Wave template projection. All of the price projections are complete with one click.

➢ The user has the choice to develop their own price projection template with any ratios desired.

➢ Dynamic Trader projects the high probability price zones for support, resistance and trend change of any degree from intraday to monthly charts.

➢ There are no secrets, no proprietary routines in Dynamic Trader. The user is taught everything in the Dynamic Trader Trading Course. Every detail of every projection routine is revealed to the user.

Dynamic Trader and Intraday Data

The Dynamic Trader Time and Price Projection routines and reports are designed for intraday data files as well as daily, weekly or monthly data.

The chart below is 5-Bars-Per-Trading Day data. The Jan. 5 high was made at the time and price projection to complete the five-wave advance.

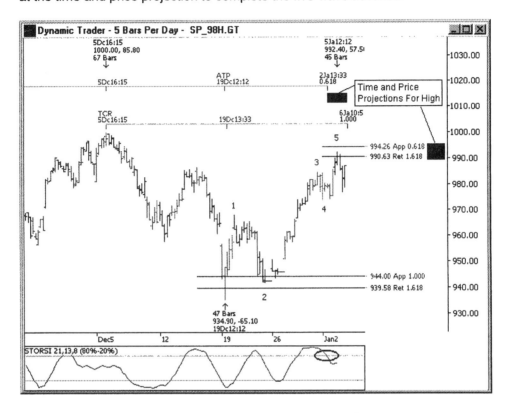

When time, price and pattern coincide, change is inevitable.
The user will learn all of the important analysis techniques and trading strategies to make the high-probability and low-risk trading decisions.

➢   Prepare all Dynamic Time and Price Projections **in advance**.

➢   Be prepared at the beginning of each trading day for the high-probability support, resistance and trend change price zones of any degree.

➢   With the Dynamic Trader Software and Trading Course you will have the knowledge and patience to wait for the specific trade set-ups with the greatest probability of success.

➢   Learn how to integrate time, pattern and indicator analysis with the Dynamic Time Projections.

See the FAQ page on our Web site at <u>www.dynamictraders.com</u> for the most current information regarding DT and intraday data formats.

Dynamic Trader Projects The Exact Price Reversal Zones, Again and Again!

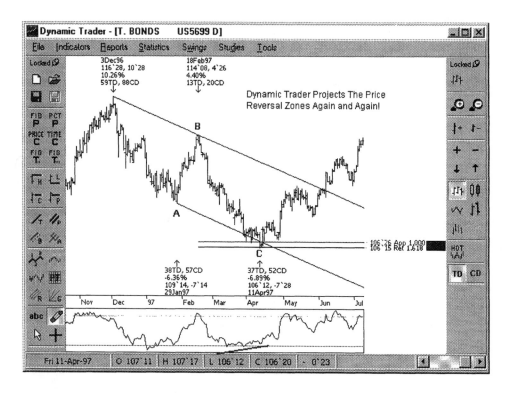

No software program or trading approach will project the precise price target for every trend change or support and resistance level every time. But no other program will provide the consistent accuracy of Dynamic Trader.

Even more important, the Dynamic Trader Trading Course that is included with each software program teaches you which dynamic ratios are the most important for each market position. No other trading course provides you with this comprehensive information.

The Dynamic Trader price projection approach is much more than just simple Fibonacci retracements. While price retracements are an important component to high accuracy price projection analysis, you must know which retracement percentages are important for each market position. You must also know when external retracements, alternate price projections and price expansion projections are valuable.

All of the Dynamic Price Projection techniques are easy to understand and implement with Dynamic Trader. The key to their practical application is to know what to use and when to use them. The Dynamic Trader Trading Course teaches you just this.

Dynamic Time Projections

While the Time Rhythm Zone projections target a relatively wide time range with an 80% probability of making a trend reversal within that time range, the Dynamic Time Projections target narrow time zones, usually just one-three bars.

Dynamic Time Projections are a unique time analysis approach developed by Robert Miner. In one three year period, trend changes were made 89% of the time within one trading day of the dynamic time targets included in Robert Miner's analysis reports. This time analysis approach has been proven over and over again in real-time analysis and trading. The comprehensive and unique Dynamic Time Projection routines and reports are only found in Dynamic Trader.

There are several Dynamic Time Projection routines and reports available in Dynamic Trader including: Fib Time Lines, Trend Vibration, Dynamic Time Projections Report, Fib Time Blitz Report and Custom Time Projection Report. The Custom Time Projection Report gives the advanced user unprecedented power and flexibility.

Fib Time Lines

Fib Time Lines may be quickly placed on the chart. The chart below shows the 50% and 100% Time Retracements. The Dynamic Traders Trading Course teaches the user which ratios and which swings to project from for each market position.

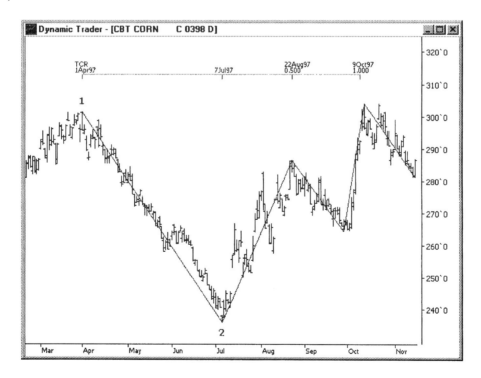

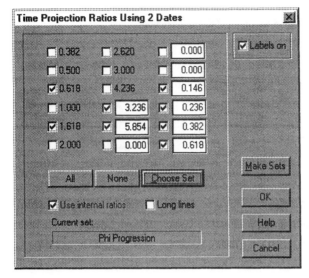

Users may choose what ever ratios they wish to use for the Fib Time Lines or they may choose to use one of the sets already created and included with the program.

The Dynamic Trader Trading Course teaches the user all about external and internal time ratio analysis and which ratios to use for each market condition.

Alternate Time Projections

Fib Time Lines may be done on any time period data. The 30-minute T-bond chart below shows the 61.8% and 100% Alternate Time Projections. The Nov. 20 high was made precisely on the 100% Alternate Time Projection. Dynamic Trader is the only software program that will project and label Alternate Time Projections on your charts.

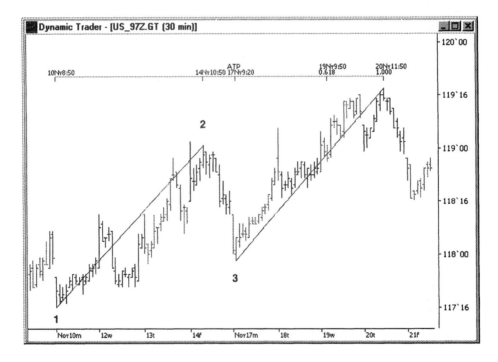

Dynamic Time Projection Reports and Chart Histogram

Now is when we show the real power of Dynamic Trader. The examples above showed how you can project the Fib Time Lines on any chart by simple marking off the high and low pivots. The Dynamic Time Projection report will instantly project all of the Time Cycle Ratios at once and show you the future dates where these projections cluster. These are the dates with the greatest probability of trend change.

The time projections from the <u>Dynamic Time Projection Report (DTP)</u> are specific as to a potential high or low. If the projections are run from a swing high, they are projecting the high probability time periods for a swing low. Vice versa if projected from a swing low. In other words, <u>Dynamic Time Projections</u> are <u>directional</u> as opposed to the non-direction time projections of the <u>Fib Time Blitz</u>.

The <u>Dynamic Time Projections</u> found in the *Dynamic Trader* program allow the trader a tremendous degree of flexibility. The trader can customize the time sets (time ratios and counts) to a specific market or a specific market condition. The <u>weight sets</u> provide a user defined weighting to specific swing comparisons as will be described below. The *Dynamic Trader* program includes template time sets for each Elliott Wave condition as well as a default set for non-specific pattern conditions.

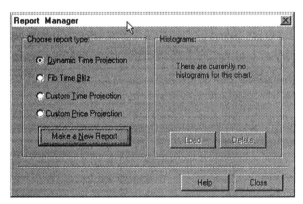

DT Time and Price Reports
Four time and price reports are available. We have chosen the Dynamic Time Projection Report, which will calculate all of the Time Cycle Ratios, calendar day and trading day counts from the recent swings.

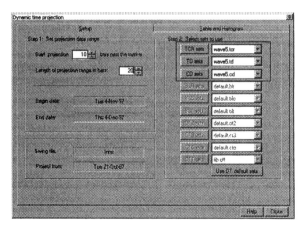

Dynamic Time Projection Report Set-Up
Dynamic Trader includes time projection templates for each wave structure as well as a default template when no particular structure is evident. Users may create their own time projection templates as well. Here we have chosen the template to project the high probability dates to complete Wave-5.

Dynamic Time Projection Results Table

The table below shows the results of the Dynamic Time Projections from the Oct. 21, Wave-4 low. As you can see, the highest scoring dates are Nov. 10 and Nov. 18. The top was complete on Monday, Nov. 7, one trading day before the Nov. 10 date.

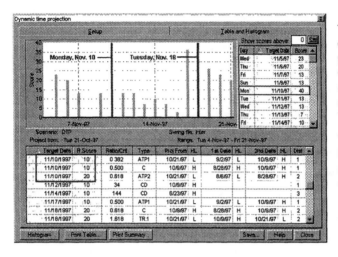

The DTP table shows the details of each time projection. The Trading Course teaches the user what each abbreviations stands for such as ATP.1 (First Alternate Time Projection).

The same information shown in the histogram below may also be brought up on the chart.

Remember, this projection was made weeks in advance.

Dynamic Time Projections On Chart

The indicator window below the chart shows the high probability target dates of the Dynamic Time Projection. The DTP report projected that either Nov. 10 or Nov. 18 had the highest probability of making the Wave-5 top. The top was made just one trading day early on Nov. 7. How valuable do you think the Dynamic Time Projections will be to your trading?

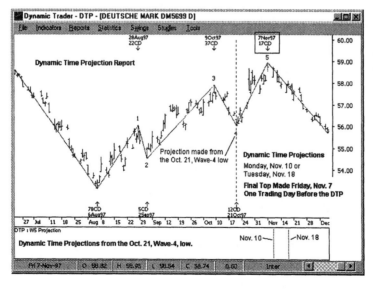

It is easy to historically test the time projection templates.

All you have to do is move the vertical market and the histogram automatically updates from the new projection date.

Dynamic Trader's Time Rhythm Zones

Time Rhythm Zone (TRZ) projections are one of the many features that are unique and exclusive to the Dynamic Trader software program. The TRZ routine projects a zone of time with a high probability of completing any degree of trend from long-term to very short-term. The user should first project the TRZ for the larger degree swings followed by projections from the smaller degree swings. The highest probability time zones to anticipate trend change are when the short-term projections overlap with the longer-term projections.

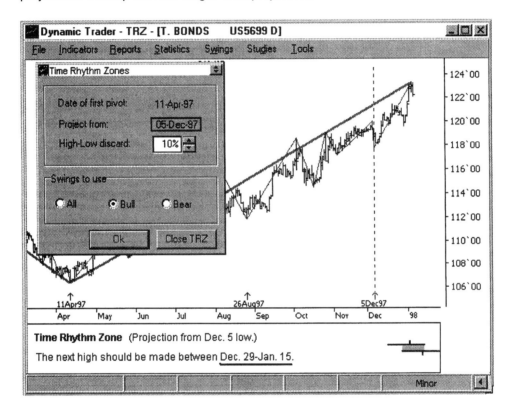

Time Rhythm Zone projections are similar to what may be considered traditional cycle analysis, but with a big difference. Traditional cycle analysis projects "average" cycle lengths based on history from the current lows and highs in order to project a time band for trend change. Dynamic Trader automatically calculates the <u>actual</u> recent highs and lows of a degree of change chosen by the user, and projects the cycle lengths of the actual, real-world cycles that have been made, not averages. Dynamic Trader's Time Rhythm Zone projections are market dynamic, they reflect the most recent cycle history and do not rely on average cycle lengths that may be out-of-date.

Dynamic Trader's Technical Indicators

Dynamic Trader includes a fairly limited selection of technical indicators compared to some of the popular analysis programs made for oscillator junkies. Traders must avoid implementing multiple colinear indicators. That is, indicators that are derived from the same data input who's output provides identical information. The *Dynamic Trader Trading Course* not only provides instruction regarding indicator analysis and trading strategies, but also provides instruction on complementary (non-colinear) indicators.

Indicator Trading "Systems" - The One Way Road To Ruin

Indicators can be a valuable addition to a trading plan <u>when used in the proper context</u>. If you want to spend endless hours developing a trading strategy based solely on indicator signals, prepare for a one way trip to the poor house. Countless indicator "trading system" have been developed and sold with outlandish claims. None of them result in a reasonable net profit over time when traded in real-time. Successful trading requires the trader to gain knowledge, experience and make decisions. If you would like to know more about the Trading System Myth, visit our Web site (<u>www.dynamictraders.com</u>) for a comprehensive article in our Traders Education Archive page.

<u>Indicator signals are only relevant within the context of the time, price and pattern market position</u>. Once you have projected the time and price of trend change and trend targets with Dynamic Trader, indicator signals may be an excellent trigger to enter a trade.

Below is the menu of indicators provided with *Dynamic Trader*. We have selected a variety of indicators that provide a wide range of relevant information. Many potential *Dynamic Trader* purchasers have asked if *Dynamic Trader* includes an indicator they have read about or may be included in another program. I always ask them if they have tested the indicator or can show how it will be useful in real-time trading. The answer is usually no.

Dynamic Trader only includes indicators that we know have value and can be put to practical use to make high-probability trading decisions. We have included several indicators that professional traders who use Dynamic Trader have recommended and have left out many more that have not been found to be valuable.

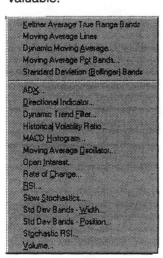

Dynamic Trader's Indicator Menu

Dynamic Trader includes a variety of useful indicators.

The most important thing for a Dynamic Trader user to know is that an indicator signal must only be used within the context of the time, price and pattern position of the market.

DT Daily Trade Scanner

Do you have a completely objective method to identify low-risk and low-capital exposure trend continuation and trend reversal trade set-ups? Dynamic Trader does. Version 2 of Dynamic Trader has greatly expanded on the DT Daily Trade Scanner, which now includes 20 different studies.

The DT Daily Trade Scanner will scan any portfolio of data files for the most reliable trade set-up conditions and provide the entry and stop-loss price triggers. The DT Trade Scanner includes both trend reversal and trend continuation trade set-up signals. This is a <u>very powerful and time saving</u> report, especially when used in conjunction with the dynamic time and price projection routines.

One of the most difficult challenges for a trader is to determine how to get into a trade with a minimum of risk and capital exposure once a trend is underway. The DT Daily Trade Scanner includes several high-probability, trend-continuation trade set-up signals. Many of our users will only enter a trade on one of the Scanner signals.

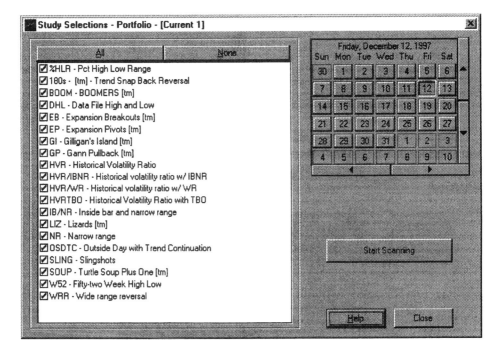

Several of the trade set-ups in the DT Daily Trade Scanner are described in two excellent trading books, *Street Smarts* (Connors/Raschke) and *Hit and Run Trading* (Cooper). The Scanner will scan a complete portfolio of data files (stocks, indexes, futures, etc.). The user may choose which studies to include in the scan. The user may also adjust the parameters of each set-up or use the default parameters.

Scanner Daily Report

At the end of each trading day, the DT Trade Scanner will show which markets meet the trade set-up conditions and what is the buy or sell trigger price for each set-up. The report below ran all 20 set-ups. Each market met more than one set-up condition.

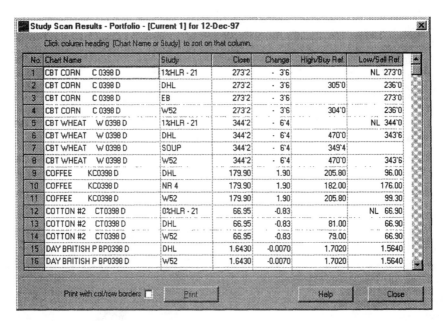

Study Scan Results - Portfolio - [Current 1] for 12-Dec-97

Click column heading [Chart Name or Study] to sort on that column.

No.	Chart Name		Study	Close	Change	High/Buy Ref.	Low/Sell Ref.
1	CBT CORN	C 0398 D	1%HLR - 21	273'2	- 3'6		NL 273'0
2	CBT CORN	C 0398 D	DHL	273'2	- 3'6	305'0	236'0
3	CBT CORN	C 0398 D	EB	273'2	- 3'6		273'0
4	CBT CORN	C 0398 D	W52	273'2	- 3'6	304'0	236'0
5	CBT WHEAT	W 0398 D	1%HLR - 21	344'2	- 6'4		NL 344'0
6	CBT WHEAT	W 0398 D	DHL	344'2	- 6'4	470'0	343'6
7	CBT WHEAT	W 0398 D	SOUP	344'2	- 6'4	349'4	
8	CBT WHEAT	W 0398 D	W52	344'2	- 6'4	470'0	343'6
9	COFFEE	KC0398 D	DHL	179.90	1.90	205.80	96.00
10	COFFEE	KC0398 D	NR 4	179.90	1.90	182.00	176.00
11	COFFEE	KC0398 D	W52	179.90	1.90	205.80	99.30
12	COTTON #2	CT0398 D	0%HLR - 21	66.95	-0.83		NL 66.90
13	COTTON #2	CT0398 D	DHL	66.95	-0.83	81.00	66.90
14	COTTON #2	CT0398 D	W52	66.95	-0.83	79.00	66.90
15	DAY BRITISH P	BP0398 D	DHL	1.6430	-0.0070	1.7020	1.5640
16	DAY BRITISH P	BP0398 D	W52	1.6430	-0.0070	1.7020	1.5640

Print with col/row borders ☐   Print   Help   Close

One of my favorite trend-continuation set-ups is the <u>Gann-Pullback</u>. Almost every trend will provide three or four Gann-Pullback set-ups before the trend terminates. The capital exposure with a Gann-Pullback trade set-up is usually very small.

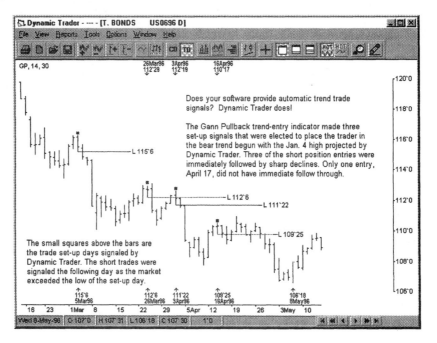

The Dynamic Trader Trading Course

Included **FREE** With Each Dynamic Trader Software Program

Included with the *Dynamic Trader Software* is the *Dynamic Trader Trading Course.* This 400+ page course is the most comprehensive time, price and pattern analysis and trading educational material available. The course includes instructions on how to develop and stick to a trading plan and how to integrate specific trading strategies for minimum risk and minimum capital exposure. The *Trading Course* is in addition to the *Dynamic Trader User's Guide.* The DT Trading Course takes off where the Dynamic Trading book ends.

Below is a partial list of the of the subjects covered in the trading course:

Market Dimensions
Dynamic Price Analysis
Dynamic Time Analysis
Pattern and Elliott Wave
Practical Application of Indicators
Reversal Signals and Trading Strategies
Stop Loss Placement and Adjustment
Statistical Analysis of Trends
Dynamic Indicators
Chart Analysis
Trading Guidelines
Developing a Trading Plan
Practical Option Strategies
And A Whole Lot More!

This is the only trading course that puts all of the factors of trading together in one course. The *Dynamic Trader Trading Course* will teach you all of the factors for you to develop a trading plan around the features in the *Dynamic Trader Software*.

The *Dynamic Trader Trading Course*
will become the most valuable reference work in your trading library.

Total Support With Dynamic Trader

Our technical support is an 800 number. Support is also available by e-mail. Technical support is open each business day plus half a day on Saturday. What other software support do you know that thinks of the customer first?

➢   800 Number

➢   Available Saturdays

We are committed to your success!

Order The Dynamic Trader Software and Trading Course, Today!

Make Trading Your Business, Not Your Hobby.

Unique Time Analysis and Projection Routines
- Fib Time Blitz
- Dynamic Time Projections
- Time Rhythm Zone Projection
- Custom Time Projections
- Built-in Elliott Wave Time Projections
- Complete Instruction How To Apply Time Analysis and How To Use It In Your Trading

Unique Price Analysis and Projection Routines
- Total Price Projection Flexibility
- Custom Price Projection Reports
- Price Rhythm Zone Projections
- Built-in Elliott Wave Price Projections
- Complete Instruction How To Apply Dynamic Price Analysis and How To Use It To Make Trading Decisions.

Comprehensive Charting Techniques
- Quick, Easy and Accurate Market Geometry Charting
- Easy Text Labeling On Chart
- Easy Chart Manipulation
- Attach Notes To Any Chart

Practical Indicator Application
- Learn Which Oscillators Are Valuable and Why
- Dynamic Indicators Included
- No Indicator Duplication

Elliott Wave Analysis
- Practical Elliott Wave Instruction
- Built-in Elliott Wave Time and Price Projection Routines

Fibonacci Time and Price Cycle Projections

Trading Guidelines Tables

The Most Complete Trading Course Available To The Trading and Investing Public

All Of This And A Whole Lot More!

What Others Are Saying About Robert Miner's
Dynamic Trader Software and Trading Course

Let ***Dynamic Trader*** users tell you why they like this exciting and unique trading package. Read these <u>unsolicited</u> comments from ***Dynamic Trader*** users around the world and decide for yourself whether you want to be a part of the cutting edge of technical analysis. None of these comments is from a magazine review or from my buddies in the business. Every one of these testimonials was received unsolicited from users of ***Dynamic Trader***. Each of these users is so excited about ***Dynamic Trader*** that they have allowed me to share their comments and their name.

1060% Profit In Three Years

Dear Robert:

I would like to thank you for your great contribution to my successful trading. I have now completed three years of trading my own account. My profit stands at approximately 1,060% for the past three years. This was achieved trading seven markets.

Your <u>Dynamic Trader Software</u> is a superb piece of work. I am really impressed. *It is the best software program I have ever seen.* I cannot begin to put into words how good it feels after years of unsuccessfully messing around with standard technical analysis, including all of those silly system software programs, to be actually trading consistently with confidence.

I am regularly trading from the actual day of a top or bottom or at worst, one day later. For the first time in my trading life, I am now making regular profits. I now see the obvious mistakes the other 98% of traders are making. When Time, Price and Pattern coincide, change is inevitable, just as you teach in your course.

Your <u>Dynamic Trader Software and Trading Course</u> is an outstanding achievement. Any trader who doesn't utilize this great material can't be serious. Thanks again for your great contribution.　　　*S. E. Griffiths, England*

18 Year Old Son Learns To Trade

Bob:

In my wildness dreams I would not believe your course material. I closed out my first soybean trade for a 43-cent profit after finishing your trading course. I closed the trade out because the time and price projections were pointing to a reaction. And react they did. I just can't thank you enough. I still can't believe I have accomplished this much in such a short period of time. I feel I now understand and have a better feel for what is really happening in the markets more than I ever did before. Using your course as a guide (my trading Bible as I call it), sure makes things a lot easier and understandable.

As you know, I have been studying and putting into practice your educational material for years. Your newsletter has been like having an ongoing real-time workshop. I can't believe this program (<u>Dynamic Trader</u>). Why aren't you selling it for ten times its price? Any person who is serious about trading and wants to learn about the markets should study your course and use the <u>Dynamic Trader</u> program first before they waste a lot of money on all of the useless and overpriced products.

Thanks again for turning my trading life around. I can't thank you enough and congratulations again for <u>Dynamic Trader</u>. It certainly is the crowning achievement of your service to us traders and investors.

P. S. I almost forgot to tell you about my 18 year old son. He saw your course and began reading it. Within 3 weeks he was asking me if he could start trading. I have him paper trading. He is still a bit rusty, but out of 5 trades, 3 had profits averaging about $700 in the cattle and grain markets. The two losers averaged only $300 per trade. Not bad for an 18 year old kid who got curious, is it? - Don Holtzinger

$5,000 To $13,000 In Two Months

Your Trading Course has <u>taught me how to finally trade the market</u> in a way that I can enter with complete confidence knowing there is a high probability that I am going to make money. Through your course I have been able to develop a good trading plan that I never had before. You have also backed up your program and course material with a great Technical Support staff.

The other thing I would like to commend you for is that you are the first person that I have ever brought a trading product from who is willing to take the time to answer questions over the telephone. Keep up the good work. This industry needs more people like you.

P. S. After learning your course and using the methods you taught with Dynamic Trader, <u>I have been able to take a $5000 account to over $13,000 in two months</u>.

Sincerely, Tim Ducroz

Wished He Had DT When He First Started Trading

I really wish I would have had this material when I was getting started. It would have saved me a lot of money and taught me good trading habits right from the beginning. <u>I'm sure *Dynamic Trading* will become the most important training and reference manual</u> for all serious traders and investors as it will be for me.

The education in the *Trading Course* is worth the very competitive price and certainly far cheaper than learning at the school of loosing trades.

For me, the satisfaction from learning *Dynamic Trader* comes from the <u>confidence I now have</u> when I wish to enter the market. The Dynamic Trading techniques not only help me know when is the most opportune time to get into a trade, they also provide specific price targets which let me know my risk before entering." - Frank Strawn

"I've used every imaginable software program for traders. *Dynamic Trader* is the only serious contender amongst them all. It recently nailed the Sept. 3 reversal in the OEX to the day, <u>two weeks in advance</u>! This one trade in OEX calls paid for the program many times over. Thanks Bob, you've really outdone yourself this time." Paul Boughton

"*Dynamic Trader* is just awesome. <u>It's the first program to put it all together</u>. For years, traders have successfully applied Gann and Elliott techniques to the markets. Robert, you have isolated the best of both those worlds and developed your own unique method that I believe will stand the test of time." - George Fizer

"You have created a <u>new standard in technical analysis</u> software and education." - Hanspeter Ehrsam, Switzerland

"I've traded for 30 years on and off the floor. This is the most outstanding educational material I've ever seen."

John Wellford

"I like your emphasis on the <u>practical</u>. One of the most valuable features is your commitment toward those who

purchase the material. I appreciate that commitment. It is rare to find it in this business." - Alan Jezek

"I can definitely say that my trading <u>has improved dramatically</u> since becoming a student of *Dynamic Trading*." - George Poor

"Thanks for the <u>practical trading instruction</u> in your Dynamic Trader Weekly Report." - Mike Jame

Are You Ready To Become A Successful Dynamic Trader Along With These Folks?

The complete Dynamic Trader Software, Trading
Course and DT Weekly Report Package is available for
$1700 plus shipping (Price subject to change).

Unconditional Money Back Guarantee

Your satisfaction is absolutely guaranteed.
You be the judge of the value of the DT Package to you.
It is sold with an unconditional, 30-day money-back guarantee.

Order The Complete Dynamic Trader Package, Today!

A definition of insanity: Keep doing the same thing and expect different results.
Are you ready to make the change to Dynamic Trader
or are you going to keep doing the same old thing?

For more information and an order form, go to our Web site at

www.dynamictraders.com

Robert Miner's

Dynamic Trader Futures Report

Delivered Four Days Each Week By E-Mail

Four days each week, traders receive comprehensive analysis and trading strategies of the position of many of the major financial and commodity futures markets.

Comprehensive Analysis and Specific Trade Recommendations

Each issue provides specific high-probability trade recommendations and general trading strategy recommendations for traders who formulate their own specific trading strategies. What ever your level of experience, the *Dynamic Trader Futures Report* will provide the critical analysis and trading strategies necessary for your success.

Trading Education Tutorials Each Week

Each week includes a special research report or trading education tutorial.

The Timely and Comprehensive Analysis Found Each Day In The Dynamic Trader Futures Report Is Simply Not Available From Any Other Source

At just $25 per week, the cost of this four days per week service is extremely low relative to the comprehensive information provided. A three-month, trial subscription is available for $300.

Each week on our Web site we include an excerpt from the Dynamic Trader Futures Report on the Current Trade Recommendation page.

Dynamic Trader Futures Report. Delivery by e-mail as an Adobe Acrobat PDF file 48 weeks each year. One off-week each quarter.

Three months: $300 for e-mail delivery.

For more information or to order the
Dynamic Trader Futures Report, go to

www.DynamicTraders.com

Dynamic Trader
Mutual Funds Report
Delivered each Saturday

The weekly Dynamic Trader Mutual Fund Report provides comprehensive analysis and trade recommendations for mutual fund traders and investors using the unique Dynamic Trading approach for index and sector funds.

The DT Mutual Fund Report is for Traders and Investors

Investor recommendations are to be in or out of S&P index bull fund positions.
Trader recommendations are to be in or out of S&P and Nasdaq bull or bear fund positions.
Sector recommendations highlight which sector funds have the best potential.

For complete information, go to our Web site at www.dynamictraders.com. You may download a recent free issue for your review and the DT Mutual Fund Report subscribers guide.

Dynamic Trader Mutual Funds Report. Delivery by e-mail as an Adobe Acrobat Reader file 48 weeks each year. One off-week each quarter.

Annual Subscription: $377.

For more information or to order the
Dynamic Trader Mutual Fund Report, go to
www.DynamicTraders.com

Coming Soon

Dynamic Trader Stock Report

The first and only report for individual stocks based on Dynamic Trader's unique time, price, pattern and trend analysis.

Highlights those stocks each week from the S&P 500 and Nasdaq 100 with the highest probability trend reversal and trend targets for both long and short trades.

For more information about the
Dynamic Trader Stock Report, go to
www.DynamicTraders.com

TRADERS PRESS, INC.®
PO BOX 6206
GREENVILLE, SC 29606

Publishers of:

A Complete Guide to Trading Profits (Paris)
A Professional Look at S&P Day Trading (Trivette)
A Treasury of Wall Street Wisdom (Editors: Schultz & Coslow)
Ask Mr. EasyLanguage (Tennis)
Beginner's Guide to Computer Assisted Trading (Alexander)
Channels and Cycles: A Tribute to J.M. Hurst (Millard)
Chart Reading for Professional Traders (Jenkins)
Commodity Spreads: Analysis, Selection and Trading Techniques (Smith)
Comparison of Twelve Technical Trading Systems (Lukac, Brorsen, & Irwin)
Complete Stock Market Trading and Forecasting Course (Jenkins)
Cyclic Analysis (J.M. Hurst)
Dynamic Trading (Miner)
Exceptional Trading: The Mind Game (Roosevelt)
Fibonacci Ratios with Pattern Recognition (Pesavento)
Futures Spread Trading: The Complete Guide (Smith)
Geometry of Markets (Gilmore)
Geometry of Stock Market Profits (Jenkins)
Harmonic Vibrations (Pesavento)
How to Trade in Stocks (Livermore & Smitten)
Hurst Cycles Course (J.M. Hurst)
Investing by the Stars (Weingarten)
Magic of Moving Averages (Lowry)
Market Rap: The Odyssey of a Still-Struggling Commodity Trader (Collins)
Pit Trading: Do You Have the Right Stuff? (Hoffman)
Planetary Harmonics of Speculative Markets (Pesavento)
Point & Figure Charting (Aby)
Point & Figure Charting: Commodity and Stock Trading Techniques (Zieg)
Profitable Grain Trading (Ainsworth)
Profitable Patterns for Stock Trading (Pesavento)
Short-Term Trading with Price Patterns (Harris)
Single Stock Futures: The Complete Guide (Greenberg)
Stock Patterns for Day Trading (2 volumes) (Rudd)
Stock Trading Based on Price Patterns (Harris)
Study Helps in Point & Figure Techniques (Wheelan)
Technically Speaking (Wilkinson)
Technical Trading Systems for Commodities and Stocks (Patel)
The Amazing Life of Jesse Livermore: World's Greatest Stock Trader (Smitten)
The Opening Price Principle: The Best Kept Secret on Wall Street (Pesavento)
The Professional Commodity Trader (Kroll)
The Taylor Trading Technique (Taylor)
*The Trading Rule That Can Make You Rich** (Dobson)
Top Traders Under Fire (Collins)
Trading Secrets of the Inner Circle (Goodwin)
Trading S&P Futures and Options (Lloyd)
Twelve Habitudes of Highly Successful Traders (Roosevelt)
Understanding Bollinger Bands (Dobson)
Understanding Fibonacci Numbers (Dobson)
Viewpoints of a Commodity Trader (Longstreet)
Wall Street Ventures & Adventures Through Forty Years (Wyckoff)
Winning Edge 4 (Toghraie)
Winning Market Systems (Appel)

Please contact Traders Press to receive our current catalog describing these and many other books and gifts
of interest to investors and traders.
800-927-8222 ~ 864-298-0222 ~ fax 864-298-0221 ~ TradersPress.com ~ Tradersprs@aol.com

Visit our Website at http://www.traderspress.com

•View our latest releases•
•Browse our updated catalog•
•Access our Gift Shop for investors•
•Read our book reviews•

Contact us for our latest catalog.

TRADERS PRESS, INC.®

PO Box 6206
Greenville, SC 29606

Tradersprs@aol.com

800-927-8222

864-298-0222

Fax 864-298-0221